Birthday Numerology

Dusty Bunker & Victoria Knowles

1469 Morstein Road
West Chester, Pennsylvania 19380 USA

Birthday Numerology
by Dusty Bunker and Victoria Knowles

Library of Congress Catalog Card Number: 82-60411
International Standard Book Number: 0-914918-39-7

Typeset in 9 pt. Paladium on Compugraphic 7500
Printed by W.P. on 55-pound Natural shade offset paper.
Edited by Marah Ren and Shaun Levesque
Cover art by Plunkett Dodge Corrigan
Typeset by Jean King

Published by Whitford Press,
a division of Schiffer Publishing, Ltd.
This book may be purchased from the publisher.
Please include $2.00 postage.
Try your bookstore first.
Please send for free catalog to:
Whitford Press
c/o Schiffer Publishing, Ltd.
1469 Morstein Road
West Chester, Pennsylvania 19380

Manufactured in the United States of America

Contents

This book is dedicated to
the Spark of Divinity
within every being.

Introduction

This book was born because of a question that I, as a numerologist, am frequently asked: Does the *day* of birth itself have a specific meaning apart from the month and year of birth? Many numerology books have sections on the meaning of the number of the day on which you were born but the treatment is short and unsatisfactory. Because I had not found a satisfactory basis for the importance of the day's number, I did not work with the birth "day" as a single entity. However, I kept my mind open and aware, waiting until I could uncover enough evidence to convince myself that it had validity. I have finally been able to do that and am so excited over this information that I want to share it with you.

Many incidents led to this discovery. One of them came from a conversation some months ago with a friend, the co-author of this book. Vikki is a fine psychic and sensitive who counsels many people. We are in the habit of discussing ideas and off-the-wall thoughts that often lead to discovery for both of us. During the course of a conversation one morning, she asked if I had any feelings about the meaning of the number of the day on which a person is born. Vikki said that she was finding similarities among people born on the same day, not necessarily the same month or year, but the same day. As I said, I had been asked this question many times, but suddenly, when Vikki commented on her experience, I realized there must be a connection somewhere that I had overlooked. Later that day, a thought struck me. I sat down at my desk, pulled out some scratch paper and began sketching the divine triangle. This figure, used by Pythagoras, the father of mathematics, is the focal point of my first book, co-authored with Faith Javane, *Numerology and the Divine Triangle* (Para Research, 1979). As I completed the figure and sat staring at it, the significance of the day of birth became clear to me. I had looked at the triangle for years without this realization and suddenly—I saw it.

The Divine Triangle

Let me briefly describe the triangle and some of its uses before I continue. The divine triangle is a blueprint of your life, based on the Pythagorean theorem that in a right triangle, the square of the hypotenuse is equal to the sum of the squares of the other two sides. Most people do not realize that Pythagoras was primarily a mystic and philosopher. His triangle had a much deeper meaning than is realized in most mathematics classes. Set up your own blueprint using this example:

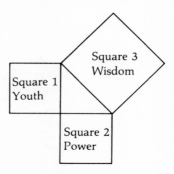

The right triangle occupies the center. Squares are built on each side of the triangle. Each of the three lines drawn to complete the squares represents nine years of life. The first square with its three outer lines covers the ages from birth to twenty-seven and is called the Youth Square; the second square with its three outer lines encompasses ages twenty-seven to fifty-four and is called the Power Square; and the third square with its three outer lines represents ages fifty-four to eighty-one and is called the Wisdom Square. Pythagoras' theorem stating that the square of the hypotenuse is equal to the sum of the squares of the other two sides is a mathematical way of saying you will reap what you sow. You will reap the rewards of your life in square three, your Wisdom years, because of what you have sown in the first and second squares of your blueprint, in your Youth and Power years.

Your birthdate is placed on the triangle: the number of the month on the vertical line, the day on the horizontal line and the year on the oblique line. For example, November 5, 1937 or 11–5–1937 would be set up in the following way.

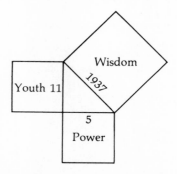

The day of your birth lies on the horizontal line of the triangle. It rules the Power Square, ages twenty-seven to fifty-four in your life. Between twenty-seven to fifty-four are your power years in the sense that, at these ages, you are no longer under parental or guiding authority. You become established as an individual with power over your own life and with certain abilities and traits that can be used to implement that power. You come into your Power years.

Visually you can see that the Power Square is the foundation or supporting block of the entire life blueprint. Squares one and three and the triangle rest upon this Power Square as if they draw strength from its solidity. We draw our impetus and motivation from square two, our Power Square. It is in this Power Square, as you approach your late twenties, that cosmic forces begin to meld your personality, abilities and traits into a cohesive whole. At this time we begin to find out who we really are, how we relate to others, what it is we want to do with our lives and what talents and abilities we have to work with.

As children, how many of us had secret dreams and yearnings? We fantasized about them during our play time games: "I'll be the doctor and you come to me because you're sick," or "I'm a great scientist and I'm working on a secret formula to save the world." Many of us can remember such fantasies from our youth. But were they fantasies or did they contain a seed of truth for us? For me, they held the truth. From the time I was five years old, I wanted to be a writer. To me, writers were the most important people in the world. Today, I am a writer. I am also a wife and mother with four children in various stages of growth. With this, my fourth book, I believe I am slowly achieving my childhood dream.

My husband always wanted to be a forest ranger. He loves the outdoors and vowed he would never sit behind a desk five days a week. Today he is a banker sitting behind a desk five days a week. And sometimes six. But every weekend he is hiking, skiing or canoeing. During the week he jogs and takes Kung Fu classes. Somehow he wedges his work in between all this. Although he claims he hates to read—his nose is in a wilderness magazine every night as he falls asleep. And as far as wilderness equipment goes, L.L. Bean's inventory pales beside his arsenal.

When my son was a little boy, he wanted to be a cartoon hero like Zorro or Spiderman. Today, at nineteen, he plans to go to art school. He is fascinated by *The Hobbit, The Lord of the Rings, The Chronicles of Thomas Covenant, the Unbeliever* and the works of Frazetti, and he plans to develop a career in fantasy art. His room is a museum of fantasy posters and figurines.

It is important to look at our childhood fantasies, to examine them in a new light. Sometimes in early adulthood, we forget or put aside our youthful dreams as wishful thinking or impractical ideas. It is here that we lose contact with who we really are. And although we have heard the whisperings in our childhood and have been pulled and tugged by the power resident in square two, we may live through those years half asleep, flowing with the tide, influenced by outside forces that may be well intended but nevertheless misdirected. We do what others think we should do, we shelve our own secret yearnings. Then we find ourselves floundering for many years—often into our fifties, sixties and beyond—unsure of the purpose of our existence, searching for a meaning to our lives, and scrambling for a niche in life where we can best express our potential.

As I looked at the blueprint on that afternoon I suddenly knew why the day is considered so important. It is the major factor in the Power Square of the blueprint. It is a major factor in determining what you will be as an adult, what kind of a mate you choose, what profession you select, what your strengths and weaknesses are and what tools you have to work with—it represents the path to fulfilling your childhood dreams.

Every numerology book I had read realized that the day was important, but no one explained why. Finally, through the Pythagorean blueprint I found an answer. Excitedly, I called Vikki. As we talked about the blueprint and the Power Square and her recognition of similar traits in people born on the same day, we knew we had material suitable for a book. As it evolved, we realized that if the day of a person's birth is important, then there must be significance in the day an event occurs as well as the numbering of a product or a drug, and the numbers in the title of a book or a movie, and so on. Whenever a number is used in the name or title of someone or something, it has been chosen, consciously or unconsciously, to correctly identify a part of that thing for others to recognize, even if they recognize it only at subliminal levels.

The Symbolism of Numbers

That we subconsciously know truths which we express every day has been made evident to me so many times that I accept this truth totally. One incident that comes to mind occurred during the taping of a television show which was exploring the new decade. I was a guest along with a number of other people from various professions. A representative from the phone company was asked why the WATS line, a free telephone service for the customer to a place of business, was an 800 exchange. The man stated that the number was chosen arbitrarily and that it could just as easily have been 300 or 700. When my turn to speak came, I remarked that the phone company had chosen the only number in the one through nine series that represents big business—eight. They had chosen it so it would correctly identify the service as business. Of course, the chances were one in nine that they would have chosen this number purely by accident and if this particular example were the only case of such a "coincidence," I would dismiss it along with everyone else, but because numbers are my profession, I observe, and I see them expressed correctly all the time. The man from the telephone company was judging the choice of that number as *coincidental* based on just that one incident. However, he is not in the business of noticing numbers, and I am basing my judgment on years of experience. Once you become aware of the millions of "coincidences" that occur each day, you suddenly grasp the fact that all the tributes laid at the feet of the great goddess coincidence only give validity to its truth.

Because we believe that the "naming" or "numbering" of a thing identifies it in a unique way as well as drawing to it other things of a similar vibration, a similar wave length, we have undertaken this book to show the correspondence between the events that occur within a specifically numbered day because of the number itself. You may want to start your own notebook where you can record relevant and interesting information, or chart the similarities you discover in personalities who share the same birthday, under the appropriate numbers so you can further verify the influence of the numbers for yourself.

This book is divided into an introduction and thirty-one days. The first part explains how numbers are commonly used in today's world in meaningful ways, of which most of us are unaware, how the calendar has changed over the years thus influencing nations and peoples and finally, how to read this book to get the most out of it.

The second part contains thirty-one sections, one for each day of the month, which offer feminine and masculine profiles for the person born on that day.

Through your reading, you may begin to recognize a commonality that occurs under each number. The famous Swiss psychologist, Carl Jung, spoke of a like phenomenon in his theory of synchronicity which states that two events occurring at the same moment in time take on the qualities of that moment in time. Similarly, the vibration of the number of the day draws to itself similar vibrations. No event is an isolated happening in the cosmos. Every thing is linked to every other thing in some manner. "You cannot pick a flower but you disturb a star." And if two events occur at the same moment, they are linked by the commonality of that moment—they have something sympathetic between them because they happened at the same time, under the same number vibration.

This universe and our solar system are seething with invisible energies that work in mysterious but rhythmical ways. That being the case, how can we be so presumptuous to declare that something is "impossible." Impossible is a word that stunts growth. Once we start believing things are impossible, we stop growing. We lose the wonder and vibrancy with which a small child experiences a new world and believes all things are within his or her reach. We become crystallized and then begin to decay. So let us wonder and suppose and imagine. Let us look at the world with eyes full of initial acceptance. Once we allow that something is possible, we can examine it with an open mind. If it does not work for us, we can discard it but if we discard it before examination, we have gained only ignorance. Too quickly we make judgments on things of which we have no knowledge. Sir Issac Newton remarked to Edmund Halley when Halley chided him for his belief in astrology, "Sir, I have studied it, you have not." And Hamlet spoke to Horatio, "There are more things in heaven and earth, Horatio, than are dreamt of in your philosophy."

So, with open eyes, we welcome you on our journey through the thirty-one days. If you are happy with life and your role in it, this book can corroborate and perhaps add dimension to your understanding of that role. If you are still uncertain, unsure or unhappy with your present circumstances, this book may open a door and shed new light upon your destiny.

One last but very important note. People often fall into the trap of believing they have no free will, that certain things will happen to them because it is somehow preordained, that there is a Great Being in the sky who points a judgmental finger and proclaims, "You are next!" This is no more true than saying winter will give you pneumonia. Of course, winter *can* give you pneumonia if you do not dress, eat and sleep properly, and most of all, if you do not have the proper attitude. However, pneumonia is not a foregone conclusion because of winter. We cannot change the seasons but we can choose how we will act within those seasons. So it is with numbers and astrology and bio-rhythms and whatever else with which you choose to work. You are born with specific qualities, traits and abilities. These cannot be changed; they are part of you. Your astrological chart, your bio-rhythms, your numerological blueprint are the *result* of what you already are, not the determiner of what you will be. Your chart is what it is *because* of you—you are not what you are because of it. So, when you look at your number and its accompanying information, please, please, do not say, "Oh my God! I knew it! Look at all those horrible traits." Each number is merely an energy. It is neither good nor bad. It just is. The good and the bad are left up to us. It is at those points that the good and bad come into play—because we have chosen. The freedom of choice is the analogy played out in the eating of the apple in the Garden of Eden. We choose to exercise our own free will and to make our own mistakes. The Bible says, "Ye are gods." And in the sense that we choose to act in certain ways that determine our future, we are truly gods. Action and inaction are predicated upon choice, an internal and personal decision. We think: "I will do this," or "I will not do this." We have chosen. At this point we have determined the good or the bad that will come upon us. We caused our present circumstances and we will determine our futures. So, decide right now that your present and your future are already just the way you want them to be. As you think, so it shall be.

Anything for a Lucky Number

In 1980, in Hong Kong, an audience of bidders shifted nervously in their seats while valuable merchandise was brought forward for sale. Ripples of "oohs" and "ahhs" greeted the auctioneer as the items were sold, one by one, for sums often into five figures. Priceless art objects? Thoroughbred horses? No. The retail value of the items was a mere two dollars. However, the Chinese were eager to pay large sums of money for this particular two-dollar item—numbered license plates.

Although the official in charge of the auction commented, "The sense of luck brought by the license plate is only imagined by bidders," the audience firmly disagreed. When the auctioneer pointed at the license number CC323 written on a blackboard and said, "I've been assured that this is a very lucky number. It means an easy life for someone," they responded. The number quickly sold for $3,367. CA88, which means "double prosperity," brought more—$12,499. CC1 reinforced the belief that the number 1 is best. Within minutes, it brought in $32,653. But the record price to date is $70,000, paid by Hong Kong film mogul, Sir Run Run Shaw, for the single number 6. Shaw said it had personal sentiment.

You probably have a lucky number, a number that appeals to you because you were born on that day, or because it is the number of the day you were married or for any one of many reasons. You may have certain digits that keep popping up in your life in strange ways—your telephone number, house address, license plate, social security number, the date a special event occurred or a number with deep personal significance.

We all have specific numbers that are more meaningful to us than to someone else. The premise of this book is that the number of the day of the month in which you are born influences your personality, relationships, career choices and attitudes. For instance, if you were born on the 5th day of any month, you are involved in some form of communication; if the 20th is your day, then you are very intuitive and psychic.

The following key words and phrases introduce the basic symbolism of the numbers 1 through 9 and the zero. The single digit numbers, and their combinations, reflect the nature of the individuals, ideas and objects with which they are associated.

Key Words For Numbers 1–9 and Zero

1 - The beginning, active, aggressive, dynamic, pioneering, energetic, unusual, unique, first and best, alone, ego, self.
2 - Partnerships, cooperation, instinctive, intuitive, passive, reactive, aware of both sides.
3 - Expansion, growth, creativity, self-expression, long distance travel, lucky events, social, positive thinking, generosity, multi-talented, scattered.
4 - Order, budget, form, organization, home, land, security, work, the body, deliberateness, tenacity.
5 - Communication, change, activity, freedom, nervous energy, quickness, speed, experience, the five senses, sensual appetites.
6 - Love, family, responsibility to home and community, balance, counseling, love of beauty, activity with home and family, family health, service.
7 - The mind, rest, analysis, meditation, reserved, aloof, reclusive, perfectionist, personal health.
8 - Responsibility, discipline, big money, business, sex, leadership, power, endurance.
9 - Universal wisdom, understanding, detached compassion and caring, completion, inclusive, broad-minded, finishing cycle, regeneration, generosity.
0 - All or nothing at all, cycle completed and begun again, power behind the numbers, holding power.

How We Use Numbers Today

An examination of the way we use numbers today reveals interesting patterns. It is said that things happen in threes. Three is the number of expansion, growth and fertility—a social number. Anyone or any thing operating under a 3 is creative and makes things happen. We innately know this so we associate activity and growth with the number 3. Three is also the number of faith, the symbol of the trinity.

Many marriages suffer the "seven-year itch." Seven rules the mind and cyclically represents those times when the mind is active. We begin to analyze where we have been, where we are now and where we are going. When partners begin to ask such questions, unless the marriage is a strong one, separations can occur because one partner or the other finds that their needs are not being met. The seventh year or groups of 7—7, 14, 21, 28, 35, 42, etc.—in any relationship can be very difficult because of the acute analyzing process that occurs.

Have you ever felt you wanted "the whole nine yards"? Nine represents the end of a cycle. It's the final digit before we begin again at 10. In this sense, it is all inclusive. It contains all the other digits, 1 through 8. We associate 9 with having done it all, or having it all. We also say, "A stitch in time saves nine." We know that if we take preventive measure, we can save ourselves the task of doing the whole thing again. If we correct our mistakes along the way, we will not have to repeat the entire process.

Your house has a personality of its own and it influences the way you will live in it. If we were more aware of this aspect of our living, we could save ourselves many headaches. Our largest investment will probably be in our home, yet we are unaware that we need to examine the personality of the house to see if it will be compatible with our own personality. What is your house number? Really. If your house number adds up to a 7, you'll either never be there, or you'll spend all your time sleeping. You may do solitary research in your 7 home, but you can be sure it will not be an active, busy household. Seven is a quiet, introspective, analytical, reclusive number.

Conversely, if your house number adds up to a 5, the phone will never stop ringing. There will be doors banging, meetings held, and the patter of more than little feet. The feet of the entire neighborhood and town will use your home as a way station. Install revolving doors. It'll save a lot of wear and tear.

If your house adds up to a 6, you probably move the furniture around every other week. You want your home to be comfortable and inviting. You will be the Mother/Father Confessor figure to every stray person wandering by, and you probably make the best toll house cookies in the state. All the family problems will filter through your home because you can solve them.

At some point, a major magazine decided to designate the five hundred businesses in the United States with the highest yearly sales as the Fortune 500. Why was 5 chosen rather than 4 or 7? Somehow the Fortune 400 or the Fortune 700 doesn't have the same ring. Five, as a number, represents activity, liveliness, alertness and quick energy. It symbolizes communication, and rules sales among other things. A salesperson has to be quick and alert. It is in the first minute that a product is sold. Much of sales success is determined by the way the individual presents him or herself to the prospective buyer. Five also represents the human being's five senses. A salesperson's senses must be keen and ready to react to changes in the customer's responses. The Fortune 500 could have been the Fortune 50 or 5 with varying shades of strength, but the 5 itself was essential because it rules sales. The Fortune 500 members achieve this status through their sales records.

An unwritten rule in the restaurant business is that meals priced so the last digit is a 5 sell better than those ending in other digits. A seasoned restaurateur would never price a meal at $4.98. For a package of T-shirts or socks, yes, but not a dinner. Experience has proven that the same meal will sell significantly better at $4.95 than $4.98. One very successful restaurant owner shook his head and said, "I don't know why this happens but it does." Most people don't like to eat alone—they want company. Dining out is a form of communication, a key word for the number 5, that satisfies the five senses: sight, hearing, smell, taste and touch. Pricing a meal with a 5 as the final digit conveys a message to the customer that the dinner will satisfy those requirements. The 5 reflects the end result of the experience.

One vacuum cleaner company teaches their sales representatives to say that the regular model has a quarter less suction, whereas the deluxe model has 25 percent more suction. The company doesn't know why, but these two ways of phrasing the same information places the deluxe model in a more desirable and salable light. The word, "quarter," implies a fourth and 4 is the number of work. Conversely, the term 25 percent, ending in 5, suggests a quick, pleasurable experience.

Books, hardcover and paperback, are invariably priced so that the 5 ends the sequence: $2.25, $2.75, $10.95, $14.95. Granted some paperbacks are $2.50 but, since zero is technically not a number, it carries the 5 through to the end so we still see the 5 as the predominant ending digit. Five is communication (information and entertainment), freedom and change, certainly experiences books bring to their readers.

On occasion, a book will be sale priced at $6.98 or $7.98 but its sales will be prompted by a very different reason. The book is on sale, that means you are saving money. The price tag ends in an 8 and, yes, 8 represents money and discipline.

As a digit, 8 symbolizes power, discipline, responsibility, big money and big business. The Big 8, the top eight accounting firms in the country, is a group of businesses entrusted with the responsible handling of the finances of other big businesses. The Big 9 or the Big 7 does not convey the same solidity and strength for dealing with large sums of corporate funds as does the Big 8. We sense the power, strength and responsibility behind the number 8. There are eight accounting firms involved but 8 was chosen rather than 7 or 9 because whoever decided 8 was the right amount and coined the term, "The Big 8," somehow "knew" that 8 conveyed the correct message.

In sports we find the Indy 500 and the Daytona 500. Five hundred designates the number of laps the racing cars speed around the track but that distance was chosen rather than four hundred or six hundred laps. Five represents speed and the quick alertness to deal with sudden situations. Certainly the drivers need these qualities. As far as the five senses go, they are keyed to fever pitch, excitement is high as the cars whiz around the track. The audience is tuned in to the same sensual excitement. Five hundred tells the world what they will experience if they attend a race at the Daytona or Indy 500.

Sports figures who wear specific numbers on their shirts for any length of time will be influenced by that number. Their approach to the sport is identifiable through the digits they wear.

Players wearing a 4 are the foundation of the team. They play hard, deliberately and methodically, no fancy dramatics. They believe in the one-step-at-a-time method and getting the job done without theatricals. Because 4 rules the body, theirs is usually strong and sturdy although it may be prone to physical injury. Four is tenacious, so these players are enduring. Hockey's Bobby Orr is a good example of number 4.

Any player wearing a 7 is going to be a thinking player because 7 rules the mind. This player may be smaller than some of his or her team mates and, if strength is part of the game, he or she will have to use wits rather than physical strength, brains rather than brawn. This player will use many strategies because he or she will think like a computer. This player will approach the game with precision and skill. A 7 player is not showy. Because 7 is a private number, he or she will not be as well-known outside the profession. In football, the Washington Redskins quarterback, Joe Theisman, wears 7. He is not as famous to non-sportsminded citizens as Joe Namath, who wears number 12. Twelve reduces to a 3 (12 = 1 + 2 = 3) and 3 is more flamboyant, social and noticeable. It also has long distance power. Therefore, Namath, as a football player and quarterback, is recognized by many people as a celebrity. His fame covers the same long distances he covers on the field.

The number 8 on a shirt bestows leadership. Because this player is serious about his or her profession and takes the responsibility given him or her by others, he or she is looked to for guidance. He or she also feels responsibility toward the team. This player has great physical strength, an awareness of the need for discipline and a fine sense of balance. Eight is a long-lived number, like the 4, but with more power behind it, therefore this player will outlast many others. Eight is also a big money number so, if lived up to its potential, it not only commands a big salary but may have some influence on the financial arrangements for the entire team. In baseball, Carl Yastremski of the Boston Red Sox, and Yogi Berra, former New York Yankee, are number 8s.

Double numbers on a shirt can be reduced but you can also read them as a group. For instance, the number 32 reduces to a 5 (32 = 3+ 2 = 5). Here we synthesize the qualities of the 3 and the 2 with the 5 as the basis of the two numbers. These players are fast and agile (5), able to cover long distances (3). They have a natural instinct for anticipating when they should move and when the opponent is going to move. They seem to know where to be at any given moment (2). Showmanship (3) is instinctive, natural with them (2), and they are good communicators with the team, press and public (5). In football, Jim Brown and O.J. Simpson are number 32 players.

In a general sense, this is the idea behind using the numbers in your everyday life. By knowing the key words for each of the digits 1 through 9, you begin to understand the purpose, use and motivation behind whatever or to whomever these digits are attached.

Numbers are a specific language. We may not be consciously aware of it, but each digit represents qualities that we innately understand. We assign these qualities to the appropriate products, ideas or persons. We speak the language of numbers everyday. When we begin to understand this language consciously, we can convey ideas with a simple number or two. The number of your day of birth speaks volumes about you as a personality to the person who knows the number language, and even to those who do not. They are, at some level, picking up valuable information about you. The day may come when, upon introducing yourself to a stranger, you'll say "I'm a 5. Who are you?" If you're appealing to a 7, you may not get an answer, a 17 may ask why you want to know, and a 23 will tell you more than you anticipate.

The History of Numerology

Historians believe human beings had words for different numbers long before they had the symbols to identify them. However, evidence of numeration (counting) has been found in the earliest traces of civilization. Various methods of counting were used by ancient cultures: simple horizontal or vertical bars, pebbles in slots, beads strung on wires, and knots in ropes. We cannot dismiss the role played by the fingers and toes in numeration. In fact, one would expect that the fingers were the easiest and most accesible method with which to begin counting.

Although not too many years ago, children were reprimanded in math class for using their fingers to help them solve problems, today finger math, or Chisanbop, is all the rage. Children are taught to use their right four fingers as units of one and their right thumb as five, and their left four fingers as units of ten and their left thumb as fifty. They are not only exercising their brains but their motor responses as well, with astounding results.

Since we have ten fingers (including our thumbs), it is not surprising that many numeration systems are based on ten. Four thousand years ago, the Egyptian system of numeration was based on ten as were the Babylonian, Chinese, Hindu and Mayan systems. Throughout the long history of numerals there have been systems of numeration using different bases but the one that predominates today is the base system of ten which matches the number of fingers on our hands.

Our present system of numbers arose from many sources, but primarily from the Hindu and Arabian systems. The writing of Arabic numerals was introduced to the West about 800 A.D. by Hindu traders from India who visited the booming capital of Baghdad. From there, the use of these numerals gradually spread to Europe. However, immediate acceptance of them was not forthcoming. In fact, a law in fourteenth century Florence made it illegal for bankers to use Arabic rather than Roman numerals. Gradually, however, the Arabic system won out and developed in Europe into the one we use today. It took many years for this system to evolve and no one knows exactly when the zero began to be used to designate a missing element, although Peter Barlow, in the *New Mathematical and Philosophical Dictionary* (1814) said this "was perhaps one of the most important steps that has ever been made in mathematics. . . ."

The esoteric history of numbers reveals a belief in a system that "always was." In the beginning there was the One from which all else evolved. The ancients had a veneration for numbers as the permanent structure and operational mechanism of our universe. They saw in numbers spiritual principles that separated numbers from figures. Pythagoras, father of mathematics, the great mystic and philosopher, taught his students that figures were for measurement—how much, how far, how heavy—whereas numbers represented spiritual qualities and processes. The meanings of figures are exoteric, or easily understood; numbers are esoteric, with hidden meanings. He believed that the numbers one through nine symbolized the underlying structure and orderly progression of all life and that number ten completed the cycle. And as we progress through the thirty-one days in the main text of this book, you will be introduced to some of the esoteric proof that supports Pythagoras' claims that qualities are inherent in the numbers themselves and that they have been observed over the centuries to express their specific essences. Suffice it to say here that your name and your birthdate can be numerically reduced to reveal your character, qualities and the rhythm of your life. In Greece, Rome and among the Hebrews, certain letters of the alphabet had numerical value.

We do not name or number things arbitrarily but with exact purpose and reason. And whether the designation of a thing is an accumulation of letters forming a word or the numbers themselves, the thing has been named so it can be identified—just as Adam was required by God to name all the creatures so they would be known. The true essence of a thing is revealed through its name.

A change in name or title is always accompanied by a consciousness change. If the name of a thing is changed, the thing itself is in a process of transformation. In the Bible, certain individuals, after experiencing profound events, had their names changed: Abram to Abraham, Sarai to Sarah, Saul to Paul and so on. These changes were necessary to identify the alterations that occured within the individuals. Their characters were altered because their thoughts had changed. The emanations they projected took on a different vibration which was recognized by everyone and understood by a few. The name change was inevitable.

Traditionally, upon marriage, the woman changes her name. As a result, she experiences a profound consciousness shift. It is easy to see why. When a man marries, he continues his same occupation and working hours, pursuing the same goals. A woman may do so for a while but she often decides to become pregnant and begins bringing children into the world. Her traditional role as nurturer and protector of her young requires that her entire consciousness adapt to her new role. Often her whole life for many years revolves around the raising of children. The husband and father naturally plays a role in this, but his main concern is his job, career and income to support his family. I realize these are traditional roles that are changing for some people. However, some women elect to follow a domestic career for the first twenty-odd years after marriage.

Think of authors' pen names such as Mark Twain for Samuel Clemens and George Sand for Mme. Aurore Dudevant (nee Dupin). Movie stars have adopted names that portray an image they wish to project. Marion Michael Morrison does not have the same flavor as John Wayne, or Roy Scherer, Jr. as Rock Hudson. Somehow we just cannot relate to these two superstars as Marion and Roy. These are fine names but they do not project the image that the movie studios want us to see on the screen.

The Calendar and Consciousness

A change of numbers, like a name change, represents a consciousness change. When the calendar was changed at intervals over the centuries, the consciousness of the people using the calendar changed. To explain this, we need to discuss the calendar and its history. The history of the most widely used calendar, the Gregorian, is long and complicated; the changes it wrought through the centuries reflect profound consciousness shifts within the nations and people who adopted those changes at the time.

A calendar records the division of time into years, months, weeks and days. Conventional systems of determining time are based on natural phenomena: the earth's twenty-four hour revolution is a day, the moon's twenty-eight day orbit around the earth constitutes a month, and the earth's 365-day revolution around the sun comprises a year.

In 4,236 B.C. a civil calendar was introduced in Egypt. Around 2,773 B.C. this lunar calendar was superceded by a solar calendar of three seasons with four months each. The twelve thirty-day months were followed by five days, making the 365-day year. The Egyptians used this calendar for three thousand years. No other group adopted it until Julius Caesar's reign. The Roman calendar had accumulated an eighty-day error when Sisogenes, an Alexandrian astronomer, explained the merits of the Egyptian solar calendar to Caesar. Caesar officially adopted it in 46 B.C. with one modification. The new Julian calendar would alter the permanent Egyptian 365-day year to recognize the 0.25 fractional yearly error by adding one additional day every fourth year.

Even the fraction of a day was an error, however. It should have been 0.2422. This seemingly minute difference amounted to ten days by the sixteenth century. So in 1582, Pope Gregory XIII declared the Gregorian reform, omitting ten days from that year. October 4 was followed by October 15. This brought the calendar and the sun into sync again. The Gregorian calendar further prescribed that only those centuries divisible by four hundred would celebrate leap year, e.g. 1600, 2000 and so forth. The new calendar also designated January 1 as the beginning of the legal year rather than the former March 25. The error in the Gregorian calendar will amount to one day in 3,300 years.

Catholic countries adopted this calendar readily, but Protestant countries clung to the old calendar for a few hundred years more. England finally accepted the Gregorian calendar in 1752 and Russia in 1918. Much of the world now uses the Gregorian calendar, the notable exceptions being the Chinese, Moslems and Jews.

It was mentioned earlier that calendar changes represent profound shifts in the consciousness of the people affected. Reviewing the history of our present Gregorian calendar, we find the following significant dates: 46 B.C., when the Julian calendar was introduced in Rome; 1582, when Pope Gregory declared the Gregorian reform; 1752, when England and her colonies finally accepted the change; and lastly, 1918, when Russia changed to the present-day Gregorian calendar.

One of the most far-reaching events in history occurred forty-six years after Julius Caesar adopted the Julian calendar—the birth of Christ, an event which shook the foundation of the Roman empire (curiously enough, the head of the Catholic church resides in Rome) and eventually caused a shift of power from the Caesars to the Popes.

The year 1582, when Pope Gregory announced a new calendar, fell in the midst of the Protestant Reformation which officially began in 1517 when Martin Luther posted his ninety-five theses on the door of the Wittenberg Palace Church in rebellion against the indulgences of the Catholic church. Europe was attacking the church's authority on three fronts: the princes wanted to cut off the flow of money to Rome and seize the educational and moral authority from the church, as well as the church's possessions; the people wanted Christianity to overcome its weakness as expressed by the church at that time and become a righteous power against the wickedness of the rich and ruling classes; and within the church, an element sought to regain the essential goodness of the church and restore it to power. All over Western Europe, people poured over the newly translated and printed Bible. A profound consciousness change was taking place at deep basic levels within the people, and the church was floundering.

In the year 1752, England and her colonies adopted the Gregorian calendar.This act foreshadowed a string of events that changed the power structure of the world. In 1775, the American Revolution began with the battles of Lexington and Concord. In 1776, the Declaration of Independence was drawn up and signed, marking the birth of a nation. In 1783, the British surrendered at Yorktown, Pennsylvania; in 1788, the United States Constitution was ratified; and in 1789, George Washington became the first president of a nation that would become a major power in the world.

Russia adopted the new calendar in 1918 upon the conclusion of a terrible and unprecedented upheaval in her history. Because of her involvement in World War I, Russia collapsed early in 1917. As H.G. Wells said in *The Outline of History,* "...Russia suffered first and most from this universal pulling up of civilization from its roots." Finally, in the March Revolution of 1917, a devastating war and governmental mishandling of the war effort caused the fall of the Romanov dynasty. The royal family was assassinated, bringing the Russian monarchy to an end. Much haggling ensued until the Bolsheviks under Lenin remained the sole power. The Bolsheviks were then renamed the Russian Communist Party.

It would seem that the calendar changes not only brought nations into more accurate synchronization with time but also signalled the need to start over again, begin anew, change the old vibrations. Throughout history, changes in the calendar affected vast groups of people, just as the numbers on that calendar affect each individual born on a specific day.

Finding Your Number

To find your number, simply look under the number of the day you were born. If you were born on the 3rd day of any month, you are a Three Man or Woman. If you were born on the 18th day of any month, you are an 18 Woman or Man.

If you were born on the fourteenth, you reduce that number by adding one and four to get five $(1 + 4 = 5)$. A twenty-nine reduces twice, to an eleven and then a two $(2 + 9 = 11 = 2)$. Larger numbers or years are reduced the same way: 1943 $= 1 + 9 + 4 + 3 = 17 = 8, 726 = 7 + 2 + 6 = 15 = 6$ or $2001 = 2 + 0 + 0 + 1 = 3$. With numbers, whenever you want to reduce, you simply add the numbers together until you arrive at a single number.

In this book there are thirty-one character sketches, one for each day of any month. As you note from above, all the double-numbered days can be reduced to a single number. If, for example, you were born on the fifteenth day of any month, your number 15 reduces to a 6. This means you belong to the 6 family, just as the person born on the twenty-fourth day of any month belongs to the 6 family $(2 + 4 = 6)$. This does not mean that people born on the sixth, fifteenth and twenty-fourth are exactly alike. They are not. The persons born on the fifteenth and twenty-fourth will have qualities similar to the person born on the sixth, but the double numbers bring in variations of the basic 6. The person born on the fifteenth uses the qualities of the 1 and the 5 to express the underlying 6; the person born on the twenty-fourth uses the qualities of the 2 and 4 to express the underlying 6. Think of it as similar to an address. Three people can live in the same city, but in different sections or on different streets within that city. In this context, the double-numbered birthday people could read the single number to which their double number reduces to give them further insight into their double number's underlying meaning. Throughout the text of the character sketches under the numbers 1 through 31, when we speak of your 6 sister or 8 brother or your 7 family, we are using these terms in the above context.

The number of the day you were born influences your everyday personality, the way you look at life, the window through which you view the world. In astrology, it is similar to the ascendant or rising sign in the horoscope. This number colors your approach to the world in general and regardless of the month or year you were born, the number of the day itself influences your daily approach, the mechanics of your everyday thinking processes: the way you dress in the morning, eat your breakfast, drive your car, approach your relationships and career, and in some respects, the philosophy you embrace. The day is ever with us.

The authors recognize basic differences between the sexes. Viva la difference!

When we talk about male and female traits, we are discussing the universal or cosmic polarities, the yin and yang, the positive and negative poles. It takes two to tango, and there would be no dance of life without these two expressions of divinity.

You might find it wise to read both the male and the female of your number because the qualities can be interchangeable. What we speak of an Eighteen Man doing, you could find an Eighteen Woman doing as well, and vice-versa. The woman might be doing it in her home or with children because more women than men are in the home raising children. But we do not wish to leave the man out of the home or the woman out of the business or professional world, and have tried to include these aspects in the text as well.

We have included famous personalities within the text to show how the traits of individuals fit their birthday number. You may find many others with whom you can identify in some manner. In our research, we have found remarkable similarities. A Seven Woman, after reading the 7 profile, commented that as a child she was called "Tokyo Rose" because she liked to play mind games. Another woman remarked that she has been told she looks like Lauren Bacall, who shares her birthday number 16. You may find this kind of identity with some of the people born on your day.

In your personal lives, understanding that certain birthday numbers belong to the same family members can account for affinities within families or with close friends. For instance, if you were born on the thirteenth, you may discover that you understand why your son, who was born on the fourth, acts the way he does, because a 13 reduces to a 4. Or you may identify with a friend more readily because her birthday is on the twenty-second, another member of your 4 family. You identify with these people because you all belong to the same number family.

One last suggestion. When reading your number, please keep in mind that every situation mentioned in the text may not apply to you but the principle behind it will. If you are a Six Woman, for example, you may not cry when reading birthday cards, but you will express the principle behind the situation which is emotional love, caring and compassion. Your outlet may be nursing, where that emotional feeling nature can readily express. It would be impossible to touch upon every possible expression of each number's characteristics so, in this context, it is necessary to read between the lines.

Again, it is suggested that you read profiles for both the woman and the man because, although there are stereotyped roles for men and women, in this liberated age, you could easily find that attributes and values long associated with only one sex or the other are now welcomed and expressed by both.

Dusty Bunker
January 5, 1982

The One Woman

The One Woman is—above all—noticed. Whether she's embroiled in the business world or the domestic scene, she's the one in front—pounding the gavel on the long mahogany table in exasperation at the snail's pace of her less fortunate colleagues or standing acrest a rocky hilltop waving her exhausted brownie troop onward and upward. Any flies on her will need seat belts and a race driver's mentality. She's quick, active and pioneering. And heaven help the male who thinks she will flutter her baby blues or browns at him in a helpless posture, waiting for him to dash to her rescue, whisking her off the tracks before an onrushing train, then capturing the black-mustachioed forecloser on her family home. All by herself, she will burst the ropes, leap off the tracks and lasso and hog-tie the evil banker with a piece of his own rope.

She can out-run, out-drive, out-think and out-anything any male—or will die trying. To say she is competitive would be an understatement. There is no competition. She's the best. The hapless male who dates a One Woman and thinks he is going to drive his own car will discover that he has greatly misjudged the "weaker" sex. There is no coyness or subtlety. As they approach his car, she simply states that she loves to drive. As he walks around to the passenger side to open her door, she gets into the driver's seat with a "thanks for letting me drive." He doesn't know her well enough yet so he silently gets into the passenger seat thinking he will straighten it out later. That's his first mistake. She drives like a kamikaze pilot, and he learns early on to take his tranquilizers.

Positions of power attract her—indeed, they are almost a necessity. She has a strong will and likes to plan but not necessarily to build. After all, there are leaders and there are followers. And she wants to wear the bonnet. She must beware that it does not become a war bonnet in her drive to the top. She likes to tell others how things should be done but does not always want to do them herself. She's most unhappy if she has to take orders from someone else because her quick and frequently brilliant mentality often envisions a better mousetrap. Others sense her ability to intuit more creative solutions—probably because she comes right out and tells them so. Those around her would have to be two of the three proverbial monkeys—seeing not and hearing not—and living on another planet to overlook her leadership and executive powers.

She can run a slick advertising agency on Madison Avenue or the PTA and the Garden Club with equal ease. Her daring and innovative ideas not only spark new ways of doing things but may ignite a few tempers along the way. She's so intent on her place in the sun that she may seem selfish and egotistical at times. To prevent severe sunburn, she needs to be aware that the earth supports more than one human being at a time. Once this monumental task is accomplished, she is on her way.

There is a One Woman who may fool you by her quiet withdrawn demeanor. Actually, she's not shy or insecure. She's just not interested in what is going on in her present environment. She prefers her own thoughts and her own company or—at the most—the select company of one or two others to a cast of thousands. Her fiery energy is then concentrated on mental conquerings of new worlds. She may silently formulate the latest law of physics or outline next year's smash Broadway play while you're trying to impress her with the family jewels. Forget it. She's not interested in what your family did or what they passed on to you. She'll be more impressed by what you're doing now—if it's gauged by revolutions per minute—and where you are going—if it's to the top. Don't spin your wheels however. She's only interested in action.

When her mind is absolutely set on a goal, she pounces on it with all the fervor of a hunting tigress. Nothing exists outside that goal. She becomes so engrossed by the object of her attention that she is totally absorbed by it. She then displays her famous one-track mind which can work for or against her. Note the dog who ate his dinner on the slightly inclined roof of his dog house. Whenever his mistress approached with food, he leaped to this roof and awaited with consuming joy. One morning, she placed the remains of an espcially tantalizing sandwich before him. He attacked it with fervor, backing up in frantic frenzy to capture each morsel that rolled toward him. His attention was so taken up by his desire to devour every crumb that he backed right off the dog house. Similarly, when a One Woman decides upon a goal, she must not attack life with blinders on, falling off dog houses with predictable accuracy. The negative One Woman can be a loner, withdrawn and set apart by her uniqueness and driving energy. Marilyn Monroe, actress, born on the first, was a complex, lonely woman "obsessed with becoming a serious actress." Ironically, the title of her last film, *The Misfits,* symbolized her life. Your One Woman should use her creative, alert and sensitive personality in ways that allow her to focus on her desires with understanding and common sense. She tends to have an all-or-nothing attitude because she is really an extremist. She is the most individualized of women and needs to find a proper focus.

She dislikes weakness in a man but may try to rule him. If he succumbs to her charms and allows himself to be dominated or is by nature a passive individual, she will soon lose interest in him. She wants someone as active, direct and determined as herself. Underneath it all, she likes to be challenged. It makes life so much more interesting.

Take her on a safari, to the rifle range (where she'll beat you, hands down) or to a drag race but don't take her home to mother and a quiet evening in front of the

1

TV. If your mother is an old-fashioned girl, she'll have trouble coping with your One Woman anyway. Maybe it's your woman's Havana cigars or that cute little rose tattoo that your mother finds alarming, but whatever it is, your woman is not the demure kitten that mama may want for you. The One Woman, actress-singer Bette Midler, is described as a chain smoker, a hard drinker, a night animal with strong compulsions. Her "raunchy memoir," *A View From A Broad,* published in 1980, drew much attention. If you want sympathy and a lot of attention, the One Woman is not for you. She expects you to be as resourceful as she is. But if you need ideas and someone to fire you up, her creative juices begin to flow and her enthusiasm is sufficient for you both.

Can you picture her as a child? She was the first one down the stairs and to the Christmas tree, leaving a pile of rumpled bodies in her wake. As an adolescent, she wore braces, carried a newspaper bag over her shoulder and flung the Daily News from a speeding bicycle into your rock garden every weekday. And now, as a One Woman, she has the magical ability to appear and disappear at will. When you go looking for her, you will swear she can walk through walls. "She was just here," everyone says as they look around in astonishment. "Yes, I know," you'll grumble. "I can still smell the Havana cigar." And then off you'll dash, while the smoke trail is still warm. And when you finally find her, on one of your lucky days, she'll be bubbling with enthusiasm over a new discovery or idea. She'll say, "Wouldn't this be fun, honey. Let's try it, O.K?" And off she'll dart.

Like the Queen in *Through the Looking Glass* she believes in six impossible things before breakfast, and another half dozen to round it off before lunch. She is larger than life—forceful, commanding and confident. Kayaking the Colorado in spring or single-handedly preparing a dinner party for thirty guests on one day's notice, she will literally take your breath away. No one can move that fast and be that efficient. It isn't decent, you'll think. But your eyes don't deceive you—although they may be mighty weary following her movements in any given day.

Given the chance, she will be the sparkle in your life—a firecracker on the Fourth of July. Her extraordinary energy dazzles and magnetizes everyone in sight. And as she seeks new worlds to conquer, she may leave you panting, a half-used bottle of Geritol in one weary hand. Give her a cause and she will lead it. And if she's up there on the stage with Gloria Steinem, spouting feminist rhetoric, she's not expounding on women's lib as much as fair treatment for all. She will exercise all her passion and personal power to assure that each individual has the freedom to live life unencumbered and unrestricted by the archaic chains of sexism. She is truly a free spirit.

She likes a man who is a dynamic go-getter and the more successful, the better. A little experience in the one-mile-dash is suggested. Her own uniqueness carries over into her expectations of a man. She is distinctive even to her dress— Midler popularized "tack"—and would expect her man to be the same. She won't be startled or object if you show up on your first date in soiled Addidas and a torn "Dirty, Mean and Nasty" lettered T-shirt. After all, she respects your right to be you, just as you must respect hers to be her. However, don't think her feathered hair style is the product of a stylist. Rather, it's the result of the law of physics—for every action there is an opposite and equal reaction. A constant forward motion creates a constant and equal back draft. You may notice that she stands at a slightly forward incline—that is, if you ever find her stationary. This isn't an idiosyncracy but rather the result of good planning. She's ready for action at the drop of a hat.

With your One Woman you will need to cling to the Boy Scout motto with all tenacity—Be Prepared. It may take you time to get used to her unexpected frankness, especially in public places. You will have to ignore the startled stares in posh restaurants when she suddenly exclaims from out of nowhere in her crystal clear, if loud, voice, "Look! Don't get any wrong ideas. I'm not inclined to tumble into bed with every man I meet. I'll let you know when I'm ready for sex." She'll fling you a dazzling smile then dig into her shrimp scampi. And whatever you do, don't try to "shush" her. Her proud head will lift royally, she'll look at you with wide-eyed innocence, accompanied by a few uncomprehending blinks, and with all the rich crescendo of Beethoven's Fifth, declare that you might as well know where she stands on sexual intercourse from the start. If you don't develop ulcers by the end of the first month, you'll know you can handle that direct part of her nature.

She is ardent and romantically dramatic but dislikes displays of gushy sentimentality. She will not waste your time with trivia or circumlocution as your first few dinner dates will graphically attest.

In relationships, she can be cool and hard to get, and if you want her, you will have to don your Nikes and sweatsuit just to keep up. She has a mental and physical strength that attracts men and an aloof manner that intrigues them. Don't patronize her and don't call her a broad, unless you want to be eliminated as a narrow prospect. If you are not ready and willing to treat her as an equal and stand with her, but apart, like the pillars of Gibran's temple, you can forget about ever enjoying her magnetic, passionate intimacies.

On the other hand, if she decides you're the one she wants, she can be downright aggressive about it. Come on, now. Admit it. You wouldn't balk about being pursued by Wonder Woman, hogtied with her golden lasso and swept away to the depths of the Amazon jungle where her primitive intentions can be deliciously carried out.

When it comes to tying the marital knot, she surrenders her freedom most reluctantly. And for heaven's sake, don't expect that a piece of paper will change your wild, lynx-like woman into a domestic tabby. She'll not remain pregnant, barefoot and on the edge of town. Forget the pipe, slippers and home-cooked meals because she will determine her own lifestyle. The One Woman, Betsy Ross, was no wilting lily, spending languid moments by the fireside with her needle and thread. She was disowned by both the Quakers and her parents for marrying outside her religion. Later, she met secretly in her back parlor with George Washington, Robert Morris and her husband's uncle, Colonel Ross, to discuss her sketches for the first American flag. Not a healthy pasttime then, but neither danger nor public opinion could deter her once her mind was made up.

The One Woman writer, George Sand (Aurore Dupin) was touted in her lifetime as a female genius but ostracized as the "pipe-smoking, pants-wearing mistress of Frederic Chopin, Alfred de Musset and numerous others." She "captivated and scandalized" Paris during the nineteenth century.

Your woman can seem impulsive and headstrong but once she is totally involved in a relationship, she is faithful—a one-man woman. Although she may not voice it or even recognize it, somewhere in the deep wells of her consciousness, she

1

believes in true loyalty. And once committed, she expects the same from you. She is emotional, idealistic and far more vulnerable than she appears. She seeks unity—whether through a concentrated drive to the top of the business ladder or in a true, deep and devoted personal relationship, and perhaps both. But when all is said and done, she is her own person, refusing to be dominated or subjected.

She is direct, uncomplicated, honest and loyal. As long as you recognize her individuality, she will work with you into the wee hours of the morning, year after year. She will love you unflinchingly and passionately. And she will whisk you through life on an adventure that makes Tarzan's escapades look like child's play on a schoolground jungle set. And if you're smart, when you are confronted with this woman, you will say yes and follow her with dispatch.

The One Man

Take a deep breath because you'll need it. Your One Man will leave you gasping. He's a combination of superhero, superlover and superego. Whether he's leading an archaelogical dig in Mesopotamia or training wild Bengal tigers for Barnum and Bailey's, he leaves no doubt as to who is in charge. His driving energy propels him to positions of leadership early in life and his courage and personal faith in himself carry him quickly past his darker moments. Part of his prosperity—if that is what he chooses—is due to his high intelligence and another part to hard work. When he's dedicated to a task, he's inexhaustable and totally inspired.

His movement is jet-propelled and he leaves a trail of stardust in his wake. Rub it out of your eyes because, if you want to survive your One Man experience, you must have no illusions about who he is, where he's headed and what he wants. First—he's number one. As long as you acknowledge that up front, you'll be in his good graces. With some men, groveling is required but with your One Man, respectful kowtowing should be sufficient as long as you keep your eyes lowered in deference. Remember, he's the type who wants his name in the *Guiness Book of World Records*—you'll find a copy in his apartment. And he enjoys parties where people know who he is rather than just know him.

Second, he is headed for the top—wherever he's decided that happens to be. He has an alert, intense power—the match of Genghis Khan, Napoleon and Rocky Balboa rolled into one, and once he gets his mind cemented on a goal, he's hell bent for leather and the devil take the hindmost. So he'll get there . . . You may think the top is a two-garage home with an olympic-sized swimming pool, set back on a sprawling lawn in the suburbs and two vacations a year—on the Riviera and in the Swiss Alps. But this may not be what he has in mind. It may mean 341 days at the apex of the White House flagpole—if he can remain stationary that long. Or the top to him might mean the presidency of Exxon Oil. He could accomplish either, or both, probably at the same time. You never know with a One Man. So, if you've planned a comfortable and secure future, you'd better iron out those wrinkles at the start or, better yet, invest in wash and wear clothes. At least then you'll be prepared for any and all contingencies. This life you've chosen with him may not always be secure but it will certainly be exciting.

And third, he wants it all. His mind can conceive of no half-way measures nor entertain uncertainties. He is totally committed to living life to the fullest and he puts body, mind and soul into every project with complete confidence. He can accomplish more in half-a-day than most people can in a week. He's in one big hurry—he's got a lot to do and a lot to see so it's fortunate that his body is strong and his vitality limitless.

His ego is strong and must be handled with TLC (tender loving care). He needs your honest praise and admiration. And it wouldn't hurt if you stretched the truth a little—well, even a lot—once in a while. He'll eat it up because he believes it anyway. He knows it's true. So don't wait for him to be surprised or flattered when you compliment him because he won't be. He needs your adulation but he also expects it.

He's a rebel, extremely independent and self-willed, an original thinker, an inventive pioneer, living in a world of his own making. The nineteenth century performer and One Man, Le Petomane, was called a "novel" entertainer. His performances were in demand more than any other entertainer of his time. The "rage of royalty and Europe," he simulated sounds—music, machine-gun fire and so forth—by breaking wind. He discovered this unique talent when he was a boy. Your One Man dares to defy convention because he envisions a world where innovative methods are not the exception but the rule. He's the person Edison spoke of when he said, "Give me a man who doesn't know it can't be done and he'll go ahead and do it,"—with one difference: A One Man doesn't necessarily know that it can't be done, he just doesn't *believe* it can't be done. In his mind it can be done and he's the one who can do it. He sees that all things are possible if one looks for new ways to overcome old impasses.

He often follows the impulsive promptings of his head rather than his heart. He's not intentionally forgetful of your needs or your presence, it's just that he's so intent upon his own role in the drama of life that people and things become props for his scenarios.

His strong ego allows him to believe in himself. Heaven forbid you should doubt his ability to lock muscles with Arnold Schwarzenegger and come out first. He may need the heating pad that night but he will prevail. He's the archetypal hero—Hercules performing the immortal Twelve Labors without as much as a batted eye and Arthur freeing Excalibur from the stone when all others have failed. The One Man is a trend setter. Clark Gable, the One Man "King" of motion pictures caused undershirt sales to plummet when he appeared bare-chested in *It Happened One Night*.

As a child your One Man was beckoned toward the heights—king of the mountain on the school playground, the boy hanging from the highest limb on the biggest tree in his neighborhood, the kid in the red soap box who won the derby hands down. In his teen years, he probably excelled at every sport—baseball, hockey, soccer—and was captain of the team, the one who rallied fellow players and inspired team spirit. As a man his unflagging energy, drive and single-mindedness place him first in the chain of command wherever he focuses his penetrating mind for any period of time. His vitality defies the laws of medical science and if it could be bottled, pep pills would be a thing of the past.

Your One Man is charismatic, exciting and sexy. He appeals to both men and women in the same way Clark Gable did. He doesn't move, he swashbuckles. And if he's chosen you, you'll know without a doubt that you've been swept off your feet

1

by a bold, seductive man who craves constant action. When he takes you out, you'll never know where you'll end up but you can be sure it won't be commonplace or calm. There's nothing commonplace about climbing the Matterhorn and nothing calm about wrestling a crocodile. You won't forget him! He exudes an excitment and energy that spills over into his environment.

He'll adore the drama of the first glance, the smoldering flirtation and the short but oh-so-sweet courtship. He's not one to pussy-foot around so don't tell him you need time to think things over. There's one big word in his vocabulary—yes! So if you're not interested in a passionate adventure, stay home and practice your knitting. But if you have always yearned for an exotic experience, you don't have to armchair travel anymore. Develop your cardiovascular system and get ready. He is magnificent. Just ask him. He's imaginative and dynamic and he makes things happen. He is unique—be prepared for a few pioneering techniques and an energetic workout. He's not interested in tradition in bed; that is, if he climbs in at all. He wants what he wants when he wants it and an amorous mood is just as likely to strike him in the supermarket aisle, in a hurtling speedboat or on a crowded avenue. He won't leave you disappointed and he certainly won't bore you. He has enough pride and satisfaction to make sure that his satisfaction is yours. Like James Bond, "nobody does it better."

Don't be deceived if your One Man appears the quiet type on the surface. Some of them do. He may be reserved and aloof at your first meeting, staring down his nose at you as at some bug under a microscope. You find him terribly dashing so you smile provocatively and launch into your most stimulating conversation. Fifteen minutes later you begin to notice that you misjudged his attentive silence. Actually, his glassy eyes are locked on you but his mind is in the cosmos. Snap your fingers in front of his eyes. If he blinks and starts, you'll know we're right.

This One Man likes his solitude, away from the maddening crowds. In fact, he may be paranoid about crowds, preferring his own company and that of a very few select friends. If he becomes too withdrawn, and has difficulty releasing his energy positively, he can be irritable and reclusive, smoldering over imagined hurts and silently blaming others for his difficulties. When his laser-beam mind turns to revenge, beat a hasty retreat. Discretion is the better part of valor.

Your quiet One Man is still as passionate, unique and creative as his more outgoing counterpart, but he requires less public adulation. If his accomplishments are lauded—his inventions, plays, books, executive abilities, athletic prowess—he may not be there in person to accept the laurels. It's enough that his accomplishment has been recognized. His work will always have the strong stamp of uniqueness on it. It will never be like the work of anyone else. Whatever you do, don't suggest that your One Man's achievement reminds you of so-and-so's latest book or architectual triumph.

Under his silent exterior beats the same rebel's heart as his more cavalier brother. They both have an innate sense of their own superiority, although this one may be more quiet about it.

A One Man honestly believes that he can do it better than anyone else. The unsuspecting soul who tries to thwart a One Man's plans will end up as chopped liver. You can't toy with a One Man's ego. He has a sense of humor but your Attila the Ham can metabolize into Attila the Hun if his goals and self-image are tampered with. Fool around here and your normally humorous and cavalier One Man will chew up nails and spit out heads. But don't despair. Free your clothing and yourself from the wall, smile humbly at your wild and delirious mistake and explain that you foolishly lost your head. Of course you didn't mean that so-and-so was as good as he, and of course everyone recognizes that his work is very avante-garde. He'll mutter, "Well..." and then, because he knows you're right, he'll generously forgive you. His anger dissipates as quickly as it arises. He seldom holds a grudge.

A One Man is in a unique position—enviable as well as frightening. He desires the highest achievement and the applause of others. But when he gains these, he is still alone. Being at the top is scary—where does he go from there? It's a long fall from this exalted position and any mistakes he makes from this vantage point will be seen by the multitudes. He is caught in the eternal dilemma expressed by Lord Byron in *The Corsair*. The crew is ignorant of their captain's responsibilities and envious of his position. Byron says, "...but let the wretch who toils, Accuse not, hate not him who wears the spoils. Oh, if he knew the weight of these splendid chains, How light the balance and his humbler pains!"

But when all is said and done, your One Man gets a genuine kick out of life. He finds it exciting, stimulating and challenging. Danger is a way of life—he smiles in its face—and no matter how many last minute rescues, close shaves, and skin-of-the-teeth escapes he has, he'll go back for more. Danger makes him feel alive. He rushes in where angels fear to tread and possesses a toughness that is truly awesome. He is aggressive action personified, with the spirit of a warrior and the optimism of a god. He's pledged to live life 111 percent—with no discounts—and if you decide to buy, you're guaranteed your money's worth.

The Two Woman

Your Two Woman is subtle, oh is she subtle. In fact, you probably barely noticed her at that party in the beginning. The dazzling blonde with the hour-glass figure and the high-pitched laugh had your attention most of the night. But your Two Woman was there on the fringe of the gaiety and strobe lights, her eyes sweeping the room like a lighthouse on a foggy night. She appeared demure, completely helpless, almost shrinking from the aggressive merry-making of the rest of the party-goers. She made a subtle impression on you and weeks later, you find yourself thinking about her, searching your mind for more than a memory of a figure in unadorned black satin. She was with a friend, no, she was by herself. Wait a minute...it seems there were a few men around her...and with that thought, you're driven to call the friend who put on the party to find out who she is. You dial her number a little nervously, wait, and as the receiver lifts, a soft velvety voice floats over the air waves. You might as well get her pinky finger ring-size now because you'll be wrapped around her little digit before you can blink and say Rumpelstiltskin. She's not the kind to make male heads twist. She has a delayed effect. She is one woman you won't forget.

Because your Two Woman is so keenly sensitive to her environment, she may appear nervous, a little jumpy at times. She seems subconsciously to pick up subtle nuances and hints of coming events. She feels things and cannot always explain why. If she tells you not to park your red Ferari next to that pick-up truck in the public

2

parking lot, listen to her or you may cry crocodile tears when you come back and find the pick-up truck gone and your Ferari fender crumpled. Or when she suggests you change your seats at the movie theatre after you've comfortably settled in, don't argue. Pick up the buttered popcorn, napkins and Pepsis and climb over the six people between you and the aisle. We can practically guarantee that seconds later the ceiling tiles will come crashing down into your vacant seats. Don't ask her how she knew. She doesn't know.

Decision making can be difficult for your Two Woman. For instance, when her birthday rolls around, you may decide to take her out somewhere special, a favorite place of her own choosing. The conversation may go something like this:

"I'd like to take you someplace special on your birthday, honey," you say. "Where would you like to go?"

"I don't know," she replies. "Where would you like to go?"

"It's your birthday. You decide," you return. "Would you like a dinner and a movie, or a concert or what?"

"Would you like the concert?" she asks sweetly.

"Honey, it's your decision."

"Well, let me think about it."

Three hours later, you approach the subject once again. "Honey, have you decided?"

"Decided what?"

"Where you want to go on your birthday?"

"Oh, I don't know. Where do you want to go?"

Don't scream and tear your hair. Just count to ten, ten times. She'll turn your brain to cerebral succotash more than once and if you raise your voice in exasperation, she will lift her heavy-lidded eyes toward you in abject dismay. "Oh, darling," those eyes will say. "What have I done to displease you?" You'll wear a hair shirt the rest of the day.

Because she sees both sides of an issue, she can feel the needs and potentials of opposing points of view. She is the stuff of which mediators and peacemakers are made. The talent for gentle persuasion is her gift. Remember the last vacation you took to Bermuda? You thought it was your idea, right? Wrong. Think back. You originally wanted to go mountain climbing and she said what a wonderful idea that was. After you got all the proper pamphlets together, she lay a slim white arm over your shoulders as she placed a Bermuda brochure on the table edge purring, "Look what Ed and Veronica left here today." She bussed your ear and left. Where did you go? Bermuda. And you loved it. But you do remember her saying, "Gee, honey, that was a great idea you had, going to Bermuda. I really enjoyed myself." She'll get exactly what she wants and you'll thank her for going along with you.

Your Two Woman is genuinely warm-hearted and craves affection. Her love nature runs deep and true. As a little girl, she was the quiet one you didn't notice much. She didn't like going to the store unless accompanied by a friend. She hated having anyone angry at her, becoming moody and withdrawn if her feelings were injured. Family disputes were very upsetting for her. As a teenager, she originated the "pairs to the ladies room" routine. And now, as a woman, she is a partner and mate, first and foremost. Her life revolves around her relationships with others. She does not work well alone but shines when working with another or in a group. But, she would rather work alone than with those who disapprove of her or her methods. And she can sense others' disapproval, even if it's unspoken.

The Two Woman, Farrah Fawcett, poster-famous in 1977, said, "I was never a rebellious child. I listened to my parents, helped my mother with the dishes, and studied hard in school." Her teachers said, "She was a very cooperative student...and an honor student. She was outgoing and friendly but never a show-off." She dated less than other girls in high school and most of her dates were "family affairs." "I was always protected by my family," Farrah says. "I liked being protected. It kept me from getting too wise too soon."

Your Two Woman is caring and compassionate, and sensitive to other people's needs. As a result, she is well liked by others. The truth is that she needs people.

She has a talent for gathering hidden or unknown facts and surprising everyone with her insights, which she utters so casually. When you do a double take at her wisdom, you'll surprise her as well. She is not always aware of her own pearls because so many of her responses are intuitive.

Your Two Woman is happy to stand in the background, the power behind the throne. Although she is a feminist's nightmare, she manages to achieve results without overt displays of power. Whether she's the top executive of a national insurance company or in charge of a herd of offspring, she'll get the job done quietly and efficiently.

She enjoys a small intimate group of friends or just having you all to herself over a checkered tablecloth, a spaghetti dinner and candlelight. She is a romantic and your cleaning bill will sky-rocket during the rainy seasons. Cloaks over mud puddles and all that. She is geared to companionship, love and harmony.

A Two Woman can be a perpetual damsel in distress. She likes the drama of knights in shining armor, fire-breathing dragons and last-minute rescues. Her quiet demeanor often masks this taste for romance, but if you find her letting her braids grow long and thick, piling stones up in the back yard to form a tower, and signing her checks Rapunzel, then you've unmasked her and you know what your role must be if you are to win her heart.

When your Two Woman is not centered or in balance, she can be moody, unsure of herself and subject to periodic depressions. Her sensitivity to the constant stimuli from her environment can cause her to scatter her energies. She then appears absentminded and unfocused. That vacant stare, those glassy eyes, the motionless form do not mean she's in a coma. She really is interested in your new promotion. After all, she's the one who has been pushing you toward it for years. Just wait until the fog lifts and then you'll be deluged with congratulations, kisses and hugs and your male ego will swell like the surfer's ninth wave.

A more agressive person might say she is too easygoing and too concerned about what others think. However, she should remain true to herself. When a Two Woman begins to feel like a doormat, it's time to reconsider her relationships with others. And if she feels she is becoming one, she needs to go off by herself—to her room, the country, the seashore—where she can find a quiet place to sort out and process all the data she has absorbed unconsciously and how she is reacting to it. She needs to learn to walk that fine line between caring and needless martyrdom.

A Two Woman often underestimates herself, as do others when they first meet her. And perhaps this reaction is part of the reason for her self-image. But those

2

who do know her recognize her power and ability to subtly influence others, often long before she does. The Two actress, Julie Harris, thought herself so plain as a girl that she took to acting "as a means of becoming other people." Along with her slight five-foot-four stature and features that lack "emphasis," she has a "presence that can fill a stage." And remember your Two Woman on the phone? Columnist Roy Newquist said that Ms. Harris has "one of the most hauntingly lovely voices in the theatre." Critics said of her first performance, in a play called *I Am A Camera*, Ms. Harris proved "her subtlety and emotional range as an actress." Your Two Woman's subtlety carries over into family quarrels or company difficulties where she is the one who is chosen to re-establish peace and harmony. She unconsciously fosters cooperation in her environment, often identifying a problem long before it is recognized by the other parties involved. And she is the first one willing to say let's do something about this. She can achieve results without discord because she can be impartial and pays attention to the little details and nuances that others overlook.

Music, poetry and dance put her in touch with her intuition. She is finely tuned to rhythm, feeling rather than knowing it. And part of her occasional absent-minded trances is a direct result of her communication with a world you may never know. You may arrive home for dinner one night and find her wafting out the window on the wings of a song. Try explaining levitation to the new boss you unexpectedly brought home with you. On second thought, don't try. Grab her ankles and pull her back. Then watch her stuff. She can charm the skin off a snake. She'll have your boss eating out of your hand, congratulating you on your fine choice of a wife. And you'll agree. You still haven't realized that she had chosen you long before you began to chase her.

Your Two Woman knows the art of passive resistance. Indeed, the day will come when you will look at her in wonder, shaking your head. You can't explain it. You know how clever and intelligent you are, but somehow you feel that she's the one who's winning this game. If you attempt to discuss your feelings with her, she'll look up shyly, a little confusedly, and say, "What do you mean, honey?" And you'll say forget it. After all, you know you're the boss. And besides, there's no one quite like her in the whole world.

The Two Man

You know that crazy guy down the street—the one in the yellow slicker who's just finished building an ark in his backyard and you're in the middle of a drought? He's not crazy. He's a Two Man and he knows something you don't. His instincts are uncanny. Wait a minute...was that a drop of water you just felt? It's time to move—haul out the galoshes, vulcanize your house and take in a forty-day supply of food. And don't worry about water. You'll have plenty.

Your Two Man isn't going to shout messages of impending deluge from the White House steps or circulate a petition for more rain barrels. He'll just set quietly about doing what needs to be done regardless of what others think.

He watches as silently as the eternal Sphinx while others beat their breasts and clash their symbols. The sands may pile up around his feet, the would-be riddle solvers come and go but he remains stolid, unshakable and enduring. And he knows. He knows things he doesn't even know he knows.

Take the Two Man as a little boy. His mother caught him, after a summer rain storm, crushing little frogs under his heel on the driveway. She watched from the doorway for a moment and then called out, "Johnny...frogs know."

Johnny hesitated, looked from her to the frog beneath his foot and back again.

"No, they don't," he replied, uncertainly.

His mother was firm but kind, "Yes, Johnny, they do."

Johnny thought a moment, then walked away. He never crushed another frog.

What frogs know may remain a mystery to the rest of us but not to your Two Man. He has an innate subconscious connection with life, its meaning and the subtle energies that pervade his environment.

As a teenager, your Two Man may have been as nervous as a long-tailed cat in a room full of rocking chairs. He still hadn't adjusted to his sensitive ability to pick up other people's feelings and emotions, and all that stimuli could have made him jumpy and uncertain. He was not aware that others did not pick things up psychically as he did. He thought everyone perceived things that way. When he finally realized they didn't, he would stare absent-mindedly, a defense mechanism, to shut it all out. And all along you thought you were just boring him.

As a young adult he might have put aside his childhood dreams in order to fulfill other requirements. He is keenly aware of his duty to others—and is willing to wait patiently knowing that one day when his obligations are fulfilled, he'll get back to those dreams. He needs harmony and the knowledge that he is serving others. His instincts told him at an early age that his dreams would wait for him.

Now, as an adult, he has learned to deal with his uncanny intuitions and rely upon his instincts. When he says, "I don't know why, I just have a feeling we should do it this way," you'd better listen to him. Set common sense aside because you may never be able to find out what he's thinking or why, or get him to explain—if he knows. But beneath that placid exterior seemingly unrelated data comes together and voila! Solomon in all his wisdom pales beside your Two Man and his instinctive knowledge.

Like Inspector Columbo, complete with wrinkled trench coat and forgetful manner, his dishevelled appearance lulls you into a complacent state. You'll smile patronizingly as you think, "This disorganized creature really needs my help." Then, when your complacency is at its peak, the trap suddenly springs shut and there you are with your teeth hanging out. How did it happen? It happened because he has a mind like a steel trap and you'd better not forget it if you want to play parlor games with him.

Then there is the Two type who appears to stumble unintentionally on truths. Like the bumbling Inspector Clousseau, no matter how inept and totally at odds with himself he appears to be, no matter how often, while stealthily pursuing a thief, he trips over a cat whose yowling screech startles the burgular who swings his flashlight through the glass library doors alerting a passing policeman who captures the offender as he dashes down the drive. Your Two Man inevitably comes out on top of the heap—your hero!

It's useless to try to keep secrets from him. You'll swear he's wiretapped your brain when he casually remarks in front of your father-in-law that you hate Chinese modern (and your father-in-law just gave you that little red pagoda lamp with the gold tassels last week). You never told your Two Man how you felt about little red lamps with gold tassels, but you did think it. And as you watch your father-in-law's brows close like thunder clouds over his eyes, try to get out of that one gracefully. The more you say, the guiltier you'll look.

Believe it or not, your Two Man can be tactful and diplomatic when he wants to be, he's a natural at it. Butter melts in his mouth and you won't find a more agreeable and friendly individual this side of the Mississippi. Give him a problem that involves two parties and he's in his element. You'll be amazed at his ability to subtly convince both sides that they are getting exactly what they want, and shake your head in disbelief when they come away from the conference table smiling broadly at their own cleverness. And this is the guy whose major accomplishment each morning is deciding what color socks to put on.

Like Bud Abbott of the comedy team Abbott & Costello, he's willing to play the straight man while others get the laughs and accolades because he enjoys working in partnerships. He needs people around him. But if he is thwarted too often in his early years he can become withdrawn, moody and unpredictable, taking refuge in his subconscious where hurts can fester and grow. His mind simmers what he experiences and if he cannot let the steam off gradually by finding a balance point, he boils. But, because he's so aware of your feelings, he usually handles life's experiences with care and forethought before reacting.

He may dislike ostentatious displays of affection in public but his seductive glances or pressure on your hand under the table are as thrilling as a bear hug from most men. He tantalizes you with subtle movements and nuances, promises of more exotic things to come. When he finally gets you "behind closed doors" and lets your hair fall down, the promises will be fulfilled.

Back in the bright light of the everyday world, you'll find him warm, sensitive and responsive. When he can please you, he is in tune with himself so what would appear placating or vascillating to more aggressive types is his way of bringing himself into harmony. He needs to fill voids, always subconsciously gravitating toward the troubled spot or to the weakest position so that he can bring balance to his environment.

Like a chameleon blending into its background, your Two Man is more comfortable off stage. And like the chameleon which turns red when it is afraid, your Two Man may blush when he's singled out. He has a strong protective mechanism built in, causing him to lay back in public. If there are assertive, strong personalities present, he'll stand back, be agreeably quiet and attentive. If his companions are passive and disinclined to take the lead, he'll tactfully move into the leadership position effectively and efficiently. This continuous awareness, however, can make him nervous until he recognizes in what direction he needs to go at any given time.

The great Indian nationalist and spiritual leader, Mahatma Gandhi, born on the 2nd, knew the art of passive resistance. He moved quietly, yet firmly and with great dignity, to lead his country toward freedom and human rights.

Your Two Man may feel he needs to be all things to all people, needing to do everything for everyone and knowing there's not enough time to do it all. A thirty-hour day would please him no end. Then perhaps he could get closer to the end of his list of things to do. He's probably a "list" person, carrying them about with him or tacking them on the walls of his home or office, continually checking things off and adding more. The problem is he makes a habit of adding more then he checks off.

Because your Two Man is so adaptable, what you see is not necessarily what you get. He has a hidden side that may not be intentional. He epitomizes the inscrutable East, an enigma even to himself, a melding of paradoxes: assertive and passive, open and closed, confident and uncertain, and always, it seems, at the most inopportune times. Yet his instinctive sense of timing and his awareness of the needs of the moment direct him as surely as the swallows return to Capistrano.

And although the Two Man was born to partnerships and to react by filling the voids in his environment, he has to learn that he needs time by himself to clear and process the constant stimuli that he absorbs. If he denies this part of himself, eliminating these necessary moments of solitude, he can become rattled, nervous and uneasy, finding it difficult to sleep at night. And if you're living with a sleepless Two Man, you're living in a sleepless Two house because—remember—he doesn't do things alone. He'll loudly wake you up and then ask what the two of you are going to do since neither of you can sleep.

You'll have to learn to take the worse with the better because your Two Man wants you doing what he's doing at the same time that he's doing it. And you can imagine some very interesting scenarios in which you're likely to be involved.

Once experience has taught him his strengths, he can master most subjects easily, including himself. At this point he finds his balance and becomes a sanctuary and a refuge. He'll be there when you need him, playing the sounding board for your ideas and emotions. He's quick to recognize the facts and analyze the angles and his insights will surprise, please and comfort you. He loves and respects life and his role in it. He is sensitive and spiritual, sensing the artistic symmetry of his world. Obscure esoteric subjects, science, music and mysticism may appeal to him because they shore up his innate knowledge about the purpose and rhythms of life. He will cling to you when all others have departed, love you when all others are indifferent and teach you to laugh at the seemingly inequitable distributions in life. You will learn to trust his intuitive feelings and find a world of peace and contentment in his arms. And, after all is said and done, what else could you possibly do?

The Three Woman

Your Three Woman is a ray of brilliant sunshine, a bright spot on everyone's horizon. She can illuminate the darkest corner, bring a Cheshire Cat grin to the sourest face and dazzle the eyes of any observers with her luminous charm. Foster Grant sales skyrocket in her path, as she moves with ease and grace in all circles. Like the sun, she draws others to her because of her warmth and genuine sociability. She makes you feel as good as a crackling warm fire on a blustery winter's night or a cool refreshing shower on a hot August day. She has a way of revitalizing others with her enthusiasm and joyfulness in life.

Your Three Woman also has a flare for the dramatic. You'll never figure out how one person's entrance can create the excitement of simultaneous openings of the Ziegfeld Follies and the Folies Bergere. Trumpets blow, heads turn and a red carpet unfolds mysteriously beneath her feet. Don't try to understand the phenomenon, just follow her with an appointment book in hand, noting the engagements she

3

makes as she flows through the attentive crowds. Yes, Sarah, lunch on Tuesday, I'd love to... Of course I won't forget, Harry. Wednesday at 9:00 to discuss my part in your new play... Oh, Hilda, darling, how wonderful to see you. Her head swivels your way for a fleeting moment and then she's off, disappearing into the crowd with a laugh and a wave. You'll end up sprawled out on the patio chaise, trying desperately to remember your name.

Your Three Woman will change your life. She'll fill it with wonder and magic and delightful impossiblities. She believes all things are possible—of course, she's going on the camping trip with you this weekend. What's one broken leg? And naturally you'll get that new job. It doesn't matter that 3,749 people have applied, you're the one they'll choose. I mean, they are intelligent, aren't they? And don't cry, little one, absolutely there's a Santa Claus. Really now, have your friends ever been to the North Pole to check out the real estate and doesn't the whole world, I mean just everyone, believe in Santa Claus... and elves, and the Easter Bunny and the Tooth Fairy too? Your friend Alice doesn't? Well, don't you feel just horribly sorry for her?

Seeing is believing for some women but imagining is believing for your Three Woman. Whatever she can imagine in her mind she knows is possible—nay, even probable—in the world around her, and she can out-positive-think Earle Nightingale, Reverend Robert Schuller and Norman Vincent Peale combined. She's the threes that things happen in. She can believe without seeing because she has an abiding faith and optimism, and it's these very qualities that produce the results she's sure she'll get. A positive Catch 22. She knows it will work and it does because she knows it. What you think is what you get.

She seems to have an inexhaustable energy pack hidden away somewhere. She can burn the midnight oil, dance in her slippers and then drink champagne out of them, into the bewitching hours of the night, and then bounce out of bed at the crack of dawn the next morning, raring to go while you're prostrate on the bed with an ice pack on your aching head. For her, life is her stage, and every night's an opening night and every day's an opening day, and she isn't about to miss one moment of the excitement and fun. She's seldom sick—she's too sociable and eager to participate to be ill, and lying in bed is a waste of time—she might miss something. And besides, there's no need to be sick.

What was this bundle of solar energy like as a child? Very emotional, talkative, eager to please, love and be loved. And it all gushed out. Sure as cats have kittens, someone affectionately tagged her "motor mouth." She loved to talk and be in the midst of the action.

As a teenager she needed to belong. And if you put her on a string, wound her up and called her a yo-yo, you'd have some idea of her range of emotions at that time. She may have used some of them in the drama or debating club in school. She has more talent than Carter has pills, but she must guard against scattering her energies too widely. The pitfall is becoming a Jane-Of-All-Trades and mistress of none. She needs to concentrate on one subject thoroughly before going on to another.

Her energies may still be scattered as a young adult. She wants to do too much all at once. Her abundant artistic inclinations and her unsurpassed imagination may plunge her in over her head. About the only thing in her life that is unspoken is her fear of overindulgence. When you go to work wearing damp undershorts and the dog is on the porch with a can opener prying at the lid of a can of dog food and your teenage son is stapling up the cuffs on his work pants, then it's time to have a head-to-heart talk with her. An intimate dinner would be the perfect setting—perhaps something simple like the Waldorf Astoria with twenty-inch Austrian crystal wine goblets, a tuxedoed waiter and a harpist on a dais in the center of a plush Victorian drawing room decor. But approach your subject gently or you'll have Waldorf Hysteria on your hands. And believe it—the last act will belong to her. She may even swoon—gracefully, of course—over the English wedgewood, one arm artistically draped over the table's edge.

She can listen to troubled or depressing conversation just so long. She is genuinely sympathetic and caring but when her sought-after advice is given, after she has offered some positive ideas and affirmations, she becomes impatient with those who will not try to help themselves. She wants to have a good time and socialize with cheerful people. Therefore, as a young adult she tends to leave less happy people behind. As she matures, however, she learns patience and can truly become a loyal, stable and inspiring light for those who are in great need. Her positive attitude has a healing effect. Her presence in a sick room can work miracles.

Your Three Woman cannot hide her light under a bushel. Cover the heads of one hundred people with paper bags and she'll be the one picked out every time. Her glow, like the eternal flame, illuminates her aura, invisible to most but definitely felt by anyone in her presence. She cultivates people through her efforts at being charming and gracious. She likes and needs the company of others. She is really not a laborer—she does best in self-expression through the arts. They are almost necessary for her happiness and fulfillment. But she is adaptable. Your Three Woman would definitely not be happy shipwrecked on a desert isle by herself but would try to make the most of her situation. She'd build a shelter—she's very clever—and you can be sure she'd have the most elegantly decorated thatched hut in the annals of maritime survival. And for want of a different audience, she'd learn to talk to the animals and they'd be only too enchanted to talk back.

She can be very funny. There's a touch of the comedienne in her. The Three Women actresses, Doris Day, Zasu Pitts and Jean Harlow were all known for their theatricality and ability to communicate humor. Ms. Day, singer, dancer and comedienne, "vivacious and popular," has starred in many comedies; Zasu Pitts, who also played humorous roles in films during the thirties, was known for her "snappy replies"; and Ms. Harlow became a legend as "the brash, wise-cracking, provocatively sexual, teasingly tarty girl with a figure and formation that were pure art-decor."

Although your Three Woman is a witty conversationalist and you may not think of her mouth as being oversized, you'll often find her foot hanging out of it. She has such a rush of ready answers that in her exuberance she often lets things slide out that are better left unspoken. And to compound the problem, she has an uncanny ability to hit the mark unknowingly. If you have a sore spot, a weakness, she'll find it and let her innocent Cupid arrows loose unerringly until you feel like a porcupine's victim. But she's so delightfully charming and honest, you don't know whether to throttle her or laugh along with her. In preparation for an enduring relationship with her, look up the term dementia praecox and, while you're at it, look up a good psychiatrist. Your Three Woman may appear to be a schizophrenic but actually she only drives other people crazy.

3

Your Three Woman devotes much of her time and attention to keeping her friends happy. You can depend on her to dash off a charming note of praise when you're bursting at the seams over a special accomplishment.

She knows etiquette. In fact, the writer and authority on etiquette, Emily Post, was a Three Woman. Although she wrote novels and short stories, had a "passion" for architecture and interior decorating, she would be best remembered for her 1922 creation, *Etiquette in Society, in Business, in Politics and at Home*, which came to be known later as *Etiquette: the Blue Book of Social Usage*. This book went through ten editions and ninety printings during her lifetime. Her radio programs and daily syndicated column "made her known to millions of Americans as the prime authority on correct social conduct." The perfect hostess.

Fun is important to your Three Woman. She cultivates it by continually seeking new and exciting outlets which she imbues with her abundant energy and creative ideas. Think about it—how many people do you know who find an astrologer in the yellow pages and set up a party around the astrologer? And have the operator asking for an invitation. Or for a summer eve's party, fills brown shopping bags with sand, places lighted candles in them and lines the driveway with a thousand lights. We know a Three Woman whose husband returned from a five-day canoe trip to find his saffron-walled bedroom with its wooden floor and colonial pine furniture transformed into a cloud of white lace puffs, pillows and linens, with an ornate brass headboard, sink-up-to-your-ankles powder blue carpet and sky blue and sunset pink wallpaper. When you re-do a room, you are also re-doing that part of yourself which the room represents. This canoeist had another exhilarating trip that night. His Three Woman is full of surprises and she makes his life *verrrryy* interesting.

On the domestic scene your Three Woman is artistic, creative and versatile. She can take an old bedspread, the braid from a discarded Indian sari and your favorite diamond stick pin and create a gown that will leave you gasping. You might even forget about losing your stick pin. And notice that she made a gown, not a housedress. After all, that would be a dress for a house not a woman. The joys of a happy housewife may be words of wisdom for some women but in your Three Woman's chronicles, they degenerate into the "diary of a mad housewife." It is essential that her versatility be allowed expression. She needs to move in more than one world, especially if that world isolates her from others. She requires being with people, having friends, mingling in social settings where her natural wit, vivid imagination and warm personality draw others like bees to honey. She has a knack for story telling and can make the simplest happening appear exciting and thrilling beyond belief. She's a pied piper, moving gayly through life with an entourage of adoring followers at her heels. There is always a stage, a microphone, or a movie camera at hand and she never disappoints her audiences.

Nothing lifts a Three Woman's spirits more than arriving at a place she likes, or leaving one she doesn't. And that applies to her relationships as well. She'll give you a lot of her time but doesn't want to be heavily burdened with insurmountable problems. She has too many things to do, too many places to go, too many wonders to see, to be confined by constant negativity. She needs her space. She needs companions in the plural who are mentally compatible, who are willing to dash off at the drop of a hat to climb Kilimanjaro or swim the English Channel. She'll soon be off to the sports center making mental notes...let's see, we'll need heavy rope, cramp-ons maybe, a good back pack, Vasque climbing boots, and then...a comfortable swim suit, some kind of body grease, what do they use, I wonder?... You'll sigh and shake your weary head. But a secret smile will hover on the corners of your lips. She's a marvel. She fills your being with unspeakable joy and hope and fun and life...and there just aren't enough superlatives. She's some woman and although you can't really say she is yours, she loves you.

The Three Man

Remember the first time you saw your Three Man—well, part of him anyway. You were at a friend's party and he was the one with the lampshade on his head. You thought—oh, this is too much—but you found yourself genuinely laughing with him along with everyone else. The twinkle in his eyes and the three-foot grin on his ruddy face eclipsed everyone in the room. You could almost feel his magnetism swirl out around you, drawing you toward him. He has a regal magnificence about him, in spite of lampshades, and wherever he is, the spotlight is on him. He's the center of the universe and if you revolve around him, your life will be warmed and nurtured by his ardor, faith and optimism. Your Three Man is an actor, and an actor needs an audience—an approving, appreciative audience.

He might have been the class clown, the one found headfirst in the trash barrels on the school ground or the joker short-sheeting beds at scout camp and sprinkling them with crackers to boot. Or he may have been headfirst in the cosmos, imagining all sorts of fantasy worlds inhabited by elves and goblins and Hobbits.

As a teenager, he found his golden tongue and learned to talk his way out of a paper bag. He could give his mother 104 reasons why he should not take out the trash. If she had the patience of Job, the wisdom of Solomon and the determination of Genghis Khan, she would eventually outwit him, getting him to perform, but the grumbling that would accompany his performance would be endless. Her Three teenager's subsequent exhaustion would result less from overworked muscles than an overworked larynx. This mother probably kept two muzzles on the back porch—and only one was for the dog. Her Three Son always had the last word. He could be heard mumbling all the way out to the trash can and back.

Now, as a man, he still manages to have the last word, not necessarily in an argument—he really wants to have fun—but in any conversation. He wants to be remembered so he always has a last quip, joke or comment to toss out as he rides off into the sunset. But he won't ride too far because he does want people around him. All kinds, all shapes and all sizes. He's very cosmopolitan. And his home will reflect this. When you have an argument and he says he's going home to mother and he doesn't even have to leave the house, you may feel the camaraderie is a bit overdone. When you plan to take a vacation by yourself on the dark side of the moon, you'll know it's finally getting to you. Aspirin, Tylenol and Sominex won't help, unless you give them to *him*. Then, like the distraught mother who accidentally mixed the tablets and gave her children the tranquilizers while she took the vitamins, you'll experience the best day you've ever had.

Your Three Man is a socializer. He loves to communicate in grand ways, like the Three Man, Wayne Newton, who plays so many instruments that he's called a one-man band. He learned to do this because he wanted to be a more versatile

3

showman. Your Three Man is also a showman. He doesn't just write letters, he writes long, long letters because he can't leave anything out. On top of that, he tends to embroider the facts so that even his ordinary experiences have a grandeur about them. You know that three-mile-long note paper you see in novelty shops? Oh, yes. People really buy that—Three People—because, first of all, their letters will stand out above any others and second, they have so much to say. Really. Your Three Man was absolutely ecstatic when casette recorders came out and offered a unique, new method of letter "writing." Now he can "talk" his letters. His joy is unbounded. Communication comes naturally to him and he tends to magnify whatever he does. Subtlety is not for him. He prefers embellishment.

The phenomenally successful Three writer, James Michener, *(Hawaii, Centennial)* often crams his stories "so forbiddingly full of information and reflection, at times even exhortation, that he has himself insisted that he cannot account for his popularity."

Carved on stone tablets in his wallet are the words: "Variety is the spice of life." This motto applies to his women as well. The list of femme fatales he has known makes James Bond's date book look like a directory of house mothers. Remember that voluptuous belly dancer who made the front page a few years ago, and the woman wrestler who won the U.S. Wrestling Championships (she had him in knots), and the quiet brunette down the street who shocked everyone when her cover was blown. Imagine, a sweet girl like that, a secret agent! He dated them all. Excitement and variety keep him going. He could be heading for his thirties before he makes marriage a serious consideration. Once he has decided upon you, this knight-errant embarks on his crusade. He'll make the plans. On the appointed night, he'll gather you up on his white steed and silently sweep over the crusty moonlit snow toward a towering cathedral where throngs of invited guests await in its hushed sanctuary, lit only by huge wrought iron candelabras. After the ceremony the mighty doors of the church swing open and amidst flowers and cheering voices, he lifts you to the saddle, leaps up behind and off you ride.

At least, that's how he'll tell it years later as your little ones gather around his feet. A smile will curl your lips as you think back: It really was something like that. As a matter of fact, it's been like that ever since. The honeymoon never ends with a Three Man. So, remember, once the knot is tied, in satin and lace of course, you need to be all things to your Three Man in order to keep his life happy, exuberant and enchanted. Surprise him often. He doesn't care if your scrambled eggs are the worst and the toast is a sheet of crusty carbon. It's your black lace negligee that has caught his imagination. And when you attend a starlit concert, spread out a Chantilly tablecloth, bring out the wine goblets and a bottle of Dom Perignon. The tablecloth could be red gingham, the goblets from the dime store and the wine a $2.98 special. It really doesn't matter. Just don't do things in the ordinary way. Make the ordinary extraordinary. He'll love you for it because what he desires most is a partner who will share his creative enthusiasm and spontaneity. At maturity, he begins to get weary of experiencing everything by himself. He recognizes that half the fun in life is sharing it with someone else. So he seeks a partner who will treat each day as a unique opportunity for adventure, self-expression and growth. He is attracted to superachievers, those who believe they can do or be anything.

Your Three Man is highly emotional. His fiery temperament can run the gamut from A to Z in the same time others go from A to B. His emotions swing like the pendulum on a clock and he can become very depressed. But it doesn't last long because he's basically an optimist. His glass is almost always half full, seldom half empty.

Your Three Man scatters enthusiasm, energy and ideas the way Johnny Appleseed, who traversed New England in the nineteenth century, scattered appleseeds—paying for his room and board by telling wonderful stories. There's a bit of metaphysical magic in him. As his audiences gather round, a glow lights his smiling face and his eyes take on a wise and far-away look as he visualizes the thoughts that give form to his words. He moves in prophetic and philosophical realms that capture the imagination of the stoniest minds. One of the greatest storytellers of all time, the Three Man, J.R.R. Tolkien, captured the minds of adults and children alike with his books, *The Hobbit* and *Lord of the Rings*, a fantasy unequaled in this century.

Because your Three Man loves the limelight and has a natural ability as a conversationalist, coupled with an emotional nature, he must be careful he doesn't get carried away and talk for the sake of talking or because he loves to hear his own voice. If this happens, he can exaggerate issues and become the town bluejay who, in order to alert the forest creatures, streaks through the woods at the first approach of a human foot. Occasionally, he needs to stand still until he has regained his equilibrium.

He should be careful not to scatter his vast resources. Because he has so many talents, is extremely adaptable, enjoys and uses a vast imagination and his inordinate optimism, he has periods of overindulging in life's bounty. He thinks he can be all things to all people—a "man for all seasons." Periodically he should remove his suit of armor, hang up his banner and plan his strategy for the next glorious campaign in search of the Holy Grail. He needs to gather his forces, drink from the well and restore and refresh his soul.

Although scattering is a real danger for your Three Man, he should not become the dog-with-a-bone type whose attention cannot be diverted by the playmate of the month, the yearly monsoons or an act of God. He needs more than one outlet for his endless ideas. He would shrivel up and die if he were cooped up in a box-like job or environment day after day with little social contact. You surely won't find him in a lotus position on a rock overlooking a solitary beach. He needs people and activity. It is essential that he have interests outside his job and outside his home in order to keep his talents in motion and his mind occupied.

When you find your Three Man snarling at the roosters on your kitchen draperies, then it's time for you two to be off on an exciting, exotic vacation. Warm sun, tropical nights and pina coladas will fill the bill. Then watch your Three Man blossom. It's like watching time photography where a seed breaks through the soil, shoots up and leafs out, buds, then bursts into glorious beauty and color—all in sixty seconds. That's what it takes to keep him happy—a little imagination and a lot of love.

Mentally, your Three Man moves in overdrive. As long as he keeps a steady foot on the accelerator and a keen eye on the road, there are no heights to which he cannot rise. Since his leanings are definitely artistic and creative, he will probably choose to mate with the Muses. Here polygamy will reign in his need to satisfy his numerous artistic desires. He could use his creative flair in business and politics but he tends to be better suited for the arts.

3

Your Three Man is eager to learn, to experience and to grow through social contact and discourse with foreign cultures and peoples. Books and formal academic training are not necessarily as effective for him as spending three hours in the jacuzzi with an Indian snake charmer and the French charge d 'affaires. He'll have the snake charmer spellbound and the charge d'affaires asking for his recipe for turtle soup. In the meantime, he'll pick up some fascinating threads to weave into the tapestry that he'll spread before the next group he meets. He has difficulty with books because the exchange is only one way. The book does all the talking and what's he to do besides scrawl his brilliant comments over the outer margins. Who's going to appreciate that? Who's going to laugh at his witticisms and bask in his radiance? Certainly not the fibrous remains of a hemlock or spruce. The traditional classroom can be just as stifling for him. He learned long ago that his behavior in those hallowed halls earned him the undying exasperation of the principal and caused an unprecedented decrease in the teaching population. It was time to change his behavior.

Today, he chooses to educate himself through social contacts—clubs and organizations, parties, theatres and concerts, and travel. The Three Man has a big investment in the good life. His stakes are high and he plays all out. As long as he doesn't become jaded from overindulgence and lose his wonderful vibrancy and expectant optimism, he is a moving force in the world. He is the one who makes things happen. He is the energy behind manifestation. He is the Three Muskateers and Santa Claus, sunshine and smiles, ice cream and strawberries. He'll tickle your funnybone, tug on your imagination and capture your heart. And with the gift of his love, you'll know you've made it. You'll have it all.

The Four Woman

So you've got yourself a Four Woman and now you don't know what to do with her. She has all those qualities you admire in a woman—she's loyal, loving, organized and dependable. She likes food, animals, gardens and children. She nurtures and cares for you when you're down, bursts her buttons when you're up and fills your soul with desperate longing when she's away. She's everything you could possibly want. So what's wrong. Coupons and the Good Housekeeping Seal of Approval? Certainly not agents eligible for alienation of affection but the picture is clearer now. She is a coupon saver—although that's not the real problem. It's being greeted by rectangular gaps in the sports page each evening and standing in line ahead of a throng of hurried, harried shoppers while the clerk adds up five cents off on baggies, seven cents off on large sized toothpaste, fifteen cents off on six ounce cans of sardines.... You could even have lived with *that* until neighbors began picketing your supermarket carrying placards reading: Down with coupons!

Second, why should you submit to wearing pastel jockey shorts just because they have the Good Housekeeping Seal of Approval. It's downright humiliating. You don't mind wearing them in the privacy of your own home but the other day you forgot and changed clothes at the health club. Pale pink rosebuds are nice in corsages but...on your shorts in a male locker room? But, she explains, research has shown that colors affect your moods. Pink, she goes on to say, is the color of love.

"Love—right!" you return vigorously, as your heart thumps against your chest like an eagle in a canary's cage. Suddenly either her reasoning is overwhelmingly clear or it really doesn't matter. She's your woman, and coupons and rosebud jockey shorts aside, you wouldn't trade her for one hundred others.

You should realize that your Four Woman is a builder. Whether she chooses to build an empire or a home, she'll do it by the same exacting and methodically painstaking process. She believes in one step at a time, making certain each step is secure before the next one is attempted. Her methodology is the result of an innate sense of the necessary solidity strong foundations require. A strong house cannot be built on a weak foundation. She's into foundations the way other women are into decoration.

Since the four is a square (made up of four lines), it represents places that contain—the body, the home and larger institutions, even those that confine, such as prisons. The Four Woman, American philanthropist and writer, Dorothea Dix, started teaching Sunday school in the East Cambridge (Massachusetts) House of Correction in 1841. The conditions were so abhorrent that she began investigating other institutions including houses for the insane and the poor. It became her life's work. She established "over thirty asylums for the mentally ill, promoting humane treatment. . . ." Her most effective writing was *Prisons and Prison Discipline* (1845).

To your Four Woman, money is also a foundation, a resource that allows her to build a comfortable present and secure future so you must forgive the idiosyncrasies she builds up around this medium of exchange. Just because she wears her moneybelt to bed at night doesn't necessarily mean she doesn't trust you. It's really not a matter of trust. Actually, it's a matter of life and death. To your Four Woman, money is security and security is an essential part of her being.

When she was a little girl, she had the neighborhood kids lining up in front of her house every Friday afternoon. Her mother thought the children had come to play but when the hand-lettered sign "Children's Bank and Trust" appeared in her daughter's bedroom window, she quickly got the idea. Loaning money is one thing but exorbitant interest rates from playmates is another. However, business is business, and if you borrowed you paid. Strong-arm tactics were not beyond the realm of her childish imagination. After all, that money was her security for the future. Pension plans were started by people born on the fourth.

As a teenager, she was probably the first one to own a car, bought and paid for by herself. Although her parents taught her, through care, proper guidance and wills of granite, to share her vast collection of earthly resources with others, she was known to swallow her car keys each night with regularity.

By now, your Four Woman has learned to give of herself and her possessions with love and joy. She goes out of her way to do favors for loved ones and friends, and can be depended upon to say yes to most requests for assistance. She has a lot of common sense when it comes to everyday matters. The Four Women, twins Ann Landers and Abagail Van Buren, offer advice on everyday concerns to millions of readers through their syndicated columns, Dear Ann and Dear Abby. They share the practical experience they have gained through life and people trust their judgment.

Along with her sharing nature, your Four Woman has recognized her strong sense of values in the proper light. She knows that if she takes care of her money and possessions, they will take care of her. She values items that have a practical use. She's the original string saver, storing spheres of the stuff in every available nook and cranny. Her cellar is full of empty cans, bottles, secondhand gift boxes, wrapping paper and ribbons. Old rubber tires are stored on that vacant lot she bought last winter—just in case. She has an uncanny sense of what you'll need next week, next year and next century.

With a history like that, you were extremely flattered when she tacked your Valentine on the bathroom wall. You felt it was a strange place to hang a card but it was the thought that counted. She cared enough. When you coyly asked why she chose that particular card to display, she replied that it was just the right size to cover a hole the kids had pounded in the bathroom wall.

But she is sentimental. In fact, some Four Women take over where your mother left off, saving your personal notes, dance programs, the stubs from your first movie, the socks you wore on your honeymoon, and snapshots. Everywhere, in albums, on the mantel and walls, in wallets, on T-shirts and over pillow cases. Home and family form the framework of her life. She is super loyal—here today and here tomorrow. Once she has decided to nurture you, she is like the little shadow from the childhood poem who goes in and out with you wherever you go. When you turn too quickly, you'll trip over her because she's glued to your form, following right along behind to be sure your tie is straight, your hair is combed and your fingernails are clean.

That loyalty carries over to her country as well. She's patriotic, standing up for her nation and its system. Her opinions about it can be very fixed. Well, let's be honest. She can be downright stubborn. Once she has cemented her mind on a point of view, it takes a chisel and hammer to make any impressions to the contrary. Actually, it would take a super nova or an act of Congress to change her mind. An Act of Congress would have more effect on her. She's very geared to law and order. For thirty years she wouldn't allow anyone to tear off the "Do not remove under penalty of law" tag from the mattress. She'd be downright appalled if anyone even suggested such a thing because she knew that if this offense were committed, waves of S.W.A.T. teams would descend upon her home. And her home must be defended at all costs. Her intrinsic belief in the law and tradition gives support and protection to her home and the roots of her being. These systems provide a stable framework upon which she constructs her life.

You are dealing with a personality whose roots go deep into earthly things. She's Mother Nature, nurturing, responsible and constant. Be aware that "it's not nice to fool Mother Nature." You know, storms, lightning, tidal waves and all that. Her passion and strength know no bounds when sacred issues are under attack.

Back on the domestic front, she takes in stray animals and people, feeds and comforts them, then delivers them back into the everyday world with mended souls. Her home looks like a cross between a tropical rain forest and the local S.P.C.A. Orphanages send their overflow to her. You will find kids, animals, birds and slithery things swirling in a kaliedoscope of movement around you. You learn to shake out your shoes in the morning before you put them on. You still haven't forgiven her for not telling you about the python in the shower—even if it was there for only one night as a favor to your neighbor, the zoo keeper. Life with your Four Woman is memorable. Three thousand years from now you may even laugh about it.

Speaking of memory, your Four Woman has a staggering one. The past is important to her because it is the foundation of the present and the future. So she remembers everything and forgets nothing.

It's wise to stay in her good graces. Because she has such a good memory, she retains things longer than most people. It's not that she holds a grudge but...how

4

many four-year-olds do you know who took contracts out on their mothers. Today she may still be debating about following it up, but then her naturally warm and loving nature wins out and she'll bend over backward to make her home comfortable and her loved ones happy and well fed.

Your Four Woman loves ritual. She finds habit patterns comforting because within them she knows what to expect. Change confuses her so she tends to stick to what she already knows. Heaven forbid you should ask her, on a Wednesday, if you can have beans for supper because it's practically a foregone conclusion that she'll reply, as if to a small child, "Of course we can't have beans tonight! This isn't Saturday." And she'll march off shaking her head at your impetuosity.

Watch your Four Woman at the dinner table. She loves food and all the accoutrements—but here again, ritual rears its regulation head. She's a compulsive silverwear straightener, always tempted in restaurants to rearrange any stray pieces. More than once she's dangled parts of her anatomy in a stranger's vichyssoise. At home, if you face the cutting edge of the knife away from the plate rather than toward it, you'd better gather up your garters and make a dash for it. My god! Everyone knows it's not done that way. And if you have the audacity to ask her why the knife must face in, she'll scowl at you, pause, then say, "Because it's just done that way, that's all." Her peas should never touch the mashed potatoes and the two must keep a respectful distance from the meat loaf. If you want a raving maniac on your hands, set a plate of goulash before her. When you come back three hours later, you'll find her muttering over the plate, still separating the peppers, onion and noodles. There are a lot of very thin Fours.

These idiosyncrasies result from her desire to finish one thing at a time. She is a wonderful organizer because she's such a careful planner, separating the flotsam from the jetsam. When you give her a project, she will extract so many details from you before she begins that you feel like a sponge that's been in the sun for forty years. "There isn't one possible question left in the entire cosmos that could be asked about that project," you'll gasp, while you wonder why you didn't do it yourself. It would have been easier. Easier, perhaps, but never as well done.

There's no use telling your Four Woman she can't have something she's decided she wants. You might as well tell the tide it can't come in. You know how much good that would do. Besides, you'd look rather foolish standing on a wind-swept cliff with your arms upraised and your robes flapping about your legs, looking like a great black crow, commanding the tide to stay out. Moses did it, but he had a little help. So, as you stand before your Four Woman in all your glory, gesticulating about why she cannot have that food processer, try to imagine how ridiculous you must appear to her. The outcome is already decided by forces beyond your comprehension. You're dealing with a woman in control.

She really is something else. When the party's over and the lights go out, you'll reach for the woman who makes your life worth while. Her soft arms will allay your fears, build your hopes and fulfill your wildest fantasies. She is the Earth Mother, the creative principle, the epitome of womanhood. She is life itself. She can calmly face the winds of failure and lay waste the forests of fear. She has a serenity and a solidity that belies her feminine frame. She can take whatever life has to dish out and make it more than palatable. So, if you have a taste for the finer things in life, with your Four Woman, you will enjoy a banquet.

The Four Man

You were at the Flower and Garden Show when you first saw your Four Man. He was squatting before the tulip display with a thoughtful look on his strong face, making notations in a large lined notebook on his knee. There was something about him that caught your attention. He looked so...symmetrical. Also, the twenty-two different colored pens and matching color-keyed tabs in his notebook piqued your curiosity. You thought he just had to be a big buyer, cataloging his purchases. You cleverly bumped into him, sending colored pens skittering across the floor. Amidst apologies and scrambling for the rainbow of ink, you found yourself looking into one of the most sensual faces you'd ever seen. Much to your surprise, you discovered over lunch—a brown bag affair because he had brought his own and there was plenty for two—that gardening was his hobby. His explanation for the pens, tabs and notebooks was that it's much easier to be organized. As he smiled the corners of his eyes crinkled. Beams of credibility flooded over you.

Your Four Man needs organization, it is the cornerstone of his life. He needs to know where the boundaries lie and what the rules are so that he can establish himself securely in a central spot. He feels safe and comfortable when the guidelines are clear. You'll seldom find him bucking the system. He innately understands that rules are made for order, and he does like order.

When he was a little boy, he had respect for authority. One evening his parents were to visit a next door neighbor. His mother explained carefully that once he locked the windowless wooden stormdoor, he wasn't to open it for anyone. She emphasized this order a number of times. The door should not be opened for anyone. When his parents left, he carefully locked the door. Seconds later, his mother, realizing she had left her pocketbook on the kitchen table, returned to the door and knocked loudly.

"Son, are you there?"

A small voice replied, "Yes."

"I left my pocketbook on the table."

Silence.

"Son, open the door."

"I can't open the door," he replied.

"Why not?" his mother querried.

"Because I'm not supposed to open it for anyone," he said proudly.

His mother sighed deeply. "You can open it for me, dear. I'm your mother."

He fared better during his teenage years because he discovered the art of asking questions. His questions, however, were specifically centered about the order of tasks assigned to him. He did not indulge in what he deemed superfluous information. Once a responsibility was placed in his capable hands, he began to operate. A skilled surgeon with the hands of an artist could not dissect a task into so many essences. He is so thorough he makes corporate accountants look sloppy. He knows that strong foundations cannot be built without the proper tools. He'll justify your confidence in him by taking all the facts and building the eighth wonder of the world. He's the cosmic mason who constructs cornerstones upon which the world builds its structures.

His deliberateness carries over into other areas of his personality. Like conversation. Conversations with your Four Man are long—very long—and silent. On occasion, you'll wonder if you're talking to yourself or if he's gone to sleep. When you're on the phone, it's impossible to tell. Even when you're in the living room with him, it can be difficult.

You might say, "Honey. I was thinking we ought to side the house in the spring. What do you think?"

He lays his newspaper on his lap as his head falls back against the couch. A few minutes go by. His eyes are closed. You think, I'll wait one more minute. Then you repeat your question.

His body remains motionless, the eyes still closed. You wonder if he's comatose, then he says, "Side the house, hmmm?"

Another seven or eight minutes of thunderous silence march by. His eyes are glassy now.

"Well, what do you think?" you ask, a bit impatiently.

He cocks his head at you. "Don't rush me, dear. Rome wasn't built in a day, you know."

Not if it was built by Fours, it wasn't. That's probably why it lasted a thousand years. You see, your Four Man is after posterity. He believes in leaving part of himself, something valuable, to the world, his community and his children. In order to do so, each step he takes must be well-thought-out, planned and carried through. He's capable of doing all three. He reflects Albert Einstein's statement to a young scientist eager to impress him, "Don't rush, young man. I'm a slow thinker." Slow but sure and very deliberate, the tortoise wins the race. When the hoopla is over, he'll emerge—calm, confident and secure in the knowledge that he's left no stone unturned regarding the tasks that have been entrusted to him. He inspires trust. Who wouldn't trust the fatherly Walter Cronkite, newscaster, who expresses the homely virtues of honesty, dependability and integrity? During the 1980 presidential campaign, the talk of him running for the Presidency was not entirely humorous. He gives the impression that you could count on him to be ever alert to look out for our interests and the interests of our country.

Like Argus with the hundred eyes, fifty of·which never slept, the Four Man notices everything, especially when it comes to the budget. He has every cent accounted for, down to the last gram of copper. Without question, banks immediately send letters of apology when he says they've made a mistake on his checking account, and each year his completed income tax form is framed for display in Washington. With a record like that, don't think you're going to get away with slipping a few dollars out of the weekly budget.

He may be the kind of Four who believes everything has a place, insisting that those things be in their places. Spices are arranged alphabetically in the kitchen, pictures are hung with levels and tools are crossed-indexed by size and weight. He can be so organized at these levels that if he didn't have one place where it could all hang out, he'd hang up his pencils, turn in his ledgers and go to that great accounting place in the sky. That strangely disorganized place is usually his bedroom where clothes pile up to such dangerous heights that a deep sigh could be the cause of his own suffocation. His bed is often unmade and crumpled candy wrappers are littered around the room. But the paradox is, his shoes are usually well-cared-for. He has a

4

thing about shoes. He likes them. Hundreds of them. Often when he changes his clothes, he'll change his shoes because he wants them to match. He feels that no matter how good you look, if your shoes are shabby, your entire appearance is ruined. His fixation with his feet may have something to do with the obvious fact that feet are the foundation of the body. And he's into foundations.

Then there are those Fours who seem totally disorganized, living in what appears to be the aftermath of a B-52 bomber raid. Don't be fooled by these types. Organization is still an issue with them—they just haven't got it together yet. Rest assured, the multiple madness in which they live bothers them whereas other types wouldn't even notice it. Fours know that, if they are to express the best part of themselves, order is necessary in their lives.

Your Four Man loves his home. Often, getting him out of it is like pulling teeth. Why should he want to go anywhere. He's got plenty of food, his television and newspaper, and, if he has strong business inclinations, probably his office, all within arms' reach. He's also got you, you gorgeous creature. He'll pull you down into his lap and before long, you'll forget where it was you wanted to go or even that you wanted to go in the first place.

The Four Man, Stephen Foster, wrote songs—"O Susanna," "My Old Kentucky Home," "Old Folks at Home," "Jeanie with the Light Brown Hair"—that were "simple and easy to remember and sing...he expressed fundamental emotions with straightforwardness and sincerity."

Your Four Man's love of home extends to his country. He salutes the American flag in a parade and is never driven by any car manufactured outside the good old U.S.A. Patriotism is a special word for him. He probably loves patriotic tunes. They stir up his deeply-held emotions about home and country.

Your lovable teddy bear has claws. He can be patient a long time and take a lot of irritation, but when he explodes, mothers pull their children indoors, brave men tremble and old people say their prayers. Because he tends to let things bottle up inside him, he must learn to work out his frustrations through exercise or hobbies.

Exercise also increases his awareness of discipline and his respect for the laws that govern his body and his world. Although others might not notice, he dislikes it when he sees someone parking in a no parking zone or crossing the street against the light. He is such a law-abiding citizen that if he were waiting for the signal at a crosswalk and a mad dog, foaming at the mouth, were barrelling down behind him, he wouldn't budge until the walk-sign flashed green. Really, he's cool. Or maybe it's just the impression made by the cold sweat washing over him. At any rate, he is single-minded, stalwart and honest, with an integrity that often outweighs his survival instincts.

Your Four Man is great at giving practical advice. He has a natural instinct when it comes to anything that smells green. He may have trouble visualizing fantasies and far-away places, and when he flies in his dreams, he may never leave his neighborhood, but ask him to write a series of booklets on sound ground values then watch his mind whirl. He'll turn out titles like How To Save Money Without Pain, How To Work And Have Fun Too, How To Grow Old And Rich, How To Live With Your In-Laws And End Up Their Beneficiary, How To Grow A Garden For Profit, and How To Raise Kids And Stay Solvent. He knows all the How To's because he's done them. He'll never give you advice that hasn't been checked out thoroughly by the CIA, the FDA and Emily Post. He'll even try it out himself, just to be sure.

Because his world's a study in cement, he is naturally a deliberate thinker and speaker. His words are physical forms that frame the ideas behind them. He cannot understand how others can blurt things out carelessly. He believes that if people say things, they mean them. As a result, he's often hurt by those who speak thoughtlessly or in frustration and anger. It takes years of experience for him to understand that not everyone's words will be carved into stone and set on a mountain top for eternity as his will. He is a genuine personality, sincere and unpretentious. What you see is what you get. What you hear from your Four Man will echo down the halls of truth.

Some Fours become boxed-in by their views. Their loyalties can overcome reason. Then they'll stick to an idea or belief even when the facts have proven them wrong. They must be careful they don't narrow down the types of people they can accept. Fears and enmities then creep into their world. Shadows of the Hatfields and the McCoys, the Montagues and Capulets, arise. At this point, their marvelous walls of strength and security transform into prison walls, keeping them in and others out.

Very few Fours are lazy but there are some who are infected with terminal lethargy. You need a block and tackle and twenty sticks of dynamite to uproot these rare mutants. It could be that their systems have become clogged and leaden. Vitamins, healthy foods and a good exercise program can stimulate them into action.

But your Four Man recognizes and lives by the law of cause and effect. He doesn't expect to gain or be rewarded without putting in his proper share of the work. He is a hard and willing worker, courting the danger of becoming a workaholic by trying to do everything himself. If you want something done right, he is often heard saying, do it yourself. But all work and no play makes Jack a dull boy and perhaps a sick one as well. He needs to learn to relax so that his physical body, which he values, can recuperate from the stress he often lays upon it in his search for perfection.

In his search for perfection, he found you. You should be flattered. He does not dispense his affections carelessly. He chose you with the same care and thought he puts into choosing all the lasting structures in his life. He is your strength, your security, your lover. He'll teach you how to live life to the nth degree, savoring every sensual earthly morsel.

The Five Woman

Remember the first time you asked your Five Woman for a date? She replied, "Why?" You wanted to say you asked her because she's sexy, exciting, magnetic and fiery but instead you just stood there with your elbow in your ear trying to figure out why she asked you why. And it's been that way ever since. Sometimes you'd swear she was the editor-in-chief for the *Encyclopedia Brittanica*. She's a walking...no, racing, encyclopedia herself, filled with all kinds of fascinating information as well as trivia. Really, how many people do you know who know that an ancestor of the newscaster, Roger Mudd, was the physician who attended John Wilkes Booth, and that the expression, "Your name is Mudd" comes from that doctor's attendance on

5

Lincoln's assassin. She'll remind you that when you write out that expression, Mudd is spelled with two d's, after the physician, not after wet dirt.

She has a fascination for words: written, spoken, single or in the hundreds of thousands—that is—in books. Books are an addiction with her. She rents apartments and buys houses contingent upon the square feet of shelf space for books. Then she'll have them piled up in corners and under tables. Certainly there's a stack beside her bed where she enjoys more than one stimulating pleasure. Most likely, there's also a dictionary and a notebook handy so, in that extremely rare instance of coming across a word she hasn't heard, she can look it up. The notebook is for collecting lists of words that sound good in her ear. It's not grammar that rules her discernment of literature but the sound of it. Once she's read a sentence aloud, she immediately targets in on any wayward participles. If she's had no formal training, she may not know your participle is dangling but she'll certainly know it's askew.

She's always been this way. When she was just a thought, she practically lived in the Cosmic Library accosting the angelic librarian with clouds of querries. That's why, when she was born, she was the only baby in the nursery with a question mark branded on her forehead. God thought it was wise. Now you know why she always wears bangs.

As a child, she could drive people to thoughts of suicide. She really didn't understand that her constant barrage of questions had a debilitating effect on less adaptable minds. When she passed first grade, her parents received a note from school: "Dear Mr. and Mrs. Smith: Your daughter has been promoted. The teachers are staying back." By the time they lifted her bangs it was too late. She had been taught that words made sentences, sentences paragraphs and paragraphs books. Words, paragraphs, books, libraries and teachers were storehouses of information from which she could learn. After that, in her home town, her first grade teachers' names were Mudd. They had set loose upon the world the fifth rider of the Apocalypse—a questioner. Institutions were never the same. She asked questions like, "How did Moses part the Red Sea?", "How do people walk?", "Where does the wind go when it isn't blowing?", "Why are blackberries red when they're green?", "Why aren't little girls supposed to do that when little boys can?", "If God is a man, where is his wife?" and a thousand other questions that are usually answered with: "That's just how it is. Don't ask so many questions." But she couldn't accept empty platitudes so she set up her own detective agency. Her neighborhood task force of six mini-sleuths pillaging bedroom closets and secret drawers came up with the most enlightening information. Parents should make an attempt to answer her childish enquiries on the spot or at least introduce her to the local librarian, explaining her needs and obtaining a library card for her.

During her teen years the "little grey cells" were still athletically active. Her thoughts flowed quickly, intuitively and imaginatively. She was always probing and questioning. In addition, her versatility was a source of pride. She could handle more mail and telephone calls than the United States Post Office and Ma Bell over a busy holiday.

She also discovered her sexual magnetism. Her thirst for more and more experience most likely left a trail of frazzled and dazed hearts wondering what happened. Trying to capture her affections was like trying to net a butterfly. Trying to possess those affections would have been pinning that butterfly to a display board. She needed to flutter from one flower to another, seeking the taste of honey.

Today she still needs her freedom and delights. She is the living example of the law of physics that states that the only constant is change. However, she needs to discriminate as to when change is positive and when it's destructive or she may end up throwing the baby out with the bathwater. If she allows her natural need for change to degenerate into restless sensation-seeking escapades, then, like the dislocated butterfly, she will light on this and that, here and there, never finding satisfaction. She becomes the rolling stone gathering no moss. Although she would probably ask why she should want to gather moss.

Since you've met her, your life has been one big merry-go-round. You think the laws of gravity have been displaced because you never know which end is up. There are occasions when that can be exasperatingly embarrassing...

There's more to your Five Woman than meets the eye...and ear, nose, mouth and hand. She's an experimenter, delighting you with the imaginative ways in which she conducts her investigations. She'll know ninety-nine ways to make love, then conduct extensive research to find the one-hundredth. In a passionate moment, don't be surprised if you roll over on a clip board with a pen attached. The rustle of paper behind your back is only her leafing through her notes. These are just minor distractions however, detracting little from your pleasure or the intensity of the moment.

Your Five Woman is mischevious and playful. You never know what to expect from her. Buy a pair of comfortable ballet slippers because she'll have you on your toes. You might come home to a spaghetti and meatball dinner in the bath tub—full of water, yet. She just wanted to know what it felt like eating in the nude. Her excitement is contagious. You'll wonder why you didn't think of it.

She is extremely efficient, hurtling through assignments like a hot knife through butter. She's the big executive at the horseshoe desk with scores of ringing phones, half of which she's answering simultaneously. With cords hanging from her head she looks like a Madison Avenue Medusa, wired for sound. Her job will certainly include much travel because she's not going to be stuck behind a desk for long.

At home, she'll have a phone in every room plus a dozen or so Ram beepers scattered around the house, including the bathroom. You never know when you'll be reading in the tub. Science and psycholgy magazines jam her mailbox while the UPS man makes monthly deliveries of Agatha Christie novels. By now you've got the idea. She's into communication. Her ability to use words is a natural talent. She surpasses others in professions that depend on vocabulary and the human voice. She should train herself in these areas.

Your Five Woman is a clone of the original snake-oil salesman. She can sell anything—a Buick to a Japanese, hair tonic to Yul Brunner and oil to an Arab. It's because she has such a way with words. She almost caresses them in sensual contact. Watch her hands and facial expressions as she talks. She puts her whole self into her delivery. Even so, you'll never hear her say that actions speak louder than words because words are her power. Bette Davis, one of the greatest living American actresses, and a Five Woman, has made her characteristic gestures legendary—"a defiant toss of the head, a dramatic lift of the chin, and a distinctive vocal

5

inflection." Her gestures and her manner of speaking set her apart. She loves literature and is known as an outspoken and articulate woman.

Your Five Woman is a wonderful conversationalist. One of her strengths is the vast background of experience from which she draws. From the Yogi in the saffron robes in the temple to the dowser with her twenty acres of vegetable gardens, she has gleaned reams of unusual anecdotes, insights and information, all of which she conveys in stimulating and witty ways. She can talk until Rip Van Winkle stirs his sleepy head but she doesn't just talk to hear herself. She has something to say. You won't be bored. You will need an alert ear. Her tongue can move like the wings of a humming bird.

The Five Woman, actress Raquel Welch, also has something to say. Besides being enormously sexy, she is witty. When asked to identify her "most errogenous zone," she "stunned and delighted the television audience with her response: 'The brain.'" She performed a one-woman stage show to prove she is more than "a cash register with glands," although she admits she loves being a "world-famous sex object."

Your Five Woman's mind travels far. She envisions far horizons awaiting her. She wants to get there yesterday. No meandering down rose-covered paths or flowing leisurely up the Nile for her. It's supersonic jets all the way. She leaves jet-lag for less curious types. She has too many mysteries to unravel, questions to ask, libraries, museums and old ruins to investigate.

Your Five Woman has a fixation with time which works in one of two ways. She may always be ready ahead of time, chewing her nails while waiting for her less speedy colleagues. She has a lot to do and wants to get it done right now. Her insides churn as if something hidden were constantly nagging, "You're late, you're late, for a very important date." Like the White Rabbit, she's constantly on the run, trying to get something done—anything done. Part of this syndrome results from the fact that she's so efficient and mentally quick that others pile responsibility on her shoulders. They know she can handle 555 things at once. She's a good administrator in that sense, solving a myriad of problems quickly. She can reach out, take seemingly unrelated bits of data, and, like a detective, piece together quicker than the eye can blink. As a result, others get used to depending upon her.

And then, she may be eternally late. Here, some part of her is rebelling against the restrictions that all that responsibility has placed on her freedom. When she gets to the point that she feels too much has been laid on her doorstep, she uses tardiness as a sign to everyone that she can do what she wants. Now you know why September 5th has been declared Be Late For Something Day by the Procrastinators' Club of America.

Watch your Five Woman shoot out orders with the rapidity of a machine gun. Because she can think simultaneously of so many things that need to be done, you need an interpreter and a photographic memory to be able to decipher and remember what she's said. She can speak quickly when she's excited, tripping over her words like an adolescent in her first pair of heels. She also has a habit of repeating her orders five times, probably because 1) she's not convinced you're listening, 2) she's afraid you won't remember and 3) she wants to be sure you'll follow through so she's emphasizing her requests through repetition.

Your Five Woman is impatient at times. Because she can do a week's work in five hours, she expects everyone can do the same. Her resourcefulness, versatility and quick mind equip her to handle enormous amounts of information. She eats up tactical problems like a division of earthworms in a garbage heap. When she's done, you have fertile, mineralized soil awaiting a season of growth.

She lives in the fast lane. Heaven help you if you're out for a Sunday drive in front of her. The view from the rear-view mirror may turn you to stone. Horns, reddened eyes and spurting clouds of sulphur tend to upset the casual driver.

She does need freedom of movement. If she doesn't travel far and wide physically, she most certainly will mentally. In fact, mental freedom is her first priority. She may be confined to a small space for any number of reasons but no one will enslave her mind.

Your Five Woman can soar to the heights and sink to the depths in consecutive moments. Her probing mind takes her to the starry heavens to "touch the face of God" then back to her sensual pursuits of earthly experience. She needs to learn to deal with the opposite sex as well as her own personal magnetism and appetites. Her ceaseless search for the new, the unique, the different can become an addiction to sensuality or the philosophic struggle to transmute lead into gold. But she knows, deep within her soul, that she can handle it all. She will teach you the delights of your sexuality, the joy of the "why's" that fill her being and the wonderment of the universe you share.

The Five Man

You first noticed your Five Man in that little cosmopolitan restaurant that caters to the arty set. Dressed in loafers, casual slacks and a pullover, he sat, weaving a tale of his tantalizing travels to a group of bangled admirers. You watched spellbound as his hands and arms circumscribed the room, embellishing his stories with a feeling of motion and life. He listened too, leaning forward over the table with a slight furrow on his brow while someone else spoke. Then he nodded his head emphatically while rubbing his fingers together. You could almost see the wheels of his brain spinning.

Then he noticed you—one brief look, then a double-take. With the second glance, an alluring smile spread across his face. Within seconds, he had you by the hand leading you to his group of friends. "Of course you don't want to dine alone," he stated. "Come and join us." You did.

Your Five Man is the most exciting thing that's happened to you since your discovery of sex. No doubt he's also shown you a few unique chapters to add to *that* "Everything You've Always Wanted To Know...But Were Afraid to Ask" book! His charisma is overwhelming. Take him out in public and every female within a five-mile radius catches his scent.

His awareness of the opposite sex began at a very early age, exemplified by the joke told about the two five-year-olds who saw a western movie. In the film, the hero grabbed a woman, accidentally tearing her blouse. His words, "I take what I want when I want it," impressed the little boy. Later, outside the theatre, the little boy decided he would try the same thing. It seemed rather interesting. So he clutched and tugged at the little girl's blouse repeating, "I take what I want when I want it." To which the little girl replied, in a condescending voice, "You'll get what I've got when I get it."

5

Yes, experience tugged at your Five Man early in life. As he went through adolesence, his past escapades provided him with a resourceful foundation so that he wasn't apt to be stymied by a quick retort. He learned to duel masterfully. Words and ideas were his rapier. He loved to take things apart as well, to see how they worked. When he was five it wasn't so bad. His mother just sighed when she found fifty-five parts of her grandfather's pocket watch in a neat semi-circle around her small inquisitive child. Things progressed from bad to worse when, in his teens, he began attacking the television and the family car. For one thing, there were a lot more parts strewn around the property. For another, his parents missed many television specials and weekend picnics.

By now, your Five Man has learned to get it all together. Thank God other people bore the brunt of his insatiable curiosity before you got him. But don't hang by your teeth until he changes. You could have lockjaw before a glimmer of sanity lights his darting eyes. Besides, you want to be free to follow him to the five corners of the earth. You thought there were only four? Oh my, has he got something to show you.

He knows things about people, places and ideas that some people have never heard, others might suspect and a few don't want to think about. There are no secrets that he cannot unearth. He may not have talked to you for five days but when you walk through his door, he'll sweep you into his arms, kiss you passionately, look you over quickly and ask you how you enjoyed your visit that morning to the Scotch woolen factory ninety miles away. He'll brush his deduction aside with a wave of his hand. "How did I know? Elementary, my dear." Then he'll proceed to tell you he noticed a heavy magenta thread on your short-sleeved blouse. That weight thread had to come from a heavily woven woolen cloth. That particular shade, he knows, belongs to a certain Scotch plaid that's sold in two outlets—one seven miles away, the other ninety miles away. It's clear from the sunburn on your left arm, which you obviously had out the car window on this sunny spring day, that you've been traveling some distance. The burn is still red so it was probably this morning. Obviously, this time of year the woolens are on sale. And on and on until you raise two hands to stem the tide.

Motion is important to him. He needs freedom, plenty of wide-open-spaces in which to move. Don't let him leave the house unless he's on a very, very long leash. He's the stereotyped individual who goes to the store for a pack of cigarettes and comes home five years later.

"Well, I got talking," he explains, as he comes in the back door after a half decade absence, "and this fellow was telling me how he had just dropped into the drugstore for bug spray. Seems he was off on a safari to the Amazon and, just by sheer luck, they needed a fifth—that was me—and how could I pass up an opportunity like that? I mean, things like that only happen once in a lifetime. Sorry I didn't have time to call but it all happened so quickly. You understand."

He busses your ear, flops down in his favorite chair and proceeds to watch the news.

The news keeps him up-to-date. He is progressive. Keeping abreast of current events helps him prepare for the next business transaction, the next lecture, the next trip. He's always ready for the next something because he knows that next something will be ecstatically exciting, something he can sink his teeth into.

There's nothing your Five Man enjoys more than mental jousting with clever people who can parry his verbal thrustings. It is the food of life to him. Actually, he needs people, all kinds.

The Five Actor, Gregory Peck, confided in an interview that he really wanted to be a writer. Peck once worked as a carnival barker—he has a way with words—at the World's Fair in 1939, and as a tour guide at Rockefeller Center. He can hardly wait to start his day—pedaling five miles on a stationary bicycle each morning before breakfast. Words and communication are his sustenance, as they are the food of life for your Five Man. Actually your man doesn't want to converse with himself although, if he finds a really good book, one that holds his interest, he enters a state of suspended animation. For hours, he is locked in thought, as the words rush through his mind. He gathers this information because he is first and foremost a dispenser of knowledge, the itinerant teacher, traveling the globe searching for those with eyes to see and ears to hear.

Food for him is necessary. He doesn't live to eat, but rather eats to live. It is necessary fuel to keep him going. But he very seldom eats without some kind of company whether it be a magazine propped up in front of the juice bottle on the table or you propped up in a chair opposite him. If he is desperate, he'll take his plate out to the doghouse and eat while conversing with his German shepherd. Not a real German shepherd...a dog. During mealtime he won't talk about the inevitable things most human beings discuss—birth, death and taxes—but about the curious shape strings of DNA molecules form, the computer that programmed itself and took over CBS, and the curare poisoned dart found protruding from the governor's pet canary.

Your Five Man courts the danger of catapulting from one experience to another. He needs self-discipline to channel his fine inquiring mind. Formal educational training can be most beneficial. He learns quickly so that sheepskin is just a hop, skip and a jump for him. He'll sail through his studies with the ease of a schooner with a brisk wind at her back.

He may choose to ignore a structured classroom scene, steering toward unchartered waters and open seas. "Around the world in eighty days," he'll learn more than some people who spend eighty years in the sacred halls of ivy. As a result, he's often the brunt of comments from more sedantary types who think you're never going to amount to anything unless you're a study in white stone, your elbow on your knee and your chin in your hand. But the world is his school. He'll learn well. At age thirty-two he'll surprise everyone, including his mother, when he writes the world's greatest classic or discovers the lost city of Atlantis. Or he may be like the Five Man, P.T. Barnum, the most extravagant advertiser ever born who always presented a show "worth more than the price of admission." "An acute businessman, well aware of the value of publicity," he claimed the public delighted in being "humbugged" as a way of escaping reality. He is reputed to have said, "There's a sucker born every minute." The dwarf "General Tom Thumb" earned him money and a reputation when he presented Tom to Queen Victoria at Buckingham Palace. He induced the great songstress Jenny Lind to tour the United States and eventually he created "The Greatest Show on Earth," the famous circus now known as Barnum and Bailey's. He was a sales man par excellence, always on the go, looking for the excitement and variety life had to offer.

5

Routine jobs will have your Five Man cutting out paper dolls. He needs to be physically and mentally active. He can move like greased lightning, completing manual jobs with ease, but physically working isn't enough. He isn't cut out for an assembly line or a job that requires that only his body be present. He needs mental stimulation to go along with his work. In fact, if the task is sufficiently mentally challenging, he can remain motionless for many hours. But then, he'll leap up, walk around the room, and do a few odd things that require only minutes to complete. Once he feels limbered up, he'll be back at the job again.

His versatility is legendary. He's always ready with an answer, and a question. Answers that satisfy most people are not enough for him. He needs to know more and more. This knowledge is part of his ability to be so adaptable to other personalities and situations. The only time information escapes him is when his nervous temperament propels him into hasty and impulsive moves or conclusions. He will arrive at the correct point but might overlook some factor in his haste. All the ramifications of the situations at this point are not obvious.

Your Five Man has a mind as swift as the silver-heeled Mercury, messenger of the gods. He often speaks hastily, a result of his curiosity and desire to get to the point quickly. Because of this trait, his words can appear sharp and cutting. He needs to learn to criticize gently, even if it is "only for the other person's own good." In reality, he's not trying to hurt you but only attempting to cut through the husks of illusion to get at the kernels of truth.

His children know that he has an X-ray mind, that he sees through walls and ceilings. He'll be sitting in the living room watching the news—one of his favorite programs—when he'll suddenly call upstairs, "Put those comics away and finish your homework!" How did he know? He knew because the rustling of pages was accompanied by a loud silence instead of the grumbling usually associated with doing homework.

Surprising him on his birthday or at Christmas is impossible. He knows a week before you do what you're going to buy for him. Sometimes that can be just plain scary. You would swear he's been programming you subliminally through the stereo system during the day.

He has a wonderful imagination. His memory bank would stagger the ethereal hall of Akashic records, where the cosmic accounts of every thought, word and deed are stored. Therefore, when he tells a story, he isn't so much embellishing his tale to impress you but rather drawing from all the possibilities and probabilities of the situation. His charisma, enthusiasm, mercurial mind and compelling voice bestow upon him a power that can sway the multitudes. This, coupled with his storehouse of knowledge, makes him a formidable foe. He's majestic in a debate and impossible in an argument.

Experience is his foundation, language his strength and communication his forte. He cannot be bound mentally. Your Five Man wants to explore the world with you. Together you'll explore the breadth and depth of this planet. No stone will lie unturned, no book unopened, no land unvisited, no exotic experience untasted. Even if he travels from an armchair, he will overwhelm you with his infectious vitality for life. You will feel your blood pressure rising, your adrenalin flowing, as you prepare to embark on life's journey with your gypsy lover.

Can you imagine life without him? Hardly. You never liked routine anyway. He'll captivate you, body and soul, with his whimsical wit and passionate gallantry.

From sun-up to sun-down life will be a merry chase in pursuit of what's around the next bend in the road. He'll stir your imagination with questions of wonder. Your day may not begin and end with a song but it will surely begin and end with a question. And one day, you'll smile secretly to yourself because, after all these years, you really are caught up in the enchantment of wondering.

The Six Woman

See that beautiful angel floating toward you, the one with the hearts all over her sleeves. She's your Six Woman. She may appear fragile, almost ethereal. She's the epitome of femininity and womanhood. Her one purpose in life is to love and be loved. She will do anything to make you happy—cook, sew, keep your home, nurse your wounds, and love you with a fervent devotion. In return, she asks only your appreciation and companionship. She is the "ideal" woman.

But don't let all that sweetness and light fool you into thinking she's a weak sister or easy prey for a male chauvinist. Once she's deeply motivated or committed to a cause, she's the equivalent of a band of Carrie Nations, armed with keenly-honed hatchets. At that point, unless you're partial to close haircuts, you are well advised to cut a wide path around her. When her loved ones or her principles are involved, she is justice, reared in righteous anger, swords in both hands and a blindfold bound so tightly over her eyes that no glimmer of light can seep through. She is mighty, swift and terrible.

Her values and principles were well set in childhood. She can be impossibly stubborn about what is right and what is wrong. To her, truth and justice are ingrained laws which, if threatened, release a hell that "hath no fury like a woman" on a crusade. History depicts graphically how devastating wars of idealism and religious fervor can be.

People began to recognize her devotion to truth and justice when, as a child, instead of building snowmen like everyone else, she erected replicas of the Statue of Liberty on her front lawn. Then, the neighbors began to complain about the gathering of the huddled masses. Charity is one thing but her social programs for six-year-olds were beginning to bankrupt her parents, to say nothing of tying up traffic in her neighborhood.

She was very devoted to her family. How many kids do you know who frame the family's birth certificates and hang them on the bedroom wall? She had a compelling need to belong. She hated family arguments, which disrupted the much-needed harmony and balance of her environment. She would go out of her way to avoid unpleasantness.

As a teenager, she had to guard against runaway emotions and the need to give herself unselfishly to others. She could be taken in by a good sob story. But also, her innately loving heart went out to those who seemed rejected by their peers. She would date a boy when nobody else would, just to make him happy. She was in love with love, and with those who didn't receive any.

Now your Six Woman has laid her heart and soul on the altar of love for you. She worships that gentle goddess, Venus, incorporating her qualities into every thought and action. She has the sensualness of the Venus de Milo—with arms—and the allurement of the enigmatic Mona Lisa. She is kind and understanding, building

6

towers of love whenever possible. She has a strong domestic inclination therefore, her home is her castle, which she'll drape in comfort and beauty. Her concern is for everyone, especially children and animals. And if you know someone with a face only a mother could love, she will love him or her because she is the Cosmic Mother, pouring out universal affection toward everyone. She doesn't love the weak or afflicted in spite of their plight but because of it. She can see the true beauty that lies deep in every soul.

The danger for the Six Woman lies in her being a slave to her passion. She must keep her emotions in both hands or she can give too much to her partner or family. She becomes her mate's alter ego, his second self, losing her own individuality in the process. Foolish martyrdom is not appreciated by anyone. She can also end up tied to a bad family situation because she doesn't know when to say "enough." Her complaints of lack of appreciation will fall on deaf ears. If she insists on being a door mat, there are only a few who will walk around her.

Your Six Woman is attracted to beauty and comfort. For some Six Women that means wealth, luxury and all the "good things" in life. Your Six Woman believes in beautifying her environment. Her own personal adornment can be high on her priority list. Her shopping list often reads like a description of the ten best-dressed women in the world. You'll have to watch your credit cards carefully. Names like Sax Fifth Avenue and Cartier on your monthly statement can be an unnerving experience but when you find the crown jewels on your Mastercard, you know you're done for. Sixty dollars a month for the rest of your life won't even make a dent.

Hopefully her tastes will run to simpler things like three carat diamonds, Yves St. Laurent originals and silk sheets. When you slide between those silk sheets, it will suddenly become crystal clear how effective a well-dressed body can be. This woman is the essence of seduction.

She'll slide her satiny arms around your neck and purr into your ear, "You know that little castle on the Rhine? . . ."

"Put it on Mastercard," you'll murmur, as you slip into oblivion.

Your Six Woman also finds beauty in a life of service. Some Six Women remain single so they can devote their entire being to a religious principle or political or social cause. Their idealism and search for perfection leave no room for a life of personal love and fulfillment. They are willing to give themselves to the world. Such a sacrifice was evident in the life of Joan of Arc, born on the sixth.

Beauty is everywhere for your Six Woman. She often finds it where others see only plainness or futility. She can bask in the glory of a sunset and thrill to the melody of a spring robin. She can lose herself in a lilting tune or the song of a running brook. But she also sees beauty in the gnarled hands of an old woman and the tired, bloodshot eyes of an exhausted mother. She thinks you're beautiful, even on one of your off days, when you have the personality of Oscar Madison.

If the family is the keystone of your Six Woman's life, either she will control it or it will control her. Some Six mothers are like blustery brooding hens, fluttering their wings amidst much ado, while their chicks nestle happily against their ample bosoms. This Six Woman reigns supreme, as far as the eye can see, from one end of the house to the other. Her home is her kingdom; you and everyone there are her charges. And take charge she will. You'll have more than you could ever dream of or want. She handles her home with a capability that would startle most efficiency experts.

The other Six Woman is rooster-pecked, allowing others to take advantage of her naturally sympathetic and kind nature. She'll pussy-foot around her tom, catering to his every whim like a slave at his beck and call. She has set him up as head of the family, a figure not to be crossed or contradicted. She not only kills him with kindness while losing her self-respect but she displays no will, desires or opinions of her own. If she discovers that her Rorschach ink blot tests are identical to her husband's, then she needs to take a serious accounting of herself and her role in the family. She needs sustenance from this relationship as much as her mate does. All Six Women need to discover the balance between giving and receiving. If it is blessed to be able to give then it is a blessing to be able to receive.

Your Six Woman is not cut out for hard physical labor but she really enjoys work which serves others. In helping others, she will work long, hard hours, almost to the point of exhaustion. She has such a strong belief in her work, coupled with a strong driving force, that she can work miracles. If she decides to work outside the home, don't plan on babysitters. She'll take the entire family with her, like the Six Woman, Lucille Ball, whose long-running comedy series, "I Love Lucy," featured her, her husband and her children. Her divorce from Ricky affected the entire country which so identified with her family. It was a terrible blow to which she commented, "Divorce is defeat."

This woman is also extremely sentimental; the more flowery the thought or deed, the better. Talk about tears. An unexpected bouquet of flowers may cause sprinkles, remembering your wedding anniversay, a heavy shower, but a long-versed romantic birthday card will surely open the Aswam Dam. Cards really get to her. She seems to grow more sentimental each birthday. This year she couldn't get past the envelopes. Sometimes you wonder if it's the sentiment or her age that she's thinking about.

One thing she's probably thinking about is that she could write those love poems just as well, maybe better, than the greeting card writers. The Hallmark approval board is probably comprised of people born on the sixth anyway, who sit around in pools of tears reading the selections presented to them. Their criteria for acceptance is most likely a resounding sob.

Your Six Woman would do well writing about affairs of the heart. She has the soul of a poet, unequaled when it comes to understanding the depths and intensity of love. Her love poems would be poignant, passionate and universal. Elizabeth Barrett Browning, born on the sixth, wrote "How do I love thee? Let me count the ways. I love thee to the depth and breadth and height my soul can reach..."—one of the most beautiful love poems ever written.

And this woman loves you. You must have earned your boy scout points along the way, helping little old men cross the street and tying all your knots correctly. Or maybe you won her through divine intervention. You must have done something right. At any rate, your Six Woman has decided to decorate your life, inside and out. She shares her love and companionship, her compassion and understanding. She is your wife, mother, sister and mistress. She is each or all at once, but she's always a woman. It's a role of which she's proud. It fulfills her every desire and will certainly fill yours. When you come home after a long day, she'll be waiting for you, and when you pull her into your arms, you'll know why God finished work on the sixth day.

The Six Man

6

It is written that it is better to have loved and lost than never to have loved at all. Whoever wrote that did not know your Six Man. For him, maintenance is absolutely essential in love. He cannot live without a deep abiding relationship with his woman. If that woman is you, you're in for a romance to equal the intensity of Romeo and Juliet, but one that will endure, in this world of musical chair partners, and become a legend.

You are the light of his life, around which he'll build his family and his fortress. He'll lavish you with attention and seek to fill your every need. His feelings flow from the hidden reaches of his soul. His three little words, I love you, speak more eloquently than pages of love sonnets. When he utters those words in your ear each morning, you'll register 6.6 on the Richter scale. When he has you alone, on a beach under a midnight sky glittering with millions of stars, you'll rocket into space where Richter scales don't even register.

With all due respect to Mr. Freud, who was also born on the sixth, your Six Man has his own theories on sexuality. His began when he fell in love with the little girl with the long pigtails, who sat in front of him in first grade. He soon found out that tying his love's pigtails into square knots was not the way to her heart. His was broken when she whipped around and whacked him in the nose with her lunch bag. His heart hurt almost as much as his nose. She carried apples every day. Of course, he felt responsible so he tried to make amends by stuffing the Valentine box in her favor. Alas, all to no avail.

He chased that little girl right into high school. Against all odds, plus a few burly football captains, he persisted with the Valentines. The seasons came and went, but he remained. Today that little girl with the long pigtails is you. You suddenly woke up to what you had in this dreamy-eyed romantic. "Where have I been all my life?" you asked yourself, when the light finally dawned on your beautiful pony tails. But there was no danger. He had chosen you when he was six years old and he's not fickle. In fact, he's more like barnacles on the hull of a ship or gum in your hair. You'll never get rid of him. But isn't it strange that now you don't want to get rid of him. In fact, he is so much a part of you that you doubt you could survive without him.

Your Six Man is also into community events. You never know when you'll open the newspaper to find his dedicated face splashed across the newsprint. Remember the time he fought city hall when their idea of community development was to cut down a row of ancient maples to widen the road a few feet so the cars could tear by your house faster. The newspaper ran his article which began with the lines from Joyce Kilmer's poem: "I think that I shall never see, A poem, lovely as a tree." That was fine but when he stationed himself in the arms of one old maple with a stack of books and a portable reading light, you knew the city was under seige. You understood his dedication to causes but, community responsibility or not, he had to come down to sign his weekly pay checks. The kids were hungry.

He may keep scrapbooks, bulging ones, because he likes to read about his own campaigns. He eats up flattery like kittens lap up milk so he's compiled his successes into that large gilt-edged scrapbook on the mantle in the living room. His less notorious ventures are kept in the plain-covered scrapbook in the cellarway. Obviously, his successes far outweigh his losses. Who's going to do battle with a fire-breathing dragon unless, of course, they have an extra supply of fireproof dragon scales laying around somewhere. Yes, your gentle, loving man can be that fierce when his principles or his loved ones are at stake.

The Six newsman and one-time co-anchorman of the morning "Today Show," Tom Brokaw, was not bothered by the grueling "Today" schedule. His concern however, was for his three daughters. "I don't want my children to grow up thinking they are better than the rest of society," he said. "We're very much aware of our middle-class roots. We want to maintain those roots for the sake of the children."

Maple trees aside, your Six Man sets his goals extremely high. Once done, he strives with every ounce of his considerable determination to achieve them. Burning the midnight oil is a foolhardy measure to take in today's market but he dares mighty things because he is willing to pay any price to reach his objectives. You know. You were one of them many years ago.

At first you may suspect it's his curly hair and straight white teeth that have women lining up wherever he goes, but look closely, there's a generous sprinkling of men and children too. His shoulders are broad, strong and bountifully absorbant. This is necessarily so because everyone cries on them. He is a natural psychologist, understanding human emotion from firsthand experience. He has a knack for the right words, a sense of the fairest solution, an awareness of everyone's feelings. Since he's going to make it a lifetime practice, he might as well hang up a shingle and get paid for it.

He's not good—he's very, very good. Solomon, in all his wisdom, runs a close, very close, second to your Six Man. Was it mentioned that he's sexy? Love is more than a clinical interest with your Six Man, however. But you needn't worry. After he finds out what it's all about and how to do it properly, he's going to do it with you.

An unwise woman may take advantage of her Six Man by trying to dominate or betray him. But his love can take a beating. He'll stand beside her through sickness and health, through hen-pecking and slovenliness, and for richer or poorer. He'll have faith enough to believe in the flimsiest stories—all true, of course,—and he'll lock jaws with anyone who speaks to the contrary. But, she can push him too far. Then, one day, her strong and gentle lover will reach Farenheit 212. Boiling cauldrons and fiery regions are to be preferred to his righteous wrath. So, it is advisable to make love, not war, with this wonderful man who loves you.

Like the American Revolutionary War hero, Nathan Hale, who was born on the 6th, your Six Man regrets that he has "but one life to give for his country." Once he's decided upon a cause, he's committed. And don't mutter under your breath, "If he isn't committed, he ought to be." You're just tired of rolling bandages and tripping over the wounded. You never signed up to be a nurse. But you do admire his unselfish devotion to issues greater than himself. It's the refugees he insists on bringing home that have you the most worried. But you can always get another job. Maybe the hospital has an opening.... At any rate, those are the cold realities. Your Six Man is bound to take on the troubles of others. Sometimes you think he overdoes it but that's the nature of the beast. He is everyone's Big Daddy.

6

Your Six Man is attracted to nature. He recognizes its beauty, symmetry and balance. His own home may reflect the landscaper's eye with cascades of roses climbing over picket fences, blushing bleeding hearts (how appropriate!) and privet hedges pruned to read from the air: Give me your huddled masses. He has an eye for the interior as well. Your home may look like a page from *House Beautiful.* He might try to decorate you as well—hair style, cosmetics, perfumes, clothing, accessories—then try to improve your posture and stride because he doesn't want anything to spoil the overall effect. Humor him. If your back begins to ache because you're draped over that French provincial chaise he picked up for the living room at an old antique shop, just grin and bear it. And don't move. You'll disturb the folds of your silk gown. It doesn't matter that he's watching television. He can see you out of the corner of his eye. You want it to look right, don't you? Besides, he would sense it if something were out of place.

Some Six Men fail to avoid certain pitfalls. Their desire to serve those they love can become a mask for meddling in family affairs under the pretext of wanting to help. Then their battle cry becomes, "I'm only doing this for you." Complaints of self-sacrifice turn off the most devoted lovers. No one wants to be told how much someone else has done for them.

There's no doubt that your Six Man wants to be of service in some capacity. He fits in naturally with people because he willingly and graciously assumes responsibility. He also genuinely cares. Chances are he'll never be without some kind of task or assignment because his services and qualifications as a man of wisdom and tact place him in constant demand.

Your Six Man looks for more than necessities. He likes bread but knows that he cannot live by it alone. Add a jug of wine and thou, beneath the bough, and it will do nicely. Even beyond that, he is in touch with the spiritual principles that underly all life. He is truly inspired. Any creative work done by him has a touch of perfection, beauty, or truth. He strives for these qualities with his every thought and action. People listen to what he has to say because he exudes a natural beauty that uplifts and refreshes their souls. He speaks to them and they respond willingly.

Sensitivity to beauty encompasses an appreciation of all the sensual phases of living. Your Six Man can settle down comfortably into his home, letting the vines grow thick and heavy around his castle, like Sleeping Beauty's, until he needs a strong arm and a keen sword to cut a path to the outside world. If his trousers begin to look like "slipcovers for a pyramid," you'll know it's time to cut down on the "good life" and begin a balanced diet.

He needs to channel his strong sexual and emotional nature as well. Six and sex not only sound phonetically similar but they are symbolically synonymous as well. A sprinkling of sexuality spices up his life but a steady diet can become addictive. He should direct his sexual drive, aiming to achieve a balance, always a key word for any Six. Some Six Men choose to sublimate their sexuality through specific religious or philosophical persuasions, but a life of total abstinence can be just as devastating to your Six Man as a life of sexual submersion. He should use his driving creative force with discrimination. If he finds mental and physical satisfaction in his selection of a path, then he has chosen wisely.

Your Six Man is the culmination of all your cherished girlhood dreams. He has fulfilled your wildest fantasies in delicious ways, inbuing your life with a love that knows no bounds, understanding all pain and comforting all wounds. He has wrapped you in a caring cocoon wherein you have been nurtured with a gentleness beyond belief.

You often glance his way to find him watching you.

"What are you looking at," you ask, smiling.

His eyes absorb your very soul. "You," he answers, in a soft, husky voice, breaking with feeling.

You don't care to know anything else.

The Seven Woman

Like Isis behind the eternal veil, your Seven Woman is a woman of mystery. She has a classic, almost forbidding beauty that drew you as the music of a snake charmer's flute draws the serpent from its basket. Actually, she hypnotized you at your first meeting. You've been in a dreamy fog ever since.

You knew from the beginning that she was different. She didn't play the coy female game many women do to attract a man. Quite the contrary. She gave the impression that you were as desirable as a sunburn. In her climate-controlled world, that is most distasteful. Her eyes swept unemotionally down your frame—just once. You're not used to such fleeting observations and your ego was a bit deflated. Then she floated out of the room leaving a layer of frost behind her. But you weren't to be daunted. You've always enjoyed a challenge.

"Who was that masked woman?" you asked a friend. Your friend replied in an awed voice, staring after her, "They call her the Lone Lady."

You discovered that your Seven Woman has little interest in frivolous pasttimes or minds. She is a thinker, a seeker after knowledge. Her world lies in the realm of the unknown where minds trample untrod paths.

She's always had an inquisitive nature. When she was a pre-schooler, she would disappear for hours at a time. A simple task seemed to take eons. Her mother would send her to wash up. Later, realizing the water had long stopped running and the bathroom was strangely silent except for a gurgling noise and a periodic flushing sound, her mother dashed to the door and opened it. Her little Seven daughter stood beside the toilet bowl, a small finger on the flush mechanism. The cat, with a fish bowl inverted over its head, was going down for the third time. A pamphlet with pictures about deep sea diving lay on the floor.

Through experimentation, your Seven Woman became the smartest girl in her grade school class. She was reciting atomic tables when you were stuck on your times. She also learned to keep a stiff upper lip if things went wrong. No one ever knew what she was thinking because she had a cool reserve unusual in a child.

Teenage years could have been difficult for your Seven Woman. Although she can charm the skin off a snake, she' was probably not aware of her charisma then. Less secure young men, although admiring her from a distance, were intimidated by her apparent superiority and aloofness. Her quick, witty responses were too difficult to parry. She may have felt that since God "didn't give her a body, she'd better develop her mind." It wasn't true but her belief in it was a self-fulfilling prophecy. Use of her growing mental prowess as a defensive mechanism turned

7

away those who would have liked to have known her better, thus confirming her opinion of herself.

Today, she's got the round pegs in the round holes, and the square pegs where they belong too. She is very selective of the company she keeps. That's why you got the cold shoulder when you first met her. She is a cool cucumber. It takes her time to decide whether she wants to step into a situation so she uses her considerable intelligence as a buffer against unwanted or premature intrusion.

A negative Seven Woman plays mind games. She is extremely adept at it—actually unequaled. She hones in on your Achilles heel like a blister from new sneakers. Then, using her keen intellect, she presents such a logical, calm flow of ideas that you will swear on a stack of Bibles that black is white. During the second world war, Tokyo Rose, born on the 7th, carried on a propaganda program over the radio aimed at demoralizing the American military by playing on their fears. In her silky voice, she gave secret locations of American troops, then, between the playing of top American tunes, urged the men to give up the battle.

You've discovered by now that verbal darts is not your game. There's no contest with your Seven Woman. You've looked like a porcupine once too often. Pit her against seven brilliant minds and the odds will be even. She needs to learn patience, however, with less brainy types. She doesn't necessarily expect speed from others but she does expect understanding. If you really want to impress her, tell her you have a brain like a prune. Don't worry that they're really rather badly wrinkled. Don't argue. Just carry a nice wallet-sized picture of your head muscle along with the results of your brain scan. These items will provide you with more clout with her than your American Express card, both of which you should never leave home without. You'll be in like Flynn. What's the secret? Well, each time you learn something new, another wrinkle appears in your brain. Therefore, wrinkled brain = prune = smart person. It's quite logical. She must have approved of your test results because she chose you. You can't be anyone's dummy or she could not live with you. Your brain muscle had to match your body muscle. The first is necessary; the second is merely a bonus.

Your Seven Woman is skilled with her hands, a fact which presents interesting possibilities. Some Seven Women have to train their hands to keep up with their minds. She may not be slow with her hands as much as deliberate because she is extremely painstaking and thorough. Once she has learned a new technique, she is faster than a speeding bullet, able to leap tall buildings with her mind.

Specialization is tempting to her because, in whatever she does, she tunes her laser-like mind to perfect pitch. The trouble for you may be that she did not choose the kitchen. That's O.K. if you like TV dinners and eating out. She gave up cooking the night she dared her bravest venture—cooking you a meal. Emerging from the land of dirty pans and food wrappers, she proudly announced, "These are the two things I cook best—meat loaf and lemon meringue pie." To which you replied, "Which is this." You blew it.

Off in broader pastures, your Seven Woman is a relentless pursuer. Whether she's trailing a satellite or stalking a quark, she'll bag her quarry because she never ·gives up. Born on the 7th, Marie Curie, a brilliant and persistent scientist, became the only person to be twice awarded the Nobel Prize in Chemistry.

Your Seven Woman should always seek avenues of expression where her fine intellect and acute powers of perception can be put to proper use. If mysticism calls her, don your conservative black suit; if science beckons, white will be more appropriate; if invention invites, remain calm when you unexpectedly confront a coffee-pouring robot in the kitchen one morning; if literature lures her, you be the coffee-pouring robot; and if the occult calls, cast out all your preconceived ideas about reality. Whatever she chooses, she'll make it work. So you'd better be ready for anything from weightless experiments in a home-built vacuum to levitation over your bed at midnight on the full of the moon. Because she's going to investigate every angle. She won't just believe. She's from Missouri. She wants to be shown. And she'll show you things you won't believe even when you do see them.

You'll accept as commonplace telephone calls from U.S. Steel, the White House and Betty Crocker, although the latter may confuse you at first. She has answers and solutions filed away in her computerized brain that make HAL envious. Unlike HAL, the computer from the film *Space Odyssey: 2001,* which tried to kill the astronaut and take over the space vehicle, she is not into power trips in that sense. She just enjoys using her inventive mind. If she is to be fulfilled and happy, she must use it. She's a one-woman brain trust. One of these days, her cloned brain cells will be the first donation to the International Brain Bank.

Even though your Seven Woman may appear reticent upon first encounter, she isn't afraid to say what she thinks, as you have certainly found out by now. She can banter words with the best. In fact, she can be downright intimidating. It is advisable that you compliment her with care. Don't be surprised if, after telling her how beautiful she looks, you end up with frost on your pumpkin. What is deemed a compliment to most women can be positively insulting to your Seven Woman. Rather, tell her that her deep limpid eyes contain the mystery of lost stars, her soft lips form words that stimulate your mind, and the curves of her inviting body remind you of Athena, goddess of wisdom. If you're lucky, you might only confuse her but at least you won't get iced.

Your Seven Woman is observant. She notices everything from the movie manager's frayed belt to your boss's plucked eyebrows. Her X-ray vision strips off all outer camouflauge, exposing the naked truth. Armed with only that truth and an I.Q. of 170, she may offer you cool commentaries on what you're doing wrong and why, and what you need to do to correct it. Some Seven Women can be icily sarcastic about other people's blunders. In fact, sarcasm may be her biggest fault. In her search for perfection she needs to realize that mentally she is far ahead of the pack. She must make allowances for those poor souls struggling along with I.Q.'s of a mere 140. Be patient with her. Teach her to be tolerant of human foibles. Show her the fun in making mistakes and being able to laugh at your own errors as well as at the faux pas of others.

Also, try to understand that your Seven Woman needs quiet periods of time by herself. It isn't your mouthwash, your deodorant or your lagging mentality that has caused her to seal up her bedroom door these past seven months. She had an idea and needed an undisturbed environment in which to work it out. Hang in there like a brave soldier. She'll soon emerge, starry-eyed and victorious, looking like the Greek warrior Queen, Martesia, who expanded her Amazonian empire through many battles and conquests. Not bad for seven months without manicures and a

7

hairdresser. The issue has been dealt with, the problem solved, and you're next on her agenda. She'll approach you with a wild and hungry look. Maybe it's the disheveled hair or over a half-year on K-rations that's creating the effect, nevertheless, she is a woman with a mission which only you can fill.

Because she trusts you, she is unafraid to show the depth of her feelings for you. As your minds and bodies meld into one, you know why they say, "Still waters run deep." You braved the wintry hunt to drink where few others dare. Now you have tasted the crystal-pure water from the spring of her soul. You've been initiated into the mysteries of love.

The Seven Man

You're upset because you fell in love with a cigar store Indian. Fret not. That strong, handsome, aloof demeanor that has so captivated your fancy actually belongs to a living, breathing man.

Some Seven Men give the impression they are living in a perpetual cataleptic state but that's only because their minds are in outer space. No, they're not spacy...not really...well...perhaps it's just that, to mere mortals, they appear slightly removed from the mainstream of life. They always seem to have their minds on something no one else can see or fathom, as if they were in continual communion with a secret voice that whispers in their ears. When you find your Seven Man sitting on a pedestal with his chin in his hand, staring stonily into space, you'll get the picture. He's a thinker. Thinking does not necessarily require physical motion, therefore your Seven Man can come across as a study in cement. However, he can get his point across most effectively without moving a muscle or twitching an eye. Gary Cooper, the movie star born on the 7th, was a perfect example of the charisma a stone statue can exude. More excitable types are driven to jumping, screaming and flailing around the immobile form of a Seven, just to get his attention. Then, as if through ventriloquist's lips, the Seven Man issues the quiet words, "How may I help you?"

Tears and hysterics aren't going to get to him, just confuse him. He won't understand why you get so emotional when all you have to do is remain calm and think it out. It's such a reasonable approach. Your birthday just slipped his mind. He's been working on that new formula, remember? He hands you a dollar and says, "Here. Go out and get yourself a nice card. Something you like. I'll sign it, O.K.?"

He fidgets as your tears fall. "Oh my God, you're impossible," you cry.

Nervously, he stubs the toe of his shoe into the carpet. With a pained look on his downcast face, he murmurs, "Look. I'm really sorry."

You stop and sigh. This big hunk in front of you suddenly resembles a small boy being scolded by his mother. Your heart skips a beat as he smiles a placatingly crooked smile down at you.

"Oh, alright," you mutter, only half grudgingly. You still feel you need to put on a bit of an act.

His body relaxes. "Thank you, darling. I won't forget again. Besides. You know I love you."

He turns and ambles off to his laboratory. You watch him move away, reminding yourself that you knew he needed a keeper when you first met him.

Remember when you were introduced? You reached out to shake his hand. He took yours as if he feared you had just contracted a case of Bubonic plague. When one of the more vivacious women in the group greeted him with a "Hello darling," and planted kisses on each cheek, she suffered a severe case of frost bite. But you sensed something beneath that cool exterior, something warm, mysterious, tantalizing. When the niceties were over, the conversation turned to meatier topics. Then your Seven Man began to shine. You loved the animated look in his eyes and, was that a hint of a smile hovering at the corner of his lips? After you made a rather intelligent statement, you noticed his eyebrows lift ever so slightly your way. You knew it wasn't your imagination that he looked at you differently the rest of the evening. You had scored a point in his most exacting game. He is cerebral. Or perhaps it would be better to say, he's a mind person.

Your Seven Man has a mind. At times you may think he *is* a mind. He had a superior look when he emerged from the birth canal, took a look around and thought, "Ah, yes. Just as I imagined it."

When he was a little boy, his mother never had a hard time finding him. It was getting to him that was difficult. She finally resorted to sliding a food tray under his bedroom door. When the tray reappeared in the hallway, picked over, she knew he was still alive somewhere in the far reaches of his room.

During his teenage years, he still had his nose in a book and his head in the clouds. The girls would have loved to have known him better but could never get close to him. Maybe the deterrent was the invisible force field he set up around himself to discourage intruders.

Today your Seven Man is still totally absorbed in mental pursuits. If, by age twenty-five, he hasn't disproved Einstein's theory or founded a new religion, he's one of the slower breed, which still puts him far ahead of everyone else.

Fundamentally, there is no man finer or stronger than your Seven Man. He is the cool, pure water from the mountain stream or from the very depths of the well. Such purity and depth are not common in this everyday world, therefore he is often misunderstood. He cannot accept facts at surface value but must know why, linking the known with the unknown. His analytical mind is constantly urging him on to discover the esoteric, the hidden side of life. And he gets involved. How many times have you lost him in corridors? You're walking along, talking to him over your shoulder—he's a slow walker—and the next thing you know, passers-by are staring at you. It seems you've been carrying on an extremely animated conversation with yourself. "There was someone here with me," you explain, somewhat foolishly. They nod their heads knowingly, cutting a wide path around you.

You've also learned to treat bruises and bumps, common ailments for your Seven Man. Walking and reading simultaneously don't mix. The problem is that reading's more important to your Seven Man, therefore he never looks up. Lampposts, curbings and motorists are real hazards. Sometimes you're afraid someone will report you for man-beating. How many times can you say your mate has walked into a door? Even if it is true.

He really needs you around. Not only because he loves you but also because it's a matter of his survival. He just isn't aware of the mundane, everyday duties that he has to attend to in order to survive, like eating, paying his bills and returning his 1040 form. Sometimes you've even held a mirror under his nose to convince yourself he's still breathing.

7

Your Seven Man is not colder than a well digger's lunch, no matter what your mother says. He's just naturally reserved and quiet. He couldn't survive without blocks of peace, silence, and seclusion. In the beginning, his silence used to upset you. Remember the time you told him he never laughed at your jokes? He looked at you seriously and said, "Tell me a joke. And listen carefully. I'm only going to laugh once." He wasn't being sarcastic. It was just that he had other things to think about.

He has a thing about time. It's not that he's in a rush. Nothing could be farther from the truth. It's just that he values time. He places a very high premium on it. In fact, he guards it as zealously as the troops guarded our national treasure, Mae West. He has such a detailed mind that he needs time to order his thoughts. He marches long, complicated ideas around in his head with the ease of a master drill sargeant.

There are some Seven Men who cannot communicate their ideas in ways that the ordinary person can understand. They get so caught up in the world of their mind that they lose contact with the everyday place in which their physical body resides. These Seven Men may feel repressed or suspicious of others so they can only find relief by themselves or with others of the same ilk. Fear of rejection and misunderstanding has caused these types to become cynical and patronizing, using their fine intelligences as weapons rather than tools.

Your Seven Man is not going to rush his mental processes. He doesn't want to forget any tiny piece of information in his search for truth. He may be a fine writer—some Seven Men are. But don't expect to dash through his novels in a night, or even a fortnight. He writes the way he thinks—comprehensively, thoroughly and in great detail. The length of his sentences will surely break a Guiness World Record. Charles Dickens, born on the 7th, wrote sentences that trudged on and on until, exhausted, they fell upon the blessed period. He was wonderful! Today we have a twentieth century woman, Taylor Caldwell, also born on the 7th, whose writing style was certainly very detailed and lengthy. If you agree to edit your Seven Man's manuscript, have handy a very large dictionary—he loves big words—and an abundant supply of pretzels. You'll be at it for a while. No one will ever accuse your man of being hasty.

No one will ever accuse your Seven Man of being undignified either. As an author once said, when writing about the English, "One must admire the silent dignity with which they do idiotic things." So it can be said of your Seven Man. He keeps his composure first, last and always—when he's awake, that is. Be aware that he can still be moving and not be awake.

During what you consider his waking moments, he is unforgettable. He is the light-bearer, the seeker of truth, magic and mysticism. He must choose his path carefully because, once started, he finds it almost impossible to give up the search. He is as relentless as the eternal flame that burns inside him. A mystical quality lies beneath his seemingly cool demeanor. Intuition guides him more than he knows or may care to admit. He responds at deep levels to dreams and metaphysical musings, nature and heavenly things. His strong invisible link to his divinity reveals itself in his need for seclusion, meditation, quiet moments when he communes with those inner aspects of his being.

He can be too serious, therefore you should teach your Seven Man to play, like moonbeams on dancing water. Teach him to laugh, even if it's only once, at your jokes. Help him look outside himself for his balance. If you do, he'll touch the inner chambers of your soul as well.

Love him long and well. But keep in mind that timing is everything. When he says, "Not tonight, dear. I have a headache," you must realize he probably does. He spends much time thinking. However, when he is ready, you'll know. Just watch the control panel on his chest. At specific intervals, a green light will flash, an even voice will state, "You have exactly seventy seconds to respond." Although your life together is cool and tingly, you won't wear your woolies that night. After dinner and a slow stroll along the deserted beach, you'll probably end up wearing just your birthday suit as together you dive into the chilling midnight surf. Afterward, as you lie in the damp sand, at one with the earth and sea and heavens above, you'll wonder why all the fuss about those fiery lover types. You've got a cool perfectionist, skilled in the art of discovery. You don't need heat to drive your temperature up.

The Eight Woman

Look upon her lightly, admire her well-sculptured beauty, entertain your secret thoughts about her personal intimacies, but don't touch the merchandise unless you're prepared for a mighty powerful exchange. Regardless of her ultra-femininity, your Eight Woman is not the type who can be domineered or patronized. Her dazzling smile strikes you full force, like a golden shock wave. She'll have your blood pounding in your veins while you move to impress her. She does look up to strong men but, if you try to muscle her, your golden girl will smoulder. And then things will rip. You'll have a tigress by the tail.

Your Eight Woman won't take orders like a "good little girl." She is too aware of her own power to throw herself upon the judgments of others. Laying prostrate at the feet of the great god Humility is not her idea of a daily function. She knows she's good. Before she's through, you'll know it too.

She left lasting impressions on her childhood playmates. In her old neighborhood, the children now play Queen of the Mountain and Blind Woman's Bluff. It's not that she deliberately set out to change the English language, it's just that she is such a moving tower of strength and solidity that changes follow in her wake.

Through her teenage years, she developed a reputation for dependability and independence. You wouldn't find her draped over the high school jock or giggling behind her hand with a gaggle of girls. She had things to do and places to go. Life is an ordination for her; she is about serious business.

Your Eight Woman has risen to full stature now, her gentle curves belying the straight-and-narrow path she has chosen. Her drive and discipline have left more than one hapless male on the road to the funny farm. Etch a firm look on your face because you'll need it. Not that it will do any good. Just because you tell her you love her, will provide for her and keep her safe forever so you want her to stay at home and be a "good wife" to you, don't expect she'll plunk herself in the kitchen, pounding bread for the next eighty years. She's not the Pillsbury Doughgirl. She'll snap those domestic chains with a flick of the wrist and be out pounding the pavement for ERA. And that's not real estate. But then, it could be. She loves to own vast tracts of land.

8

Possessions enhance her image of herself. They represent the culmination of her efforts in the physical world. The more elaborate, unique and expensive the items are, the more successful she feels she is. Your Eight Woman finds beauty and fulfillment in the ownership of objects. She has a spiritual bond with the material world, sensing the pleasure of God's physical universe. As long as she continues to own her possessions, rather than letting them own her, she will fulfill her destiny.

A negative Eight Woman becomes obsessed with money and the power it bestows. She can become cold, ruthless, and unfeeling in her drive to positions of control. She becomes addicted to her relentless ambition which drives her toward a barren mountaintop where she'll find only loneliness and desperation. The Eight Woman must learn to share the fruits of her labor with others. Only then will her rewards have meaning and pleasure for her. In the sharing is her joy.

Your Eight Woman is a born leader whether she expresses her executive capabilities in the home or in the world outside her home. If she has chosen a career—temporarily—as a wife and mother, don't be lulled into a false sense of security. There are little tell-tale signs which indicate her natural bent. You find your socks rolled into neat balls placed in rainbow order in your bureau drawer along with an index card upon which you are to note the durability of nylon versus orlon. On the bathroom wall there hangs, not a Picasso, but a large graph with a bright red zigzag slash across it, noting the children's cavity count since the first of the year. Every Friday before they get their allowance, the kids must turn in a carefully detailed expense sheet. Twice a year, your performance on the job as a husband is reviewed. (It does keep you on your toes.) When the day comes that she asks the kids for a profit and loss sheet on their lemonade stand, you may decide it's time to encourage her to find a job outside your home. You might as well encourage her because you certainly can't stop her. She has a mind like a steam roller.

Once she moves out into that big wide world full of opportunities, you'll be in Schaeffer City. Let's hope your ego can stand the competition because, when she gets rolling, she'll probably bring home more hard cash than you do. Not only can she "bring home the bacon and fry it up in a pan," but she'll never let you forget you're a man. You'll wonder what the catalyst is that changes your neatly tailored woman into a tawny Amazon. But yours is not to question why. You'd probably just get smacked across the knuckles with a ruler anyway. So, enjoy the transformation. She is powerful and exacting. When she's through with you, you'll know that your assets have been thoroughly examined. You're still around so obviously she's approved of your ability to perform useful functions.

Your Eight Woman has a strong practical side coupled with keen analytical ability which will eventually assure her a solid position as head of the World Bank. Don't play chauvinistic games or expect favors from her. Behind her quiet eyes lies a finely oiled mental machine that chews up little boys with big egos without interrupting her revolutions per minute. Don't get emotional because your best suit is in shreds and your ego's hanging out, tattered and torn, for everyone to see. It's just business. You can't expect her to allow personal considerations to influence her decisions, so just go home and start dinner. The Eight Woman, Mary Pickford, famed film star, with her gentle, kittenish eyes, "although typecast as an innocent young girl ignorant of life's seamier realities and ever in danger of losing her purity," offscreen Ms. Pickford "knew her way around the fine print of a studio contract." Aware that her presence boosted profits considerably for the film moguls, she "renegotiated her own salary from forty dollars a week to an unprecedented ten thousand a week in less than two years." "America's Sweetheart" then proceeded to set up the Mary Pickford Corporation in 1916 and began turning out films of her own.

Money and power are no strangers to your Eight Woman. Her physical body is also very important to her. It is her most highly prized personal possession. Sometimes she identifies too closely with it, thinking that she *is* her body rather than realizing it as a temple for her soul. If she becomes too enamored of her appearance—her eyes, hair, skin, bodily shape—she becomes conceited or dissatisfied, depending upon how her physical body meets her standards.

She may use her body as a means of recognition in the eyes of the world. Her capacity for long hours of discipline combined with her sense of balance makes her a potentially fine athlete. Esther Williams and Sonja Henie were born on the 8th. Or she may choose a career where her natural healthy good looks shoot her to stardom, as in the case of Lana Turner.

She may take on heavy physical and mental responsibilities that require a schedule only an Amazonian could handle. The Eight Woman, Elisabeth Kubler-Ross, pioneering psychiatrist in counseling terminally ill patients, keeps such a grueling schedule. She travels two hundred fifty thousand miles a year giving lectures and workshops because she feels the heavy responsibility of her work. At one time she lived in a house designed by Frank Lloyd Wright, an Eight Man. Those who know her speak of her incredible mental strength and deep understanding.

There is the Eight Woman who allows the pressures of life to close in about her and dampen her warrior's spirit. If she feels overwhelmed by the responsibilities of living, depressed by too many difficult experiences, she may become somber and disheartened, shutting herself away in a prison of loneliness, complaints, fears and resentments. But, she always has a choice. She is incredibly strong and enduring, and can decide at any moment to break her bonds and charge forward, crossing the finish line long before her nearest challenger.

When your Eight Woman is operating at full efficiency, she'll get a lot done and so will you. She'll keep you well supplied with work. She actually loves labor and the thrill of attainment. It may be your labor and her attainment but you must realize that there are the followers and the leaders, the drones and the queen bee. There's no question in her mind who's capable of handling all that. It matters not whether her glove be velvet or iron, she'll rule. You might as well get used to the fact that the woman you love with all your heart and soul is having an affair with the world.

She's always set her sights on the top and aimed for the best. She won't take no for an answer and won't believe she can't have something if she wants it. She does listen...sometimes. Remember when you told her she was looking for a god but she'd have to settle for the next best thing, a man. She listened, right? She chose you. You might have to scratch around for another example of her listening to advice, but one incident always proves that at least it's possible. Rare, but possible.

Your Eight Woman has a warm and outgoing personality. People like and respect her. She minds her own business...very well, as a matter of fact. She doesn't care if the neighbors are skinny-dipping in their new heart-shaped pool at two in the morning or if the minister's son ran his family's car through Miss Hunnicut's picket fence and into her frog pond. Coffee klatches strike terror into her heart. Now, if they want to discuss importing half a million tons of coffee beans before the prices go up, she'll be interested.

As far as she's concerned, diapers, soap operas and a husband's latest brand of body soap are subjects discussed on another planet peopled by those in penal servitude. Her domesticity leaves much to be desired, for those who are giving home-making points. Your Eight Woman is the one who makes the commercial or plays the lead role in the continuing story of Laura Kent, girl from the wrong side of the tracks. Then she talks about the money she made and the influential people she knows. And she does make big money and hob-nob with famous people. Like few others, her boasts have foundation in fact. She's on a first-name basis with well-known personalities and political leaders. At home, her walls are covered with framed photographs of the rich and famous with their arms around her lovely torso. If she's a sportswoman, trophies line her bookcase shelves. She's been known to charge admission to her living room. She's always the entrepreneur.

Although she appears matter-of-fact at times—how many women do you know who calmly file a broken nail when 880 shares of her common stock have just split?—she really does have strong feelings. It's just not her style to get excited and bounce around. She knew it was going to split anyway. It was good stock or she wouldn't have bought it. And if you had listened, you would have bought some too. Oh, did she forget to tell you the stock is in her name? Of course you share everything, but one of you has to make the decisions. That's O.K. She'll share her shares. A little thank you wouldn't hurt. And please say it as if you meant it. Oh well...who wants to argue with a woman who has a bank account like hers. Besides, she's magnificent. She is the woman who challenges your male instincts like no other. She is so clever, capable and intoxicating, you don't know whether you want to seal her in a basket and toss her into the bullrushes or throw in the towel and sign up for life. Of course you'll decide to do the latter. You couldn't possibly let her get away. She combines the creaminess of pearls with the fire of rubies to become a stunning jewel of womanhood. She sparkles like crystal in sunlight and fills your life with treasures beyond compare.

The Eight Man

See that fellow in the loin cloth, trudging down the street, carrying a globe of the world on his broad shoulders? He is your basic Eight Man and he's into heavy responsibility.The more tasks and obligations that are piled on him, the better he seems to operate. He has a mental strength that is truly awesome. Long periods of stress that would debilitate lesser mortals merely work up a good sweat for him. He wipes his brow, rubs his hands together and says, "Well, what's next?"

Not only is he mentally able to sustain repeated efforts and complete arduous tasks. but he is also extremely capable and efficient. He has an uncanny business sense. With a finger on the pulse of the economic world, he knows where and when the public heartbeat requires his services. He'll supply their needs in ways that will satisfy them as well as provide financial remuneration for himself.

Your Eight Man loves the color green. It reminds him of money. When he was a tot, his mother realized he had an obsession with this shade when he insisted on dying all his pajamas green. It was tolerable for a while but then all his clothes, his bedroom, bicycle and baseball mitt followed suit. The last clover was when he spray-painted the family dog a lovely shade of chartreuse. The neighbors began to suspect his mother had given birth to a leprechaun.

In his teenage years he began to sense his power. That realization could have developed into an interest in sports where his physical endurance and strength became legend. Some Eight Men decide to channel their drive for success and recognition into the world of sports where they are still able to fulfill their intense need for money, which is power painted green.

If your Eight Man chooses athletics, he will be outstanding. He has a natural balance and rhythm, coupled with strength and endurance, which is absolutely essential in an exceptional athlete. He'll make it big because he is relentless in his drive to the top. That's where he wants to go and that's where he belongs. If he decides to model panty hose along the way, so be it. At least his endorsement will bring in the megabucks.

Your Eight Man has a genius for making money, a Midas touch, which transforms everything he handles into wealth measured by the ounce. He can take a hot dog stand, eight hundred dollars and a few years and transform his enterprise into a billion-dollar-a-year restaurant chain featuring dogs a mile-long...or is it a kilometer? Kilometer would take more advertising space, of course, which your Eight Man will take into account. He doesn't miss a trick when it comes to getting the best value for his dollar. He's got a baby to nurture—his business—and he'll fight tooth and claw to see to its well-being.

When he wants something, he gets it. If you're the object of his mission, he'll move heaven and earth to find you. He just won't settle for less than the best. If you're not interested, keep your hair short and your running legs limber because your Eight Man has been known to resort to cave-man tactics when all else fails. He has intense physical needs that need to be returned. He'll want your all—body, mind and soul. In that order. Remember, he recognizes his physical needs first. However, he knows that physical conquest is empty without the spiritual bond that unites two people when they truly love. Of all the types, he is able to experience and understand total unity in a relationship—the perfect balance that results from sexual fulfillment between two souls in spiritual accord. He'll enjoy it all, taking unabashed pleasure in his body, your body and your mutual satisfaction.

Your Eight Man is deeply into the things of the material world. He believes in rendering unto Caesar. Togas are a large part of his wardrobe. He takes great pleasure in owning clothes, jewels, cars and houses. He enjoys the status and power they give him. Since you are his prized possession, you could be draped in mink and dripping with diamonds. He loves display and you're his Taj Mahal.

One of the dangers an Eight Man faces is his driving intensity toward material gain. He can work himself to the point of physical and mental exhaustion. Constant stress will wear out his greatest possession, his strong physical body. He must take care that he doesn't drive others as ruthlessly as he drives himself with an attitude that's "hell-bent for leather and the devil take the hindmost." He must not allow his physical appetites to imprison him. It is harder for him to break habits than for others because his attitudes can be so intense and rigid.

8

Your Eight Man knows better. He is intelligent. He learns very quickly from direct experience and observation, and he doesn't forget his lessons. His past experiences are the basis of future successes. He is extremely aware of cause and effect because his life has been one long string of karmic events. After he's been burnt once, you can bet your bottom dollar he'll wear asbestos gloves the next time. He won't keep away from the fire, but he'll be totally prepared for any future immolations.

His good judgment and common sense inspire confidence in others. He doesn't make hasty or unwise decisions. His criteria are: is this practical and will it work? His calm and unperturbed demeanor in the face of a crisis is well-known. Everyone knows better than to question his opinions whether they be on falling skies, economics or world politics. He is well-respected, admired and down-to-earth, with few illusions about the world as it appears, and with tremendous insight into the world as it really is. He makes you feel as if life will continue without interruption, on schedule and from eight to five because he expects it to. Typhoons, births and acts of God will be scheduled off company time. Then everyone will be back at work Monday at 8 A.M. sharp, bright-eyed and bushy-tailed. Of course, just because his door bears the gilt-edged letters: Office hours 8–5 Monday through Saturday, does not mean that he works only fifty-four hours a week. In fact, he can outwork any eight men through sheer endurance. He loves it. He'll roll up his shirt-sleeves and dig into the work pile right along with his employees, continuing long after they leave. He's not just talk. He's action. His motto: Put your money where your mouth is, is emblazoned across all his T-shirts and laundry tags, and the office stationery. He doesn't want excuses, platitudes or high-flown philosophies. He wants action and results.

It is essential that your Eight Man have a purpose. Without a feeling that he is performing a useful and much needed function, he can flounder. He becomes sullen and despondent, sure that others are neglecting him. His keen sense of timing is thrown off and, as problems mount, his confidence dwindles. Cause and effect again reign supreme but, in this case, negatively.

No other individual has such a profound effect upon the visible power structure of the world as a positive Eight Man. The Eight Man, Frank Lloyd Wright, American "architectural outlaw," built homes designed to fit into the landscape. His biggest commission, however, came when he built the Imperial Hotel in Tokyo, "an engineering triumph" that was so solidly designed and constructed it survived the 1923 earthquake unscathed.

Another Eight Man, German surgeon, Karl von Graefe, was a pioneer in plastic surgery. His specialty was the nose, certainly the most visible part of the face.

Your Eight Man wants to do things that show, that are lasting and make an indelible impression. Perhaps your Eight Man's belief in his own ability to change and rule his world stems from the fact that the results of using his energies are so visible. Right from the beginning he found that when he set goals and worked hard and persistently, he could achieve them. As he obtained his desires one by one, his confidence grew to the point where he knew that nothing was beyond his reach if he persevered and kept his eye on the mountain top.

Today, his goals are simple. He wants money, power, possessions, fame and influence. A fulfilling sexual relationship with you will round it all off nicely. He's not greedy. It's just that it's all there so why not take it. Somebody's going to and he knows he can handle it better than the rest. Others may know that thoughts are things, becoming a reality if they are entertained long enough, but your Eight Man will prove that thoughts are things by making them happen. So, when he decides he wants to be captain of the Green Bay Packers—they wear the right color anyway—set the table for twelve. You're included, or course.

Your Eight Man is capable of obtaining and maintaining awesome influence. He lives and breathes economic, political and social power. It is not unusual that his actions or decisions have worldwide repercussions. John D. Rockefeller, Sr. and his grandson, Nelson Rockefeller, both born on the 8th, are perfect examples of power men whose influence reaches into every corner of the globe. As your Eight Man amasses fortunes, his humanitarian impulses are triggered. He can be more than charitable in giving to worthwhile causes, organizations and foundations. These donations not only satisfy his true compassion for the suffering of others but also sate his need for prestige in the eyes of the world. He'll also really like the way his name is printed in eight-foot-high letters across the fronts of museums and hospitals. He's concerned with posterity.

Taking orders is difficult for your Eight Man. If he has a choice, he'll choose a job which provides him with the latitude to use his executive talents. Even if he finds himself in a trying work situation, he can follow the rules and work within the confines of the job until he reaches the position he was destined for—that of leadership. He is a power person who thoroughly enjoys making decisions himself. He takes to responsibility like a duck to water. These qualities make him a formidable opponent. He's a tough man to put down or discourage. His actions have more reaction than those of other men because of his very nature. If he is successful, he is very, very successful—known in wide circles or around the world, influencing the lives of millions. If he gives up—which is most unusual—he becomes more of a prisoner than a lifer. He has more to lose and more to gain in the material world than other men because he is so capable. He has a responsibility to discipline his vast energies toward creating a better world for everyone. That is his task. He has the strength of Atlas and the enduring fortitude of Saturn. His works can become the eighth wonder of the world.

So, if you've been looking for the best in life, if you've decided you want it all, this is your man. He is the Eighth Wonder of the human race. He'll work until dawn's early light to provide you with treasures that equal those in King Solomon's mines. You won't have to search for him, wondering where he is when he's late for supper. You'll find him in his oval office, behind his black mahogany desk on top of a thick Persian carpet amidst one red phone and eight green ones, all of which seem to be ringing off their hooks simultaneously. He's important; he's needed. You need him too. Though you may have to share him with eighty-eight other industries and potentates, you finally decide to lie back and enjoy it. Spending your anniversary on a private jet soaring through the midnight heavens to some exotic land isn't so bad—even if your Eight Man is still answering phones. You can see his rugged profile outlined in the lights of the cabin. You rise, move over to him, take the phones off the hooks and wrap your arms about his neck. He hesitates only a moment, thinking of all the calls he should make, then returns your gaze with a look of such passion that the stars pale beside the fire you have kindled. You forget everything. You have arrived at your destination.

The Nine Woman

9

Bewitching, isn't she. There's something about her that captures your imagination. She seems to be many women in one. She can be as wise as Solomon, as naive as a child, as unpredictable as the weather, as unconcerned as the lilies of the field, as emotional as an Italian wedding and as mystical as the ancient Orient. You may live with her for a hundred years but she'll remain an unfathomable mystery. Just when you think you've taped her tune, she'll catch you on the flip side, tangling you in miles of satiny tape until you resemble an Egyptian mummy. Now you know why people have been asking you to repeat yourself since you met her. All along you thought it was because you've been babbling incoherently.

By now your lively, intelligent Nine Woman has taught you that "love is a many splendored thing." She is fun. She insists on living a full, brimming-over life and, in her exuberance, sweeps you along into situations that test your confidence. How many men, dressed in faded denims and rugby shirt, pick up their date to go bowling and end up at a caviar and champagne soiree as guests of Barbara Cartland?

Your Nine Woman does not discriminate because of sex, race, color or creed. Some of her best friends are men. In fact, she enjoys mingling with a variety of people. Her list of friends reads like the daily role call at the United Nations. She's educated you so that you've learned to be tolerant and unflappable. Remember the time you took her to your church outing and she unexpectedly brought along her friend, the disco king with the pinky rings, long gold chains and red silk tights. You were a little startled but you recovered with admirable dispatch. The congregation is still talking about it. But you all had a wonderful time and now the parson listens to the Top Forty.

When she was a little girl, she supplemented her allowance by offering counseling services for nine cents at a hastily constructed booth on her front lawn. Her parents realized she had something going for her when old men with long white beards and twisted staffs, and ancient women with deep and dreamy eyes, began stopping at the booth.

Even as a teenager, she seemed older than her peers. She could communicate with everyone but she sought out individuals who could teach her things whether they were small children wondering about a snail after a summer's rain or great-grandmothers with clacking knitting needles. She might have had restless and uneasy periods during these growing years if she didn't understand why she felt different from other people, why the ordinary pursuits did not satisfy her as they did others.

Your Nine Woman might have been a Peter Pan, living in a fantasy world where perfection and idealism could be played out, where Captain Hook is always the villain, obviously and thoroughly distasteful, and good always wins out.

If she's followed today by ticking alligators, you'll know that she's still in Never Never Land. Perhaps she doesn't want to grow up if growing up means laying aside her idealism and what others would call child-like belief in magic, truth and perfection. The Nine Woman, folksinger Joan Baez, became active in the antiwar and civil rights movements in the early 70s. She felt empathy for the downtrodden. When she spoke out against the inhumane policies of Vietnam's communist government, she found herself in the strange position of being criticized by activists like Jane Fonda. But Baez declared, "I'm against all forms of oppression, no matter whose flag it's under."

With an attitude like that...you wonder if it isn't your Nine Woman, in reality, who has the proper perspective. She does make it work. Not that she has proven her power to materialize objects out of thin air—although she's working on it—or that she has walked on water—yet—but she believes that nothing is impossible if you believe. She goes beyond believing because she knows. Sometimes her eyes, changing as they do from deep wells of wonder to flashes of fire in a flick of Tinker Bell's dust, animate you with their innocent intrigue. You wonder how she can be both naive and so wise in the same moments. Perhaps she's courageous, or just plain crazy. You doubt if you'll ever find out. Yet, time after time, her divine standards are rewarded in ways that leave you stunned.

There is a Nine Woman, however, who is inconsistent and hard to understand. She is cold, distant and interested in her own welfare and personal gain. She can shut out the ones she loves to achieve her personal ends. Then she can suddenly change, become warm and generous, giving without a thought of herself. There is also the Nine Woman who is moody and impractical, living in a world of illusions and abstractions, where much is dreamed of but little is planned and nothing carried through.

But your Nine Woman has a heart as big as a home into which she welcomes the suffering and underprivileged of the world. The Nine Woman, Barbara Cartland, prolific writer of romantic novels, has literally taken the underprivileged into her home. On her vast estate in England, she has set aside a portion of land for the gypsies to live on. She feels they have been and still are discriminated against.

Your woman feels the same way toward the underdog. She is so impressionable and compassionate she has to be careful she isn't taken in by a good sob story. She's been known to whip out her check book and write out a small sum like nine thousand dollars to save the Arabian dhow from extinction. But she's good for it. Unlike some who take their new checks to Goodyear to be vulcanized, she usually has a healthy amount of cash available. Once she learns to give discriminately and handle her affairs properly, she attracts money, favor and good fortune because she's in partnership with the cosmos. You always knew she was far out. But, to your surprise, her spaceship shuttles in frequently. She has an uncanny ability to recoup her losses and redeem her failures. Nines have been known to make, lose and make again many fortunes in a lifetime.

Your Nine Woman has the ability to bounce back emotionally after volcanic outbursts that leave residue in the atmosphere for months. While you're sputtering, choking and wiping the ash off everything three dimensional in your environment, she's somehow renewed herself and is raring to go. She seems to have a hidden pool from which she secretly drinks, a pool that restores her body and soul during long treks across emotional deserts under parched skies. When she disappears periodically, don't assume she's crept into the tent of an Arab sheik at some hidden oasis and now lies breathlessly in his bronzed arms enjoying heated passions flamed by a sultry night. More than likely she's locked herself into the sauna at the health club and is doing one hundred push-ups or has tangled tentacles with a 3800 series computer in her office at midnight and is determined to show the superiority of woman over nuts, bolts and blinking lights. She may find curious ways to relieve her tensions but by allowing her the space to do so, you save yourself a mighty big clean-up job.

9

One thing your Nine Woman has learned is that she must live her philosophy. She is not one of those people who can profess a specific belief in a way of life then turn around and do just the opposite. Of course she can but she will be caught. "Do as I say and not as I do" was never spoken by a Nine. She knows, and because she knows, her actions and words make impressions. They become most visible. She is an example for others. People remember her—her conversation, her personality—and are impressed by her vision, her breadth of understanding, her caring. As a result, when they meet her again, they recall what she said. Besides, they probably follow her in the newspapers—Nines are all over the place—or through friends' conversations. If everyone doesn't know her, at least they know *of* her and they are quick to notice when her lifestyle, actions and words don't dovetail. It's not that her observers are critical but that they unconsciously expect more from her because they sense she has so much more wisdom and wholeness than most people.

Because your Nine Woman is on a pedestal, she needs to keep a firm grip on her principles. More than any other number, she has much to lose because she knows better. Her awareness of what is right and wrong places her in a responsible position in any situation. If she fails to do right, her sin is greater because she knew what she should have done whereas others might not have known. She sins with awareness. Falling off pedestals can be tedious and dangerous, especially from her elevated position. Nines use a lot of bandages.

Your Nine Woman involves herself totally in everything she does. When she has a problem, she is into it 109 percent. Your persuasions to the contrary are as futile as the medieval argument about how many angels can dance on the head of a pin. Her experience is always a total one; therefore, she goes head over heels into the drink. Obviously she can get caught in some pretty tricky situations, but her marvelous cosmic sense can be triggered by a casual phrase or a line from a book and voila! she has solved the problem and is suddenly totally free from it. Because she lives and experiences so completely, she has the ability to let go of the past.

Personal love is important to your Nine Woman but she must learn to reach beyond it. Part of her purpose is to know and experience universal love and camaraderie. Only by letting go can she possess. Some Nine Women cling tenaciously to their mates, living in fear that they will be left alone. Such actions assure that their fear will become a reality. A Nine Woman can have her love only if she leaves space for him as well as herself to move and grow. If she is mentally free of personal bonds, then her relationship will endure and grow stronger with each passing day.

When it comes to friendships, your Nine Woman sheds them like a snake sheds its skin. She must be prepared to let go in all areas of her life. When friendships have fulfilled the needs of both parties, they will end, peacefully, casually and on their own so that she will be free to move on to new fields of awareness.

This delightful woman with whom you are in love is meant to be a globe-trotter—if not physically by traveling this planet, then certainly socially in her own area. Her contacts with different kinds of people add to her storehouse of wisdom and her capacity for tolerance and understanding. After all, if her best friend is an organ grinder, she can hardly dislike monkeys. Through her vast experiences, she grows into a loving, compassionate, truly wise woman. Others will seek her help and counsel. She not only offers truth but must live it herself, thereby becoming an example for others by her very actions.

You're right. You've got yourself quite a handful. She's not your everyday mechanical Stepford wife, programmed to move through her daily domestic duties with a frozen smile. If she decides that her home is her universe, be prepared for some jet-age living into the future or the ancient past. They both meet at some point, she will assure you. And when you find yourself not arguing about her sending your little ones to first grade in space suits or Roman togas, you'll know you're convinced too.

Security and routine aside, it really doesn't bother you to come home to find strangers carrying your Victorian bedroom set out the back door. You can handle that. At least the house still belongs to you...you think. Once inside, you realize it does. The kitchen dishes aren't packed. You sigh with relief. Your Nine Woman smiles seductively at you over the din of household noises and you know that something lies in wait upstairs where your old bed used to be. Suddenly all your tension is drained away. As you watch her over the evening meal, you know that once you step through that door into Never Never land, the heavens will open and welcome you as one of their own. Cosmic consciousness, super novas, here you come.

The Nine Man

Who is that handsome heartthrob who has been portaging a canoe across Kansas for the past week and a half? Some say he's a land-locked Wrong Way Corrigan; others claim he's a walking advertisement for Olde Town. His now famous legs are all over the newspaper and on television. Crowds are gathering at the watering holes. He hasn't lost his marbles or his way. He happens to be your average Nine Man who decided he wanted an adventure and, since he had a canoe handy, figured he'd dip his paddle in a few rivers across Kansas, Oklahoma and Nebraska. Not to be deterred by the fact that streams run downhill to the sea and that rivers between Kansas City and Lincoln are scarcer than hen's teeth, he proceeded to pack his optimism, drive and considerable energy along with a few sundry personal items and head out for the wide open spaces.

Your Nine Man finds the lure of far away places most compelling. He lives life in large chunks, leaving the crumbling pieces for more sedantary types. He is drawn toward unique experiences and contacts with people which will expand his horizons. Truly a "man for all seasons," he communicates with all types of individuals from every walk of life.

His present inclinations were fed with clock-like regularity by his parents. As a child he had to know how other people lived. One year, when he was a little boy, his parents shipped him off to a summer camp for nine-year-old bohemians. They had to. It was cheaper than sending out search parties to Greenwich, Tulsa and Carmel-by-the-sea. Besides, they had to know where he was if they wanted to claim him as a deduction on their income tax forms.

His horizons broadened as he traveled into his teens. His life became a kaleidoscope of emotions, events and experiences. He had to be careful that his need for approval did not lead him into bad habits. Since Nines attract money and assistance, he could easily have allowed peer pressure to push him into a dissipated life style.

But your Nine Man came through hail and hearty. His imaginative vision and artistic feelings create a showman who appeals to people of every age and cultural background. He can touch the universal pulse by appealing to the emotions of others. Because he moves in wide circles, he often seems to have been "born with a silver spoon in his mouth" and a silver platter to boot. But he has cultivated his present position through early hurts and disappointments where he learned to look beyond his present circumstances and needs. He has learned that pain can be the foundation for great accomplishment. Now he views life from a broader perspective, detecting the good behind seemingly negative events.

He is a generous idealist. The antithesis of Scrooge, he is the big business executive who goes against the economic wisdom of his pleading bookkeeper and gives a needy employee a fifty-dollar-a-week raise even when raises aren't being reviewed. Eventually that fifty dollar a week investment will return to him a thousandfold, in ways the accountant could never dream of.

A life of seclusion or meditating on a mountain top is not for your Nine Man. He must mingle. He needs your love, comfort and appreciation but his destiny reaches beyond the bounds of personal love and fulfillment. Universal understanding and impersonal love are the qualities he must embrace if he is to find satisfaction in his personal life. The Nine Man, astronomer Carl Sagan, has stepped outside his elite professional circle to communicate with the multitudes through his television series and book, *The Cosmos,* about issues he feels are vital. He said, "There is a great need for social reforms on earth, if poverty, starvation and injustice are to end. But just as food is necessary for the body, we need sustenance for the mind and spirit." When comparing the cost of the Viking mission to Mars to the cost of war (this mission equalled fourteen days of the Viet Nam war), he pleaded, "Life versus death, hope versus despair, courage versus fear. Space exploration and the highly mechanized destruction of people make use of similar technology and manufactured products, and similar human qualities of organization and daring. Can we not make the transition from automated aerospace killing to automated aerospace exploration of the solar system in which we live?"

Your Nine Man has breadth of thinking. He is seldom pulled down by smallness. He is like the yogi with his beads and saffron robe who was accosted on a city street by a critic who screamed and waved his arms wildly.

"Who do you think you are, you big fake. Walking around here with your stupid beads and phony robes. Everyone thinks you're nuts. You're really making a class-A fool out of yourself. Just who are you trying to impress?"

To which the yogi calmly replied, "How may I serve you?"

Imperturbably, your Nine Man faces the misunderstandings of the human race, seeking to show by his own actions how others should live. He sees the true Self behind the physical image and the emotional reaction. He is the teacher who reveals to his pupil not *his* truths but the truths that lie within the student. If he is truly fulfilling the highest potential of his number, he lives his philosophy in every way, regardless of his profession or status in the eyes of the world.

Your Nine Man may be the type who can be easily taken in. He lives truth so he expects that everyone else does too. He'll believe the vacuum cleaner salesman's pitch about the new model IR 999 that not only vacuums but washes the dishes,

9

makes the beds and patches Levi's as well. If your Nine Man is still a bachelor, there may be more motivation behind his need to believe than just idealism. At any rate, if you walk in to find an irate and indignant Nine giving orders to his Hoover, you'll know what happened. But, wait a minute...is that machine beginning to move?

Life is a wave which your Nine Man has learned to ride. Its ebb and flow influence him at profoundly deep levels. He has an abiding faith in the bounty of life so he gives freely knowing he will be taken care of, but he must also learn to give with purpose and not out of generosity alone. His act must be useful, sustaining a principle. If he has a down-and-out neighbor who has greeted him at his back door every Friday night at 5:30 for the past nine years to say he's broke and could he borrow a fin, your Nine Man must awake to the fact that the fellow might not be trying. Better he should put the money in a weekly club for nine years then send his neighbor to school to learn a trade. That way, his generosity will pay off.

Your Nine Man has the ability and vision to take objects that others have discarded and make them into something useful. He can reconstruct a human being in the same manner. Ferreting out naked truths in the junkyard of a broken soul, with clever and compassionate hands, he mends the shattered husk through visions of its own inner beauty. Like a robed priest with a neophyte, he reveals the higher Self to the outer self through educating the beginner in the basic principles of correct living and charitable loving.

He doesn't give up easily. When he sets his mind to a task, he sees it through. Leaving a job or situation unfinished offends his sense of wholeness. He is driven to tie up any loose ends. He wants everyone to enjoy the abundance of life's bounty. He has a world view like John Lennon, born on the 9th, who wrote in a song, "All we are saying is give peace a chance." Your Nine Man sees that peace is only possible in a world where one group does not turn its back on the ragged edges of humanity but gathers up all the loose souls and weaves them into the fabric of life.

In the meantime, your Nine Man has the ability to gather in the very best in material possession. He can thoroughly enjoy plush living conditions. You might say that a chauffeur-driven Rolls Royce, a fistful of star sapphires and a string of luxury hotels can jade the most principled of men and, of course, you're right. He has to learn to travel in gilt circles without becoming tarnished. Because he's impressionable he mentally absorbs what happens to those who disregard the laws of correct living. The broader his experience and travels, the greater his understanding of his own need to curb and control his natural adaptabilities.

Your Nine Man has so much love in him that he will draw women with as much ease as the Sirens whose songs lured Odysseus and his shipmates to the isle of Aeaea. Be prepared to fend off the female hordes tooth and talon because they often misunderstand his broad compassion. Women often interpret his concern as a come-on. If you find him at a party with a slinky young thing draped around his neck like a python, listen closely to the conversation. While she stares seductively into his eyes, he carefully explains Buddha's Eight Rules for right living. As she moves in for the squeeze, just nudge her and she'll slither away. Your Nine Man will smile at you, pleased as a rooster at sunrise, because he knows he's bestowed new enlightenment on a young soul. Who knows? Maybe he has.

Speaking out on issues is a must for your Nine Man. Watch his emotions rumble when a cause captures his conscience. It's his responsibility to speak, even if it is in tongues of flame, because he sees truths clearly and he can communicate them

9

in working ways to others. He really doesn't do it to embarrass you. Yankee Stadium in the bottom of the ninth in a tied World Series game may not be the place to grab a microphone to expound on saving the pristine wilderness of Maine's St. John River region, but you have to admit he has a captive audience. If you escape from New York City with only a few bruises, consider yourselves fortunate. He's got a few more permanent body markings he hasn't told you about yet. But as a rule, he doesn't need to go to such extremes. His opinion is respected; people listen carefully to what he says. They also watch what he does. If his ideas work physically for him, they'll try it too. Others expect him to practice what he preaches.

As a rule he does. You've got yourself a combination of saint and sinner. When he's a saint, children smile up at him, birds light on his shoulder and soft rich tones waft in from the cosmos. He treds with a gentle but sure foot up the mountain of attainment to spread the light from his lantern of illumination. When he's a sinner, his fall echoes long and deep like the fall of a mighty redwood in a silent forest. Many go down with him. It is the eternal law of action and reaction. He has the potential of reaching great heights as well as the danger of falling to great depths. His is a mighty responsibility. Truth lies heavy on weak shoulders so he must build his spiritual muscles early in life.

So here you are, consort to this muscular shining one. You're head over tea kettle in love with the guy and want to spend the rest of your life with him. See your stock broker. Then pick up a case of gold stars at your stationery store. You'll want those to stick on your wall charts to reward yourself for understanding in the face of his unbelievable humanitarianism. Then gather up your sea legs, your dancing shoes, your conservative greys and sleek blacks, your incredulity and your good humor in preparation for a life journey to anywhere, everywhere and nowhere. Anywhere he goes, everyone will be there anyway so nowhere becomes everywhere. Don't try to figure it out. With him by your side, it won't matter anyway.

The Ten Woman

See that lovely sure-footed creature striding confidently over those burning coals, descending ever deeper into that fiery sulphuric pit. While others tremble with trepidation, she marches in where angels fear to tread. She challenges destiny, Satan and the Infernal Revenue when her mind is made up. She knows what sacrifice means. She's been through it like no other, gaining a strength, purpose and understanding unequalled in the annals of femininity. That grim set look on her face, which only adds to her allure, is a result of her awareness that she needs to keep a tight rein on her powerful energy and drive. She was born with a mission and only an act of God will deter her. If you ask her to pick a number from one to ten, she'll refuse. First, because she knows she's a ten, and second, because she doesn't believe in chance.

Ever since she was able to talk, she tried to convince her parents that she spoke with a "big person" each night after she went to bed. Her parents snickered patronizingly behind their hands at her childish fantasies. But, the summer they took her camping and she came down off the mountain top with two stone tablets, they stopped laughing. The powers that be know visual aids are very effective.

Through her teenage years she was even more dauntless. Uncertainty and vascillation were foreign words with no meaning to her. She didn't believe in possible futures for herself. She knew there was only one future for her which required great determination and a casting aside of personal considerations. Driven by this knowledge, she was led unerringly into the correct environment in which her purpose could be carried out. This knowledge could have been subliminal through her teens and early twenties, but it led her nevertheless.

As an adult, your Ten Woman is looked to for leadership in whatever field has chosen her. Armed with a clear objective view and the knowledge that history repeats itself, she is able to make uncanny decisions, pre-empting the best forecasters. Her considerable executive abilities shoot her to top positions in her profession.

Your Ten Woman attracts wealth and fortunate circumstances almost without trying. If you're concerned that her cave full of gold Krugerands will corrupt your relationship, ask her to give them away. If she doesn't need them to accomplish her mission, she'll say confidenttly, "Of course, darling, no problem. I'll give up my wealth for you. But next month or next year, I'll make another million." She knows that circumstance will provide her the means and opportunity to leave her mark.

If you dream of domestic bliss in her loving arms, you'd better dream on because, when humility and passivity were passed out, she was obviously absent. And if your idea of womanly accomplishment is producing a basic two-egg cake, then you can bet your baking powder you're headed for a fall.

Your Ten Woman is driven. She must be careful that she doesn't ride over others in her zealous pursuit of nirvana. She is an idealist, a determined one. With her head down, flaps out and destination set, she makes Mario Andretti look like the Sunday driver who gets in front of you when you've got sixty seconds to get to the bank before they foreclose on your ancestral home. But her destination is not frivolous or self-centered. She knows her actions to dignify the individual will make a difference in the world. She comprehends the needs of the masses but won't allow the individual to be trodden under their combined feet. She has too much respect for individual creativity to allow such a meaningless and sacrilegious waste of the human spirit.

When her hackles are up, she becomes the universal solvent, wearing away all opposition through persistent and powerful poundings. It's not thunder you hear rumbling in the distance, nor the angels bowling. It's Mother Nature warning the unwary that she's on a crusade. This isn't the time to ask her to sew a button on your Van Heusen. Better you should do it yourself and suffer a needle in your pinky than experience being nailed to a cross. She does get carried away. When you start polishing your breast plate and harnessing the lions to your Datsun, you'll know that her energy and enthusiasm have overwhelmed you too. Her fiery ardor is contagious—no, not like smallpox and childhood diseases. She has a positive influence on people, motivating them into actions they might not have considered under normal circumstances. Look at you. You bought those two lions and now the people in the next apartment have hired a game hunter. A little makeup and two pairs of Foster Grants make your pets passable in the car but when walking down the street, your shaggy companions have drawn a little fire. Your Ten Woman is convincing.

10

Because she is confident, others expect her to take responsible positions—but she must work alone. She doesn't like taking orders or advice from someone else and she doesn't need to. Her own experience is her best teacher. Often she finds herself out on the proverbial limb because she takes unpopular stands. Saw sales will mushroom as opponents begin attacking her lofty position. She learns quickly to depend on her own wits and resources because she is often alone in her rarified atmosphere. Nose bleeds are a constant menace for your Ten Woman. The Ten Woman, Claire Booth Luce, American playwright, politician and diplomat, was never one to pussyfoot around. As a Republican Congresswoman from Connecticut from 1943 to 1947, she "bitterly attacked the administration, calling its foreign policy 'globaloney' and accusing Franklin D. Roosevelt of 'lying us into war.' "

If she cannot go beyond her personal ambitions, your Ten Woman will turn the tremendous power at her disposal in on herself. She becomes a mouse on a treadmill, running on and on but going nowhere in her race for self-gratification. The emptiness of it all can bloat her life-style like too much yeast in the dough. Overinflated bread dough, rising up and out the sides of the oven door, threatening to absorb anyone or thing in its wake, may seem like a B-rated monster movie but it becomes a very real danger for your Ten Woman when she hangs up her boxing gloves and gives up her fight for cosmic individuality. She is then absorbed and sacrificed to the god of self-interest who nourishes no one but itself.

But your Ten Woman is progressive. Like the wheel of fate, she turns inexorably, with the sureness of a mountain goat and the ease of a dolphin. She sees life as a series of steps taken in a logical order. If she is to succeed, she abides by the laws of nature. It's as simple as that. She assesses her priorities objectively, then with the best interests of all peoples in mind, she proceeds onward unflinchingly, if a bit intensely.

Your idealistic woman brings dignity to her world because she believes in the dignity of the human spirit. She imbues everything she touches with a devotion and style uniquely her own. She is like no other. You may have known women in the past but they pale in comparison to your fiery female lover. Most of the women you took to the park sat quietly beside you on the park bench, feeding the pigeons. Some of the more vivacious might have run you a merry chase through the woods but never have you watched the woman you love leap astride a bronze horse behind a stolid General Grant and proclaim freedom from tyranny before the gathering crowds, all the while maintaining her dignified posture. Her message strikes a harmonious chord within the breast of every listener. She is believeable because she believes in herself and her mission, and she carries it off with unbelieveable finesse.

Your Ten Woman's practical bent takes her out of the category of dreamy idealists. She has a good business head, grasping ideas quickly and putting them into action that furthers the progress of civilization. Her agile mind and fearless nature stand her well in the confrontations she will surely draw. She is not one who can put idealism aside and say, "This is business." Her principles are engraved on the inside of her eyelids so she can see them each time she blinks. So, unless she's practiced long hard stares, she can't get through any transaction without the firm finger of conscience tapping her on the shoulder.

If she is to live up to the best within her, your Ten Woman must balance her personal drive with an objective overall view of the work to be done. Emotional issues cannot distract her from the straight and narrow path she is on. She knows one mathematical theorem well: the shortest distance between two points is a straight line. If she is one point and her objective is another point, then pray for whatever lies in between. The Ten Woman, poet Emily Dickinson, was such a woman. She did not see the need for wordiness but chose to write deceptively simple, clear verse. "Her tiny condensed lyrics provided the perfect medium for flashing intuitions of God, of nature and human life, of love and death, of time and eternity. The secret of her inimitable art, phrases sharp as crystal, stanzas vitalized by delicate metrical variation and hinted rhyme, is its absolute integrity." She exemplified the clear grasp, understanding and integrity that the Ten Woman possesses.

More than any other individual, your Ten Woman is responsible for her actions. She has gone beyond cause and effect to a point where she recognizes the laws that govern this phenomenon. She isn't reaping what she has sown rather she is sewing new seeds with a clear awareness of the cause and effect of her actions. She knows what she is doing. She was born with this understanding, therefore she's more responsible and has more freedom of choice than other people. Her efforts have far-reaching repercussions not only for her but for large groups of people.

Your Ten Woman is a pioneer with an obligation to numbers beyond herself. Because she has clear vision and is experienced in the technique of proper living, she will be singled out. You noticed her. Of course, you'd have to be blindfolded and locked in a dark closet not to notice her, but more than that, you fell madly in love with this delightfully incorrigible female. Now all you have to do is figure out how you're going to live with her while maintaining some semblance of sanity. It's not that you're coming unglued—doesn't every guy at the office wear one bright gold earring?—it's just that you're beginning to walk a few steps behind her when you venture out into public. You haven't yet determined whether that action is out of respect for her or whether it's due to some basic survival instinct on your part. Be that as it may, you know that at least she has a firm grip on reality.

It's no use. You've succumbed. The Great Wall of China couldn't protect you from that look in her eyes. A dazzling smile flung your way is like a royal summons that cannot be denied. You are inexorably drawn to this ardent woman whose shinning fervor turns life into a romance. In the evening, when a crescent moon hangs low in a pewter sky and she sweeps across the terrace floor in her flowing scarlet pajamas toward you, your heart leaps and you quiver like a bowl full of jelly. There's no question about it. This woman of yours is magnificent. She is a 10.

The Ten Man

Probably the greatest single invention in the history of the world is the wheel. It's a symbol of motion, freedom and progress. Undoubtedly, the wheel was invented by a Ten. Visualize, if you will, your primitive Ten Man thudding along in a cart with square wheels. Thump...thump...thump...thump...in quarterly rhythms. Cave people had a lot of upset stomachs and blinding headaches, clubs notwithstanding. One memorable day, the Ten Man's cart hits a deep pot hole (times never really change) and, as luck would have it, the identical corners of both square wheels break off. As our hero continues onward, he notices a change in the wheel's rhythm. Thump...thump...thump...silence...thump...thump...thump.... The fourth

10

thump is missing. His brow furrows. He scratches his shaggy mane. Something's different. Then a light goes on in his head. He races home. While his friends stand around laughing and pointing fingers at him, he chisels away at the remaining three corners of the wheels. Then, he leaps into his cart, growls a commanding grunt to his mastodon, and off the cart rumbles...but it doesn't thump. A statue of this Ten Man holding his wheel, which his people erected in his honor, now stands in a famous museum in a large city. The archaeologists claim it's a primitive expression of an ancient god who held up the sky. Oh well...to each his own.

At any rate, you're in love with this god's descendant. He's all man. He has this thing about getting things rolling. He wants life in motion, including you. If you plan to travel with him, keep your eyes alert and your wheels oiled because, once his interest is fired, you'll be off like a pack of hunting dogs after a fox—with the accompanying fanfare, naturally.

Enter trumpets, cameras and *Time* magazine. Your Ten Man can be egotistical. He loves to see his name in the news but he insists that it be connected with something meaningful. Just being rich and famous is not enough. He wants to be rich, famous and remembered for something incidental like changing the course of history. He can do it too. Remember who his ancestor was.

When your Ten Man was a tot he knew he was somebody special, no matter what his parents said. After he looked the words up in a dictionary, he realized they were only kidding when they called him a dictatorial megalomaniac with an overblown ego. He reminded them he was only five years old so they'd have to give him another few years to prove he could do all the extravagant things he boasted were easily within his powers.

By adolescence, his gross annual income was up to five figures and approaching six. By then, his parents had digested their words nicely and were settled into a comfortable state of speechless shock. "I told you so" was added to their menu, a phrase invented by a Ten, along with the wheel.

Your Ten Man is a grown megalomaniac now, only his claims are not fantasies. He is capable of great deeds if he directs his power and energy with the care and foresight of which he is capable. He has everything to gain and everything to lose, because he invests so heavily in life. He gives it his all—his blood, his bones and his Calvin Kleins.

Because he walks with clenched fists, don't assume he's either angry with you or preparing for the people's revolution. This peculiar pose is a result of his mental attitude toward everything he does. He has a firm grasp on ideas, hanging on to them like a hungry dog with a bone. He's had this grasp since childhood. He didn't need to take a new seed, plant it and wait for the results. He was born with his energy blooming, ready to invest it in an existing idea or established institution. He surveys social and political situations in search of an area where the individual needs to be freed from the oppression of a system. Then he attacks with the determination of a bulldog. He's made up his mind; there is no other recourse. It's "damn the torpedoes—full speed ahead." The Ten Man, Martin Luther, the founder of Protestanism, "shattered the external structure of the medieval church" with his bold act of nailing his ninety-five academic theses to the door of the Wittenberg Church on October 31, 1517. At the same time, however, he "revived the religious consciousness of Europe." He felt the Catholic church had to change because it didn't allow the individual to worship God freely within the structure of the church.

Your Ten Man has respect for civilization with its cultural advances and social institutions as long as they are willing to grow and don't hinder the expression and independence of the individual. He belongs to the new age where progressive thought is an inevitable part of evolution.

Brain twisters stimulate his creative juices. Your Ten Man eats up tough problems like a horde of soldier ants on a relentless march through a rain forest. He's really at his best when confronted with an issue. Take pot holes and city hall. Your Ten Man is driving through the city when he unexpectedly hits a pot hole that could qualify as a crater on the moon. Naturally, it's unmarked. His car sustains heavy damage. When he approaches the appropriate official at city hall, he is told there is nothing they can do. End of discussion. As he leaves the building, he turns and shakes a clenched fist at the tall marble face of bureaucracy. But he has his ancestor's blood. He goes home and for the next few months pours his creative energy into an idea. He invents a radar-sensitive wheel that anticipates depressions in the earth ahead of it. Now, when his vehicle approaches a pot hole, the tires automatically spread out laterally, nicely circumventing the hole.

History does repeat itself, a fact of which your Ten Man is well aware. He was born knowing and he learns quickly from experience. He can jump right in the middle of a problem and, with a swivel of his owl-like vision, take in most of the relevant points. But like the owl, he does have a blind spot. He can be extremely stubborn and singleminded, believing that he's right no matter what. At this point, he will not listen to reason. Damning the torpedoes here will sink the ship. Then you need to call in the U.S. Marines. It will take that much force to make an impression on him. Your Ten Man may not be noisy about his mind-set but he certainly will be indomitable.

You won't often find your Ten Man sitting on his ischial tuberosities. He's too obsessed with motion, discovery and progress to linger on his derriere for more than fleeting moments. When he does, he seems to hover like a spaceship from an old sci-fi flick. Though he's motionless, you can feel his vibrating energy. He is enamored with life and his role in it. He doesn't want to miss one pulsation of Mother Earth's heartbeat. Because he drives himself, he may find relaxing difficult, but he should force himself to periodically stop, look and listen, and to cultivate the art of patience and tact. He never did get gold stars for restraint. He can learn but it doesn't come naturally. However, it's his genuine exuberance that's so contagious. He is desire in motion, the need to be and express, but always toward a greater goal than his physical needs. He seeks immersion of his ego in individual achievement beyond himself. If he loses sight of this vision, becoming tangled in the web of personal glory, he deceives himself in the way that Sir Walter Scott spoke of when he wrote: "O, what a tangled web we weave, When first we practice to deceive." Your Ten Man must not deceive himself.

To get a firm grip on life, your Ten Man must stay within the speed limit, although he is allowed to travel in the fast lane. There may be days you feel you're traveling with a test pilot. Just slap on your goggles and flight cap, and give that long silk scarf an artistic flip around your lovely neck. Glue on a grin if you have to. Only you need know that the smile is not from pleasure or a sense of well-being but from a state of idiocy. But you know he'll protect you. It goes with the territory. Place your love and trust in his capable hands and he'll rise to the occasion like mushrooms after a rain. He also cares about those who are in need. He's like the trial lawyer, F. Lee

10

Bailey, born on the 10th, who footed the bill for a specially equipped plane to fly an injured boy from Florida to his home town in New England. He does things in a big way, to match the bigness of his heart.

It's safe to put your Ten Man on the pedestal where he belongs. As long as you're eye-level with his feet, you'll always be aware that he's human. It's the little hairs on his toes that give him away. Make sure he has a telescope handy so he can also occasionally zoom in on his feet—just as a reminder. And those feet will circulate, too. Magellan left Spain on the 10th of August, 1519, to circle the world. How's that for a little circulation? And those people had just gotten over the shock that the world wasn't flat.

Your Ten Man wants to be where the action is, where he can handle many enterprises at the same time. It is sometimes necessary that he has more than one interest so he can vent his energy reserves. Otherwise, they can build to explosive levels like a clogged pressure cooker. Along with ambitious drive that can roll over you like a steam roller, he is an excellent promoter because he is full of unusual and creative techniques with the energy to back them up. He can scandalize society with progressive ideas that haven't as yet caught on. In this sense, he's an anachronism, born before his time or at least on the very fringes of it. He can shock the public as Rhett Butler did in *Gone With The Wind* when his closing remark was, "Frankly my dear, I don't give a damn." Audiences were known to gasp. In 1935, no one "swore" on the screen, especially well-known actors in films for general audiences. But secretly, the audiences loved it. It appealed to the sense of adventure and sensual excitement that lurked within them. So relax. Does it really matter that your Ten Man is X-rated? It merely makes him more desirable. As far as the disapproving go, just watch the news to discover how many staunch and proper citizens get caught with their hands in the cookie jar. Even though these citizens may display a disdainful and superior air, privately they carry out the very acts they have publicly condemned. Be assured that people are magnetized in varying degrees by the daring innovative ideas of your Ten Man. In a few years, his ideas will become second nature to some and commonly accepted by most. Fewer and fewer eyebrows will raise as the multitudes jump into the pool after him. Besides, he seems to be having so much fun that maybe they're missing something. And that certainly won't do.

The Ten Man hears the whispers of destiny in his ear and he responds. He wants you by his side, well...maybe a few steps behind. But he wants you there. He'll assure you that it will be worth it. Not only will you have him, the supreme compliment, but your name will go down in history as well, as you're his woman. You can't doubt him. He's absolutely sure. Who else do you know who does crossword puzzles with a pen?

The Eleven Woman

So, your Eleven Woman has threatened to ride naked, on horseback, through the streets of Salt Lake City to protest excessive taxation. Count your blessings. You've got one thing to be thankful for—her long hair. Lady Godiva did it in the eleventh century in Coventry, England, as a plea to her husband to spare the townspeople additional financial burdens. The town shuttered its windows and no one looked—except Peeping Tom.

But no one can call you a Peeping Tom. You walked into this relationship with your eyes wide open. You knew she was a woman who was willing to stand up and be counted, even in the buff. She'll go against established tradition, the divine right of kings and your wishes once her mind is made up on an issue. She isn't the type who stands back on one toe when the chips are down.

She really is an engima because she often appears quiet, conservative and tactful. Then suddenly, like Aphrodite, she'll rise up out of the ocean and set the world on its ear. Like the goddess of ideal love, everything about your Eleven Woman can be charming and harmonious. She has a grace which magnetizes, then conquers. She's quite irresistible and irrepresible. It's wise to recall your mythology, remembering that Aphrodite rose out of the foam produced by castrated Uranus' genitals which had been flung into the ocean. So, you see, your Eleven Woman comes from heavenly stock and has the blood of galaxies coursing through her veins. Don't be startled when this demure and quiet woman suddenly takes on the job of reporter and charges into a football locker room after a losing game to question a 254-pound linebacker about his relationship with his hairdresser. She is as unfathomable as her mother, the ocean, and as cosmic as her sky-father, Uranus.

Your Eleven Woman is willing to tackle issues of great importance, even if they are controversial. She wants to see justice done and she's not afraid to speak out. Lydia Child, born on the 11th, was unafraid to let the world know her stand on the issue of slavery in the early 1800s when, first, it was unpopular to do so, and second, when women, like children, were to be seen and not heard. Her book was one of the first in America to denounce the injustice of slavery.

So you see with whom you are dealing. Your beautiful Aphrodite is an idealist. She strives so hard for perfection that she is in danger of overlooking the human equation. She has to remember that no one's perfect, except you, of course. She did choose you. Your moral integrity came across loud and clear at your first meeting at the counter in the B. Dalton Bookstore. After the cashier handed you the wrong change, you promptly returned the extra ten dollars he had given you. As fate would have it, your Eleven Woman was standing in line behind you. She didn't drop a hardbound unabridged volumne of H.G. Well's, *The Outline of History*, on your foot because she was surprised. That was a well-calculated accident intended to get your attention. It worked. After she commented that you ought to be an opera singer, she kindly aided your hobbling body to the car. You had lunch and, well, you've been hobbling after her ever since.

You also discovered she had another book in her arms that day, a strange little volumne titled *The Language of the Hand*, by a fellow named Cheiro. It intrigued you, although you really didn't believe in palmistry. But it's strange how, after peering into your sweating palm during lunch, your Eleven Woman told you that you'd be changing jobs before the end of the year. You laughed a little too heartily. You hadn't told anyone you were thinking about leaving your present occupation. You only entertained the possibility a few days ago. And then she told you there was a girl in your past who...well, that's when you snatched your hand back and muttered something about leaving your motor running and forgetting to put money in the parking meter...you'd be right back. When you returned, the crowds had gathered and she was reading the maitre d's palm.

She certainly is different. She'll stand behind whatever she believes regardless of the jeers and ridicule of more conservative types. She's in good company. Eleanor

11

Roosevelt, dubbed First Lady of the World, often had palm readers at the White House. She too, spoke freely, enduring unkind attacks during her lifetime.

There is an Eleven Woman whose emotions twist and turn like a weathervane in a wind storm. She seems to possess two diametrically opposed personalities, a sort of Dr. Jekyll and Mrs. Hyde. She can be cooperative and concerned about the welfare of others and then suddenly do something radical, without considering the feelings of those about her or the consequences of her actions. Her combination of quick reactions and fluctuating emotions can get her in more trouble than even she can handle.

But your Eleven Woman has probably learned to keep her balance, even when her nerves are vibrating at high frequency. She sometimes acts like a thoroughbred race horse, nervous and tense, but, like a thoroughbred, she is able to react swiftly, alertly and in winning style. She is in charge of every situation, her creative mind racing to the finish line ahead of all others. She has an above-average intellect which can override her pronounced intuitions. Her logical mind tells her there are eight steps between one and ten, and those steps need to be taken progressively. But her intuitive mind flashes from one to ten with such lightning speed that she sometimes thinks her conclusions are in error because she can't find the intervening eight steps. Setting off on a journey toward a specific answer, her logical mind is like a horse and buggy, clopping along a country road, noticing each detail of the surrounding landscape while her intuitive mind is a race car, speeding over the highway, turning the landscape into one long blur. They will both get to their destination, but the car will arrive long before the buggy. Both methods work but your Eleven Woman needs to trust her intuitions more than she does because her first impressions, her intuitions, can be startlingly accurate. So don't laugh when she comments that the classic lines of your face will bring you fame one day. The next thing you know your photograph will be hanging in the Louvre next to the Mona Lisa.

Yes, your Eleven Woman will come right out and say things you wouldn't hear on the six o'clock news, especially if she thinks it will improve someone's moral fiber. She'll tell you, the neighbors, the community and the world. If you dare to hazard the opinion that she could get slapped with a law suit or that what she's doing may not be quite within the restraints of established law, be prepared for disdainful indifference. She'll just quote what Teddy Roosevelt may have said when his advisor told him that his latest decision was illegal: "Why spoil the beauty of the thing with legalities."

She does tend toward extremes although her goal is always balance and moderation. These two seemingly paradoxical attributes are really flip sides of the same coin. Your Eleven Woman is governed by inspiration, a quality that causes curious changes in normally sane people. She envisions a world where everyone has an equal opportunity to express their deepest hopes and achieve their wildest dreams. If she can't achieve this goal through mediation and cooperation, then she'll oppose the system in very visible ways. Remember the time she became incensed over the Senator's stand on ERA, so she dressed in an Egyptian slave costume, draped herself over the front of his car and called herself a hood ornament. At least she wasn't in her birthday suit. But the papers had a wonderful time with the incident and created headlines like: *Slave Girl Buffs Senator's Car* and *Can Sexist Senator Satisfy Slave Girl?* She's sensitive, cooperative and caring. But it's not enough that she care and support those who charge out into the melee. She's learned that she must participate in the action too. She must be seen and heard, actively involved in eliminating outworn ideas, and useless laws and institutions.

Even though, at times, life with your Eleven Woman makes you feel like a turkey ten days before Thanksgiving, you have to admit she makes your life exciting. One never feels more alive than when one is on the brink of total annihilation. Why do you think people scale North Walls, free-fall from airplanes and try to break existing speed records? That's not to say that living with your Eleven Woman is courting disaster but she does tend to leave scattered rubble and shattered nerves on the trail behind her. What a litter bug. However, out of the smoking debris will arise, like the Phoenix, new life, hope and inspiration. This is when you cheer.

Eleven cheers for her. You should join in the accolades because, chances are, she'll have the money. How can she lose? She has executive ability, strong personal magnetism and a creative, original mind. On top of that, she enjoys prestige, being in the limelight, because she is naturally dramatic. Can you really doubt that the reserved and demure Lady Godiva had a little Gypsy Rose Lee tucked away inside, grinding to get out? With all these abilities at her disposal, no matter how many difficulties your Eleven Woman gets into, she usually lands butter-side-up. Look at Miss Piggy. Not to be outdone by Bo Derek, our little porcine friend donned a T-shirt with the number 11 on it to show the world that she's best—twice over, 1 plus 1. She landed on the cover of *Time* magazine.

Your woman may be very eloquent or have a quality in her voice or manner of speaking that captivates the imagination of others. She speaks with an experience gained from the tests life has presented her. If she looks deeply into herself, she gains an indestructible sense of her ability to make sound judgments and she finds the courage to voice them at the right time. Her spirit electrifies her thoughts so that whether she speaks or writes, her ideas will vibrate within the souls of her listeners. The message will eventually come through as truth.

She will light up your life. Some days you may wish you could sell some of her wattage back to the electric company. Then you'd be rich too. But you wouldn't change her for all the bulbs in Boise—a nice, quiet town, conservative and orderly, all the things your Eleven Woman often is. And that's where the mystery of her lies. She can appear cool, collected and reasonable, like a pair of "sensible" shoes you wear for a long time and love because they are so comfortable. Then, one day, you find her draped over Senators' hoods, shoeless—and you wonder where the woman you love went. But the truth is, you find this other woman equally as exciting. You may begin to feel you're collecting your own harem, two for the price of one. Your Eleven Woman may cook and sew for you but keep your mind clear. She can handle routine jobs but she doesn't necessarily enjoy them unless they offer her a challenge, a stimulation, an electrical prod, that keep her fired-up about the purpose and quality of her work. She needs to be appreciated. Then, when she's operating on AC and DC, watch her sparkle. She can accomplish miracles. The biggest miracle of all is that she loves you with a devotion and intensity that pales the brilliance of the New York City skyline at night. She'll brighten your days and fill your nights with tenderness. The cares of living will fade into oblivion. Who cares about the cost of electricity? You've got your Eleven Woman, and she'll turn you on.

The Eleven Man

No, he's not a jeweler, Your Eleven Man always carries that small pocket case with the miniature scales in it. They're very convenient when he's called upon to voice his opinion, as he often is, and there's no way he'll speak without first weighing both sides. This does not mean he's slow. On the contrary, he can be extremely witty and quick to respond but on important issues he will deliberate, examining each point of view, until you're ready to clasp an asp to your bosom in sheer desperation. It's vital to his well-being that he make fair decisions. So, when his head cocks to one side, his sparkling eyes grow intense and his teeth clamp onto his thumb nail, you'll know it's weigh-in time again.

His scales are as accurate as he is exacting. He has great expectations, high standards for achievement that haven't been matched since the Elevens built the Pyramid. These standards may be expressed in his work, his dress or his selection of companions. He isn't judgmental. He's exacting. If something doesn't measure up, he discards it. He keeps the Salvation Army well supplied and the Broken Hearts Club treasury full.

Your Eleven Man is the kind you remember. It's rather difficult to forget someone who vibrates like Burt Reynolds and has the staying power of Yul Brynner. Your man has a sparkle, an effervescence that tittilates you to your toes. Toes are a good barometer of your emotions so watch yours curl whenever he's around. Now you know why your Eleven Man goes barefoot. Unlike Inspector Hercule Poirot with his pinched patent leather shoes, your man demands the freedom to run barefoot in the park. It's symbolic of his attitude toward everything he does.

Don't be fooled by the more conservative type. There is a part of him that's still a rebel. He's the stolid banker who, after twenty years of quiet, loyal service at the same institution, grows a long black beard. New customers don't trust him, old customers are shocked and the Board of Directors is apoplectic. What happened to that poised, patient, cooperative creature who has supported the system for so many years? It's as hard for the community to believe this change as it was for the scientists to believe what the Indians said about alligators eating rocks. But, of course, they do. Rocks help them float just below the surface of the water while stalking their prey.

The escapades of a Northern Illinois businessman well exemplify the type of action an Eleven Man might take. A well-known businessman by day, by night the hero of this story donned a mask, black jersey and tights to beseige the factories fronting the Fox River. He swam in the clear waters of that river as a boy but today, because the factories had dumped wastes into the water for so many years, and continued to do so, his beloved river was polluted. Even the fish were dying. So, each night, "The Fox," as he was dubbed, shed his three-piece Hart, Schaffner and Marx and climbed into his form-fitting blacks and scaled the smoke stacks of the offending factories to stuff up their chimneys. And each morning employees found the interiors of the buildings covered with a most unpleasant smelling and damaging soot. During radio interviews, The Fox told of his adventures—how he narrowly escaped through a sewer one night, with the police in hot pursuit—shades of *Les Miserables*—and how, on one of his more daring daylight raids, he clomped in muddy, hip-high boots across the plush carpet of a very expensive office to dump a barrel of dead fish on the receptionist's desk. The factory owners finally discovered that cleaning up and repairing the damage caused by The Fox was more costly than the installation of the pollution devices that he was demanding on his frequent radio interviews. The Fox took drastic measures but all within the realm of possibility for your Eleven Man who can seek justice in effective, although some might say, unorthodox ways. Your Eleven Man has respect for his community, supporting and living within the system that he loves, but he can be driven to drastic measures by the imbalance he sees around him.

Your man began refining his sense of balance as a child, when he practiced walking blindfolded for X number of hours a day. It was acceptable when he was little but as he grew, his parents began overhearing comments like, "He must be sensitive to the light," and "Isn't that different. He thinks he's an ostrich." Parents can use certain excuses just so many times. How often can one's son be the pirate in the school play practicing walking the gangplank? Actually he was practicing his ability to make impartial judgments without being influenced by the sights and sounds of his environment. He was tuning in to himself.

Through his teenage years, he learned to be more decisive. His sense of stature and self-direction grew. He noticed that others began taking him seriously, in spite of blindfolds. People felt confident enough to rely upon his judgment of the issues presented to him. He was probably adventurous—and devilish at times—but underlying it was a core of solid surety and concern for the welfare of those with him.

He's a big Eleven now, out to make his mark in the world. No, not an X, even though that is formed with two ones. He's more apt to believe that an 11 makes him first twice. He does have an ego, drive and energy, but he may not be as overt about it as some because, in the back of his mind lies that constant awareness of balance. It takes two to tango, and your Eleven Man isn't here to sweep and dip alone. He likes belonging, feeling necessary to someone. His desire to achieve balance may show in his work, as in the efforts of Jacques Cousteau, born on the 11th, whose life has been devoted to maintaining ecological balance for future generations in the oceans of the world. The Eleven always has a unique flair, a different approach than anyone else. He can be in a diving bell twenty thousand leagues beneath the sea or leading a battalion into battle, like General George Patton, but his methods will have an electric quality about them that lights up the imagination of the world. Speaking of lighting up the world, we can't forget Thomas Edison, born on the 11th.

Your Eleven Man may have an inventive mind in which ideas strike in a flash. You can usually pick an adult Eleven out of a crowd. They're the ones with the light bulbs flashing off and on over their heads. Your Eleven Man does have moments of inspiration when he converses with the gods. He'll amaze you with his insights and prophecies but it can be embarrassing when you're with him, pushing a cart down the supermarket aisle, when suddenly the musak becomes faint, then stops altogether as a deep voice that shakes' the walls of the building thunders out his name. Clerks tend to shy away from you. When you've been on a seek-and-find mission for twenty minutes because they've changed the aisles around again, a sixteen-year-old clerk with the answer to where the lox and bagels have been stashed is to be desired over messages from the gods.

Self-direction comes naturally to him. He seems to have an inward capacity for sensing the accuracy of his decisions. It is this quality that sets him apart from others. Although he is friendly, and sometimes quite charming, there is a part of him that you can never touch. He does care what you think but it will only influence him to a point. After taking problems into his internal threshing machine, he separates the wheat from the chaff, promptly discarding the rest. At this point, a heavenly edict to the contrary could not convince him that he is wrong. He knows what is right and what he has to do. With poise and confidence in his decisions, he sets out to eliminate waste and restore equilibrium either by example or through some educational effort. He may choose to do so in some unorthodox manner, sensing that work with shock value wakes people from their lethargy. The writer, D.H. Lawrence, born on the 11th, sought to bring emotion and intellect into balance through novels such as *Lady Chatterley's Lover*, which was shocking when it was first published in 1928.

Your Eleven Man has so much vitality that there are days you'd swear he has a doppleganger, a ghostly double, and that the three of you are living in the same house. Like the ubiquitous crow, he seems to be everywhere at once, observing, picking up things. There isn't much you do that he doesn't know about. He isn't nosey. He just happens to be there, even if invisibly on the fringes, when anything happens. He can know things for years and never say a word. Like the time you funneled one hundred dollars out of the grocery money to put toward a trip to the mountains—your treat—and you told him you found the money tucked away in your bureau drawer—which was true...because you put it there. You don't like to lie. The fact that you ate canned spaghetti-o's for thirty days might have tipped him off that someone had pilfered the pantry. But he never said a word. You might not have known he was on to you if you hadn't invited him on another weekend trip to the same mountains. When he countered with, "Another month of rations, eh?" you knew the game was up. He can be exasperating.

There is an Eleven Man who is unpredictable and unreliable. He can't decide whether it's the sky that's falling or just his arches. His life runs to extremes. One minute he's super high and ready to conquer a Boston bargain basement sale and the next moment he's as nervous as Don Knotts on a first date. His affairs fluctuate as rapidly as his emotions. Ideas simmer beneath the surface until they explode in the most unlikely places and in the most startling ways. This Eleven Man must carefully weigh and balance his emotions, keeping them on an even keel. He can be either in perfect harmony with himself or totally at odds, at which time, he becomes a heavy cross to bear.

But your Eleven Man can stand the test, if you can. He has a highly nervous side which is not always apparent at first glance. But if you're driven close to insanity by just holding hands with him at the movies, you've got the picture. It's the rhythmic rubbing of his first finger that gets to you—over and over the same spot on your flesh until you're staring glassy-eyed at the screen, your mind riveted to the back of your hand. When you start babbling incoherently, "My hand, my hand!" don't expect any sympathy. Who is going to believe you're upset because the man you love is holding your hand? He'll look startled, a big "What did I do?" splashed across his face while you dash from the theatre clasping your fists to your chest in pain.

Your Eleven Man leaves an unmistakeable mark on everything he touches. Notice the back of your hand. To avoid scars, you must live your life equipped with peripheral vision. "Expect the unexpected" should be printed on cards and taped to

11

objects all over his house, beginning with the bathroom mirror. Heaven forbid that he or a family member should get caught unawares like the hapless Inspector Clouseau in his eternal battle with the indomitable Kato who most inconveniently leaps out of a refrigerator or from under a bed. Life may present your Eleven Man with occasional Katos in the form of people and events leaping in and out of his experience with astounding rapidity. Therefore, because survival is a predominant instinct and reflexes are automatic, he must develop an inner calm which will aid him in weighing and balancing such intrusions quickly and accurately. This accomplished, he is the magnificent swordsman, leaping, thrusting and parrying with perfect aplomb, a devilish laugh coming from his lips. His eyes, shining green fire through the holes in his mask, flash with the zest of living. With a sweep of his arm and a swish of his cape, he leaps upon his pawing steed and gathers you up before him. He draws his sword and leaves his final mark for all to see. No, it's not a 2. It's a Z, and it stands for Zowie!

The Twelve Woman

Lord Byron described your mystical Twelve Woman when he penned the lines:

> She walks in beauty, like the night
> Of cloudless climes and starry skies;
> And all that's best of dark and bright
> Meet in her aspect and her eyes:
> Thus mellow'd to that tender light
> Which heaven to gaudy day denies.

Your Twelve Woman probably best fulfills the image of the cosmic feminine mystique. She is a reflection of the life around her; she gives, she serves and she loves, yet she maintains a private chamber into which only she can enter. She is all yours but belongs to herself. She lets you have your way but manages to fulfill her needs. She surrenders totally in order to conquer. She may cause you to bite your nails down to the quick.

Sore and bleeding fingers won't do. To handle your Twelve Woman, you'll need ten operational digits so you can peel off the many layers she wears. What you see is not necessarily what you get. She can be all things to all people and never change one iota in the process. Magic? Hypnotism? Probably. No one has ever entered her labyrinthine mind and returned in a stable enough condition to report lucidly. She's left scissors and strings of paper dolls in the hands of many unconquerable Herculean types. Not intentionally, of course. She is a loving person with a heart as tender as a new bruise. It's just that she confuses people by adopting stands that seem contrary to the world and to her own lifestyle and upbringing. She has a large capacity for loving that extends beyond her own needs and comforts.

Your Twelve Woman also needs to be busy. She knows that idle hands are the devil's workers so she finds outlets where she can express her considerable talents in helpful ways. Florence Nightingale, born on the 12th into a family of wealth, disapproved of the empty hours and meaningless pasttimes women of her class were subjected to in the early nineteenth century. Instead, she chose to pour her love and

12

energy into a nursing career, not a highly regarded profession in 1851. Going against medical tradition, she also recognized the necessity for sanitary conditions and instituted them in the filthy wards she tended.

Likewise, your Twelve Woman has a way of seeing beyond the surface and into the heart of every situation. Do you feel rather inadequately clothed and vulnerable under her misty-eyed glances? You should. Your woman can see into watery realms you've only heard of in myths and fairy tales. She bids you to look upon her world, to see the wonder of a place that can only be visited when the logical mind is suspended in time and the imaginative mind is allowed to wander.

Mystical forms of self-expression touch the wells of her being. In their formlessness, she finds communion with an unknowable source. But you'll have to get used to her magical nature. She may do things that lesser mortals would find disconcertingly curious. At midnight you could wake to find the bed beside you empty. A rustle in the branches of the old maple draws you to your open window. The moonlight, casting shadows across the lawn, reveals a ladder propped against the trunk of the tree. In the leafy branches, you catch a glimpse of white satin and a shapely leg.

"What are you doing in that tree?" you whisper hoarsely, quickly canvasing the street.

The branches part. Her captivating mouth, like a quarter moon, curls up at you. Her eyes shimmer in the pale night light. "The neighbor's cat," she explains brightly, "chased Friskie up the tree. I heard her crying so I came out to get her."

"Why didn't you wake me?" you ask, miffed, but still speaking in hushed tones.

"Oh, I didn't mind," she sings back. "It's such a beautiful night." She slides down out of the tree, cradling a small white kitten in one arm. Truly, she doesn't mind. She is intimately connected to the rhythms of the universe—poetry, music, dance—and can even find them in moments that others would overlook—while rescuing cats from trees at midnight for instance.

But don't let her gentle and friendly aspect lead you to think she's a pussycat. She has a good reasoning mind, well-practiced in the intricacies of thought. Elizabeth Cady Stanton, woman suffrage reformer, born November 12, 1815, had an unusual education for a girl in her era. Elizabeth was admitted to the all-boys Johnstown Academy where she studied Greek, Latin and mathematics, taking second prize in Greek. She studied law with her father, Judge Daniel Cady. "Mrs. Stanton had great charm, intelligence, humor and courage." She also had seven children and her home life was a "model of domesticity." So, you see, your Twelve Woman, although charming and witty, is not about to take a back seat to anyone. She may be gracious about it but she, like Mrs. Stanton, will exemplify the best qualities of the Twelve, exerting her rights while maintaining her genuine sense of humor.

Your Twelve Woman is a trend setter. Her success in influencing people lies in her guileless manner, independent action and creative flair. She is not always conscious of changing the present methods of procedure because she goes into life with a mission, a purpose, that is an end in itself. What happens peripherally is sometimes as big a surprise to her as to anyone. Florence Nightingale went into nursing to help the sick and ended up making an invaluable contribution to the "evolution of nursing." She set a new trend.

There is a flair for designing and embroidering the fabric of life hidden deep within your Twelve Woman. She moves with a sense of drama that is delightfully lightened by a dash of humor. She can turn her child's birthday party into the fete of the decade. Her own birthday celebrations were something to behold. Her parents indulged her when she sent out party invitations covered with gold stars but when the Duke of Windsor pulled up in front of their home on the 12th, mama and papa had second thoughts about her whimsical projections. She tossed her beautiful curls and smiled enchantingly. "It's mind over matter," she whispered, with a small finger over her lips.

If fairy tales come true, it is your Twelve Woman who is responsible for the magical manifestations. Through her teens she could convince the wind in the willows to blow her way with a crook of her little finger. She knew that what her mind could conceive was a potential reality. All she needed to do was believe. Grace Kelly, born on the 12th, was a quiet, imaginative child. She enjoyed acting out her fantasies. Prophetically, in 1955, she made a film, *The Swan*, in which she portrayed a young woman who married a crown prince. Today, she is Princess Grace of Monaco. Her fairy tales came true.

Don't be fooled into thinking your Twelve Woman is a piece of feminine fluff. She has a practical mind that reasons in logical steps and she can be quite convincing in an argument or debate. After a half hour's discussion with her on the merits of the metric system, you'll begin to believe you couldn't hit a bull with a handful of rice. How is it that she can stand there looking so complacent and serene while you're pounding the same spot on the pavement in frantic frustration, as if you were digging your way to freedom and you had twelve minutes to make it.

Don't try to measure up. Chances are she prefers the linear-inch system and nothing you could ever say will convince her to the contrary. She's reasonable, that's not the issue. But how can you argue with the Great Pyramid, which was built on the pyramidal inch? The Egyptians knew something about building. They created the oldest structure on this planet and it's doubtful it could be duplicated. Besides, there's our culture and language—you'd walk a mile for a camel but who is going to walk a kilometer for a dromedary. It just doesn't have the same ring. Her practical reasoning mind is ultimately connected to a misty realm where truths are in the process of creating form, a world where believing is the same as knowing, and the proof lies in the feelings and instincts.

She knows when things feel right. Many of her actions are motivated by her instincts, which are uncannily on the mark. Maybe it's her woman's intuition, but whatever it is, if she tells you to drop the double declining method of depreciation and double check your confirmation of accounts receivable—and she's not an accountant—you better pull out your ledgers and sharpen your wits along with your pencils. You may be clean as a hound's tooth but when Uncle Sam's boys arrive, you could be categorized as anything from a pickpocket to a pirate unless you've got every mote itemized.

Your Twelve Woman will keep you on safe turf if she's intellectually alert and creatively innovative. She's so expressive and imaginative that she courts the danger of spreading herself too thin, taking on too much responsibility or becoming involved in so many fields of endeavor that she drains her excellent potentials, making them totally ineffective. This scattering can bring on nervous conditions and imagined difficulties. She can then turn inward and become negatively reclusive.

12

However, when your Twelve Woman uses her natural inclination toward meditation and quiet introspective moments in a positive way, she can be absolutely brilliant. Those suspended moments—a weekend sailing, a day on the beach, or a few hours locked in her bedroom listening to music—restore her resilency and good humor. Then she swirls from her self-imposed retreat into the moving, creative world in which she lives to finish her current projects with a dramatic flourish inspired by those meditative pauses.

Your Twelve Woman has a capacity for caring that signals the needy like a vibration on a spider's web alerts a hungry arachnid. Unfortunately, she's the one who is wrapped in a silk cocoon. Her caring is natural and beautiful, and she should express it freely but with discrimination. If she allows chronic complainers to sap her energy, she'll become the victim, tightly bound in gentle strands of silk that are as effectively debilitating as the coarsest hemp. Or, if she insists on carrying a cross, there are plenty of people with a hammer and nails who will help her out. She must realize that some people, if they are to grow, need to help themselves.

Take her to Bonwit Teller and buy her a new wardrobe because hair shirts are out of style. Besides, she finds even wool sweaters itchy. When she discovers the comfort of satin, she'll be in her element. She adapts to her world with the grace and sureness of a jungle cat. You catch fleeting glimpses of her, then she's gone, like a dream you're not sure you really had. But you know she's not a dream because this female feline is in your arms, alive and enticingly real. When you weren't looking, she slipped into your heart on little cat's paws.

The Twelve Man

That's not the jingle of loose change you hear behind you. It's the clanking of cameras hanging around the neck of that fellow who has been snapping secret shots of you since the tour began. You cast a curious look over your shoulder to come face-to-face with a zoom lens and the command, "Hold it!" You freeze, startled. "I hope I didn't frighten you," he smiles beguilingly, extending a hand. "I had to take your picture."

A quick retort hangs on your lips. You're ready to respond when his head tips slightly and he says, "The contours of your face are exquisitely soft."

That did it. He tapped the croquet ball through the final wicket and won you over.

Your Twelve Man's path through life resembles a croquet game. He knows the circuitous routes, and how to skirt obstacles and adjust to circumstances. He plays through when he can; and when he cannot, he thinks. He does need periods alone with his thoughts. Your Twelve Man enjoys a certain amount of social interplay but he isn't going to take out a full-page ad in *Variety* for attention. He'll draw recognition naturally because he is talented, expressive and has the drive to bring his talents into manifestation. Henry David Thoreau, born on the 12th, belonged to a social circle of his talented peers in the late nineteenth century. He withdrew to Walden Pond for two years in an eight-by-ten hut to get in touch with himself. When he emerged he wrote the classic, *Walden,* a discourse on his spiritual insights and growth while living with only the bare necessities.

Your Twelve Man has the same poetic nature. And you fell for him in spite of his line. Exquisite contours, hmmm. Well, who knows, you might recover.

But your life will never be quite upright again. You'll look through different lenses, viewing part of his topsy-turvey world as your own. Does he really look at everything upside down or back-end-to, or does it just seem that way because he walks backward and stands on his head a lot? You're not quite sure. It's certainly true that the majority of the world is living in the fast lane, so when he quotes something mystical from Jacob Boehme like: "Walk in all things contrary to the world," you begin to wonder if he's a gander or if everyone else in the world is a turkey. Then you remember he wasn't too impressed when you excitedly dashed in to show him your first credit card and the accompanying letter that read—welcome to the great majority—in bold enticing letters. But what can you expect from a guy who stands on his head, reflecting all day, besides a ruddy complexion, good circulation and terrific sexual magnetism.

Of course, circulation to the head increases brain functioning and he's no slouch when it comes to cavorting with the cerebrum. He's an excellent researcher. He'll spend twenty years on the Galapogos, as Charles Darwin did, watching the Camarhynchus Pallidus—that's the tool-using finch to the rest of us—dig its food out of a flower with a twig. A few other interesting things happened there too, all of which Darwin, a Twelve Man, recorded, pondered and expressed publicly in a book that sold out the first day. A run-away best seller, to say the least. Darwin's theory of evolution was certainly contrary to the ways of the world then, and is still being debated in classrooms and religious institutions around this planet today, one hundred years later. He didn't shout his ideas from the rooftops or charge into the House of Lords to proclaim his latest "truth," he merely observed, then expressed his observations in a nice, quiet book. But it's rather difficult to keep a Twelve Man's light under a bushel. Too many fires have started that way.

Even when your man was a little boy it was hard not to notice him. He had an inborn humor coupled with an instinctive sense of timing. The month his father was up for a big promotion, the company had an outing for the families. When his father introduced him to the president's wife—who was sporting the latest natural look in hair fashions—he smiled crookedly up at her and said, "Your hair hangs like swamp weed." His father was passed over at work that year and the Twelve Boy got a verbal lashing that sent him back to his dressing room to polish up his act.

He did well. Before he hit twenty, he had investigated the world of illusion and become a master of disguise. He could adapt to any situation with the speed of a chameleon. Drawing from his grab bag of talents, he could be the butcher, the baker or the candlestick maker. More often, however, he was the doctor, the lawyer and the Indian chief like Esternado Waldo Demara, born on the twelfth, who, from 1941 to 1963, impersonated a doctor, a prison warden, a Latin teacher and more. His biography, *The Great Imposter*, tells of his escapades.

Your Twelve Man has a brilliant imagination. He can play in the microscopic world of macrophages as easily as in the macrocosmic world of music. Actually, wherever he is, he touches the mystical pulse of life, feeling its synchronized rhythm. Whether he cleans the Aegean stalls with Hercules or the backyard by himself, he'll discover the vitality of being. Chain him to twelve square feet of soil in his back yard, with no more equipment than his tenacious interest and a notebook, and he'll unearth the original homunculus—the fully-formed diminutive human being believed by medical authorities in the sixteenth and seventeenth centuries to reside in the spermatazoa. And all along the world dismissed it as mediaeval nonsense. Ah, what folly.

As you can see, this man does walk contrary to the world. But he doesn't deliberately raise eyebrows and elicit gasps of incredulity. Well, maybe sometimes he does. There is a bit of the showman in him, and he can overdo it at times. He has a flair for drama although he's often quiet about it. Remember the time he took you to Las Vegas on an impulse? You had nothing else planned for the weekend so you tossed a few heavily-sequined gowns in an overnight bag and off you went. You ended up at the black-jack tables, watching, with a gathering crowd, as your Twelve Man calmly piled up the blue chips. Five years and 3.3 million dollars later, he, like Ken Uston, born on the twelfth, is refused admittance to all the casinos. Your Twelve Man has an uncanny knowledge about things. He "knows when to hold them and knows when to fold them."

The danger for a Twelve Man can be overdramatizing given situations in his life. His nerves can suffer and his pliable and adaptable imagination can lead him into deep waters where he feels swamped by the events happening to him. Choosing good companions and friends who can complement his naturally easy-going temperament is essential. Because he is so caring, negative people drain him and bad friends can get him in a peck of trouble. He could martyr himself for unworthy people or find himself in deep moods of depression. When he retreats in this frame of mind, he sinks deeper into a morass of negativity.

Even though your Twelve Man has his ups and downs—roller coasters should have so many—he does provide you with interesting surroundings. He's charming and entertaining, and often a whiz at getting an idea across. He could coax a turtle out of its shell, then convince it to donate its real estate to the common pot. He's delightful when he's in full swing, and he's never quite alone. He seems to draw curiosity seekers in droves. But then, people who suspend their bodies over Niagara Falls by the ankles while in a lotus position often attract more than mist.

Strangely enough, he's often in the right place at the right time. You may think he's just lucky but...look at the Twelve Man who invented a sorcerous little black box that captures human images on paper. Less sophisticated types thought he'd stolen their souls when they saw themselves trapped on small squares of white paper. But others subsequently discovered the world had gone black-box-crazy and hordes of otherwise normal-looking individuals are now running around, with assortments of cameras strung about their necks like primitive shell necklaces. He was just lucky, you rationalize, a Johnny-on-the-spot, but the truth is, George Eastman, founder of Eastman Kodak Company, exercised his innate awareness of cosmic rhythm—when to hold and when to fold. In this sense, the Twelve Man is a time technician. John Derek, former movie star born on the 12th, also loves photography and uses it to market the image of his beautiful wife Bo Derek.

When your Twelve Man is fully involved in that special moment when time hangs suspended and activity ceases, he knows only mind space, he becomes one with a music only he can hear. Watch Van Cliburn play. Does he really know the audience is there or is he in some magical place resonating to mystical melodies we cannot hear?

It is necessary that you recognize your Twelve Man's periodic needs for privacy. He still loves you and can't live without you, but he can live better with you if he has these moments to restore and recharge his batteries. Solitude helps him maintain the balance that his metronome approach to living requires. When he has put out too much and his nerves are stretched like a three-inch rubber band around twelve inches of envelopes, the message is clear. He's lost his elasticity and is about to snap. What he needs is some fun. Throw a costume party in his honor. Send out invitations asking everyone to come dressed as something beginning with the letter "L," from lewd to luscious. It will appeal to his sense of drama and tickle his funny bone.

While he's laughing, gather up his scattered pieces and reassemble them. You can keep his life on an even keel by respecting his private moments, encouraging his creative ideas and sharing in the wonderfully whacky moments that wash over him periodically. He's a complex man. He has an ego-centered drive that propels him to search for new ideas, experiences and adventures, and a mind that focuses like a hungry child on a call to dinner. When he is involved in the complexities of a drop of water, the torrential rains won't disturb his concentration.

He also has that observant, thoughtful, meditative side when his eyes become glossy and unfocused and you press the panic button thinking the cake you made was hazardous to his health. You take his pulse—a little slower but still within the realm of the living—then you realize he's just in alpha. So you watch and wait. When the moon passes void-of-course, he finally steps out of the mists and back into the land of the living.

He showers you with affection and love at home and in public. He isn't afraid to be demonstrative. Look! What's that up in the sky? Is it a tool-using woodpecker finch? A spruce goose? No, it's the Goodyear blimp pulling a twelve-hundred-foot-long banner with twelve-foot-high letters and it's circling your home. What does it say? You can see it now. It says "I love you." And there's your Twelve Man, hanging out of the cab, waving wildly at you.

The Thirteen Woman

Black cats, broken mirrors and thirteen for supper. Heavens, your Thirteen Woman wouldn't have stood a chance in Salem a few hundred years ago. Born on the 13th, she would have been watched carefully for the smallest telltale signs of occult powers. But she's probably as perplexed about her number as everyone else.

Your Thirteen Woman does have power, there's no doubting that. Look what she's done to you. Now there's a good case for witchcraft. She does it so well too. She has a commanding presence that's quite undeniable. Check out her forefinger. Chances are it's a bit heavier than the others. This pointing digit is called Napoleon's finger because, you guessed it!, she's adept at aiming it with authority. She can be a diminutive five-foot-two but she'll wag that well-formed finger at the biggest brute and have him cowering before her. Now, that's spooky. This darling dictator in ribbons—not necessarily medals—is often affectionately dubbed "the little general" because others do enjoy her command. She does it with finesse and a million-dollar smile. The truth is she enjoys being boss. She may not disclose it but you can bet your bottom button she feels a secret thrill when the reins of power lay in her lovely hands. Your Thirteen Woman is intimately connected with the earth and all that resides within its realm. She possesses an innate understanding of cause and effect, that is, she desires and others fulfill that desire.

The laws of nature are her guides. There is a time to sow and a time to reap, and she can do both as easily as you fall asleep on a rainy Sunday afternoon. She's a motivating force, no question about it. You won't sit idly by when she's within remote control distance. She sets you in motion toward the accomplishment of a task that she has deemed worthy of your combined efforts, then basks in the successful completion of the job. She's satisfied; therefore, you must be too because what she understands as her need encompasses you as well.

Your Thirteen Woman is not a loner. Companionship is a vital component of her makeup. You'll never find her dining alone in a restaurant. She may cross the threshhold unaccompanied but it's as inevitable as the sun in the morning that she'll meet someone she knows. If she doesn't, she'll make a new acquaintance before she leaves. You may shudder when you hear her account of such incidents. One-liners like: "Haven't I seen you someplace before?" and "You look very familiar," seem trite to you but she really means them. She doesn't eat alone even at home. You've arrived there unexpectedly to discover she's convinced the newspaper boy he's hungry and they are laughing over roast breast of pheasant and wine for her. He's drinking grape juice, out of crystal goblets yet. Setting is important.

You know better than to rant, rave and riposte because you won't make much of an impression on her. She's really grounded, secure in her actions and able to short your circuit with one glance. How she manages that look while she's smiling at you is still a mystery. When she's upset over an incident, weather patterns within a thirteen mile radius are affected. Her emotional states can change sunshiny clear skies to heavy black clouds and affect large metropolitan areas. She's the type you never want angry with you. Her dark moods cast a pall over others and they feel her emotions in a curious, unexplainable way. When her eyes flash disapproval, crowds disperse like the parting of the Red Sea. With the parting of the waters her power over physical manifestation becomes apparent.

She recognized her ability to influence and organize others at an early age. She outshone everyone on the block and they loved her in spite of it. She was probably one of the few girls admitted to the secret rooms of boys' clubhouses, and certainly the only one likely to become president. She could beat them at their own games without losing their admiration and friendship. Annie Oakley, American markswoman born on the 13th, defeated noted marksman and vaudeville performer, Frank Butler, in a public contest. He fell in love with this spunky woman who early in her career was photographed with a chest full of medals. They married and he became her assistant and manager on circus tours.

Yes, your Thirteen Woman does possess amazing powers of persuasion. You may not allow her to shoot at cigarette butts clenched between your trembling lips, as Butler did with Annie, but she can convince you in sundry ways to cooperate in her life's adventures because, sure as shooting, she isn't going to travel the trail alone.

She's a groupie, that is, she understands the need for banding together. A house divided cannot stand, she'll say, as she proceeds to work out the budget, cut down on your allowance and line the kids at the kitchen table to fold, staple and stamp fliers for extra money. When problems arise, she's a pillar of strength and a ray of sunshine.

Lillie Langtree, English actress born on the 13th, known for her beauty and winning personality, caused a sensation in 1881 by being the first society woman to go on the stage. The reason for this unheard of behavior—to support her family and pay their accumulated bills. At first, the critics didn't take her seriously but eventually they realized she was a very competent actress, a perfect description of a Thirteen Woman. She did it well. Her group instincts came into play when she opened a theatre to help young struggling talent. Among her many admirers was the Prince of Wales, who subsequently became King Edward VII.

Your Thirteen Woman is a stronghold of miracles. What she can't do, you could put in a thimble for a munchkin. She has a power over the physical world which even she may not understand. Ask her to tell you about the summer night the neighbor's dog had been barking incessantly. She lay there, in the sauna-like darkness, counting to ten, one hundred, one thousand, until, though she knew the dog could not hear her, she cried, "Shut up!" Suddenly, the dog yelped and was silent, as if an unseen hand had clamped over its mouth. Coincidence? That word is a convenient dumping ground for all the things that cannot be explained.

There's no need to forearm however. It really won't do any good. She has a magical key that opens the lock to relationships. Her charming, sensual earthy beauty calls to your primal instincts for joining together. Love, trust, physical satisfaction and safety lie in her warm embrace. You also know that somehow her magical presence will transform your life. She possesses a dormant power that awakens intermittently like a giant rousing from a deep sleep. When she stretches, the earth trembles and the contours of the land shift, never to be quite the same again. She has an intimate knowledge of the laws of change which are an inevitable part of the life process. Change is the fertilizer of progress. Without it, the earth would stagnate and die. She loves the earth and tends to cling hungrily to its offerings. Anything she can touch, smell, see, hear or eat empowers her with a sense of her earthly roots.

Speaking of power, you could make a few dollars on the side—which would please her no end—by bottling and selling some of her excess. You could borrow a phrase for the bottle's label: Win Friends and Influence People. Good advertising copy could read: A tablespoon before each meal will cure bumbling, inefficiency and laziness. Increase your social graces and improve your stick-to-itiveness. Warning: an overdose results in criticism, fear and a scattering of energies. A Thirteen Woman must beware of becoming trapped in her sensual attachment to the world, to her hungry need for the earth's resources. She must use these resources with love and respect, able to let them go when the winds of change blow her way. If she cannot, or fears losing what she possesses, then she becomes their prisoner. In her desperate attempt to have it all, she can waste her valuable talents in a search for a distant "promised land" that is nonexistent outside her self. A Thirteen Woman should have a reminder posted on the wall opposite her bed to read each morning. Jim Harrison in *The Man Who Gave up his Name—Legends of the Fall* said, "Life is, after all, what we do every day." It certainly fits the bill.

But your Thirteen Woman already knows this. She has worked at opening the windows of her mind. With her larger view of life, she has overcome her tendency to be critical, which often results when a person has an eye for details.

Don't relax, however, she still knows she can do the job more efficiently than anyone else. Or, at least, better direct those who are doing it. But she won't expect you to do any more than she's willing to do. When you build your next house, you won't bother with an architect or a foreman. You know she can handle both jobs. You come home for lunch to find her ankle deep in sawdust, viewing the frame of the picture window from behind a raised thumb.

"I tell you," she says firmly to a slightly agitated carpenter, "the opening's four inches too high."

"Lady, I already measured it," the man insists, rolling his eyes in a S.O.S. toward you.

Your Thirteen Woman steps back a few paces, sighting with her thumb again. "No, it's four inches too high. Please measure it again." Her tone of voice allows no choice.

The carpenter sighs, ambles to the window, draws out his tape and carelessly runs it up from the floor to the window base. He looks, then does a double take.

"I don't believe it," he grumbles, running a hand over his forehead.

There is something perfect about her, come to think of it. When you've decided she's the woman of your dreams and she has made you her own, she will transport you to a paradise of abundant sensual pleasures, an Elysium of delight. You'd better enjoy it now because tomorrow, at 6:00 A.M. sharp, there's a lot of work to be done.

The Thirteen Man

Your Thirteen Man is what you might call "down-to-earth" in his desires. Who else do you know who gets paid in salt? He's worth his share however, just as the Roman soldiers were who received a "salarium," or salary, of that scarce and necessary commodity. Your Thirteen Man loves earthly pleasures. Money, property, the home and physical contacts are important to him. Whether he has them in his firm grip or not, you can be sure he encounters them on a daily basis because they are part of his basic makeup. How he handles such things is another story.

If he has the proper mind-set, he has an enormous capacity for work. He knows that "honesty, diligence and perseverance" are the virtues that lead to success, confirming the old phrase that genius is 5 percent inspiration and 95 percent perspiration. He doesn't expound on the capriciousness of the muses, while draped tragically over a chaise waiting for their visitations. Rather, he puts his mind to the task, his nose to the grindstone and works. He knows where the streets lead that are paved with good intentions so he produces while others procrastinate. He's headed for cooler regions because he knows that with just a little bit of luck and a lot of determination, he will succeed.

In his "rags to riches" books, Horatio Alger, a Thirteen Man, portrayed underprivileged youths who transformed their lives and acquired fame and fortune by the homely virtues of hard work and perseverance. Although his books weren't considered literary greats, they influenced American youth by emphasizing merit and determination rather than birth or background as the road to success. If your Thirteen Man concentrates too much on work, however, you'll have a hard time getting him out of the fields and onto the primrose path.

He has a sense of humor and a fun-loving side. Actually, he has quite a flair. His actions have a grandeur that suggests he knows the outcome of any scenario in which he plays. Motivated by some sense of security, whether it be money or the herd instinct, he often gives the appearance of a cavalier, devil-may-care individual whose main purpose in life is to have fun. Don't let this fool you. Underneath it all, he has a respect for following the rules, which is another form of security. When you follow rules, you know the perimeters and you feel safe. In his own inimitable way, Butch Cassidy qualifies as a Thirteen Man. In the beginning, his Robin Hood tactics, perpetrated with great fanfare, of robbing from the rich and giving to the poor, graphically depicted his concern for hard-working groups. He also kept his word and followed the rules. In 1894, facing a two-year jail sentence, he talked his jailors into letting him out for a last night on the town, with a promise he would return in the morning. He kept his word and returned the next day. When the governor of Wyoming gave him a pardon with the stipulation he never again rustle cattle or rob banks in that state, Cassidy agreed. He went on to rob trains. But he kept his word, to the letter.

You may have to be very specific with your Thirteen Man because he takes everything literally—like the difference between robbing banks and robbing trains. There is a part of this man that loves to formulate and plan, then, with precise accuracy, carry out those plans toward a successful conclusion. The conclusion in some way revolves around the instinct to gather the wagons in a circle to protect against attack. Your Thirteen Man has a built-in defense mechanism which is heavily reinforced by his eye for details.

He will allow no cracks in his dam. Watch him in a debate. He gives no quarter and is a formidable opponent. His personal magnetism and dramatic flair serve him well in winning support. With his booming voice and his arms gesticulating wildly, it's hard to concentrate on your own point of view anyway. Your Thirteen Man has to be careful that he doesn't become so enamored of his own opinion that he refuses to hear the other side. Or he may hear the other side but reject it because it wasn't his idea. He sometimes feels he has to stick to his original premise even if Daniel Webster and the Archangel Gabriel are debating the opposing view. You should remind him that cutting off his nose to spite his face will mar one of his more valuable resources—his body.

His everyday thinking is affected by the way he feels about his body. He is aware of himself, his personal charisma, and how effective he can be when dealing with others. He can have a positively transforming effect upon those with whom he comes in contact. Through his words and actions, he sets forces in motion that would astound even him if he knew their greater or esoteric import. He has the ability to control, then transform people and situations. Is he a Merlin with magical occult powers? If he knew the extent of his influence and how to use it, he could be. The Thirteen Man, Robert Louis Stevenson, in his most famous story, *Dr. Jekyll and Mr. Hyde,* told a tale of such a man. Stevenson, recognizing this power in himself, presented the thirteen's transforming ability to the world personified in Dr. Jekyll. Things ran amuck, however, because the transformation produced a negative manifestation.

He does like to organize and oversee the bodies that carry the souls around. He enjoys the captaincy but, beyond that, he is motivated toward such positions because he feels a need to strengthen foundations in life through groups. Safety in numbers is his motto, as long as he's numero uno. (He has a one in his thirteen.) He's part of the clan, yes, but he's the Big Daddy, the sun around which the lesser satellites revolve. He is the necessary sustaining and nurturing source of the group's life. In a crowd tilting beer tankards or in a group running a home for children, he'll be the central figure—merry, gay, laughing, but solid rock underneath, you can be sure.

The Thirteen performer, John Davidson, in an effort to become the "Arthur Murray of nightclub singers," opened, on Catalina Island, a "camp" for aspiring stars. He recognized his own duality when he commented that because of his boy-next-door good looks, "producers and casting people never felt this person inside me could go through an emotional catharsis."

Your Thirteen Man inspires trust. Just look at that honest, beaming countenance. It would be easier to believe that someone you trust would run off with your life's savings than that this man would fail you in any way. You would rather put your body and soul in his hands, which, by the way, he'll thoroughly enjoy. The responsibility, that is. He is an excellent manager, and if celestial management needed a little help on this third planet from a star in a corner of the Milky Way Galaxy, there would be no better choice than your Thirteen Man. His magical powers have already been discussed, and he certainly doesn't lack in confidence.

The ancients deliberately wove superstition around your man's number because they recognized the power it contained therefore, by osmosis, the power any individual connected with it possessed. Your Thirteen Man is of the earth, grounded in body, home and money and he will live with and work out his life through these mediums. But the magic of him is that he knows the earth and its possessions for what they are—manifestations of the life force of which he is the steward. He is here to use them in ways that will transform his life and others' lives for the better. Then he needs to let them go because they are of the earth, they will serve in their form for a limited time only. Such things are transitory. Once he understands this law of thirteen, he no longer sees death in the same way. When people, situations or possessions pass out of his control, "die" in a sense, he understands it as a transformation where the refuse of the old fertilizes the seeds of new growth. He becomes the magician in the sense that he realizes and can "see" the processes of life.

Besides, he can walk on water. Well, he could if he wanted to. If he really sat down and concentrated hard for, say, thirteen years, he would be the one who could do it. Don't take our word for it. Ask him. He might even do it for you. Remember the time he took you to a ballgame and you mentioned you'd like a baseball as a souvenir. He said he'd get you one—from the player's bat nonetheless. He does have a flair. It was the seventh inning when a crack of the bat sent a pop ball high over your heads. He leaped into the air, knocking a hot dog into the face of a burly three-hundred-pounder and caught the flying white object. He caught more than the ball. Didn't you love the way he dashed down the aisle with a lumbering figure in hot pursuit, all the while motioning at you that he got your souvenir. Coincidence? Maybe. Did you notice how he had his eyes clenched tight each time the batter swung at the ball? That strange reflex was not because he didn't like the noise. He was concentrating, using his considerable will and belief to direct the ball his way.

His parents think it magical that they survived his early years. It can be difficult living with a facsimile of divinity. Although his ego is as obvious as a flashing neon sign in the Saskatchewan provinces, it was much more fragile in his youth. It was exasperating for him to know that he was right and not have everyone else acknowledge it as well. He may have unconsciously shouldered too much responsibility, thinking he should correct any family problems that arose. When he was not able to—only because of his physical size and lack of experience—he may have become temporarily timid.

But "temporarily" was as long as he could endure that condition. As he grew into his teens, he began to notice the influence he had on others. He became the happily acknowledged leader—happily for him and for the group. They wanted his leadership because they felt safe in his capable hands. He was at the All State level then.

Positive feedback insured his growth to his present exalted position—king of your universe. And because you love him, you may have to point out that he rules your universe but not *the* universe. Douse his dictatorial deliberations with a good dose of understanding and love and he'll be fine in the morning. The new day always fills him with a mystical expectancy and excitement. There is work to be done, and he's ready. No one can do it quite the way he does so he must be there to supervise and transform the ordinary task into a miracle of accomplishment. You're the first to admit he transformed your world from the beginning. You heard him boast that he always does things right but when you decided to spend your life with him, you never expected tickets to heaven. There's a honeymoon that's hard to top.

The Fourteen Woman

Have you noticed that when you bring up your Fourteen Woman's name, people take a deep breath, their pupils enlarge ever so slightly and a wave of resigned bewilderment washes over them. Designating this woman an interesting personality makes as much sense as calling St. Peter's Sistine Chapel "pretty," which it is, but neither description is adequate. Actually, your woman is quite overwhelming. Passing passively through life is not her idea of a meaningful odyssey. You won't find her pussy-footing around issues. Ask a question and you'll get an answer—clear, direct and to the point. She doesn't see the value in embroidering issues with superfluous stitchery. It may look pretty but why camouflage a deeper beauty—the truth. She knows only one direction—full speed ahead, because the shortest distance between two points for her is a straight line, and if she wants to know something, she goes directly to the source. It's been rumored that the Consumers' Protection Agency is proposing legislation to make it mandatory for Fourteen Women to wear bright yellow arm bands stamped with large black crosses to warn travelers about impending dangerous intersections. You can run parallel with your Fourteen Woman but it isn't wise to try to intersect her.

She is a warrior. And all along you thought those two golden arm bands were just decorative. Believe this—you wouldn't want to arm wrestle with her because she has a beautiful yet powerful body. She has one advantage beyond that. She can think. She uses her dual strength to convey her thoughts effectively to others.

Margaret Sanger, American birth control advocate born on the 14th, crusaded for a cause that defied existing laws. Arrested several times, her court decisions opened the way for dispensing contraceptive devices by physicians. She

14

worked to promote favorable legislation. Her book titles conveyed the warrior image: *Motherhood and Bondage, My Fight for Birth Control,* and *Woman and the New Race.*

Your Fourteen Woman has a respect for the law. She knows it is necessary to uphold and support society and the family unit, both of which are important to her. However, the law must be able to speak to the people in terms they can understand. It has to apply to their everyday lives. There must be a real communication involved that supplies the needs of the individual—body and mind. Your Fourteen Woman has a strong protective nature which encompasses others. Home and family are of vital importance in her lifestyle. They are her roots, her refuge, her sanctuary, and she'll protect them at all costs. She'll also protect their freedoms as Margaret Sanger did with her fight to give women the freedom to protect their own bodies and make their own decisions, without outside interference.

The skills of communication are one method that your Fourteen Woman relies upon to achieve peaceful change. She knows she has a power with the word, whether spoken or written. The truth is she could talk the whiskers off a cat or the spots off a leopard. But she doesn't speak lightly. She feels a strong sense of responsibility for her words because she knows they are building blocks. Her words create form. In the beginning was the Word. Your Fourteen Woman knows that sound is a moving force, a vibration that sets things in motion. Sound has the potential for great constructive or destructive acts. She'll show you if you ask. Draw a violin bow across the edge of a glass covered with sand, and the subsequent vibration or sound will cause the sand to form beautiful geometric patterns.

Yes, her words are a moving, creative force. When her lilting phrases move toward you, you're as helpless as a loose kite in a hurricane unless you plug your ears with wax or lash yourself to the mast as Odysseus and his sailors did when passing the rocky islet of the Sirens. Because, like the Sirens, she will charm you with a sweet song and forever change your life. An ounce of prevention is worth a pound of cure, as the old saying goes, so if you plan to escape her compelling persuasions, you might try wax.

Your Fourteen Woman has always admired those who could command with ease. She fondly remembers her fifth grade English teacher who preached basic skills as the foundation of good communication. Spelling, punctuation and composition skills were stressed. Your Fourteen Woman would have sooner gone without her Twinkies than misplace or omit a comma, semi-colon or exclamation mark in her English assignment. As her teacher would say, creativity is important, but if you can't get your idea across, if you can't think and write coherently, what good is it? End of discussion. Exclamation point! No wonder they got along so well. The teacher was a Fourteen too.

Your Fourteen Woman learned early that variety is the spice of life. In her teenage years, she found interaction with people essential. She loved to talk and mingle with others, especially with people who liked to do things. Chances are she was the one everyone looked to for direction. And you can believe she found a few that weren't on the compass. She liked to experiment with her senses, much to the chagrin of her parents and teachers, but no one could really be angry with her. She'd open her eyes, curl her lips into a whimsical smile, and bubble into rhythmical explanations. Before anyone knew it, they were smiling back at her, assuring her that her actions, although rather extraordinary, had really caused no harm and, yes, she could go but please, she wasn't to do it again. She didn't. She would manage to find something else to do, however, that was just as much fun, if not more so. Her parents spent a confused twenty years trying to decide if they wanted to put her name in the paper or keep it out.

One of the pitfalls for a Fourteen Woman is overindulgence in the physicality of life. She has a driving need to experience situations first hand. Listening to what others have to say about events and emotions is not good enough so she plunges into the surf of sensual experience to find out for herself. A Fourteen Woman can be caught by the undertow and pulled in over her lovely head. The ensuing struggle back to the safety of the beach can be very exhausting. She should try to approach all things with moderation. Good advice to anyone but especially to the Fourteen Woman because her senses are so keen and her bond to the earth so strong.

But whatever you do, don't carve these words in the headboard of her bed and try to chain her there. She loves you and her home and will darn your socks, eliminate your ring-around-the-collar and play the domestic game according to Hoyle—because a part of her enjoys that—but the minute you try to change the rules and box her in or limit her mobility, she'll yell gin and you'll be out of the game.

There's an elusive, will-o-the whisp quality about her, now you see her, now you don't. She seems to be solidly with you physically and emotionally, then suddenly she's off on an adventure, full of excitement and fervor. She is impatient and aggressive at times, like the Fourteen actress, Faye Dunaway, whose approach toward life exemplifies many of the Fourteen qualities. She loves cooking, gardening and shopping, art and music and wants to found an American National Theatre. The Fourteen Woman likes to organize, set in motion, and then be off because freedom is in her blood. If you don't want yours spilled, as in some Mickey Spillane mystery, you'd better recognize this need at the start. Those simple sounds of respect and appreciation—please and thank you—will put you in-like-Flynn with her and she'll move mountains for you. She can do it. Whoever said the pen was mightier than the sword was unwittingly describing your woman's ability to make major changes. One lone Fourteen Woman's pen contributed to the outbreak of the Civil War. With it, she didn't move mountains but she moved a nation to its knees over a moral issue. Harriet Beecher Stowe, with her husband, made frequent trips to the neighboring slaveholding state of Kentucky where she heard first-hand accounts of runaway slaves. From her experiences, she wrote many books denouncing slavery, including the one that first ran in serialized form in the abolitionist newspaper, *The National Era*, from June 1851 to April 1852. When it was presented as a book in 1853, its success was unprecedented in publishing history. Five hundred thousand copies were sold in the United States alone in a five-year-period, and it was translated into twenty foreign languages. *Uncle Tom's Cabin,* more than any other single factor, crystallized anti-slavery sentiment and precipitated the Civil War.

Not only did the title of this book, *Uncle Tom's Cabin,* verbally depict her concern for the family unit, the cabin or the home, but true to Fourteen tradition, she dictated the manuscript in her kitchen while holding her baby on her lap and overseeing her other little ones and the household duties.

Your Fourteen Woman can do many things at once. She has more arms than an octopus and an industriousness that would shame an army of ants and she uses both to full advantage. Coupled with a storehouse of energy and overflowing ideas, she will never cease to amaze you. She's Auntie Mame and a female Mr. Spock wrapped into one delightfully dual package. You may think that conservative stripes and crazy polka dots don't mix but, on her, they keep your eyes busy and your mind curious. The secret of your Fourteen Woman lies in the convoluted curves of her medulla oblongata where a marriage of logic and imagination takes place. Does that mean she's brainy? You hope to smoke a pickle it does. Remember, the medulla oblongata is the nervous tissue at the bottom of the brain that controls respiration and circulation, and her ideas circulate like a jacuzzi with a contract. Meanwhile, your respiration rate rises to 140. Those little trouble makers—her ideas—swirl and spin, then rise like the great Phoenix out of the ashes of outworn social mores and philosophies. Caught by the four winds, they spread to the far corners of the Earth. Institutions crumble, crowds cheer, sparkling white edifices are erected, a new age is at hand, while, back at the jacuzzi, you're standing wrapped in a rather wet Turkish towel with your bare legs hanging out, wondering what happened.

Remember the time your Fourteen Woman insisted you camp out in the Amazon jungle with your feet toward the fire so the vampire bats wouldn't get you, or the time you had to cross the Jamunda River where a school of pirana had attacked a crossing herd of cattle the day before? Well, those experiences have a way of raising your body temperature. But she has a way of making things seem so reasonable. Remember the comforting touch she brought along? Tacked to a Brazil nut tree and encircled by a rather large snake was a small wooden sign decorated with a vine of roses climbing over pretty pink hearts that read: Home is where the heart is. Speaking of nuts, you began to wonder what kind you were to have allowed this daffy, dangerous, deliciously tantalizing woman to persuade you to take that trip. Well, at least you got home safely. It wasn't too bad. You did get across the river the next day with just a nip taken out of your left heel and your picture was there in the middle spread of *National Geographic* in living color—even if it was just the top of your head. That large bush you were crouched behind obscured the rest of you. Your Fourteen Woman was there too, laughing and slapping her knee beside a rotund and very bare native holding an extremely ugly, long, pointed spear. He was grinning and gesturing back at her.

Yes, home is where the heart is. And in spite of it all, or maybe because of it, she is where your heart is also. No matter if her home is in the steamy jungles of South America today and in the calm corners of Eaton Center, New Hampshire tomorrow, that's where your home is too. She is some woman!

The Fourteen Man

"Do you promise to tell the truth, the whole truth and nothing but the truth, so help you God?" Your Fourteen Man will be accosted by this question, in some manner, all his life. When he inserts the pronoun "I" into the phrase, it becomes his motto. He not only seeks truth but he's as determined as a seasoned encyclopedia salesman that you and everyone else know it. He may even sell them—they do fit his image of facts in ready form for the digestion of the multitudes.

Your Fourteen Man is into broadcasting his ideas, beliefs and opinions like a farmer casting grain to a pen of chickens. People flock to him. They tend to cluster around him, pecking at his feet to get his attention. You were there once, remember? He was in the midst of an animated group of eager adventurers, one of whom was you. He was witty, charming, down-to-earth, and had a charismatic voice that almost mesmerized you into signing up for the Peace Corps. He had already been there but now that you found him you weren't going. You suddenly had other plans.

Before you knew it, your right hand was raised and you were swearing that you were morally upright, ethically just, that you handled money efficiently and were kind and courteous to animals, children and old people, and that you didn't drink, smoke or chew gum in public. That wasn't done to get into the Peace Corps. It was the prerequisite for your first date. You would have said anything to get in his good graces.

Frank Borman, former test pilot and astronaut, born on the 14th, eventually joined Eastern Airlines as senior vice-president of operations. He soon advanced to his present position today of president, chief executive officer of the airlines. He is widely respected not only for saving the near bankrupt airline but for turning it into a profitable enterprise noted for its polite and efficient service. He neither smokes nor drinks, and allows no alcoholic beverages to be consumed by employees during business hours. It is said he runs a "very tight ship."

No matter what your Fourteen Man gets into, he will be busy. It's the nature of the beast. He has a mind that runs in overdrive. If you're very quiet and listen carefully, you can hear the gears clinking, spinning and whirring even when he's asleep. His mind never rests. Like the eternal flame, it is constantly burning, seeking fresh new avenues of expression and accomplishment. Don't expect him to come home after a hard day's work, grab a beer and cement himself in front of the television with a glaze over his eyes. He may not have fancy tastes—like Frank Borman, he could be a "hamburger and movie man" or like Albert Einstein he may enjoy "simple tastes"—but that doesn't mean his mind falls into a state of sleep when he's through his daily rounds.

George Lucas, a Fourteen Man and creator of *Star Wars*, like most Fourteen Men, is not afraid of work. He wrote eight hours a day for three years creating the screen play for a film that critics acclaimed as one of the greatest with superlatives like magnificent, grand, exhilarating, glorious.

The duality of the number Fourteen—a combination of the structural mind that needs to know what the rules are and where the boundaries lie, and the mind that must be free to express—becomes apparent in Lucas when he makes statements that claim he is "inherently conservative" and that in his work he is "trying to set up an alternative film making that allows me to do what I want within certain perimeters."

Your Fourteen Man combines the best of both worlds. He is exceptionally expressive and enormously tuned in to the physical world in all its phases. He takes special pride in his body and works to keep it functioning properly. He's fast on his feet so he may choose activities like jogging and tennis where he can keep his muscles moving in rhythm with his mind. When he comes puffing through the door after a fourteen-mile jog, his face red and rivulets of sweat streaming down his muscular body, you may wonder what sadistic motivations drive him. "It relaxes...my mind...and my body," he explains, managing those utterances between pants as he wipes his forehead and heaving chest with your clean dish towel. "Good," you reply, picking up the dish towel by one corner with two finger tips and dropping it into the laundry basket. "Now you can shower and dress and we'll visit Aunt Minnie."

14

His eyes dart toward the ceiling and fix on some imaginary point there as he bites his lower lip. You see, Aunt Minnie has never heard of E= mc² or Obi-Wan Kenobi and cares little for the space program, and your Fourteen Man is wondering how long he can sit balancing a tea cup on one knee and finger rolls on the other. He has so much he wants to do and time is of the essence. Besides, if he begins to feel trapped, then you may have some trouble explaining why his body's gone rigid and he does not respond to Auntie's querries. Astral travel isn't one of Aunt Minnie's topics of conversation either.

But your Fourteen Man does love Aunt Minnie. He is devoted to his family and the small circle of friends he chooses. He may know a lot of people but it's a select group to which he is emotionally bound, and those few he will protect most effectively. Now you know why there's a moat populated with cranky crocodiles around your house. It wasn't just a decorative touch to set off the stone castle with barred windows and heavy oaken doors guarded by enormous eunichs. He had something else in mind. Your protection and his privacy.

He does have moments when he retreats into the sanctuary of his mind, a place where no one can reach him. Maybe it was his wild unruly hair and the unfathomable abstract look on his face that made his parents think he was touched with either a lot of genius or a little madness. He was temperamental and devilish, or preoccupied and lost in another world, one or the other, sometimes both at the same time. No one ever knew for sure. He probably disliked formal education with its penchant for pedantry and examination. Why were they asking him "Why?" That's what he wanted to know and they were supposed to give him the answers.

By the time he was a teenager, his restless and unsatisfied mind either drove him to drag racing or plunged him nose-deep into classical physics—fields not so far apart when one thinks about it. They both require a technical mind and an understanding of structure.

Today he has a mind like a steel trap. He is a perpetual student, as voracious as a teenage boy who has missed a meal. He cannot ingest enough information or experience enough of life to satisfy him. He's on a hungry quest and he may have knocked a few down on his way to the refrigerator. Not intentionally, of course, it's just that he sometimes gets carried away by his exuberance.

He's "into" ideas and experience the way others are "into" eating. His need for first-hand experience can be his downfall if this desire is not handled with some discipline. If he allows his own interests to compete with each other, he waters down his effectiveness and ends up with alphabet soup, a mishmash of letters but no words or sentences. When he gathers up his past experience and places it into a mold of his choosing, then he can build an empire of ideas to feed a devoted following or the world.

Your Fourteen Man's ideas can influence the thought processes of an entire generation and outlast his own time. He may unwittingly give rise to cults devoted to his brain children.

The Fourteen Man, Einstein, whose startling ideas about such concepts as time, mass and space, aroused a popular cult far beyond his scientific confines. Your Fourteen Man's name could also become a household word.

Your Fourteen Man has a high level of standards and an impulse to broadcast. Did you think the letters ABC on his key chain represented the alphabet? Somewhere deep inside even the most quiet, unassuming and cloistered Fourteen

Man there lies the knowledge that he has something important to say. He didn't bronze his first grade work papers for nothing. He knows that one day those painstakingly worked markings will bring a big price at auction.

Your Fourteen Man also has a reverence for life. Remember Freddie? He used to come whenever your Fourteen Man called. They were great pals. But no one else could do anything with Freddie. He attached himself to your man. He was a one-man fly. Chances are there's no fly paper in your Fourteen Man's house because he has a respect for all forms of life. He's even been known to talk the ants out of the sugar bin and into the backyard. He's the type who gets involved, becoming an influential voice on issues of freedom. In 1970, by Presidential request, Frank Borman embarked on a world-wide tour to enlist the support of third parties for releasing the American POWs held in North Viet Nam. Einstein's public life was "marked by a deep concern for the freedom and dignity of man and he was always ready to lend support to persecuted individuals or groups."

Your Fourteen Man is a strange mixture of respect for the law and demand for personal freedom. He senses his responsibility to earthly things—social issues, family, the rules—but he needs the latitude to express his personal views. He's the type who shouldn't make so many social commitments that his mobility is limited and his spare time reduced below tolerable levels. He needs to be free to come and go, and to use his spare hours to experiment with his own ideas. Routine can stifle him. You want to see a grown man go stark, raving mad? Put your Fourteen Man on an assembly line in a building with no windows and you'll have a lunatic on your hands in no time!

This man is a one person relay team, a marathoner who can go the distance. He'll be dropping one foot in front of the other long after most others have fallen exhausted by the wayside, and he'll be filing his nails and thinking up a formula to save the world at the same time. He wasn't meant to specialize. He believes, as Robert Heinlein said, "A human being should be able to change a diaper, plan an invasion, butcher a hog, conn a ship, design a building, write a sonnet, balance accounts, build a wall, set a bone, comfort the dying, take orders, give orders, cooperate, act alone, solve equations, analyze a new problem, pitch manure, program a computer, cook a tasty meal, fight efficiently, die gallantly. Specialization is for insects."

This amazing man is all yours. Just think what an education you'll have before you're through.

The Fifteen Woman

Just because your Fifteen Woman is waving a wooden cooking spoon in one hand and a Magnum .357 in the other does not mean she's schizophrenic. She's just expressing opposite sides of the same coin. She feels deep family and social responsibility, and is capable of handling the expressions of both areas of her interest, even in extreme circumstances.

On the domestic scene, she is an excellent parent and teacher because she's basically kind, sympathetic and caring, and she communicates these feelings and attitudes to her family and friends. You're sick? She's there with the hot chicken soup and fifteen remedies to cure your particular ailment. And she can make a good soup!

15

She's an adventurer, an "explorer of foods," and has learned a lot through trial and error. She's like the musician who plays by ear—she cooks by taste. What about all those cookbooks standing on the kitchen shelf next to that display of stainless steel cookware? They're for decorative purposes only. Notice how the binding colors blend with the decor and are reflected in the metallic flash of the steel. But she uses her own recipes. Into her bowls go a few scoops of this, a half-handful of that—interrupted by a sniff and a taste—then a pinch of the other and, all the while she's "measuring" her ingredients, she'll be carrying on an animated conversation with you on the pros and cons of women on corporate boards and the problems the publishing committee has run into with the next issue of the junior high school newsletter.

"Any woman worth her salt can throw a few ingredients into a pan and come up with a deliciously tantalizing meal," she says carelessly, when questioned about her unusual M.O. "Just dump them in and whip them up. Voila! You have an entertaining meal." You have discovered she can carry a meal on her witty personality alone. Food just naturally tastes better when you're with her. You may think she knows a special language—that she talks to the ingredients—or else how could that mishmash of opposing substances combine to treat the taste buds so exquisitely.

Like the "fumbling French Chef on public television, flubbing recipes and wisecracking about the private parts of fowl," Julia Childs, a Fifteen Woman, says of her talents, "I'm a kind of 'what-the-hell cook'—let things fall where they may." Ms. Childs' "things" have fallen well, to the tune of 1.3 million copies of her book, *Mastering the Art of French Cooking*, sold since 1961. Her social concerns become obvious in such comments as "How can a society be called great when its bread tastes like kleenex?" Ms. Child might be surprised to know that one of her constant companions—shortening—was introduced to the public on the 15th, back in 1911.

You've been in suspense about where the Magnum 357 comes in, right? Well, that's for social issues that get bogged down. You can imagine how quickly the vote at the PTA swings her way when she rises in the midst of a debate over a purchase of a jungle set for the school playground brandishing this rather indiscreet weapon. She'd be a public leader even without her Magnum because her penchant for writing, lecturing and speaking coupled with her strong nurturing tendencies and desire to see justice done automatically place her in the public eye. It's difficult for her to remain silent on issues that touch her soul. She is courageous and will go to great lengths—miles and miles—to achieve her goals. She might not walk a mile for a Camel but she'd walk 115 miles to get in the newspaper over a case of discrimination. Although moderation is her key word, you'll notice it doesn't even apply to her cooking habits.

But that's the fun of her. You never know what she's liable to do. Remember the time you came home to find a hole broken through the kitchen wall and her standing in a pile of rubble, swinging a hammer with both hands, her hair tied in a kerchief? "What are you doing," you cried out, in abject horror. Her head snapped your way. "Oh, hi darling. I thought if we took this wall down, we could put up a bar and the kitchen would look so much bigger."

She moves walls like some people move furniture. She's also adept at moving furniture. It satisfies her traveling urges. You see, she loves to travel but she doesn't want to leave home, so moving furniture suggests motion and new locations, and somehow sates her wanderlust. So, don't complain. At least she doesn't change partners like she does slip covers. But you could come home to find your house moved to that lot she's been talking about for the last few months on the next street—you know, the one with the spruce trees in the backyard and the ancient elm with its wide, wonderfully leafy arms. In any case, you should prepare for such an eventuality. You'd look pretty silly arriving home in the dark, driving your car into a garage hole. It's not good for the alignment to say nothing of your nerves.

Your Fifteen Woman has a distinct creative flair which may show in the way she decorates her home or in her love for music and the arts. Her creativeness has a certain "homeyness" about it, a comfortable feeling with which the public can identify. Such a feeling is evident in the talents of Petula Clark, a Fifteen Woman who was "England's answer to Shirley Temple during World War II." She made twenty-five "cutesy movies" before settling into her own personal style. Today she is a "top nightclub singer, hit recording artist and mother." Her interests are "cooking and songwriting" and she irons for relaxation. You can take the Fifteen Woman out of the home but you can't take the home out of the Fifteen Woman.

Your Fifteen Woman has a naturally pleasant, harmonious personality to which people are drawn. She is a born counselor, listening sympathetically to your problems, and able to see clearly the underlying truths of the situation. Problem solving is her forte and once she is motivated, she is unafraid to tackle anything. She comes up with ingenious solutions to brain twisters that frustrate the most avid detective fan, and she makes it sound so easy and logical. One problem you may run into is getting to her through the crowds. People congregate around her because they feel comfortable, safe and nurtured in her presence.

Although most Fifteen Women gravitate toward nurturing and defending their home and family and expressing through some artistic media, there is the type who marries a cause. Her ideas become her children, whom she will defend against any and all opposition with the fervor of a female animal protecting her young. In this instance, the opposite side of this normally passive, gentle and peace-loving creature becomes visible. Let there be no mistake about it, when her children or ideas are threatened, she becomes the most ferocious of the species. She may still be smiling, but when you see that "you'll-be-sorry" glint in her eye, you'd better make like a baby and head out. You could learn a lesson from the insect world. Only female mosquitoes bite. The Black Widow spider and the female praying mantis both devour their partners after mating. And only female bees work. Take heed and don't buck this Fifteen Woman who is so dedicated to the children of her body and mind.

Susan B. Anthony and Susan Brownmiller, both born on February 15th some 115 years apart, have parallel lives. Susan B. (Brownelle) Anthony, born in 1820, was an "effective speaker and writer for the causes of abolition and woman's rights." For fifty years she made significant contributions in the face of harsh and continuing opposition. Her only marriage was to her cause. In 1919, fourteen years after her death, the "Anthony Amendment," granting woman suffrage, became law.

Susan Brownmiller, born 1935, also devoted to her work, was a college member of the NAACP and active in civil rights movements in the South. In 1968, she formed the New York Radical Feminists. Her influential best seller, *Against Our Will: Men, Women and Rape,* is the most comprehensive study on rape ever done. She states that rape is a "weapon to subjugate women in the male-female power relationship."

15

On the other side of the Susan B. Anthony coin is Phyllis Schlafly, born on the 15th, who is an author, social activist and conservative politician who has attacked ERA as a "threat to family life and the American woman." Eloquent, well-mannered in her own way, she is as aggressive and tough a fighter as Susan B. Anthony. Schlafly and Anthony represent opposite sides of the same issue.

Does your Fifteen Woman scare you now? She seems so gentle, loving and compassionate. Well, she is all those things. In fact, she has such a deep sense of obligation to you and the family that she can forget about her own needs while serving yours. She will cater to you and be downright indulgent with you. She has to be careful that she doesn't smother those she loves. Often, your Fifteen Woman finds it hard to understand that some people need privacy, time away from mate and loved ones.

Another area she must tread carefully is that of clinging to an idea when she knows it is wrong. Some Fifteen Women birth an idea, then feel obligated to nurture it even if it's been proven erroneous and futile. This is where her stubbornness rears its head. She needs to learn to see beyond surface appearances into the truth.

Truth is an issue with her. Her parents realized this when she was quite young. Most children are born believing their parents and teachers but this Fifteen Child carried a mini-Bible strapped to her waist at all times. When her parents promised her an ice cream cone if she ate her succotash, out came the Bible and her parents had to swear to tell the truth, the whole truth.... Teachers planning class parties and school trips were subjected to the same promisory tactics.

She was probably an emotional child and even into her teens, her feelings were apt to ride the roller coaster. She could have carried a certain naivete with her as well. Disliking trouble and confrontations, she avoided unpleasantness by using her natural charm and magnetism to keep relationships running peacefully.

The family unit was important to her as a child and still is today. Communication is a vital part of her interaction with her loved ones. She establishes and carefully maintains open discussion between family members. She tends to be more independent and confident in herself than her sister, the Six Woman. Part of the reason is that the Fifteen Woman is more concerned with communication and self-expression. She has a feel for language—the written or spoken word—and when she has an audience, she's as happy as a clam in deep mud. She'd probably prefer to be surrounded by people with their feet in cement, providing her with a captive audience to whom she could lecture, express her views, generally entertain and nurture, and probably feed too, and they couldn't get away.

But your Fifteen Woman knows that bondage to a person, idea or cause is limiting and destructive. She also knows that bondage is illusion, a circumstance created by the mind. When you think free, you are free though your body be draped with shackles and chains. Emily Dickinson, a Fifteen Woman, expressed the freedom of the mind in the following simple, eloquent lines:

> He ate and drank the precious words—
> His spirit grew robust—
> He knew no more that he was poor,
> Nor that his frame was dust.
>
> He danced along the dingy days
> And this bequest of wings
> Was but a book—What liberty
> A loosened spirit brings!

Your Fifteen Woman has an appreciation for beauty that is reflected in her own natural beauty—a look that can't be achieved through cosmetics. When she is operating on positive waves, she remains young from age six to ninety-six. She positively glows from inside with a radiance that emanates from her genuine core of love and compassion. One day she'll turn to you and say, "Honey, I was reading an article in the paper about the people in the South End and how the city is going to take away their homes—they're all elderly—to put in a high-rise office building and parking lot and I decided that I should do something about it. So I called a small meeting—fifty or sixty people—to see what can be done about it. The meeting's tonight and..." The doorbell rings. The murmur of multitudes reaches your ears. "Oh, here they are now," she exclaims, jumping up to answer the call.

Where does she get her energy, you wonder. Then you grimace. You'll have to share your board and her attention with fifty strangers this night but then, she wouldn't be the exciting woman you love if she didn't do these things. Life would be rather dull without her. You smile and burrow deeper into your stuffed chair. Nothing could be finer.

The Fifteen Man

Your Fifteen Man wouldn't want a house built of straw or sticks but he would be fascinated with the Paper House at Pigeon Cove in Rockport, Massachusetts. It's built of 215 thicknesses of newspaper. The builder claims that "all the furniture is made of newspaper including a desk of newspapers relating Lindberg's historic flight." Your Fifteen Man has strong ties with his home but he also loves to know what's going on in the world so, as the owner of this house, he could read the table while eating his breakfast and not be accused of hiding behind a newspaper in the morning.

It would be difficult to get angry with your Fifteen Man because he has a boyish charm, a lovableness that's hard to resist. He could resemble a Greek David or have the face of a goalie and he'd still mysteriously draw you to him. It's not just the small bouquets of forget-me-nots he sent you on non-occasions or the gentle kisses he brushes across the back of your neck when you're bent over a steaming kitchen sink. It's something more intangible but very real. It's called charisma.

Your Fifteen Man can be very sentimental however. Not too many men cry at a friend of a friend's wedding. Of course, the little boy did walk his mother down the aisle and hold her hand during the ceremony. The choker however, was when the small son turned to the congregation and stumbled through a short poem about love and sharing. Sobs echoed through the rafters of the arched ceiling.

There is a nervous, adventurous soul lurking in the heart of every gentle Fifteen Man whether he expresses it openly or not. He has a need to communicate with life in all its aspects. He's curious about this, that and the other, and searches for avenues of expression in traveling—although many Fifteen Men don't like to go far from home—reading, writing, lecturing, acting and getting involved in social issues.

Ed Asner, actor born on the 15th, is known as the "lovable Lou Grant" from the character he plays on the television series of the same name. As Lou Grant, he

15

portrays an "unglamorous, middle-aged man who nevertheless projects charm and loveability, a figure with whom millions of viewers can identify." Ed Asner is quoted as saying, "I really wanted to be an adventurer . . ." Ed Asner, as Grant, is accurately portraying a part of himself: the caring individual who must be involved in life. As the newspaperman in the series, he is involved in communication and the social issues in his city.

The adventurer in your Fifteen Man is married to a sense of responsibility for his home and community. He couldn't go off half-cocked to explore the Saskatchewan wilderness or sail a dhow to Zanzibar without first securing the home front. But chances are he would choose to stay close to home and find his excitement and fight his causes on his own home turf.

He is a strange combination of peacemaker and warrior. He genuinely seeks balance, love, harmony and beauty in his world. Yes, pin-up posters of Suzanne Sommers may appeal to him. There is a great sense of symmetry and joy in viewing a perfect human body. Your Fifteen Man does find solace and contentment in a balanced environment and fair treatment. He has a keen sense of right and wrong, peace and war, and his counsel is often sought on such issues. In him is recognized the counselor, advisor, and balancer who tries to achieve harmony through peaceful means.

The law is important to him although he would find it difficult to justify the seventeenth-century ruling in Turkey that put to death anyone caught drinking coffee or to explain why it's illegal today to hunt camels in Arizona. He would certainly advise a coffee-drinking camel hunter to stay out of both places but then he and his Fifteen Ancestor would wage a campaign to change the laws. Distributing hundreds of thousands of leaflets from a plane over Arizona poses little problem but in seventeenth-century Turkey, before his ancestor got all the printed matter handed out, he would have been stuffed and trussed.

There is a part of your Fifteen Man that is willing to sacrifice for his cause, especially when the cause is linked to patriotism and defense of home and family. Erwin Rommel, commander-in-chief of Hitler's German Army in World War II, was born on the 15th. Dubbed "The Desert Fox" because of his clever tactics in the African desert, Rommel became increasingly outspoken against Hitler's policies and leadership. When he was suspected of involvement in a plot to assassinate Hitler, he was given the choice of taking poison or standing public trial. To save his family, he took the poison. His sense of honor, personal bravery and brilliant achievements "earned him the respect of his adversaries." It seems you can't help liking a Fifteen Man even when he's the opponent. And it's not the Ipana smile. It's an underlying recognition of his loyalty, honor and fairness in love and in war. Give him five minutes with his bitterest enemy and he'd have that person eating out of his well-manicured hand.

Your Fifteen Man loves beautiful things. He enjoys surrounding you both with luxury and comfort. He has an appreciation for art objects, good literature and music, fine wines and impeccable decor. When he's in the mood, he can communicate his feelings like no other. A candle-lit dinner for two, overlooking the city skyline, the finest French wine and Mantovani or Beethoven playing softly in the background. Well, if it's Mantovani, it will be playing softly but if it's Ludwig, it will be thundering across the room in exciting waves of romantic fervor. Most likely he'll select Beethoven for you. Doubt not, it will stimulate your many appetites.

Your man's passion carries over into other areas of his life. He approaches relationships, work, politics and play with the same thirst, as if he can't get enough of its experience and has to hurry so not one delicious drop will escape his parched lips. Indulging himself or loved ones, or becoming so involved with a cause that he cannot see the forest for the trees, becomes a real danger for some Fifteen Men. At this point, they see their opinions, ideas and methods as the only ones with value and seek to dictate such principles to the entire world as Napoleon, a Fifteen Man, tried to do. In the early 1800s, as General and Emperor of France, he instituted numerous reforms in government and education, showing his concern for social and legal imbalance, but his zealousness drove him to try to conquer the world.

Because your Fifteen Man has a facile tongue, he can rationalize the most outrageous position as totally sane and logical. He is eloquent and convincing. He could talk his way out of a paper bag. As long as his keen sense of justice and fair play dominate his brain waves, then he is a paragon of virtue and justice, defender of the old, young, weak, defenseless and poor. But when he turns to pursue his own indulgences, he is very dangerous because he is so convincing. A Fifteen Man should read his speeches out loud, to himself, while standing before a mirror. He should record those speeches and play them back at night while he's sleeping to reinforce his knowledge of the truth. He should repeat over and over, "I know this is right; truth is more important than victory."

But your Fifteen Man is incorruptible. Even when he was a youngster, he couldn't be bribed with candy, baseball cards or a free pass to the movie *Star Wars*. Now, there's a kid with staying power. He probably cried a lot over it, jumped up and down on little sneakered-feet and rolled around in the mud with his new jeans on—he's very emotional—but he wouldn't give in. And all his parents were trying to do was get him to take his sister to the grade school dance. But he had reasoned it was unfair to ask a boy-child to do that and it became the principle of the thing.

As a teenager he may have become involved in the student council or school newspaper or just have decided to chuck all responsibilities and have a good time. There is a devilish side to him. But he was well-liked and managed to get through school without too much of a hassle. Besides, if he can talk his way out of a paper bag, the principal's office must have been a cinch.

He's grown now into a clever, witty, intelligent, charming and caring man—he could think of a few more adjectives because he's very good with words—with a talent for winning friends and attracting good fortune. He's one of those people who always seem to be in the right place at the right time. He's the thousandth person to make a purchase at that large newly-opened department store, and suddenly there are photographers flashing bulbs in his eyes and the store manager clapping him on the back with one hand and shaking his vigorously with the other. Clerks are piling gift boxes on the counter in front of him, champagne is being uncorked and the crowds are gathering. And this is the day you decided to wear your baggy blue jeans and give yourself an afro perm. You grin sheepishly and slink off to the women's room, pink plastic curlers protruding from beneath your scarlet scarf. You wish you had his sense of being in the right place....

His sense of timing carries over to his relationships. He is a diplomat of the first order. There is no one who can get to the crux of an issue—and do it with such finesse—as your Fifteen Man. He's the type you thank after he's fired you from a job. Somehow you go away thinking he's done you a favor. You might be more prepared for such an eventuality if you "key in" to certain phrases such as "I feel that your work here is unique" and "Your presence in the organization has made quite a difference," neither of which tells you whether you're about to get a raise or lose your position. He isn't deliberately misleading you. He just wants to start the conversation out well-balanced. Then he can go either way.

Your Fifteen Man should tune in to the hymn to the Egyptian sun god, Ra: "Thy priests go forth at dawn, they wash their hearts with laughter." For your man, each morning is the beginning of a new adventure, one that requires hope, faith, optimism, and an abiding dedication to spreading truth. He knows he is a gifted messenger, one who speaks with the tongues of gods. His words will reach and touch the hearts and minds of many. Throughout his travels, he should maintain a sense of joy and of good humor. A smile and a laugh are balm for a weary soul. He must be able to laugh at the seeming inequities of life, not in a scornful or derisive way, but with the knowledge that bondage is illusion and laughter is—after all—the best medicine.

This facile mixture of man and boy is really a camouflage for the medicine man, the shaman, the miracle worker in him. In his compassionate hands, the troubles of your outside world melt away. He holds you in his loving arms as you swing gently in the backyard hammock, while he tells you tales of queens and princes and wondrous places. You nestle deeper, lulled by the warm summer breeze and the sound of his voice. When you feel as if you and the rhythm of the swinging hammock are one, he nuzzles your ear and whispers, "I'm running for governor."

The words "Oh no!" hang suspended in your mind. If you had the energy, you'd argue. But then, you can almost see him now, on his white horse, armor gleaming in the sunlight, lance tilted toward a shrouded enemy of truth, justice and the American way. Yes, there's no question about it. He will make a fine governor. And just think—his name will be all over the newspapers. Save enough of them and you can update your house. But if paper houses aren't his style, you can always build a gingerbread house. He loves good food. Then, if campaign expenses grow beyond your budget, you'll always have something to eat. You wouldn't want him to have to eat his words, now would you!

The Sixteen Woman

Your Sixteen Woman has the grace and ease of Botticelli's Venus, symbol of Spring, Beauty and Divine Love. She has a cool elegance, an abstract lyrical quality that belies her earthly form. You reach out to touch the woman and find a bit of magic beneath your fingertips.

What is this mystical quality that has you so intrigued? There she stands in her climbing boots, shorts and loose sweatshirt, a band around her classic forehead, perspiration streaming over her body, beckoning you up the last few feet to the top of the mountain. You look up at her, outlined against the teal blue sky, and swear she could wear a gunny sack and still appear more regal than the greatest queen in history. She was born to a bond with nature. She finds solace, comfort and a healing magic in natural settings—a rocky mountain top, a solitary beach, a country lane—as if she were conjured up out of the mists of time. These settings stimulate her mind.

Her mind is as magnificent as her figure. She's got your number and the sooner you figure that out, the better off you'll be. You haven't got an "endearingly half-witted bombshell" like Chrissie from ABC's number one comedy show, *Three's Company*, on your hands. What you've got is a Suzanne Somers who, unlike her character on the show, has a B.A. from Lone Mountain College and has written two volumes of poetry. Ms. Somers is described as contemplative and introspective.

However, your Sixteen Woman does have charm. She could charm the leaves off the trees and a big tip out of Jack Benny. She doesn't even have to flutter her long sweeping lashes at you. A mere lift of those limpid pools in your direction and you're paddling like a sailor with a thirst to accommodate her in any way you can. She has a strange magnetism that draws you near yet keeps you at a distance. You want to sweep her into your arms and cover her with passionate kisses but you're not quite sure who would end up the conqueror. You are bigger and stronger but she is, somehow, in control and if you're not careful, you know that, at any moment, she could point a long slender finger and a violet vapor would arise from the ground beneath your feet, enveloping you in a mist, and a ceremony reminiscent of the myths of Woman, the moon and magic would commence.

If you told her this, she would probably laugh. There is a very analytical side to your Sixteen Woman which makes her an enigma to herself as well as to you. She senses this metaphysical side of herself but isn't quite sure what to do with it so laughter relieves some of the anxiety she has about it. After all, if she can't reason it out logically, then there can't be anything to it...can there? You can be sure there will be a time in her life when a thunder bolt will flash through the heavens and strike her—metaphorically, of course—and she'll find her old ideas of matter, form and reality completely shattered. She will have glimpsed into another world where matter is energy, and time and space stand still, where mystics, shamans, oracles, and metaphysicians are one with scientists and realists. She will have discovered her "analystical" mind, that perfect combination of analytical and mystical.

It is not hers to accept without asking or seeking. She has an alert intellect which concentrates on perfection. She wants to know the ins and outs so that what she produces will be a harmonizing and beautifying product. She can get involved in the intricacies of any situation. She often sets up complications for herself when her mind and her emotions become entangled. Then, instead of procrastinating, which is one technique she can use to avoid settling a situation, she needs to go off by herself where she can sort things out. It's important to realize that although you are the one and only man in her life, she needs time by herself where she can disassociate herself from her feelings, lay them out before her and carefully analyze their parts. You can tell her that she can't control feelings, that they just happen, but it won't do any good. The need to understand is a part of her makeup, like lipstick and perfume, so don't waste your breath.

She can be a technical wizard, sorting out the various working parts of any unit, whether it be personalities, relationships or society as a whole, and her work will always have a touch of caring concern in it. Jane Austen, English novelist and author of *Pride and Prejudice*, born on the 16th, spent her years from birth to early adulthood in a "quiet, domestic and moderately studious" environment. Her writing

16

eventually revealed a woman unequalled in the presentation of truth, humor and vivacity. Her thorough understanding of characters made them appear perfect in their humanness. It is said that as a storyteller, "she has, in point of technical construction, no superior." It was her attention to the fine nuances in personality that made her the great writer she was.

And don't think your woman won't notice your nuances. So, unless you've prepared them for public airing, you'd better keep them closely under wraps. But forewarned is forearmed so you might as well understand right now that there isn't much hope for you in this conspiracy. When she rests her chin on one hand and quietly observes you while you explain your way out of some embarrassing position, she will pick up every signal, every twitch of your jaw muscle, every change of voice inflection, every movement of your hands, until her thorough understanding of your character becomes painfully apparent.

If your Sixteen Woman expresses through the arts, then her observations of subtleties emerge in her dramatic sense of timing. How many women take empty Cheerios boxes, plastic from your discarded Fruit-of-the-Loom wrappers, a little glue and a few magic markers and build a replica of the Daily Planet building, remember Superman? You laughed but word got around and now she has sixteen people working in your basement five days a week doing the same thing and shipping the product around the world. You can't laugh now. It's no longer funny because she's making money—amazing what respect the green stuff bestows—and besides, your mouth is always full of cereal.

Her "performance" always seems to have a touch of detached caring and a cool unapproachable strength coupled with intriguing femininity. Remember how your Sixteen Woman just lifted her pretty chin and looked at you as if you were a particularly unevolved member of a newly discovered primitive society when you first kidded her about her fruit and cereal construction? Actresses Barbara Stanwyck and Lauren Bacall, Sixteen Women, also convey this alluring aloof charisma. Yes, that's the look. Your additional comments to the effect that if you ever got hungry you could eat the first three floors and have a balanced diet had no effect on her. She just continued cutting out her squares and, well, you know the rest of the story. She who laughs last . . .

Your Sixteen Woman loves her home and the security and privacy it affords. She can be sociable and fun-loving but she will always be selective. She prefers a few friends and family to large groups of semi-acquaintances or strangers. Some time spent with friends and loved ones is fine but you'll find her systematically slipping off to quiet places where she can recoup her strengths. Her mother or father may be a significant factor in her life even through her adult years so if you find her "going home to mother" as regularly as the world turns, don't be offended. She loves you but she's also into roots and hers run long and deep. You'll have to learn to accept her family and recognize her need for solitude. When she needs either one, she won't be totally with you. But then she never really is. She is difficult for you to grasp; someone elusive, mystifying, even when she's climbing mountains or building skyscrapers.

Active aggression is not her style. She has an independence about her, no question about that, but it's not threatening. She seems to say to you, come take care of me . . . if you can. The break in the message is what trips you up. You are in such a hurry when you hear the first encouraging words that you never hear the last three. Then, when you've bitten—hook, line and sinker—you're out of the fire and into the frying pan.

But if she's the cook, you surely won't mind. Because if she does—cook, that is—she's going to do it with the same finese that characterizes all her actions. No greasy hamburgers and french fries for her lover. Au contraire, mon cher. She's a graduate of Le Cordon Bleu and La Varenne in Paris, and she'll convert you from flounder a la skillet over the campfire to Fillet of Flounder Veronique over the campfire. You'd be amazed at how expertly she can pack butter, wine, grapes, English wedgewood and Austrian crystal. But don't get excited. That's only if she likes to cook.

Her interest in food might have been prompted by childhood games in which health played a major role. She probably envisioned herself as a medical missionary in the wilds of a sweltering jungle and the little boy next door was the native hunter who had just been attacked by an army of soldier ants. She attended his tiny red wounds and recited passages from Goethe's *Faust*. One must save the soul along with the body. Somehow she escaped with her skin in tact when her mother discovered a trail of sugar from the back yard, across the porch and into the kitchen where her little daughter had set up ant traps to capture them alive. The screams from the playmate upstairs further corroborated her mother's fears. Her Sixteen Child liked realism but, for some unfathomable reason, the playmate objected to live ants crawling over his body.

In her teens, she developed an interest in behavioral sciences, most likely because of the strange way her playmate turned out. She always was willing to listen to a friend's problem and then help them figure out a solution.

If she has a predilection for sports, she'll be right there beside you at the Celtics game, on the home court, of course, cheering the tall boys on. She'll know every player's number, height, weight, sports record, number of marriages and children and what they regularly eat for breakfast. She's nothing if she isn't thorough.

There is a part of her that enjoys business too. Accounting I, II and III may be your idea of a lost weekend, but she finds it an exercise in mental discipline and a good outlet for her patient, persistent and analytical mind. But she's more apt to find greater rewards in the ants—oops, that's arts and professions where those same qualities will set her work apart from others.

If she applies herself to research, she will not be nose-to-microscope in an isolated setting but rather out in the field where she can mingle with life in its personal aspects. Her research will involve her in the social mores and relationships of groups of people where the I-want-to-get-personal-at-arm's-length side of her nature can be satisfied. Margaret Mead, American anthropologist born on the 16th, published many classic works on interactions within groups. After expeditions to Samoa, New Guinea and Bali, she made a study of infant and child care and sexual and adolescent behavior. During World War II she was executive secretary of the committee on food habits of the National Research Council and she served as president of the World Federation for Mental Health. The Sixteen Woman's childhood interests in body and mind keep popping up.

Don't think for a moment she's not interested in your body and mind. She has a sense of responsibility toward humanity but you're a part of her humanity—a big part. She has destroyed your stereotyped ideas about women and taught you that intelligence can be exciting. She brings flowers, music, grace and love into your life and teaches you to find beauty in a buttercup and love in a cup of hot soup. Home is in her heart but she won't let you forget that heaven is in her eyes. She is the eternal female, gentle and loving, yet unfathomable in her enduring strengths. She is a woman and an individual, and wants you to accept her as both.

16

The Sixteen Man

Regardless of what your Sixteen Man says, as far as brains go, an ant has him beat. In proportion to its body, that little creature has the largest brain of all animals—that's not to say your man is an animal, quite the contrary. Among his own species, your man has a mind as sharp as a prickly pear cactus. He's alert and observant. Not much gets past him. He'll notice your plucked eyebrows, the change in your shade of nylons and the three pounds you've lost since Monday. That's very flattering but he can take it to extremes. Like noticing your broken fingernail and that the glue that's holding the false one in place is showing under your polish. The back of your skirt's a bit wrinkled. Of course, it's not *that* bad, if you want to keep your back to the wall at the party but if not, well, you probably ought to either iron it or change into something more pressed and presentable. Much more of this and you begin to feel you've just come out of the tumble dry cycle. Really, there are some things he could just as easily overlook.

But that's his M.O. He's super observant and he drifts toward perfectionism. (He picked you, didn't he!) Thinking about it, however, "drifts" toward perfectionism isn't quite the appropriate phrase. Maybe something more like "thunders" toward or "tidal waves" toward or... The truth is he personifies perfectionism. He prefers to think of himself as the better half of the Odd Couple, and he will state carefully, in order to clarify the difference for you, that he is not Oscar.

There is a serious side to this man regardless of his profession or outward appearance. He is a thinker, with a deep "analytical" mind that can concentrate long and heavily. No, that's not a misspelling. His mind is a combination of analytical and mystical. And if you're confused about that, you can believe he is too. He is extremely psychic—he has "hunches," "feelings,"—but because he is so analytical and wants to reason everything out to the nth degree, he confuses himself. This is the guy who approaches the metaphysical section of the bookstore as if the Bubonic plague lurked behind every cover. He's drawn to these books, there's no question about it. But to watch him select them, you'd think he was buying margarine instead of butter. Someone might see him. He takes them home, wrapped in plain brown wrappers, and in the night when everyone else is asleep, he pulls them out from under his side of the mattress and reads them by flashlight in the hall closet. You can always tell when he's done this. The next morning, he'll walk a bit stiffly and keep arching his back. The hall closet's small.

Of course, when a guy has to sleep diagonally on a king-sized bed, he won't have to hide his books at all. Kareem Abdul-Jabbar (Lew Alcindor), basketball star for the Lakers, sleeps diagonally across his bed. At seven-foot-three, he's got a choice? This Sixteen Man is more than poetry in motion. He recognizes his "analystical" mind when he makes statements such as: "I can do something else besides stuff a ball through a hoop. My biggest resource is my mind." He not only has a B.A. from UCLA, a journalism major—the analytical side—, but he converted from Catholicism to the black orthodox Hanafi sect, thus his name change, and bought a mosque in Washington, D.C. for his church—the mystical side. However, one wouldn't care to argue with him about what kind of books he reads in bed.

The subtle things in life appeal to your Sixteen Man. He loves nature, and living in the suburbs or the country is almost a necessity for his health and well-being. Although home and family are important to him, another necessity, he needs time by himself to meditate, think and generally sort out his moods and feelings. Subtle things affect him, things that you might not be aware of, so he needs your understanding when he withdraws for three years. He tends to concentrate so hard on a thought or issue, that you often have to remind him to come up for air.

Although protective of his family and loved ones, there is something of the lone wolf in him. However, in the Seven family (7, 16, 25), he tends to be the lover of the group. And speaking of families, everything's relative. He's certainly not Don Juan, flaunting his sexuality. On the contrary, he has a subtle magnetism that, in spite of his natural aloofness, draws you toward him. One minute you're here, then like Jonathan Livingston Seagull, the next minute, you're there, in his cool arms, experiencing the delights of a refreshing rain shower on a hot, sultry summer's day.

He dispenses his emotions discriminatingly. He's not the type you'd classify as falling in love head-over-heels. Rather he leans toward affection selectively. But a little of his leaning can make up for a lot of some other man's falling. With him, you don't have to pick up the pieces. If there's any picking up to do, it will be just one big spot. Neater that way. With your Sixteen Man, you know you're getting true value for your dollar.

Speaking of money, he likes it. Not for the power it brings but for the beauty and order it can create in his life and in the lives of those he cares about. He may like personal adornment, fine wines and foods, as do Liberace and Peter Ustinov, or he may spend his time and greenbacks in raising money for special charities, as Jerry Lewis does. There is a generous loving side to your Sixteen Man although it's sometimes hidden under layers of armadillo skin. Your man tends to dispense his desires to serve in personal ways—to family, friends or a specific charity where he feels closely involved with the cause, rather than scattering his resources through many charities and causes where he remains an anonymous entity. He wants to nurture and see his cause through to the end, then enjoy the satisfaction that results from his personal involvement—although he'll do it at arm's length. He doesn't want to get too close.

Liberace is known for the gifts he lavishes on friends. He also has a sweet tooth and loves to cook. But he remained aloof from the early criticisms of his "saccharin delivery" and cried "all the way to the bank." He now jokes that the bank to which he went crying, he now owns. Ustinov is an oenophile—a lover and connoisseur of wines. He's also involved with UNICEF (United Nation's Children's Fund)—here's the home issue—and UNESCO (The United Nation's Educational, Scientific and Cultural Organization)—this is a combination of the nurturing and the thinking. Ustinov's first love is writing so that automatically places him in the category of lone wolf. Jerry Lewis is known for his Muscular Dystrophy telethon, for marathon fund-raising along with his acting career. He has a strong love for these for marathon fund-raising along with his acting career. He has a strong love for these handicapped children even though, off stage, he is hard to understand, a chronic worrier. All three men have strong nurturing tendencies along with an aloof demeanor.

Your Sixteen Man must guard against becoming irritable, moody and depressed. He tends to become so involved in what he's doing, that it can absorb him like a giant science-fiction sponge that falls into a swimming pool. Before you know it, slurp, and he's gone, off to some analystical world where logic and magic try to meet.

He can become most frustrated when he doesn't live up to his own standards. He's always regretted that he wasn't born permanent press and equipped with a correcting tape like an IBM Selectric. If his obsession with perfection isn't obvious in his personal dress code and his environment then it surely will surface in his attitude toward his work. When his mind is working at peak efficiency, he has the power to penetrate thick walls of the most complicated problems and zero in on the target area with the accuracy of a hungry eagle after a hare. Then, with the precision of a skilled surgeon, he'll cut out the offending intrusion and stitch up the incision with such care that you'd have to look closely to know he'd been there. You won't find graffiti on his walls. He takes pride in his work so he'll leave no tell-tale mess. Clean, efficient and well-done are his trade marks.

Although well-ordered now, he probably had a confused and emotional childhood. He was professionally precocious and began to wonder at an early age whether he wanted to open a restaurant and feed the body, start a university and feed the mind or found a church and feed the soul. That's why he set up a lemonade stand in the library of the church. Notes from the cleric to his parents were followed by telephone calls, then personal consultations. Even his psychiatrist ended up babbling over his Rorschak tests.

By the time he reached his teens, he had a sense of his own destiny. Timing was the key. A sense of the social mind and its needs was also a consideration. Putting them together, he discovered he could creatively capture the mood of his audience either through laughter, drama or second guessing his adversaries. Look what he did to his psychiatrist.

Today, as an adult, he has blended the ingredients of his complex personality and become a master of subtleties, nuances, the slightest shift in mood, so that you're as helpless as a declawed kitten when his radar is on. Look what he did to the church and his psychiatrist, not to mention his parents. They're still on their knees making recompense.

He knows your every hidden response. You can't fool him.

"Yes, I really do want to attend the conference on Heisenberg's Uncertainty Theory," you say. You really don't. You hate uncertainty but you love him and you know he wants to go.

"I can tell you don't want to go," he says, shaking his head as if he thinks anyone who would miss a chance to hear about Heisenberg's Uncertainty Theory must have mush for brains. He tries to be kind.

"It's O.K. I don't mind going alone." That's half true.

"I really want to go," you reply, trying to put some conviction in your voice.

"Look, darling," he says. "Just admit it. I really don't mind."

16

He throws you a kiss and off he goes. Maybe you should have gone. The lecture might have given you a few clues on how to dispel your own uncertainty whenever you're with your Sixteen Man.

His recognition of other people's body language allows him to recreate their mannerisms. He is a wonderful mime, and can have everyone in stitches if he applies himself to comedy. In France, Jerry Lewis is idolized as a comedy-genius second only to the great Charlie Chaplin who, by the way, was also born on the 16th. Lewis and Chaplin, along with Ustinov, are great mimes. If your Sixteen Man is of a more serious note, his ability to recognize the subtleties of specific personalities produces a dramatic artist such as Eugene O'Neill or Oscar Wilde, both Sixteen Men.

Your Sixteen Man is truly inventive. Necessity is the mother of invention and he's not only into motherhood—he probably either sees or calls his mother six times a week—but he's also into inventing things to make the world a more beautiful and balanced place in which to live. The things he invents will have a touch of class. Like a hair dryer that plays music. An advertising slogan might run: Blow dry your hair while you blow your mind, or Flip your follicles while you bop.

Well, you've flipped more than your follicles over this mind-blowing mass of manhood. He's lovable, kind and caring, and occasionally aloof, mysterious and unapproachable, sometimes all at the same time. He'll treat you like a princess, secure you in his ivory tower, then go off and forget you're there—unintentionally and only for a short time—and when he comes back to earth, he's kneeling at your feet, full of phrases that he had to have stolen from the gods. So that's where he's been all this time. Yes, he's part mystic and part man. One luxurious night with him will demonstrate both.

The Seventeen Woman

Your Seventeen Woman may utter a provocative, "Why don't you come up and see me some time," but you'd better believe that she'll pick the time and the place. This isn't your stereotypical female who sits passively and helplessly by the wayside, awaiting the favors and direction of a strong, divinely shaped hero. She's made her own decisions up to now and is perfectly capable of continuing to do so. Oh, she'll be impressed by your well-exercised muscles—she's into health and the body—but don't try the muscles out on her unless you want to end up rather badly twisted. She has some pretty good moves of her own. That black belt she wears is not for decorative purposes. She earned it.

Exercise not only keeps her physically fit but it stimulates her mind. You look pale. Are you alright? Yes, she has a mind. All that and she can think too. Well, she considers it an advantage and if you don't, then you're not right for her. Beauty and brains are a powerful combination, as you're soon to find out if this is the first Seventeen Woman you've ever encountered.

You see, she wants something more from a man than a wide-through-the-shoulders, narrow-through-the-hips type. On second thought, can she change her mind? No, she wouldn't really. Oh, she'll happily take the above package if it can converse with her. She appreciates and admires a beautiful body but if that's all she needed, she could buy a paper doll that she could call her own. However, don't be surprised if a full length Burt Reynolds centerfold adorns the back of her bedroom door.

17

You found yourself staring at her, and how. She has tremendous magnetism, and you can bet that when she's pushing eighty, she'll still be magnetizing you and probably every other man with operating twenty-twenty. She's in the same category as Mae West and Lena Horne. Born in 1892, Mae West, voluptuous sex symbol of stage and screen, was honored by the World War II GI's when they called their inflatable life jackets "Mae Wests." Her hour glass figure and roles as a dubious-virtued, flippantly good-natured siren brought her enduring fame. Into her eighties, she was still considered a "glamorous presence." Lena Horne, in 1978 at the age of sixty, was chosen one of the most beautiful women in the world by *Harper's Bazaar*, along with Farrah Fawcett and Elizabeth Taylor. Her sultry sensuality reaches beyond age. Beneath the torrid femininity, Mae West exuded, as does Lena Horne, a determined strength and a cool aloofness.

Your Seventeen Woman can remain cool during the most alarming experiences. She's good to have around in an emergency. When everyone else is running around not knowing what to do, she's having her finest hour. She has staying power and would make an excellent doctor or nurse.

Leaping before looking is not her idea of forward motion. She is going to take one well-deliberated step at a time so don't rush her. It doesn't matter that the auctioneer is on the "going, going" part, about to sell that nineteenth-century print you've wanted for seventeen years. She's got her forefinger raised at you as she calmly says, "Now, wait a minute, honey. Are you sure you want to spend five hundred dollars on this?" She is conservative. "Maybe you ought to think about it for a moment." You don't want to think about it for half a moment. You've been thinking about it for seventeen years. At this point, you've bitten your nails to the quick and are working on the knuckles. You open your mouth to protest as the gavel resounds a final sold! Your body goes limp. You'd cry but that might lead to more demonstrative expressions of your frustration like rolling on the ground and screaming, and she'd never understand that. Five minutes later, the auctioneer's assistant calls you aside to say that the winning bidder changed his mind and since the gentleman is a good customer and they don't want to embarrass or antagonize him, would you like to purchase the print at your last bid of four hundred dollars? You look at your Seventeen Woman who is smiling straight ahead as if at some invisible Marx Brothers movie.

Maybe you will scream. She would deny that she's into crystal-gazing, but you're very suspect on that point. She's always wearing that thirty inch chain around her neck with a crystal dangling on the end. You've always thought it looked a bit incongruous with her black belt but now a pattern is beginning to form. She has the radar-like ability to focus in on what people are thinking about—usually practical things like business and money, and wherever she decides to use her creative talents, you can be sure the greenbacks will roll in. It's a natural phenomenon with her.

If you come home to find her in her bentwood, rocking like a tenacious metronome, gazing glassy-eyed across the kitchen, not noticing that the potatoes are boiling over on the stove, the puppy's just wet on the linoleum and your little one is splashing barefoot through the puddle, don't scream. If you did all the screaming you'd like to, you'd have a very sore throat and also raise some speculations about your stability. You must keep in mind that this woman of yours is very inventive and she's probably on the verge of discovering a better mousetrap. So, who needs a better mousetrap? Not you perhaps, but millions of other people would be willing to pay $3.98 for a neat, fool-proof method that keeps the little creatures from dying in inaccessible spots between the walls. It's also cheaper than four dollars a week for cat food and fifty-dollars-at-a-whack veterinary bills. Beginning to sound interesting? So, let her think. Turn off the burner, wipe up the floor and wash the baby's feet. This time by herself will keep her busy and maybe she'll forget about her nightly Kung-Fu classes. It's always been a problem for you to explain to business associates why your Seventeen Woman likes to kick people at night.

But she won't kick you unless you get out of line. Relationships are important to your Seventeen Woman. They form the foundation of her life. When she was a tot, she probably had two friends with whom she did everything. She liked small groups because she was timid and shy. Or at least, a bit cautious in reaching out to others. She also had chores and though she'd complain like every other child, she somehow felt more responsibility toward her duties than most.

In her teens, your Seventeen Woman began to blossom somewhat, though she was still cautious in relationships. But others began to sense her intelligence and ability to handle affairs so she may have been president of school clubs and organizations. Sports also interested her either as a player or spectator. She's always admired a good pair of strong legs. She's got a good pair herself, as you've probably already noticed.

Her loyalties remained with her early friends and today, as an adult, she probably still writes, calls or visits them. After all, they are a part of her past, her roots and her security. She's into such things as traditions because the past has been proven reliable. One can count on it to repeat itself. She'll quote statistics until you think she's a human computer. She places great value on facts because they help her separate the wheat from the chaff. Now you know why your house has threshing floors. She's a seeker after knowledge and if circumstances don't permit her to use her mind, if she allows "responsibilities" to interfere with the refining of her mind, she will always regret it. She knows that it is one of her greatest resources.

Her ability to think can put her well-ahead of others in her field. She has good judgment and can manage the finances of family or the business affairs of others with good common sense and often with great success. As a rule, she's conservative with cash but she has her wild and crazy moments. If she comes home with a ton of coal and your house runs on oil, don't be shocked and chagrined. Remember her inventiveness. Coal and diamonds are made of the identical element—carbon. Now, there's a technique you could call a better mousetrap. No matter how difficult her finances become, she always manages to find a source of income, usually quite substantial.

For one thing, she can find help because she probably knows people in high places. No, not flag-pole-sitters and high-rise window-washers. You'd better be careful that your sarcasm doesn't cut off your allowance. Not only will her business acumen stand her in good stead during financial crises but she invariably knows that one person who just happens to be the head of that company that dominates the field

17

she's into. Birds of a feather flock together so she cultivates people like herself who have a homing instinct when it comes to success. She's not a name dropper, regardless of those little letters scattered around her feet. She really does know the people she talks about. You'd better not laugh because, with friends like Harry Reasoner, you could end up on "Sixty Minutes" with more than your bare face hanging out.

There is a Seventeen Woman who doesn't know her own strengths. Because of past conditionings, she can feel bound and limited by circumstances, afraid to reach out and grab a hunk of life. Her natural caution and need for security degenerates into fear of not having; therefore, she clings to what she has, meager though it may be, with all the fervor of an overpossessive mother. She limits her horizons because she believes nothing more is possible for her. But once she latches on to her self-confidence and realizes the mountains she is capable of climbing, you won't see her moving for the dust. She'll be off like a herd of mountain goats—proud, confidant and sure-footed, singing, "If they could see me now."

Your Seventeen Woman has a serious, thoughtful nature. There is little danger of her being classified as a superficial entity. Even if she is a glamorous queen, people will sense a deep mystery about her that is not easily identifiable. She has a strong link to her subconscious mentality that prompts her to investigate the unseen, to discover the secrets of the unknown. Her natural intelligence needs quiet moments of meditation or seclusion in which her reservoir of mind stuff can be contacted. She seeks an inner light.

Marian Anderson, black American contralto, knows such a light. On Easter Sunday in 1939, she was scheduled to perform at Constitution Hall in Washington, D.C., but the Daughters of the American Revolution would not allow her to sing there. Ms. Anderson's friend, Eleanor Roosevelt, resigned her membership in the DAR, and made arrangements for the singer to perform at the Lincoln Memorial. One biographer said: "Her voice, her dignity, her acceptance of her responsibility not to bend under horrendous circumstances...to stand on the steps of the Lincoln Memorial and sing in an atmosphere of hate. Where did she find the strength?" Ms. Anderson's repertoire usually includes Southern spirituals. Her depth of tone and feeling moves listeners of all backgrounds.

But you'll appreciate those qualities in her when the world is tumbling down around your head, when everything you do seems to come to naught, when you feel like one big cipher wandering around in a world of definite values. She'll imbue you with a knowledge of your true worth and inspire you to go forth to conquer the world. What else can you do? Each morning you leave the house to find your white steed saddled—actually it's a Volkswagen idling rather noisily—the family colors planted on the front lawn—or is that your high school sweater flapping in the breeze—and the neighbor children—whom she hired—lined up blowing those rather long horns. She believes in tradition and perseverance and the simple values in life but she's not above using a bit of ostentation if it will accomplish her purpose. If she loves you, you are her purpose and her life, and she will support you with every ounce of her considerable intelligence and strength. And a woman's intelligence is nothing to fool around with. Keep in mind that she's had centuries to nurture it underground thus imbueing it with unbelievable strength, and now that the age of Aquarius is dawning, she is in the process of emerging as an—hold your breath and gasp—intelligent being! And all these years you thought she was merely beautiful.

The Seventeen Man

So, your man is a Seventeen, you lucky woman. You must have done something right! He's got it all. He's charismatic, ambitious, courageous, vital, intelligent and wealthy. He isn't? Well, if he isn't now, he soon will be—wealthy, that is. You know he's already all the rest.

The motivating force behind your Seventeen Man is the drive for success. He wants to be at the top. He knows power and how to use it, and since it comes so naturally to him, it won't be long before he's in that elevated position. He's not prone to nose bleeds, shortness of breath and lack of vitality as are other men who can't tolerate the rarified atmosphere at his height. On the contrary, he moves in that atmosphere with ease and grace. He was born to be there.

Your Seventeen Man is such a natural leader that others automatically look to him for direction. He'll find himself in the limelight whether he wants to be there or not, and often he likes the power but not the spotlight. Regardless of his hesitation, he is invariably the one chosen to be the spokesman for the group. If he takes to wearing turtle necks and dark glasses, you'll know the light is getting too bright but notice he never takes off his leather gloves. He's always in the driver's seat whether it's under the noonday sun or the moon at midnight.

Part of the reason for his success is his mind. Gillette should know his secret. His mind is honed as sharp as a razor twenty-four hours a day. When he's in a sound sleep, sawing logs like a dedicated lumberjack, all you have to do is whisper, "Did you hear that the prime rate dropped five percent this morning?" and he'll leap from the bed and race to the nearest telephone with all the dispatch of a Bache broker. On second thought, he won't have to leap. Chances are he has installed a telephone within arm's reach of his side of the bed. There's probably one in the bathroom, too. If you decide to wake him in this decidedly annoying manner, you'd better have a pretty good reason for it. He takes business seriously.

Get used to telephones ringing at all hours of the day and night because, no matter what career your Seventeen Man chooses for himself, he'll have wide-reaching influence. Monarchs, presidents, prime ministers, sheiks, stock market brokers and heads of international business chains may call him for advice and counsel. Some will forget that the time changes four minutes for every one degree of longitude and when they're talking from a distance of 180 degrees of longitude, that's twelve hours on one side or the other of your alarm clock, and at two in the morning, you may be asleep. Try to be polite. A string of prize camels tethered to the driveway lamppost of your quiet residential street may be your reward.

Even if your Seventeen Man chooses art as a profession, he'll always be interested in the business side of it. He has such an acute business acumen that he can handle his career better than an agent.

The public senses your Seventeen Man's ability to make wise fiscal decisions. It's hard to ignore a Lumbergini, a BMW, silk suits and a villa in Naples. This is the fellow who last year started a hot dog stand at the beach and worked seven days a week to make ends meet, and he did it on his own! He has an instinct, an inner understanding that he would find difficult to explain. He knows when to fight and when discretion is the better part of valor. He has insight and foresight and the

17

courage to carry his plans through once he has made a decision. John Jacob Astor, born July 17, 1763, left Germany at age sixteen to come to America. His first job was selling musical instruments in New York City. He later developed the fur trade which Lewis and Clark's expedition to the west coast had opened up for transcontinental trade. However, his greatest investment was buying large tracts of land on Manhattan Island, far beyond the city limits. This wise purchase secured his family's fortune. Astor was "a business organizer of extraordinary energy, range and foresight, and he died the richest man in the United States, with an estimated fortune of $10 million." You might want to tuck two other Seventeen Men in here as well—J.P. Morgan, Sr. and Montgomery Ward.

Now, that's encouraging. It would take care of the MasterCard bill too. It also brings up another point. To say your Seventeen Man has energy is to put it mildly. He's a whirling dervish in a business suit. He can come across as cool as a cucumber on a cloudy day but you'd better believe that under his conservative threads there beats the heart of a well-trained Kung Fu black belt. If the occasion arises, he can perform mental side-kicks and spinning-round-kicks with the agility of a cat. Even when his temperature's normal, he's running on all eight cylinders.

Don't let your Seventeen Man get too puffed up. There is another aspect to the Seventeen type. Evel Knievel and Al Capone represent the shrewd Seventeen Man of power and energy. These are clever men who crave the attention of others, and stop at nothing to get it. Capone controlled a city and Knievel commands the attention of millions of viewers as he performs his motorcycle stunts on national television. All three used their instincts to put them in power positions.

A Seventeen Man must be alert so that, in his drive to the top, he doesn't trample people underfoot. He can do it with great finesse because he has the intelligence and agility to move quickly when outwitting less clever associates. He must apply his principles of loyalty and honesty to business just as he does to family and friends.

Your Seventeen Man has high principles in all areas of his life but he seeks truth in his own way. You'll never find him in a loin cloth with a shaved pate—unless he can make a profit at it—and seldom find him having his palm read or his numerological chart done. In fact, the Seventeen Man was almost not written because he probably won't read it. But then, you will, so, at the last minute, it was included. However, you never know. He might take a peek. The point is that your man tends to be more materially inclined, demanding proof in all matters. He suspects things that are non-material. This is the type of man you can find in the bank, law office or brokerage. Background training for these jobs does not include courses in mysticism, the stars or ommmming, and one wonders how much business they'd pull in if their shingles displayed moons and stars. Although Vidal Sassoon hasn't done too badly with his interest in yoga and meditation, and one recently deceased, successful commodities expert left charts with tiny astrological glyphs scattered over the zig-zaggedy lines. But if your Seventeen Man is going to do that, he certainly won't advertise it.

There is a mysterious side to this man. He's short on conversation when it comes to his personal life and feelings but he's so sensible and trustworthy that, when you first meet him, you find you've told him your life's story, down to and including the part where you got that little scar on your navel. All the while, he's leaning back in his chair, slowly puffing on a pipe, and he hasn't told you his first name. You're not likely to find out either unless you've got a good reason. Well, you'll probably find out because he was drawn to you right at the beginning. But he doesn't kiss on the first date.

Your Seventeen Man may be the strong, silent type. There are a few strong and not-so-silent types also but usually a Seventeen Man is more laid back and observant. Rock Hudson and the late William Holden exemplify the strong, silent Seventeen Man. Hudson is described as calm, articulate and semi-reclusive; Holden was soft-spoken, polite and avoided the Hollywood scene. Their financial success kept pace with their professional success, and both skyrocketed over the years. You see what walking softly can do.

Speaking of walking softly, your Seventeen Man probably does. Or jogs or lifts weights or plays baseball or racketball. His concern for tangible items includes his body and he spends time keeping it in shape.

Since physical strength often shows up in this number, it is not surprising to find athletes here. Men who can think, are clever in business and inclined toward making megabucks. Here you find thinking, business-minded stars like Tom Seaver who has his B.S. in dentistry and has endorsed "everything from Sears menswear to Phillips 66." For pure strength, there's Paul Anderson, known as the world's strongest man, who in 1955 lifted 6,270 pounds on his back—more weight than anyone in history. Once an athlete's playing career is over, he is often drawn to business because it's a perfect arena for expressing the power urges that drive him. He's usually very good at it. Can you see anyone slamming their door in the face of an encyclopedia salesman like Paul Anderson. He'd pull their house from its foundation and toss it into next Tuesday and not twist a teeny muscle.

But your Seventeen Man doesn't have to use strong-arm tactics because he's a smooth talker. It all started when he was very, very young. He did sell his parent's house twice and pocket the difference but he got into a bit of trouble. It seems his title wasn't clear.

He was out of jail by the time he entered his teens and he'd decided to play the game according to Hoyle. He wasn't deliberately dishonest. It's just that he failed to read the fine print. What do you want from a grade school kid? In high school, he learned, and became an achiever either in the classroom or in the sports arena. He had so much drive that he needed an outlet for it.

You notice he made it and aren't you glad. Today, your Seventeen Man has strong ties to family and close friends, in spite of the fact that his parents took his real estate proceeds away. He is steadfast and loyal, and always willing to lend a helping hand. You need four hours and another pair of strong hands to move your player piano up three flights to your new apartment, he'll be there. If he can't for one reason or another, he'll hire someone to help you. Although he is basically conservative, he has a generous side and can do extravagantly crazy things at times. Not that helping you move a three-thousand-pound piano up three narrow flights of stairs is crazy. Wait a minute, maybe he knows Paul Anderson. Then your prize piece would be safe. Three thousand pounds. That's only half what Anderson's lifted. And you wouldn't want your piano crashing down three flights of stairs, not after the beautiful finishing job you did on it.

Losing friends would affect your Seventeen Man. He is sensitive when it comes to his feelings, although most people will never know it because he comes

17

across as confidant and in control, which he is when he's dealing with the public. But when he's with you, he'll let as much of himself hang out as he possibly can, given his character. He'll never reveal himself completely but he will be able to release his feelings more easily.

That's the fun of him. Remember, he's a "tangible" person. He has to know things are real. He wants to see and touch and taste. Now, apply these needs toward your relationship with him and, with a little imagination, you can entertain some very interesting encounters with your wonderful Seventeen Man.

The Eighteen Woman

You've got a date with an Eighteen Woman and you want some advice, right? Well, first of all, what you see is not all you're going to get. There's much more to her than the surface suggests. That's not to say there's anything wrong with the surface. On the contrary, it's extremely well laid out but if you want to maintain a grip on your mind and reality in this relationship, you'd better acquaint yourself with the facts.

She is a powerhouse. She's the kind of woman who can wear ribbons and lace or denims and T-shirts and still command a formidable presence. You know when she's walked into the room. Curves in her life are more than part of her anatomy. She's intimately familiar with those undulating lines as they move over graphs and charts indicating the inclinations of the public mind. But she's interested in more than fashionable trends. She will watch, then analyze, and her conclusions can affect the status of the Fortune 500.

It's your good fortune that she noticed you because, if she decides you're the one for her, she will move heaven and earth to support you and ensure your success in whatever field you choose. When her love is truly given, there is none more enduring or stable. She's a rock of Gibraltar with a tempting apple tree tucked off to one side. A little spice is nice, yes? You will become her hobby and her cause, and heaven help the unsuspecting or devious souls that step in your path. A lazer beam flash from her beautifully quiet eyes and they'll end up smoldering rubble at her feet. Opponents get the message. She's also been known to whip out that large rubber stamp that reads "Cancel," that she carries everywhere she goes, and plant it on unprepared foreheads, in indelible ink yet. Like cancelled checks, people who are not useful are disposed of. In a man, that quality would be deemed good business sense; in a woman, it's often construed as hardness. But your Eighteen Woman is far from hard. She is devoted, loving and compassionate, and her heart reaches out to the helpless and suffering in the world. She has her ideals and the strength to see them through so she'll stand tooth to fang with the most invincible forces. She's no weak sister.

Rosalynn Carter, former first lady, born on the 18th, is no stranger to power circles. With previous political experience behind her, in 1975 her "political skills were honed finely enough" for her to embark on a two-year journey through forty states to promote her husband's presidential campaign. Once in the White House, her influence was quiet but pervasive. On occasion, she was sent on solo missions with personal messages to the heads of foreign governments. Rosalynn's "overriding devotion to her husband and his political ambitions...earned her the title of 'the Steel Magnolia.' "

Yes, this is one woman who isn't going to fall all over herself to get your attention and then be thankful the rest of her life that you looked her way. She knows her true worth and she's proud of it. She'll stand tall and look you in the eye as an equal and if you can't stand the heat, you'd better get out of the kitchen. Although, there are no guarantees that she'll spend much time there herself. Oh, she can do it if she has a mind to—there isn't much she can't do when the spirit moves—but often her mind is far from Betty Crocker and copper-bottom pans. More likely it's focused on bears and bulls and the Dow Jones Industrial Average like Sylvia Porter, whose nationally syndicated newspaper column on economic advice has earned her the respect of business people, politicians, economists and the person on the street. Her new book, *Sylvia Porter's New Money Book for the 80's,* is designed to educate what she has called "a nation of economic illiterates."

Your Eighteen Woman has the need to invest in life. She has tremendous strength and discipline which you will find her expressing in some area of her world. She may pour that energy into relationships and family molds but you can be sure she'll be, not the mother of a family, but the matriach of a dynasty. It's inevitable because she is a pillar of strength and principles so it's only natural that family members cluster around her for advice, solace, reinforcement and protection. Not only can she be loving and compassionate but she can do it in a detached way so that her broad vision is not overrun by personal emotions. She knows what is good for the individual and the situation involved so she sets the proper wheels in motion, probably with a "This is going to hurt me more than it will you." An unbelievable line when you're at the wrong end of a long switch. Cosmic law is her guide; discipline and adherence to principles of right action are the rules that lead her to correct the problem. So, in her greater overview, she can dispense wise advice and counsel in spite of personal feelings.

She knows the paradoxical truth that only in discipline is there true freedom; that once you follow the rules, you no longer need them. But herein lies great temptation. She has the knowledge of human personality and the wisdom of greater good plus the everyday savy of the working mechanics of life. Outwitting less well-endowed individuals is no great feat. This is her test. Can she walk the fine line between the material world of money, glamor, negative sexuality and physical power, and the spiritual world of ethics, morality, positive sexuality and the greater good of all? The light dawns. That's why she's been out on that elevated one-by-three in the back yard in her ballet slippers, practicing her balance. You wouldn't mind except she's been drawing more attention that usual. Perhaps you could ask her not to carry those two inscribed stone tablets while she's balanced so precipitously eighteen feet above the ground. She might drop them—that's one way to break cosmic law—and you're not keen about having little gopher hole digs all over your carefully tended lawn.

You really can't get angry though. She has a way with words that has you at a disadvantage. She brings her wisdom right down to earth when she looks you straight in the eye and says, "Don't worry, darling. I'll have new turf laid if there's any problem." That means the one-by-three, the ballet slippers and the tablets are here to stay. But what can you say? She can pay for it. She has an absolute genius for ferreting out ways to make money. She's seldom without cash in her wallet or, at the very least, a source from which she can readily get it. Who is going to refuse her? She'll make them an offer they can't refuse. Besides, no one wants to walk around

18

with a cancel imprint on their forehead. Actually, the real reason she can raise funds so quickly is that people put trust in her ideas and plans. They know she is efficient, dependable and capable of handling large enterprises and sums of money. She works with tangibles, things you can see, touch and taste, so whether she's marketing her physical body—her looks, body discipline or health items—or a physical product—like money and how to best invest it—she will make it a lucrative venture.

She has a practical side. Surprise! You couldn't have guessed that by now, could you? She has her day organized from dawn's early light to the last flicker of the evening candle, and the work she packs away in between would stagger a sturdy elephant. You may need to participate in one of her recommended daily allowances—jogging, swimming, skiing, tennis—just to keep up with her. She manages to wedge some measure of exercise in between her daily appointments and duties because she knows a healthy body is necessary if she is to accomplish the many tasks she has set for herself.

You've learned not to argue with a woman who lifts weights. Besides, it would do no good. You have noticed, haven't you?, that she has a mind of her own. Ever tried to give her advice? No Advice. Buy yourself a pack of posters and a red magic marker and print in large, easy-to-read letters, NO ADVICE.

She won't get physically violent if you do give her advice, not most of the time anyway. Actually she is quite calm, controlled and self-possessed. It takes a lot for her to pop her cork and maybe once, every time Halley's comet returns, she does, whereupon she merits and will receive the same close attention.

When she uses this same passionate approach to life in your more intimate moments, you'll find you will forget about the daily lacerations. She knows the meaning of physical contact, and what's more, she really enjoys it. It satisfies the deeply sensual part of her, the part that knows that physical contact with the one you love is a communion with divinity. She has a highly developed spiritual side that others are not often aware of because of her seeming preoccupation with the physical. But it is in the physical that she finds her spirituality. She needs to take time off, to spend moments in nature, getting close to the earthy side of herself. Mother Nature will heal and regenerate her so that, back in the busy everyday world, she is able to reach, once again, for the stars.

There is a certain air of reserve, an in-built caution, in your Eighteen Woman. She's certainly not going to gush all over you or anyone. She handles affairs and relationships with loving but disciplined and thoughtful hands. Her first reaction is one of practicality and caution. A reporter interviewing John Lennon, shortly before his death, found John serving tea and cake while Yoko Ono, his wife and an Eighteen Woman, "labored for the Lennon enterprises in her office downstairs, recalling the lyric on their latest album: The Queen is in the counting home/Counting out the money/The King is in the kitchen/Making bread and honey." John had turned over the running of the business to her. When she returned, John fixed her tea and cake, asking how her day had gone. She had been up at 5:00 A.M. for her walk in Central Park. Yoko said: "I have learned that I have strengths too. I can use my talents." She uses them well, tending the Lennon business, worth more than two hundred million dollars.

There is an Eighteen Woman who is so defensive, that like the lobster, she enters her burrow tail first. Because she doesn't trust anyone, she ends up in an isolated position, cut off from friends and those who would be friends. Her insecurities are so great, she is afraid to reach out to the world for fear of attack or loss of what earthly possessions she has. She is unaware of her inner strengths.

But your woman knows her strengths. She has exercised them from childhood where she may have faced early responsibilities. Even if she were a happy child, she took life more seriously than most and saw duties where others did not. She probably didn't have much free time to play with her little friends. Running a health spa for grade schoolers took all her energies.

Through her teens the response to her physical power and magnetism convinced her that her destiny lay in broader pastures. She had a world to see, and she developed a longing to travel, to get in touch with other people, countries, ideas and cultures. She knew that something out there was waiting for her. Nights under a full moon did more than stimulate her amorous inclinations. Gazing at the star-sprinkled heavens, she wondered about life and its greater purpose and plan. She felt pulled out of herself toward a greater self. She may not have understood these feelings but they led to a greater understanding in adulthood where she approached her relationships and transactions with more depth and awareness.

The stars are still in the heavens; some are there in her eyes. She has become a pillar of pulchritude and prodigious accomplishment. If you had the hundred eyes of Argus, each one would follow her with intense desire and awe because she is magnificent, a wonder and a myth in her time. She has taught you a courage and steadfastness unmatched by lesser mortals. The spirit of matter and the spirit of divinity meet in her. She has invested her all in this life, and you are privileged to be a part of her experience. Buckle your seat belt. You're about to blast off on a cosmic journey. Your Eighteen Woman will make Haley's comet appear as a mere flash in the eye of God.

The Eighteen Man

There's no question about it. Your Eighteen Man is the greatest, and when one is as superb as he is, it's hard to be humble so don't expect him to be. He knows his self-worth and places great value there. Positive thinking is a way of life with him so if you see him wandering about the world shouting, "I am the greatest!" don't be surprised. He believes it—we learn through repetition and God knows he's said it often enough—and chances are everyone else believes it as well.

By now you've guessed who else was born on the eighteenth. Right. Cassius Clay, now known as Muhammad Ali, and it's hard to deny that he is the greatest because Eighteen Men have such a universal appeal. They are so believable. Part of your Eighteen Man's believability is that he genuinely cares. He is compassionate and understanding and has a sense of his responsibility to the physical needs of the world. He understands earthly values—the need for money, relationships, home and family, career, status—as well as comprehending the necessity of working with but rising above them so as not to become their prisoner. Your Eighteen Man's everyday actions are motivated by his search for these true values in life and until he comes to understand this aspect of himself, he cannot find true happiness. He needs to live and give beyond himself.

Like Paul McCartney, a member of the Nine Family (18 = 1 + 8 = 9) to which his partner and co-writer, the Nine Man John Lennon, also belonged, your Eighteen

18

Man may know power as a test of his sense of values. "Will Success spoil Rock Hunter?" or will your man use his power, money and influence to create a symbol and send out a message of universal caring and concern." Wings" is an appropriate symbolic name for former Beatle Paul McCartney's new group because wings is what an Eighteen Man needs to rise above the world and its temptations for a cosmic overview of the real purpose of life.

Your Eighteen Man has power, there's no question about that either, and he knows how to use it. He must exercise discipline in his life so that he uses this power wisely and is not manipulated by it. He becomes an example for others to follow because his influence is so wide-reaching. He cannot hide his light under a pile of gold bars—although security is an issue with him—because he is a "man for all seasons," "all things to all men." He is a symbol of achievement and success coupled with wisdom and love, the best of both worlds.

Although he may spend a lot of time in the cosmos like John Glenn, Jr. and Alan Shephard, don't think you've got an angel on your hands. Your Eighteen Man has feet of clay. He's into his senses and may experiment with much of the world's deceiving glamour before he's through. He can be tempted to believe that power is an almighty god and he must fight daily to keep his feet on the narrow path between the extremes of materialism and spirituality. He needs to understand that he cannot live exclusively in one with no awareness of the other. He must keep his feet on earth and his head in the heavens.

There may be times when you think those feet have been grounded in cement. Try to give him advice. Remember, this is the man who dropped out of college because he figured he knew more than his professors. He's not conceited, he'll tell you, those are just the facts. Far be it for you to argue. He has a mind of his own—a very good mind as a matter of fact. Muhammad Ali made the statement, "I'm not just a boxer. I'm very intelligent." Your Eighteen Man, like Ali, has a native intelligence which is a far cry from intellect. Intelligence is wisdom whereas intellect is knowledge. A man can be knowledgable but not necessarily wise. Chances are your man is a combination of both.

Your Eighteen Man will have a life which will test both his strength and his wisdom. He is up to the task because he is courageous and unafraid to roll up his shirt sleeves and put his shoulder to the wheel. He may be physically strong, as many Eighteens are, but his strength is merely a means to an end. His purpose is to set an example in right living. A fine example of an Eighteen Man is Pope John Paul II, at fifty-eight the youngest Pope in 132 years, the first non-Italian in 455 years and the first Polish Pope ever. He is adept at skiing, volleyball, swimming and canoeing. He loves to sing and joke with his colleagues. His daily schedule is exhausting, up at 5:00 A.M., literally rolling up his shirt sleeves at his desk. He has such universal, down-to-earth qualities that although his choice delighted, it also stunned the world. Here was a Pope to whom people could relate. It was time for a bridge between the secular and religious communities.

Your Eighteen Man has the inexhaustible strength, drive and zest for life that would challenge the endurance of Atlas, the ambitions of Mars and the appetites of Zeus himself. He needs a life that is full and active so he can exercise his many talents. He loves travel and change, and must be ready at all times to adapt to both in his experiences. You'd better too, if you plan to spend any time at all with him. It can be disconcerting, to say the least, to plan an intimate evening for two in the basement of that cozy Italian restaurant with the fine wine and the wandering minstrels—you know he's going to pop the question—and you've just bought a silky little thing to wear that cost two weeks pay, only to find yourself a few hours later on a plane to Buffalo bound for his high school hockey team's ninth reunion. It was rather exciting, however. Cary Grant and Reggie Jackson stopped by to say hello. Eighteen Men do stick together.

By now you know he could charm the skin off a snake and talk his way out of a paper bag. He has the gift of oratory, a great force behind his ability to reason. He shares this "way with words" with two other Eighteen Men, Peter Roget, surgeon of note and author of *Roget's Thesaurus of English Words and Phrases,* and Daniel Webster, statesman and orator, who debated and won over the greatest opponent of humankind—the devil. Though *The Devil and Daniel Webster* was a fictional account of a debate between Mr. Webster and Satan himself, the story nevertheless reflected the public's opinion of Webster's great persuasive and oratorical talents.

Your Eighteen Man may love to debate and argue. He has a fondness for using his keen perceptions in matters that exercise his mind. He usually takes very good care of his body and, seeking balance, puts his mind through systematic workouts as well. But rather than spend isolated hours studying for his own satisfaction, he prefers to use his accumulated wisdom in an exchange with an opponent in a, hopefully, friendly debate or detached exchange of political or philosophical views. However he approaches it, you can be sure he will be heard.

Life holds no surprises for your Eighteen Man. He cannot be easily shocked. He has seen and experienced much of what life is all about. He has an inclusive understanding of human weakness which is innate and whether he has experienced it himself or not, he possesses a comprehension of the psyche that, along with his innate strength, draws needy people to him for assistance, support and direction. You should have suspected his flute playing was more than just entertainment when, passing through towns and cities, he drew crowds that followed him to the outskirts and beyond. Your camping trips are always a bit crowded and you've yet to get to that Italian restaurant. Well, maybe next weekend.

There is an Eighteen Man who can be very manipulative, who uses his flexible mind and astute reasoning powers to build walls and hide facts that he fears could undermine him in some manner. This man has a strong ego to protect. He doesn't want to lose his exalted position at the top of the heap so his thirst for power and his natural caution become a shackle, and his walls of protection become a prison. Because he is so influential, in this condition he can be a very dangerous man. But, in most cases, his feelings for the universal good and his responsibility toward the power that is his, overrides his little ego and guides him on a just path.

Of all the numbers, this is the one that can have the most far-reaching and most enduring influence. At some level, your Eighteen Man knows this, therefore, he probably exercises discipline in many areas of his life in preparation. Training his body is one method of training his mind for the great things that are expected of him. He has the independence, the efficiency, strength and sense of responsibility, the wisdom and the talent to broadcast his philosophy. He's a winning combination.

He began building his spiritual muscles early. When he was quite young, he spent his first two dollars on a beautiful necklace for his grandmother. It took him a long time to understand why his grandmother, a staunch Puritan, would be shocked over his gift. It had lovely beads and a cross and the word on the box read: Rosary.

18

He had a cosmic mentality even at that tender age, and it may have been difficult for his family to understand why his ideas were different from those of others. He had to strive to adjust to the conflicting circumstances in his environment.

His teen years may have tested him more severely. His inclination to participate in the fun and camaraderie of his peers may have had its temptations. His friends looked to him as a leader, the one who usually knew what was going on and how to get out of it, if need be. But experience eventually taught him to follow the rules. It was more productive and satisfying in the long run.

Today, he follows the rules if they make sense to him. He answers to his ideals first, the rules second. Don't forget, this is the man who left his professors shaking their heads in hallowed halls. Such questions and arguments haven't resounded through those revered structures since Daniel let go at the devil and Scopes and his monkey performed in a Tennessee courtroom. He isn't one to avoid an issue. If you want an opinion, you'll get it and sometimes more than you bargained for.

Your Eighteen Man can be somewhat emotional. He may hide it well but there are times when his idealistic fervor is aroused and then, unless you want to see the destruction of a planet, you'd better blast off. If he directs that megapower into social, political and philosophical areas, he will go down in history as a moving force, a man who made a difference. Robert Redford, actor born on the 18th, is an avid environmentalist. He feels responsible for maintaining the pristine beauty of the earth. The *Wall Street Journal* recently announced that he's considering running for Senator from Utah. Watch his political acumen and persuasive force. He is a man whom others had better take seriously.

When you met your Eighteen Man, you met your Waterloo. He is dramatic history in the making, and he's about to make your history book. One of these days, when you turn a page, you'll find a quiet scene, a few secluded moments. You two are alone, the wine is sparkling in tall goblets and a minstrel plays haunting love songs from the shadows. You will have made it to the restaurant, and it will happen. He will pop the question. If you say yes then you'll live happily ever after, maybe not peacefully, but definitely happily.

The Nineteen Woman

If you're expecting a submissive, easily-impressed woman who stands in awe of authority or fame, you'd better look somewhere else because your Nineteen Woman is not anybody's poor relative. She may have been born on a remote farm, in a trunk or in a charity ward, but she knows who she is and she'll keep pace with the best of them. Her wit and intelligence often surprise those who meet her for the first time. Before they know it, they're gathered about her like moths to a flame.

Your Nineteen Woman has a deep dislike of inferiority. At a Washington barbecue, she'd think nothing of telling the President he had corn stuck between his teeth, then offer him a toothpick and have him eating out of her hand before the conversation was over. The Nineteen American Woman, Wallis Simpson, was such an individual. She had a headcold the evening she was first introduced to the future king of England. Edward asked her if she missed American central heating, to which she replied, "I'm sorry, Sir, but you have disappointed me." The Prince of Wales asked why. Mrs. Simpson answered, "Every American woman who comes to your country is always asked that same question. I had hoped for something more original from the Prince of Wales."

Edward later wrote a definitive description of the Nineteen Woman when he said of Mrs. Simpson, destined to be the woman for whom he abdicated his throne, "In character, Wallis was, and still remains, complex and elusive, and from the first I looked upon her as the most independent woman I had ever met. This refreshing trait I was inclined to put down as one of the happiest outcomes of 1776."

A handful of American men and women did free the Colonies from English rule and the Declaration of Independence stated that "all men are created equal." However, it said nothing of women who, along with criminals and lunatics, were denied the right to vote until 1919, when the 19th Amendment finally passed, granting females their "inalienable" rights. Yes, the Nineteen Woman is not daunted by power people or power structures because she was born independent and not, as the Prince of Wales assumed, a product of her culture or times.

Your Nineteen Woman is complex and elusive. Besides being a Nineteen, she's also a woman, a combination that's bound to rouse your libidinal instincts. It's not that you're lustful or unable to control your sexual drive when she's around, but you're really not quite sure how she would react to aggressive advances. She might lift her chin and look down her nose at you as at a baby's diaper, she might just smile patronizingly at your feeble attempts—yes, she deems them feeble—or she could surprise you and respond most willingly. The problem is you never know. If your ego is the least fragile, it will consistently lie scattered in thousands of glittering shards about her feet. But you'll never give up because, when you found her, you happened upon that rare oyster that yields one hundred pearls.

She is a treasure. All you need to do now is find the map. If it's a treasure hunt you're on, most likely she'll go with you because she loves variety, change and adventure. Her strong emotional nature, although often cleverly camouflaged, requires many outlets. If she is restricted in her mental or physical mobility, she can become moody and unreasonable, playing power games in order to manipulate those around her. Because she is playing with a full deck and able to comprehend situations so quickly, she becomes a formidable opponent. Prime Minister Indira Gandhi of India, after her military victory over Pakistan and her victory in the national elections, was charged with election tampering by her defeated Socialist opponent. The High Court ruled against Mrs. Gandhi, and within two weeks, she had declared a state of emergency, imprisoned political opponents and issued a string of laws limiting personal freedoms. She postponed the March 1976 elections. In the elections of the following spring, she was stunningly defeated "in perhaps the greatest election upset anytime anywhere..." But on January 14, 1980, "slightly stooped and forcing a shy smile, the little woman in the red and gold sari stepped softly into the Parliament Building in New Delhi" to be sworn in for the fourth time as Prime Minister of India.

You can't keep a good woman down, and your Nineteen Woman isn't a splash in the pan. She has the incredible ability to keep rising before the count of ten. She may lie there maddeningly until the count of nine—she likes cliff hangers—but you'll seldom hear a ten in her ring so don't ever dismiss her from the picture until that great referee in the sky decides she's down and out. Or perhaps it should be up and out.

Your Nineteen Woman might make a mistake—a rare possibility—but the time will come when she sees the light. She can be very opinionated on certain issues because she's learned to reply upon her own inner information center, not on what others tell her. She has found this source to be the most reliable. All her life she's been told "you can't do that" or "that's impossible" yet she's gone right ahead and done it. With this as her experience, you can understand her reluctance to listen to advice. Dear Abby would never get a letter from her and the only psychiatrists she knows are the ones who switch places with her, to lie on her couch and tell her their problems.

She has an understanding heart, deep wisdom and a comprehensive awareness of the fancies and foibles of the human creature. Even though there is a certain elusiveness about her, on a one-on-one basis she is someone you can confide in with the certainty that she understands your feelings and can offer some constructive solutions. She grows on you like corn under a hot August sky, tall, straight and curiously enigmatic. You never know what you're going to get until you strip away the husk, yet the whole package promises mouth-watering, nourishing delights.

She stands in a field of waving humanity yet she is one of a kind, an original. If you pick her up and look at her feet, you won't find "made in Taiwan" stamped on her little soles. How many Dolly Partons do you know? Yes, there's nothing conventional about your Nineteen Woman. She may subscribe to proper behavior publicly but underneath lurks a most unconventional woman who, at times, like a periscope, emerges. We know one Nineteen Woman bank employee who, during a Halloween promotion, dressed in a monkey suit with accompanying long tail, slid down the bannister of the circular stairway in the bank and cavorted across the lobby to the delight of many customers. You'd never know it was possible if you met her during normal business hours.

There's nothing normal about your Nineteen Woman, however. Normal means devoid of any outstanding characteristics, hardly an apt description for someone as independent and creative as your woman. Someone with a milktoast personality, someone who is mild, ineffectual and easily dominated doesn't get a whole loaf named after them as did Dame Nellie Melba, Australian operatic singer. A Dame of the British Empire by 1881, she appeared regularly at Covent Garden in London and at the Metropolitan Opera in New York City. Her remarkably pure and agile coloratura voice—a voice that could trill and run with the notes like a cheetah with the wind at its back—flowed with a "flawless and effortless skill."

There is one quality about your Nineteen Woman that consistently astounds you. She makes handling the most awesome tasks appear as easy as falling off a log. She can be the perfect hostess as were Wallis Simpson, the Duchess of Windsor, and Indira Gandhi, hostess to her father and prime minister, Jawarhalal Nehru. You need peach Melba for five hundred dinner guests by 7:30 tonight. No problem. She's so versatile that she can pick the peaches, stew them up in a pan, and still prove that she can...succeed at many other things as well. She'll keep the dinner conversation witty and entertaining. Are you inviting the President? Order extra toothpicks.

Your Nineteen Woman is not a social butterfly. Far from it. There's no question of her handling parties and conversations brilliantly and performing the functions required of her with propriety and efficiency to shame an accomplished English butler, but her insistent individuality keeps thrusting through the layers of expectability. She can enter a noisy crowded room with a rustle of amber silk and a catlike tread and have every head instinctively swiveling her way. She can speak in hushed tones yet, like the shot fired at Concord, be heard round the world. Her influence is intangible but unmistakeable.

Her teens may have been more emotional as she swung between expressing her own strong opinions and feeling the pressure of blending with her peers. But her personal ambition probably drove her to find her place in the sun on a singularly isolated beach. She needed room and time alone. She also wanted to make it on her own. She may have been too poor to paint, but she was also too proud to whitewash. Dreams of being the best and doing it her way beckoned her with bejeweled fingers. She traversed her early years with courage, strength and a vision not seen by many eyes. She gathered knowledge to her bosom with unyielding arms.

In the secret place she visits regularly, she finds a sustenance and completion that can not always be supplied by her relationship with the opposite sex. In her wisdom she will understand the solitary moments she spends within a partnership or marriage, knowing that it is right and good that she experience those times because they bring her closer to her personal divinity. You must understand and allow this part of her to function in your life together if you want to keep her. What she can give you in return is more than most can give when they give their all. Like She, the queen in H. Rider Haggard's romance by the same name, who lived for thousands of years by bathing in the fire of the Pillar of Life, your Nineteen Woman can renew her mind and her body by entering her personal sanctuary of wisdom. Don't bother her. She's adjusting to the constant changes that dog her through life, that tax and test her ability to learn through experience. That's why her resource center is so full of ideas and why she always seems to come out on top of the heap even when she's started out on the bottom. When you're down to your last dollar, she'll come up with an idea that will save the day. You've depended on her before and you will again, many times, because she has an endless font of creative energy. Some of the things she comes up with have been most surprising.

The latest has you baffled. You say she's been collecting kindling and has it piled high on the bedroom floor. You're a bit alarmed and wonder if you should call the firefighters. Don't. You won't need them unless it's to put out your fire. You see, it's renewal time.

The Nineteen Man

Notice those huge eyes scrutinizing you. They look a bit distorted because they're behind two strongly-magnified monocles. That's ridiculous, you think. No one wears a monocle today, never mind two. But there's your Nineteen Man, sporting a pair, and looking rakish, debonair and downright upright, and he can get away with it. One reason may be that your attention is immediately diverted to the tape recorder strapped to his waist and the television cameras that are following him. Well, you see, he just happened to hear that you do business with a firm that produces defective ping-pong balls and he'd just like to ask you a few questions. Be careful because you're likely to end up on "Nineteen Minutes."

He did call you the next week for an evening on the town, an event at which he excels. He is thorough and he knows the ropes, every tiny little knot. His logical

19

mind progresses from one to nine with the speed of a greyhound and just as smoothly. He makes his reasoning seem so effortless. In fact, he has a natural ability to feret out information and, once on the track, has the tenacity of a bloodhound on a hunt. But he does it with such ease and finesse that you're tagged and bagged before you know what hits you. So, if you have the good sense God gave a goose, you'll give up now. He's decided he wants you and he doesn't take no for an answer to questions from which he expects a yes. Besides, do you want to end up on "Nineteen Minutes"?

This is one man you cannot easily outwit. He has done it all, seen most of life, and what he doesn't know or can't find out, you could put in the nest of a hummingbird and still leave room for the newborn. Like the hummingbird, which is the only bird able to fly backward, your Nineteen Man can backtrack over information and the years past to resurrect unnoticed or buried facts that shed new light and understanding on present day situations. At his best, he is a beacon of truth, seeking to better difficult and unjust conditions. His perception of matters is clear and inclusive, and his penetrating insight scatters attempts at camouflage like ashes before a fan. He's quick, and gets where he's going yesterday while everyone else is still packing. He says the early bird gets the worms. You're more than willing to let him have the worms—not very tasty little devils anyway—and you'll take him. He is many people rolled into one and, if you like a bit of spice in your life, he's got Heinz beat.

You see, he craves change and variety. If he isn't moving the furniture around the house every other week like a frustrated traveler, he's moving himself to the far circumferences of the earth. How can the earth have corners when it's round? Your Nineteen Man will remind you to keep the facts clear. Jack Anderson is a good example of the Nineteen Man with a penchant for exposing the "inards" regardless of the pressures and machinations of the "outards." There is no substitute for truth. He knows that truth can set you free.

Not that you want to be free of him. Where else can you find a walking fact finder? But you'll need your own resource book to understand his many moods. He is a person who is subject to extremes, falling into the pits one day and flying to the heights the next. Keep your intercosmic passport handy. You never know when you awake on any given day where you'll end up with him as your traveling companion.

He has a nervous temperament, his emotions fluctuate and he can anger easily but he soon forgets the incident that rose his wrath, and he seldom holds grudges. He is capable of greater understanding, a larger overview. Then again, sometimes he's just so much into his own thing that he's not aware of the petty bickerings that go on around him. If he does tune in to it, he may find it amusing. It really depends upon whether you catch him on a Monday or a Friday.

Your Nineteen Man is as independent as a hog on ice. You'll seldom find him subservient to a taskmaster. He's his own taskmaster and his own boss. He has a sense of himself that keeps a segment of him apart from others, no matter how close the relationships are. He knows he's different, is aware of his individuality and uniqueness and must be careful this awareness doesn't degenerate into supreme egotism and megalomania. His wisdom and drive place him in positions of authority from whence he exerts great influence without half trying. At first, he may be surprised at the breadth to which his ideas and actions spread and the masses of people he seems to influence. He is most persuasive, the golden-tongued orator who, like the Nineteen Man William Jennings Bryan, is often recognized for his eloquent pen and tongue.

If you haven't noticed, there's something of the explorer in him. He's just as likely to drop the boring, boring, boring! routine of the work-a-day world like a hot potato and get lost in that big world out there. Oh, you have noticed? Where are you calling from? A way station on the upper Zambesi? Your Nineteen Man wanted to retrace another Nineteen Man, David Livingstone's, famous footsteps. That's Dr. Livingstone, I presume? What did you say? Really! Then you're off to follow the tracks of George Rogers Clark of Northwest Territory fame, and you want to know what you should pack? Well, fur and heavy boots are in, but you'd better drop off a subscription request to *National Geographic.* They're better informed on these matters of weather and terrain and they probably aren't that far behind your Nineteen Man's trail.

Your Nineteen Man is rather dramatic. He does seem to get into the thick of things, not without an impish delight. He does so without fear because he knows his versatility. He has tremendous resources from which to draw, and unlike the average person tangling with an opponent, he manages to emerge victorious, while adding another story to his vast repetoire.

He has a strange regenerative power. No matter what happens to him, no matter how many doors are closed in his wonderful face, no matter how many rejection slips are deposited in his mail box and regardless of the ultimate failure, the refusal of his application by MasterCard, does he give in, give up and take to crunching gingersnaps and staring at last year's calendar? No. His disappointments can be as numerous as hairs in a brush yet he'll still grin and try again. He knows he's good; he knows his ideas will work, and he has a secret source of sustenance. Don't fret because he disappears into that locked room in the attic with the huge skylight during thunderstorms. He always looks and feels years younger the next morning when you greet him, right? And he's been up all night. You have shadows under your eyes and you've had eight hours sleep. But he's feeling better and that's what matters. Besides, a little alchemy never hurt anyone. Just be sure you put your foot down if he tries to buy a barony. He shouldn't be too obvious.

Your Nineteen Man is extremely creative, inventive and original. Cosmic Mother threw away the mold when he was born. He's not a man who takes advice easily—that white fluffy stuff sticking out of his ears is cotton—therefore, he doesn't know that it can't be done. He sees all things as possible, and is not easily programmed by the negativity and the "yabuts" in his world. Yabuts are those people who, in answer to your every proposal or idea say, "Yeah, but..." He dismisses such people and concepts—that is, if he even hears them in the first place—with a wave of his hand. When he births an idea, he is as inexorable as time in seeing it through to a conclusion. There's a whole lot of will, perserverance and tenacity in him when he's latched on to something. He approaches life's experiments in the same way a doctor approaches chicken soup as a cure. It may not help but it sure can't hurt, and your Nineteen Man is going to give it a try.

When he was a little boy, he knew he was special. His light shone so brightly that people would stop on the street to smile at him. They innately recognized his brilliant aura. Even on those occasions when he was called in to spend a few sticky minutes with an austere principal, his winning ways softened the verbal blows.

19

In his teens, he began to recognize that his ideas and techniques were different than those held and utilized by his peers and teachers. He knew things he couldn't explain in any rational way to the logical minds around him or even, at times, to his own logical mind. He had an uncanny grasp on the workings of things, whether it was personalities, situations or machines. He either camouflaged his lightning perceptions well and flowed through school with the ease of a hot knife through butter, the class leader in just about everything, or he left school to pursue his own unique paths. Either way, he grew to manhood and here he is today, lighting up your life in wondrous ways.

He's a man who knows what life is all about. He doesn't want it all, he has it all. As Balise Pascal, brilliant mathematician, physicist, philosopher and writer, wrote in *Pensees* that the analytical mind needed "l'esprit de finesse" which comprised of "grasping a thing at a single glance and not by the process of reasoning," your Nineteen Man has a reasoning ability so swift that he often fails to realize that his process is "reasonable" and logical, it's just that the speed with which he traverses the steps one through nine is measured in machs. His intellectual and philosophical mind tends him toward politics, religion and art where he can exercise his deep metaphysical connections, rather than business. Anyone who tangles mental tentacles with him is in for an inordinate amount of frenzied frustration. Handfuls of hair strewn about his feet are mute but eloquent testimony to his mental prowess. When a committee gathers before his house with a large cup of hemlock, you'll know he's overstepped his bounds again.

This man is hard to convince in many ways. You may have to ask him to marry you every day for nineteen months before you get a response. Michelle Triola didn't have much luck with Nineteen Man Lee Marvin during the six years she lived with him, although she was awarded $104,000 for "rehabilitation purposes" in the first major "palimony" case.

But your Nineteen Man made a decision, that is, he wants you, so if you're in the mood for a soap opera drama, try to get away from him. He won't use physical force, locking you in his bedroom for nineteen days and nights with only bread and water to convince you to change your mind, but he will use every ounce of savoire faire and smooth adroitness he can conjure and he's a masterful conjurer. Remember the attic room during thunder storms. He knows your every mood, likes and dislikes, strengths and weaknesses, and he'll use this knowledge to wine and dine you in the way you secretly dream of but have never told anyone. If your idea of royal treatment is a drink from a plastic water bottle at the top of a mountain after an arduous six-hour climb, he'll be there, uncorking your canteen, smiling enticingly into your sun-speckled eyes. Or if you're the type who dreams of champagne in frosted stem glasses on a bedroom veranda overlooking the Mediterranean, he'll be by your side, dressed elegantly in a white dinner jacket, toasting your future together, as the strains of violins from beneath your portico drift up to mingle with the scent of the two dozen blood-red roses that now sway gently in the warm summer's night breeze.

Don't fight it. Lie back and enjoy it. Your Nineteen Man has everything under control. He's the center of your universe, warming you with brilliant rays during the day and wrapping you in a glow of tenderness at night. He's first, last and always in your mind. He knows he's the best thing that ever happened to you. And so do you.

The Twenty Woman

If you want to pick a Twenty Woman out of a crowd, start examining pinky fingers. Hers has a beautiful little bend, a tantalizing curve, around which you'll find yourself wrapped before you finish introducing yourself. Don't scoff. She may appear quiet and unassuming, not the least bit dangerous to a big, strong male specimen like yourself. She's the perfect female, right? Feminine, passive, cooperative, tactful. These adjectives may fit her but you've overlooked one very large quality. Her magnetism. You felt it right at the start. First, it was curiosity. Who is that woman with the sultry look? A bit of maneuvering and you were talking to her. You felt so comfortable yet deeply intrigued. She listened to you for hours. You didn't realize until later that you had told her everything and she had told you nothing. A hopeful telephone call set up a dinner date and by then, it was all over. You were bent around her little finger.

Periodic chiropractic care, or perhaps hiring someone to walk up and down your spine to straighten it, will keep you flexible for encounters with your Twenty Woman. She's worth it. Besides, she obviously needs your protection. Your Twenty Woman may appear weak and helpless and as if she needed a six-foot, 220-pound body guard to protect her from those who would take advantage of her. No matter how vivacious she is, and some Twenty Women are, she still maintains a certain quality of aloneness, like a babe in swaddling clothes found on a doorstep, homeless and abandoned. She has a way of drawing upon all your nurturing instincts.

She is extremely sensitive. Her sensitiveness springs from a well so deep that even she is not aware of its depth. She reacts strongly, with her intuition, to the stimuli in her environment. She gets "feelings" about people. Even shaking hands often transmits strong messages about the person she is touching. Like Mr. Spock of "Star Trek," whose sense of touch is highly developed. The "little grey cells" in your Twenty Woman's fingertips seem able to "read" the person she is greeting by hand. The fingertips are the only other part of the body with grey matter like the brain. Have you noticed how she likes to touch things, handle them, feel them? If you're lucky, you'll be included in that category. If the objects are beautiful or have personal value, she gets a sensual pleasure from this contact because she is on intimate terms with them. She is communicating with them. Many Twenty Women have the ability to read objects, a feat called psychometry, and certainly all of them could develop this skill quite easily.

Your Twenty Woman may be totally unaware of her ability to respond to people and objects in this manner because this part of her personality is so instinctive and hidden. She's not aware how much like a sponge she is, absorbing the emotions, thoughts and feelings of people around her. If she has a good education, which is important for a Twenty Woman, her uncanny instincts join with a well-trained mind to produce an unbeatably accurate and tuned-in professional. Her peer acceptance depends on the fields she enters because she does react instinctively and not everyone can trace her reasoning.

The Twenty Woman, Dr. Joyce Brothers, America's best-known psychologist, is often criticized "for dispensing pop psychology remedies like so much chicken soup," but nonetheless she "strikes a responsive chord in millions of fans, adding a touch of sympathetic concern to her expert advice." Her daily column

20

is syndicated in 350 newspapers. What her peers and critics fail to realize is that Dr. Brothers has the best of both worlds—a fine education and a developed instinct—and if her remedies are like chicken soup, then chicken soup may well be the long-sought panacea for the mental sickness of the human race. Dr. Brothers instinctively tunes in to the people she talks with, sensing their deepest problems, feeling their pain and anguish. In a sense, she is experiencing what they are experiencing. Because she has trained her mind, she can work with awareness.

Your Twenty Woman's sponge-like characteristic can make her nervous because she is picking up so much around her. Crowds can tire her quickly—she is sensing their cumulative energies which, because many people carry their problems with them, can be very draining. Therefore, she needs periodic retreats to the country or to quiet places where she can shut out the constant bombardment of stimuli.

She is truly the most mystical and psychic of all women, and these attributes are furthered considerably by her ability to notice the smallest details. This woman can remember what someone wore or said a year ago last May at the family cookout. She stores incredible amounts of information that seep in through her senses, only to bring it forward at future times, in casual comments or remarks that astound you because of their accuracy or relevancy to the moment. You swear she's psychic. She's taken the words right out of your mouth more than once, anticipating it seems, your every thought. You sometimes feel she's descended from Cassandra, the prophetess daughter of the King of Troy. However, Cassandra's fate was that she never was to be believed. You have learned to believe your Twenty Woman. How can you ignore fulfilled prophecies? Remember the morning she stuck a pair of scissors in your bag lunch just before you left for work. You were on a diet and thought it was a rather sly hint to cut short your lunch hour. But you just looked down at her, scratched your chin and took the bag without question. Somehow, at work, your scarf got caught in the elevator door and if you hadn't had those scissors to release yourself, you could have modeled scarves for giraffes.

However, her intuitions can be maddening when you're trying to get away with something. All she needs is a single clue, one little hint dropped into her magic well-deep mind, and the game is up. She's got a thumbnail sketch of your M.O. that makes the FBI files look like the secret book in a neighborhood clubhouse. Sometimes you'd swear she is invisible, following you around and listening to your every thought, word and deed. She is light on her feet. Often, when you think you're alone, you turn and she's right behind you. You never heard her approach.

Your Twenty Woman is subtle, laid-back and inclined to operate behind the scenes. She doesn't require the constant up-front, center of attention status that some women do. She may like some of that but, the fact is, she often prefers working in the background. She may be shy, reclusive or just unwilling to "expose" herself in ways with which she's not comfortable. She has a strong protective need in her life. Estelle Parsons, a Twenty Woman and Oscar-winning actress, said, "I'm really absolutely no good on stage because I cannot bear to expose myself to the audience." She loves films because on the screen she can be an exhibitionist and not hear "if people are laughing at me." Twenties are sensitive. Their appealing vulnerability and protective attitudes are obvious in performers like Sophia Loren, who is "so superstitious she always wears something red and carries a packet of salt with her." Anne Murray once commented, "Las Vegas isn't for me. I'm just a turntable person";

and the late Natalie Wood, preferred, at age 43, to raise her children and run her real estate business.

Speaking of business, your Twenty Woman is better in a small one, either running it or working within its folds. She really doesn't want to go it alone. She needs people. She is sympathetic, affectionate, warm-hearted and loyal. Her success stems from her natural capacity for sympathy and her adeptness and patience with details. In a small business, she is in closer contact with the people with whom she works and there is more personal interchange and camaraderie. She is a fine diplomat and a natural peacemaker because she is tactful, has an affinity for harmony and can see the finer points on either side of the fence. She is satisfied to work with or for others rather than to be the big cheese, doling out orders to mouse-like employees.

Friends and family are important to your Twenty Woman for the comfort, companionship and security they provide. She also likes to give to them. She collects things—string and buttons, property, houses and people—because you never know when someone will need what she's got. (The people she keeps.) She is the Cosmic Executive, ready to dispense alms to the needy whenever Cosmic Law sends out an edict. She is willing to give of her mind, soul, ample larder and pocketbook when the need arises. Other people seek her out because they sense her compassion and genuine understanding of their plight.

Your Twenty Woman must learn discrimination and controled decisiveness. She can be dominated by fluctuating emotions and an imagination that seems as boundless as the sea. She may have difficulty making up her mind which color ball-point pen to buy and then buy a new car because she happened to be riding by the dealership and the car on sale in the showroom matched the pen she finally decided upon. Don't say too much. Remember how psychic she is.

As a child, your Twenty Woman probably had vivid dreams and a pretty healthy imagination during the day. If she didn't have the friends she required, she would "invent" invisible playmates. She could create an almost bubble-like world in which she saw and conversed with beings that her parents and others did not see and in whom they did not believe. With her record to date, you're not apt to challenge her on this issue.

Through her teens, she was probably surrounded by admirers, either close by or from afar. Her magnetism was operating full force by then. Boys would gaze at her across the classroom and wonder what mysteries lay behind that enigmatic smile.

As she grew into womanhood, she always seemed able to get what she needed. Unconsciously, she can manipulate others with a word, a look, a slight nuance in body language. She's not aware she's doing it—you may not be either—but you find yourself on bended knee, begging to be allowed to fulfill her every request, and she hasn't even opened her rosebud lips. She can be a vamp, like Theda Bara, early silent film star who was the first screen vamp. It was said she had "a vampire-like, coldly appealing personality which lured men to destruction." Well, let's not get carried away. But she surely was sexually enticing.

Your Twenty Woman may be a sunnier type but she has the same luring charisma. She's often better at communicating indirectly through writing, film making, musical recordings, or in a small personal type business rather than in large, open, face-to-face discussions. She may love her home and find enough peace, contentment and security there to satisfy her drives. It does go against her nature to be too open because she is extremely sensitive and vulnerable. Theda Bara, after an unsuccessful Broadway appearance and Hollywood comeback, retired. Estelle Parsons prefers films where she doesn't have to face a live audience. Anne Murray prefers behind-the-scenes roles. Those Twenty Women who do reach out for direct contact with other people have to constantly fight these protective and reclusive urgings. Your Twenty Woman belongs to the Two Family (20= 2+ 0= 2), therefore, she feels comfortable in the background, supporting others.

Whoever she is—you're never really quite sure and you wonder if she is—you've flipped over her. You know that this lively, enticing creature was not meant for manual labor. She was meant to love and be loved, to feel the joys and pains of those she loves and those she would love if she but knew them better. You want your Twenty Woman to be draped in satins, dripping with pearls and scented with moonlight because, for you, she has opened up a mystical, magical world of belonging and now you know what it's like to be really loved.

The Twenty Man

If you've ever seen a computer with a big smile and a bright red paper heart taped to the front, you've seen a Twenty Man. He's a complex, magnetic and intriguing combination of qualities. The Computer is more likely to be cantankerous, stubborn and willful, as any computer operator will attest. So how does your Twenty Man resemble a companionable computer? First of all, he has a memory bank. He has more information stored in his mind than grains of sand on the beach and stars in the sky, and he seems to be able to come up with bits of sand and star at the most opportune and even inopportune times.

Second, he observes and absorbs details. He isn't always conscious that he's involved in this osmosis process but, one thing you can be sure of, he didn't get the majority of his data from straight, hard core intellectual processes. He's not an intellectual in the true sense of the word. He is more instinctive and reactive to the stimuli in his world. You might say he programs himself. He sees, feels, touches, and then absorbs these responses into a hidden cache to be drawn upon whenever the need arises. That's why he's so deliciously dangerous. He can appear to be the most unassuming of men, then suddenly, in a quiet calm voice, say something that knocks you off your shapely pins. He sees everything. Why do you think perfect vision is called 20/20?

Like Jimmy Stewart and George Burns, your Twenty Man tends to be more laid-back, passive and reactive than most men. He wants to observe the situation before he acts. He also prefers a less obtrusive role where he can participate from the fringes, behind the scenes or in the background. When situations require him to be up front and in the limelight, it is often done with effort because it is not his most natural inclination. If he is in an executive or public position, he feels more comfortable working behind closed doors or in a partnership where another person can complement and balance any weaknesses he feels he has. Aptly, George Burns played the role of God in the film, *Oh God.* What better assignment to play God than someone with 20/20 vision who tends to play a hands-off game.

Your Twenty Man has a heart. He is sensitive and caring, finding great comfort and pleasure in close intimate relationships. He has a gentle side that draws people to him. He prefers personal contact with family and friends, and in business strives to keep it "all in the family," in the sense that he wants employees to feel part of his family. Mass production turns him off because it doesn't have the personal touch. Most Twenty Men prefer a small business to run or work in so they can get to know the people with whom they work.

Your Twenty Man does require some privacy. He goes within himself in a self-absorbed process, seeking information from his hidden computer source. The Twenty Man, Peter Frampton, English rock star, exceptionally talented guitarist and gifted song writer, was quoted as saying, "I've always had the capability to sit alone in a room and flake out, not say anything, just completely turn off, whether I'm happy or sad. I guess that's some kind of release." Similarly, your Twenty Man has this unique ability to go within and reprogram himself or to seek out new avenues of expression if things aren't going well.

No matter what he says to the contrary, he is very psychic. He's like a radio station, tuned in to many frequencies, that stands silent, unobtrusive, unmoving, yet picks up messages and communications from all over the world. Actually, thought, sound and color move in waves of energy which his internal sensing devices latch on to with detailed efficiency. The human eye can differentiate between eight million colors, the human ear can distinguish more than three hundred thousand tones. The human fingertips contain grey matter like the brain, and his are all operating at full megacycles. So, if he suddenly whisks you out of a crowded city during a shopping spree, you'll know why. He is a romantic, sensitive to your feelings and needs, and can imagine your deepest fantasies. Imagine, hah! He *knows* your deepest fantasies. So, be careful what you dream about because, with your Twenty Man, even your silent wishes will be fulfilled. It may be embarrassing but it will certainly be fun.

Your Twenty Man's ability to tune in can take on astounding proportions and implications. When Twenty Man, Uri Geller, was three or four years old, he was playing alone in a garden when suddenly, a high-pitched ringing filled his ears. All other sound ceased and the trees stopped moving in the wind "as if time stood still." Looking up at the sky he saw "a silvery mass of light" coming toward him. He knew it wasn't the sun. It was too close. Feeling as if he had been knocked over backward, he experienced a sharp pain in his forehead, then passed out. Since that event, strange phenomena occur around Geller, parapsychology's latest sensation. Silverware bends, clocks, watches, televisions, escalators, cable cars and other mechanical devices stop and start at his will. He is baffled about his own ability, expressing a childlike delight whenever he demonstrates his skill.

Yes, your Twenty Man can influence others. He may look upon your suggestions that he has these abilities as the babblings of an incoherent, impressionable woman but it's only because it takes a while for him to discover them in himself. Twenty is such a hidden number that it often takes an experience such as Uri Geller had or an influential person to be the catalyst to its awakening. Certainly your Twenty Man should not stand on a mountain top awaiting a bolt from heaven to strike him between the eyes, awakening his third eye, like a newborn unicorn. He may be led less dramatically to his rebirth but it will occur in some way, sooner or later.

20

The unicorn is a good symbol for the Twenty. He spears the truth so often that, with a little flame, you could use him as a shish kebab skewer. He nourishes and warms those who have nothing to fear and brings out beads of perspiration on those who can't stand the heat or the sudden exposure. He elicits confessions from others because of his innate sympathy and understanding. The fact that he often comes up with workable solutions adds to his credibility as a wise man.

A negative Twenty can get so caught up in the emotional vibes of others that he can't make his own decisions. He relys upon others to do that for him, following the crowd. If he gets in with the wrong people, he can be in deep trouble because he responds at such deep levels with the psyches of those in his environment, and if they're thinking evil thoughts, he will pick them up and may claim them as his own. If he is not in tune with his true self, he can be manipulated by those with power who recognize his psychic responses and inner power. They know that he can be an effective tool in their endeavors.

But your Twenty Man has it together. He's worked on it long enough. In his childhood he may have had trouble sorting out the flotsam from the jetsam, separating what others term "reality" from what he knew of his reality. Or he may have jumped into an early lead as Uri Geller did, when he was a child.

Either way, through his teens he was supersensitive at a time in life when it is most painful to be so. He probably found ways to conceal his instincts and hunches, his connections with the cosmos. Music, art, drama, or philosophical leanings may have supplied him with outlets for his mystical meanderings.

But, at any rate, nature worked her magic and he is full grown now. He may no longer be confused about who he is or what he's feeling but almost everyone around him will be. It seems that no one ever sees a Twenty Man as he really is. He remains a mystery to most people, although a pleasant, companionable, usually tactful and diplomatic one. "Seeing is believing" does not apply to him. You see him and you believe him but that's because you know him and what he can do. Other people would be surprised at his strength, courage and depth of understanding. And if his contacts knew the power of his X-ray senses, they would erect lead fortresses, surround their structures with six-foot-high chain link fence and keep a contingent of very large German shepherds on alert. The dogs would alert them at his approach so they could empty out their minds and try to present a blank face to him. The lead walls might cut down slightly on his reception.

Your Twenty Man needs an education or some kind of self-imposed training so he can encapsulate his abilities, bring them to the surface and examine them. Otherwise, he finds himself in a confusing world where his perceptions don't match those of many others and he begins to wonder if he's crazy or the rest of the world is blind. With experience, he begins to blend and fill in the blank spaces. He observes the reactions of others, he listens to other people's ideas, he absorbs life's experiences, tabulates it all and then, when the right combination of buttons are pushed, he spews out the most startling information. He surprises himself most of all. Like a well-trained doctor who knows there's more in heaven and earth than was taught him at medical school, he has his finger of the pulse of the soul. He knows what makes you tick. He knows that your pain rises from a deeper source than the three epidermal layers or the physical organs that lie beneath. He can read your feelings. Like the best kind of medical man, he heals with more than two slips of paper, one illegibly scrawled with Latin names and a few numbers, your prescription, and the other, most precisely typewritten in English, containing more understandable figures, your bill. Your Twenty Man knows that healing goes beyond the mechanics. His very presence is a soothing ointment, a healing balm for your weary and troubled soul.

Many men come and go, some remembered, most forgotten, but your Twenty Man remains forever woven into the fabric of your being. He does not praise himself from suburban rooftops or from metropolitan skyscrapers. He does not make entrances on the backs of tasseled elephants accompanied by a thousand regal, feathered warriors. He slips into your life quietly and surprises you with his physicality. He doesn't beat you over the head with the fact that he's sexy. As the Twenty Man, Art Buchwald, wrote about his subtle, laid-back manner in obtaining information for his syndicated column, "To get my stories, I use my enormous sex appeal to ingratiate myself with lonely and unhappy wives of administration officials, Congress and the Supreme Court. In exchange for spending long hours holding their hands, I manage to pry government secrets from these women which I use to further my subversive column." Was it mentioned that your Twenty Man also has an unusual sense of humor?

At any rate, there you were, kind of sauntering along through life, not really stopping to smell the flowers, just more or less existing, when suddenly, there he was, smiling at you. At first you merely raised your eyebrows, threw back a quick smile and kept on going. But then, as if a nova had exploded in your head, you stopped in your tracks. There *is* something about him. And then it was all over. Somewhere in your universe, a star was born.

The Twenty-One Woman

Who is that lovely creature up to her neck in quicksand? She doesn't seem too alarmed. A dazzling smile is splashed across her perfectly formed face and her eyes are bright and cheerful even though her pretty little chin is beginning to submerge in the gooey stuff. You break a branch off a handy tree, dash to the fringes of the oatmeal-like substance that's trying to devour this beautiful woman, and frantically direct the limb toward a calmly outstretched hand. "Stay calm," she calls to you. "Everything will be alright." After a short struggle, you've extricated her. Your heart's beating against your ribs like an unevenly loaded washer in the spin cycle. But she stands before you, smiling cheerfully and wiping the sand from her shapely body. "Thank you, darling," she chimes at you brightly, "I just knew someone would come along." Don't ask her how she got in there. You wouldn't want to know.

You are in for a treat because you've just met a Twenty-One Woman. One thing you will discover very quickly, if you haven't already, is that the world is her oyster and she knows that, any moment now, she will find a pearl. No doubt it will be the biggest, most perfect pearl any irritated little oyster ever produced. You can laugh, but she who laughs last...and believe it, she will laugh last.

Your Twenty-One Woman just doesn't want to believe in the gloomy side of life. She sees a rainbow in every shower and an oversized pot of the yellow nuggets at every end. Like Erma Bombeck, who gave up writing obituaries for a newspaper because nothing funny ever happened there, your Twenty-One Woman tosses unpleasant suggestions and reminders aside as so much trivia. The rent may be due tomorrow and she's got exactly $1.39 in her pocket but that doesn't daunt her spirit. Hell, that's no problem. All she needs to do is raise $448.61 in the next twelve hours. You know what? She will do it. Because, besides possessing a fountain of faith abundant enough to quench the thirst of the multitudes, she has the drive and determination to put that faith to work in the most unique and innovative ways.

The Twenty-One Woman tends to be more independent than her Three Sister. She has the energy and the desire to achieve, coupled with the courage to stand up and be counted. She's no flower to be pasted on someone's wall. If she believes in a cause, she'll move heaven, earth and the Republican Party to see it through. When she's behind you, you've got an ally that makes Genghis Khan look like Whistler's Mother. You can't lose. What's so amazing is that she does it with such grace and charm that no one would ever suspect that bubbling and boiling deep within her furnace lies the same kind of expressive energy demonstrated by Mt. St. Helen's in the spring of 1980. When she speaks on a major issue, she'll do it in a big way. She can be very dramatic. In fact, she is drawn to the dramatic. It's a release for the creative energy she contains. She's an effective entertainer because she is multi-talented and has the need to be recognized by others in her own right. She wants people to sit up and take notice of her so she stands center stage, playing the role of her life, with the regularity of a dripping faucet at midnight. She must be careful she doesn't overdo it.

But you won't be left out because she's very aware of you and your needs. She'll respond to your plans and accomplishments with the same enthusiasm and support that mark her own ventures. Your joy is hers, and you've never met joy until you've encountered a Twenty-One Woman. She imbues life with new meaning, a breathless inspiration, and dewey-eyed faith in her own abilities and yours to return the planet to the Garden of Eden she envisions. With one alteration, however. Adam's going to have to help with the apple harvesting. She's not going to pick the apples then let him take all the credit. Adam's apple, indeed!

That does not mean she won't bring you your slippers and pipe. She will. But you'll be expected to bring her slippers and jade cigarette holder to her.

Your Twenty-One Woman is socially inclined. She makes a wonderful hostess because she can be tactful as well as charming. Because her interests have the scope, although perhaps not the detail, of an FBI report, she can render an opinion on most subjects that her guests wish to raise. She is popular with both sexes, making each feel equally at ease and welcome.

As with her Three Sister, she must be careful of scattering her energies and talents. Her mind can flit from one flower to another, like a homeless butterfly seeking a place to light but not really wanting to stay on one blossom too long because that yellow cornflower up ahead on the grassy knoll looks especially tantalizing and just beyond that are some shasta daisies bobbing in the breeze, and the taste of those could be oh, so sweet. Your Twenty-One Woman needs to learn concentration.

If she cannot channel her energy, she becomes nervous and moody. Her emotions go up and down like a cluster of college kids on a greased flagpole. Her nerves make her impatient with others and she broods. Because her imagination is so expansive, she can enlarge upon situations in her mind, blowing them out of proportion. Then she becomes suspicious of the intentions or actions of the people she loves and of the world in general.

Don't discount the fact that this woman is a bit psychic. She picks up subtle messages that often get garbled in transmission because she is so busy in the outer world. But the information registers at subliminal levels and eventually motivates her to say or do timely things or to be in the right place at the most opportune moment. It was no accident that the Twenty-One Woman, Jane Fonda, chose to take a part in *China Syndrome,* a film concerning the dangers of a melt-down at a nuclear plant. A comment was made in the film that such an accident could destroy a state the size of Pennsylvania. The movie was released the same week that the Three Mile Island nuclear accident occurred in Pennsylvania. Miss Fonda, like the Twenty-One Woman, has stood her ground even though she often stood on unpopular platforms. She's a dramatically acclaimed, multi-talented, nervous, chain-smoking actress. She has evolved from an ingenue in light-weight roles to a sex pot in films like *Barbarella* where "she was carelessly exploited" to a mature actress with "brilliant performances" in *Julia* and *Coming Home.*

You can't keep a good Twenty-One Woman down. In fact, it's quite impossible, even using "crazy glue" will do you no good. You might try weighing her down with sand bags to keep her from inflating with the most wonderful, outlandish, impossible ideas and floating off into the wild blue yonder. But then, how do you hold down a dream? She has more than her biologically alloted share of dreams. Four to six a night suffices for most, but not for her. She even dreams when she's awake. She envisions a world of beauty—art, dance, color, form—where everyone is free to express their talents, to accomplish their individual goals.

But she often meets frustration on her own stomping grounds. One part of her loves the freedom of space, sun and empty skies in which to soar and see the beauties of nature and the universe, free from responsibility and bonds of any kind. Another part urges her to walk the straight and narrow, to explore new territory, to focus her creative abilities into stable cables of individual strength and uniqueness, a link between the past and the future. And yet a third part urges her to reach out to others, to respond to their needs and cares. And you think you're confused about her! To bring her many-faceted personality into some semblance of cohesive order, she needs all her considerable creative drive. She goes through life with a royal ease and style. She is not indifferent to her subjects' needs however. Unlike Marie Antoinette who, when told the poor had no bread, callously remarked, "Let them eat cake," your Twenty-One Woman would knead the dough, bake the bread and personally hand the loaves out to the hungry. Her heart is as big as her imagination.

Your Twenty-One Woman is, to put it mildly, an interesting personality. Ask her mother about her but allow mom a little time to sort out the experiences she should relate. How about the time she plastered setting lotion on her hair, piled it up to look like her favorite movie star and swept into the living room, startling her mother's bridge party guests with "Hello, dahlings!" That's one thing, but the black garter belt, stiletto heels and red-feathered boa was enough to feed the Harper Valley P.T.A. for a good three months. Probably because that's all she had on.

Her dramatic talents were tempered—somewhat—by the time she entered high school. Not by her parents however. Mother Nature always steps in to make young adults more receptive to the opinions of their peers. Adult opinions are superfluous. In high school, she may have been a member of the drama class, elocution or debating clubs, or just the class clown, reacting to favorable audiences.

By now, your Twenty-One Woman has flowered into a breath-taking American Beauty, with its fragrant scent and bold beauty. She has a wonderful way with words as well, and her voice can be a source of pleasure, not necessarily running the scales, but certainly running the alphabet. She resonates to an inner sense of rhythm which often produces a melodious speaking voice like the Twenty-One Woman, Senator Barbara Jordan from Texas, whose magnificently smooth, magnetic voice mesmerizes the listener. Ms. Jordan could sell oil to the Arabs at a profit, have the contracts signed, sealed and delivered before they finished marveling at her wonderful delivery.

But the Twenty-One Woman is mindful of her obligations to the second party. She is a strong individual and will always maintain her integrity within any cooperative act. She asserts herself through cooperative methods and partnerships. Her goals are as expansive as her imagination. She wants to build an empire to give or leave to others. She has a larger vision than most, a view that does not allow for failure. She expects success, rewards and triumphant entries in all her undertakings. She believes in herself and in you. And if wishes come true and there is a pot of gold at the end of the rainbow, and fairies did come from the first baby's first laugh, and wishbones, horse shoes and four leaf clovers fulfill their appointed tasks, then your Twenty-One Woman has an edge on the rest of the world because she believes in them all. She knows that "every time a child says, 'I don't believe in fairies' there is a little fairy somewhere that falls down dead." Why don't you try, just for a little while, to see the world through her gleaming eyes, and follow into her magical realm which may, after all, be the most real of them all. She's off. You'd better hurry. Why is she clapping so merrily as she dances off into a sun beam? In her imagination she hears the eternal Peter Pan whispering brightly, "Do you believe in fairies...If you believe, clap your hands!" With your Twenty-One Woman, soon the whole world will be clapping.

The Twenty-One Man

Talk about a high roller. Your Twenty-One Man was born howling lustily and clutching a pair of red-hot dice in his warm little fists. He captured everyone's attention in the delivery room—how many infants are born on a 7-11 roll?—and he has been playing center stage ever since. He's unafraid to take a big swig of life's juices and actually revels in excitement, opportunity and a touch of uncertainty, challenge and danger. He has style. Did you notice the spongy pair of dotted cubes hanging from the rear view mirror in his candy-apple-red Porsche? He has an unmistakable flair for living, a willingness to take a chance and an abiding faith in himself and the ideal of success that astounds and mystifies more timid souls. He's a man who can't be kept down.

Strip him naked and leave him penniless and without a friend in the Klondike and, quicker than a cat has kittens, he'll have turned all his adversities into advantages. A big lodge right about here with a huge stone fireplace, a skating rink over there, a gourmet restaurant tucked in that corner with maybe a cozy discotheque with flashing floor, wall and ceiling lights and he'll have the natives in their jeans, red-plaid shirts and rag socks dancing shoeless under a shower of colored strobe lights to the "ghetto growl" of Wolfman Jack.

The Twenty-One Man, Bob Smith, alias Wolfman Jack, has been "comin atcha" since he was sixteen. Today his syndicated radio show is played over twenty-two hundred stations in forty-three countries. He is "easily the most successful disc jockey of all time." There was a time in his life when rivals tried to take over his Mexican station forcibly and several attempts were made to kill him. Also, at one time he lost his astronomical income and turned to drugs but his appearance in the film *American Graffiti* revived his career and today he is a world-wide success. He just kept coming back.

This man attracts women like a sunny beach draws bathers. He can be skinny as a hoe handle or rounder than a prize pumpkin at the annual 4-H Fair, as tall as Wilt "the Stilt" Chamberlain or as short as Aristotle Onassis, and he'll still have women trailing after him, hanging on his every word or glance. Maybe it's his million-dollar smile or the secret knowledge that he knows he's special. They're both assets he uses skillfully. His sexuality is conscious as well as unconscious. He knows he could charm a unicorn into captivity. He interacts most effectively and with full awareness, and he genuinely enjoys women. But even when he's thoroughly absorbed in a project and sex is the farthest thing from his mind—at least two or three feet away—he still exudes a subtle magic that women pick up like radar.

The Twenty-One Man may not even be physically attractive, according to the world's standards, but he has a certain something that radiates from inside, a special aura that sends out unmistakable messages about his person. He is "somebody" and he knows it, and so will everyone else within communicable distance!

He has a way of communicating with your most secret thoughts and touching your greatest needs and desires, and he does it instinctively. He just knows what to say, when and to whom, and he's often in the right place at the right time. You can call him lucky, but he earns his luck because he intuitively tunes into the needs of the moment, and then has the courage to dare mighty deeds (and the audacity to believe they can be accomplished), to soar where eagles live and to view the world from a larger, loftier aerie than most mortals. Your Twenty-One Man belongs to the world. There is something grand about him. When he plans, he plans big. No nickel and dime stuff for him. And he can work magic. Watch him with a pencil and paper. He can show you, in a few artistic sweeps of ball point fluid across a restaurant napkin, how you can make a million dollars in three months. Yes, you snicker, on paper it looks fine. Don't worry. He's been laughed at before and his advice has been tossed more often than not, into the kitchen waste basket along with the table scraps but that's why there are so few millionaires. Have you ever noticed how many waiters make it big? Not everyone is willing to take the gambles your Twenty-One Man is. Everyone's hindsight is 100 percent accurate but your Twenty-One Man's foresight stacks up some pretty impressive percentages. What's his secret? Simple. He knows he will succeed. He has faith in his plans and ideas, and he's not going to sit in a rocker on the back porch and gaze into the starry heavens waiting for the hand of God to point the way or send down a shower of greenbacks to complement his lawn.

When he explains his latest scheme, you wonder how that could possibly work. But give him a few months and he manages to pull it off. You just shake your head muttering, "God watches out for fools and Englishmen...and Twenty-One

21

Men." He's Tom Edison's favorite type. Remember? "Give me a man who doesn't know it can't be done and he'll go ahead and do it." Your Twenty-One Man is the last one to believe it can't be done, and as a result the first one to do it.

The fact is, your Twenty-One Man does want your approval. He'd like nothing better than to have you behind him, supporting and knowing along with him that his "wild and crazy" scheme will somehow coalesce into a viable, working operation. He doesn't believe it will, he knows it will. And therein lies the difference between his successes and others' failures. Believing implies doubt; knowing leaves no room for doubt. He wants you to know right along with him. Partnerships are important to him. He is most aware of your needs but he fluctuates between being responsive and susceptible to your moods, thoughts and ideas, and needing to express his own, independent, personal opinions on how things should be done. He'll come to you, ask your opinion, really want your approval, but if you disagree with his wonderful plan, he'll probably go ahead and do it anyway because he knows it will work. However, he did ask you, right?

There are moments when you're convinced that you have instilled some semblance of sanity between those elegant ears and into that imaginative mind, and that now he'll settle down to a normal, even-keeled, nine-to-five routine. Wrong! You wouldn't like that anyway. That's not what drew you to him in the first place. There has to be a bit of the gambler tucked away inside you somewhere for you to have thrown in with him in the first place. Secretly, you must like to live dangerously. So, don't let that warm smile, the receptive attitude, the Chablis by the evening firelight, fool you into thinking he's reformed. How dull. Rest assured. It's just the calm before the storm, or better yet, you're just in the eye of the hurricane. Suddenly, without warning, an Aristotle Onassis image imposes itself over your seemingly sane Twenty-One Man, and he's suddenly planning to buy Saudi Arabia and manufacture sandboxes. Just think about it. How many kids are there in the world? And each order of a ruggedly-built, last-a-lifetime sandbox could come with an added bonus of a large bag of sand, free of charge. After all, there is an abundance of the grainy stuff over there. There is also the rebuilding of beaches around the world, icy weather conditions and the Sand Man. The possibilities are limitless. Somehow, you feel yourself getting excited. He's done it again. His enthusiasm is contagious and here you are, again, almost ready to invest in foreign real estate.

One thing your Twenty-One Man has to be careful of is—you guessed it—overconfidence spiced with a dash of impulsiveness. He has such a wonderful way with words that he could convince a cat to take a bubble bath. Images of your cat plunked in the midst of frothy bubbles, merrily scrubbing its back with a brush to the yowling refrain of "I'm going to wash that tom right out of my fur..." may seem ridiculous to you but stranger things have happened. You have to realize that there may be a bit of the showman wrapped around the edges of your Twenty-One Man and he can get carried away with the sound of his own voice and the imagery of his ideas. He must be taught that he will scatter his fine talents and energies in erratic ways if his emotions get the upper hand. Some good, hard, facts of life need to be spooned into him occasionally, along with the milk and honey with which he nourishes himself.

But with his batting average, who's to say what the facts of life really are. He tends to believe all things are possible. He often leaps before he looks and more than once has landed knee deep in cow flaps. So how does he always manage to come up smelling like buttercups? Forget it. Even if you knew you wouldn't believe it, so just file it away with the rest of the unsolved mysteries of the universe. Besides, it makes him all the more interesting. It's like living on the edge of a volcano and the ground's been trembling for forty days and nights. Try to keep in mind that he's a brother to H.G. Wells, Florenz Zeigfeld and Robin Williams, exciting, imaginative company, to say the least.

Your Twenty-One Man is a social creature. He's certainly not the type to cloister himself behind high, thick walls, wear a hair shirt and flail himself three times a day for naughty thoughts that just happened to creep into his mind when he wasn't looking. Au contraire, ma cherie. He rather enjoys a stray naughty thought here and there. It spices up his life. The glittering side of life appeals to your Twenty-One Man. He likes people, conversation, social contacts, drama and theatrics. He may not keep a written record but he'll fill every second of his calendar with activity. He wants to see and do it all. Knowing him as you do, you are sure that this particular goal will be fulfilled. He wants to explore the beauties of the earth. His travels may take him to faraway places. He would prefer to have you along because he likes nothing better than sharing his emotions and observations with an appreciative audience. He wants your approval even though he would never admit such a thing. He does have a certain amount of pride. Like three and one-half tons. That accounts for his strange gait. That stuff can get pretty heavy but he's up to carrying it. He'll be sinking to his knees, his tongue lolling about between parched lips and his face a strange purplish hue, and he'll assure you, between gasps, that everything's perfectly alright, that he can handle it. Just link your arm in his and lift him gently, telling him that you just want to be near him, that you feel safer when he's next to you, and he'll never know the difference. There are rewards for such subversive actions. Even though he needs more love and affection than he tends to give at times, he takes great interest and pride in you and what you do. He's like a beneficent king, bestowing his favors on those subjects who recognize his position in the scheme of things. When he has given you his love, he will protect you with his strong faith and positive outlook. The only hurt you'll know is from holding your sides while laughing at him. He'll keep you smiling and, after all, laughter is the best medicine. Even if he's not a comedian in the strictest sense of the word, his own wondering and endless stretches of imagination will catch you up as it does him. You'll play in the Milky Way and discover what it's like to ride a moon beam backward. And he'll be there facing you, grinning happily.

The Twenty-Two Woman

Your Twenty-Two Woman is of the earth. She is rich black soil and growing things, sensual summer nights and harvest moons. She is home, hearth and heaven. A little hell, if you get out of line. She is the pain in a puppy's wounded paw, the hunger pang in the bellies of the poor and the scar tissue left by those who ravage Mother Earth. She is the budget director and the broker on Wall Street. She is the pulse of the world in all its ramifications. She enjoys working with earthly problems. It puts her in contact with her senses which are exquisitely keen. But don't lay a finger on her until she tells you to or you are apt to lose both arms.

22

She is an enigma, and probably always was, because there are depths to her of which she is not even aware. Experiences strike deep within her. She watches them, pondering, allowing the waves of activity to sweep over and into her cells for computation. Then she becomes a serious study, a thinker etched in granite, unmoving and unfathomable. You're intrigued by what could possibly be going on behind those silently intelligent eyes.

As a child, her mother would notice her suddenly stop in a crowd. Hands hung loosely by her sides, legs locked back, little belly protruding, she would lift her large thoughtful eyes and watch silently, staring at a particular individual or action. It was as if she were caught in a time warp, where time did not exist for her but she could watch those around her scurrying about, as if from her void she could examine and analyze those earthly actions without interference. Then the moment was gone, and she was the playful, enjoyable child again.

Through her teen years, she was more aware than most of the feelings and thoughts of her peers and authority figures. She wanted to be accepted, needed the companionship and security of friends and family. She found ways to fulfill her needs, either by super-achieving or by clowning around, making other people laugh. Either way, she felt she belonged.

Now, as a woman, she is strongly tied to home, family and those things in her world that make her feel at home. If she dared, she'd probably carry her "ga-ga" (that's a postage-sized blanket left over from her babyhood) wherever she goes because familiar things, things from the past and from loved ones, make her feel happy, loved, secure and comfortable. They enhance her sense of well-being. By now, she has transferred her love to those around her.

She has a strong, protective, militant personality when aroused. Whether she's protecting a child, a cause or an idea, she is a formidable opponent because she has powerful instincts. She knows your weaknesses and will hone in on them like a bat to a cave. If she happens to be frail or slender, don't let her size fool you. She is a powerful woman. Her power comes from her sensitivity to the electrical energy around her. Whenever you think or act, you create an energy wave. She senses these waves, sometimes without knowing it. That's why, even if on the surface she seems calm, cool and collected, she is often nervous and jittery underneath. She is receiving so much subliminal data and trying to process it all the time. When her computers are working at full efficiency she is aware of exactly what is going on with everyone she knows. She senses things you don't reveal, so be careful, and clean up your act.

Your Twenty-Two Woman needs time by herself on occasion. Don't take it personally if you come home one night with a handful of forget-me-nots, kiss her on the back of the neck and say surprise, and she blows like an aerosol can in the fireplace. It's not you. She tends to let things build inside, piece by piece, until she has a tower of brick waving in the breeze, waiting for the slightest puff to send it tumbling down. Your hot breath on the back of her neck was that puff and whammo, there you are on the floor as if a ton of bricks had fallen on you. Symbolically, they did. But then, she will realize what she did, her eyes will fill with love, remorse and compassion—which later will turn to passion (she's very sensual)—and you'll forget all about your mortar burn. It's more than worth it. "Bring on the bricks" will become your battle cry.

Rules and order are a part of her life. After all, it is the thing that keeps the family together. She may be overt in expressing this part of her personality, as was the Twenty-Two Woman, Debbie Boone, when she announced proudly on the Phil Donahue television show that both she and her fiance were virgins—"and intended to remain so until their wedding night." This is one expression of following her rules that is so important to a Twenty-Two.

Other Twenty-Two Women may feel that following the rules of strict body maintenance and proper diet are essential because they value that most personal personal possession—their bodies. If that is the case, eating your greens and getting daily exercise becomes very important to them.

Your Twenty-Two Woman is basically idealistic. She sees that the world must be operated in a certain way if everyone is to be happy and productive. Organization, an eye for details and an uncanny intuition make her the best in the field. She can work from sunrise until the cow bells clang in the evening, and then light the midnight candle if the job isn't quite finished. She'll expect you to do the same. One of her problems is not being able to identify with those who can't or don't choose to work with the same intensity she does. She is idealistic enough to expect them to be there to help when they say they will. Often however, she ends up doing the job alone because others don't feel the same moral work ethic she does. Resentment builds and one day, crash, the walls of Jericho come tumbling down. Whoever is on the receiving end of this musical merger very quickly understands the plain honesty with which she can speak. Blunt, you might call it. This state of affairs can be very confusing to someone who doesn't know her. She can be gentle, loving, understanding, compassionate, and is, indeed, all these things. She will bend over backward and somersault to keep things running well because she respects the harmonious family unit. But when her basic beliefs or her sense of justice is tampered with, watch the family pets. When they start to scatter, you'd better follow their instinctive lead.

Some Twenty-Two Women find fulfillment within the perimeters of their home and church, as did Rose Kennedy who, at 15, was voted the prettiest senior in high school and graduated with honors. After achieving an excellent academic record in college, becoming an accomplished pianist and gaining proficiency in French and German, she married Joseph Kennedy and settled down to her family. Rose stressed an atmosphere of "affection, loyalty and intellectual curiosity." She also kept a card file on illnesses, vaccinations, food problems and visits to the dentist. Her sensitivity and sense of order are most obvious in the way she lives her life. She has been described as an "uncomplaining woman of iron will and self-discipline, of meekness combined with assertiveness, of a wry wit and a sometimes astonishing candor."

Your Twenty-Two Woman does have a sense of humor, perhaps because she can see beneath the surface of things at the way they really are. As Cindy Williams and Valerie Harper are able to do, she can make you laugh. She is a natural mimic, able to copy the actions and inflections of others. Perhaps part of her need to express comically is a release. She is so sensitive, impressionable and absorptive, that in order to relieve some of the tensions in her experience of life, she acts zany. It is a classic psychological tenet that laughter relieves tension. Her silliest days may reflect an alarming level of personal tension.

There is a serious side to your woman, and sometimes this is the dominant personality. Whether she works hard in sports, as does Billie Jean King, or in the

22

field of business, as did Beatrice Webb, author of several "masterly studies on economic conditions," she is somehow involved with the financial side of life. Ms. King became the first woman athlete to be paid $100,000 in a single year. She also soundly whipped Wimbleton champion, Bobby Riggs, in a tennis match called "the battle of the sexes." So much for the "weaker" sex. The sociologist, Mrs. Webb (1858–1943), lived and worked in the field of economics when women weren't considered capable enough to vote. So much for the less "intelligent" sex.

Money seems to play a role in a Twenty-Two Woman's life, whether she's attached to it or not. She seems to need to learn how to use it or work with it. It is one of the resources of the earth and perhaps there is an inner urge that prompts her to understand its intrinsic value when dealing with people's lives. It is a necessary part of living, therefore, a necessary part of her life's experience because she is so involved with the earth and its resources.

Your woman may be quiet, unassuming, cooperative and loving or she may be a live wire, bubbling and jumping from one laugh to another, a bundle of raw energy. Whatever she appears on the surface, one thing you can be sure, she is no lightweight. As Margaret Atwood said, "We still think of a powerful man as a born leader and a powerful woman as an anomaly." Well, your Twenty-Two Woman is not a deviation from the norm, as Bobby Riggs found out, and if what Ann Landers has said is true, "You are what you are when nobody is looking," then your Twenty-Two Woman is more of a powerhouse than you'll ever know. Ever seen her levitate? Or spin straw into gold? Or cause a big, burly man to tremble? She may laugh along with you at your suggestion she could do such things. But deep within her, such thoughts go bump in the night, straining against velvety walls. Those thoughts need only the light of day, the flicker of understanding, to send them on a bursting stream of consciousness into the sunlight.

The only danger here is that your Twenty-Two Woman may be overly conservative in letting inspirational feelings and thoughts flow freely. She has to first understand that they are logical and real even if she cannot see, touch or examine them under a high-powered microscope. She puts much of her experience under rigorous analysis, as if to confirm that what she senses has an external reality that can be seen. Since this is not always the case, she may shut out the psychic side of herself because it cannot be tested in orthodox ways.

You have a delightful, complex woman on your hands. She is a wonderful companion, reveling in the camaraderie of close relationships, responsive to your unspoken needs, willing to cooperate to create a harmonious partnership. She loves her home and family. Although she likes to travel, her home is where she is at her best. When she is back amongst the things that create continuity between the past and the present, she feels whole again. Material objects are part of her being. They don't have to be beautiful or expensive. She enjoys coming home to her favorite frayed armchair.

She can be the most logical of women, organized, detailed, patient with handwork and dealing with people, efficient with money and dedicated to work. She'll cooperate and be a helpmate. She will support and love you. But you must be aware of her sensitivities. They are alive and well and, regardless of how she acts to the contrary, she needs your love. Her no-nonsense, stately approach is so often a cover-up for emotions and feelings that would overwhelm lesser souls. Once you have proven that you truly understand this side of her and will respect it and handle it with TLC, then you have found a solid, enduring haven of rest and love. You have found, as J.R.R. Tolkien so aptly put it in his classic, *The Hobbit*, "a hobbit-hole, and that means comfort." But without warning she'll decide to leave her fine home and embark on a quest. You're it, and you're on it. So buckle up. This will be the wildest ride you've ever had.

The Twenty-Two Man

On the surface your Twenty-Two Man appears to be a walking contradiction. He is, perhaps, one of the more difficult types to describe or understand. He appears either totally dedicated to the subjective, intuitive world or committed to an objective, linear reality, but actually, he's caught up in both. His great mission is to find the balance between the two.

You never really know him. He's a man of many disguises, not necessarily intentionally so. He may not be aware of how reflective and responsive he is to his environment. His feelings run deeper than icy mountain springs; his reaction to outside stimuli is as instinctive as nature herself. He finds himself absorbing the moods, feelings and thoughts of people around him to a point where he can become that person through mimicry. On some level, he notices every lift of the eyebrow, every tremor of the lip and shuffle of the foot, the off-angle drop of a hip and the curious tip of a head. If he decides to use this talent on the stage, he becomes the unmoldable actor, the man who can be a saint or a sinner, an authority or a lunatic with equal ease. He cannot be typecast because no one can put a finger on who he really is. Even he has trouble figuring that out. Film critic Derek Malcolm says of the Twenty-Two Man, Jack Nicholson, "He is one of the few major screen actors around who . . .can change his physical identity from part to part." His features have "great plasticity." He has been described as laconic, wry, funny but very cynical, charming and intuitive. His intuitions have seen him through many difficult situations. The Twenty-Two is a complex creature. Some are intuitive, instinctive, seeming to work off-the-cuff and by-the-seat-of-the-pants and yet, underlying all the poetry resides a method, a pattern, an orderly and systematic approach, a love of form and discipline.

Your Twenty-Two Man is like an ultra-sensitive receiving station. He can pick up the mating advances of a cricket in the next county. He may not know it and, if he does suspect he might be psychic, he may not want to acknowledge it because of that strong part of him that is practical and methodical, rooted in the earth.

Your man is a powerful force in the material world. He is called the Master Builder. He must deal with the world of form, the objective, financial, practical realm in which our physical bodies reside. He has few doubts about himself and his abilities to handle this world because he has an innate self-confidence that is found in those with intellectual and emotional touchstones. He knows he can do anything, and, if given half a chance, he will. And he'll do it thoroughly. There's nothing he hates more than a sloppy job. It offends his basic sense of order and rhythm. If you, the city, the country and the universe aren't run in accordance with generally

22

accepted accounting principles, he can become very fidgety. It is the cosmic scheme of things, he will tell you. If God didn't have a basic sense of order, the planets would be bumping into each other, sending planetary fragments to litter outer space. This would certainly destroy time as we know it and what would happen to our jobs? And, after all, he'll remind you, we're here to work. He knows he has a specific purpose here on this planet, that he is meant to contribute something to the general good, that he has to leave something tangible behind when he vacates this planet.

Like his Four Brother, he has a respect for his body, the most personal physical aspect with which he must work. Sports and physical exercise are an important part of his life-style. Whether he's the head of a large conglomerate making million-dollar decisions every day or a high school chemistry teacher working with the sub-atomic world of form, he will find time to give his body the respect it's due. If he chooses sports as a career, he will approach it with the same methodical, hard-work ethic with which he approaches every other phase of his life.

He is a worker with a cooperative spirit and the need to serve others in some useful, utilitarian manner. He can take on more than his share of the load. He can handle big jobs and he likes nothing better than to take on a task that will affect large numbers of people positively. His approach is marked with vibrancy and broad ideals. He has no patience when he discovers that the promised help is lying out under the apple tree sipping frosty mint juleps while he is sweating over the stapling, folding and stamping of ten thousand programs for the next morning's mail. He can be patient for a long time but then things begin to bottle up inside him and when he realizes that he is being taken advantage of, he will pop his cork and what pours out, like vintage wine, will be strong stuff. He will let the unsuspecting party know in no uncertain terms just what he thinks of him or her. He is such a power person that this outburst can be quite devastating, leaving the victim stunned and speechless.

Your Twenty-Two Man needs to let the steam off more slowly. If he could learn to let people know along the way that certain things are bothering him rather than waiting until the fuse fire is a breath away from the dynamite, he could save himself a lot of body wear and others a lot of shock.

Because he feels the responsibilities and care of the world so keenly, he is apt to be nervous. On the surface, you may never realize this is the case but when he announces that he's going to his room to shut the door and he doesn't want to be disturbed until the frost is on the pumpkin, and you just finished celebrating the 4th of July, you'd better take him seriously. He is sensitive, and because he's a double two, he feels everything doubly. He becomes overstimulated by activities, thoughts and events, not only around him, but around the world. He needs periods of seclusion in which to sort out his emotions and find that balance between his outside and inside worlds. Give him space. He still loves you but he will love you much more harmoniously if you allow him chunks of time alone to regenerate his physical and mental being.

As a little boy, he was either a model child, adhering to his mother's rules like a little soldier or he was an irascible imp, with a perpetual, winning smile on his guilty little face. It was a toss-up as to which side would win but chances are, there was a little of both in him.

Through his teens, again, he was either the model student, getting all A's, playing on the football team and coping all the senior honors at graduation or he was the lovable, troublesome, class mimic, aping his teachers, classmates and every public personality to the delight of anyone in sight.

Today there's still a bit of the poet and soldier in him, although one will be more obvious than the other. But never fear, which ever one he is, the other is lurking in his heart, ready to pop out at the most unexpected moments. When you discover there is something hidden, secretive and unknowable about your Twenty-Two Man, you are usually surprised. "Who would have thought it," people say, shaking their heads in disbelief. "And all along I thought he was..." The final description is surprisingly varied, depending upon to whom you are talking.

The Twenty-Two Man, J. Robert Oppenheimer, American theoretical physicist who directed the production of the first atomic bomb during World War II, excelled in Latin, Greek, physics and chemistry. But he also published poetry and studied Oriental philosophy. He trained a generation of American physicists who were tremendously influenced by his leadership and intellectual independence. His sensitivity to the horror left on the face of the earth by the repercussions of the bomb caused him, as chairman of the General Advisory Committee of the Atomic Energy Commission, to oppose development of the hydrogen bomb.

Your Twenty-Two Man likes the rules because he feels safe within their perimeters. If he chooses to work within the arts—writing, music, acting—the basic rules of applied effort and awareness of rhythm and order are still necesssary in order to produce something meaningful. How many people know that the Twenty-Two Man, Kris Kristofferson, in college, was a football star, golden gloves boxer, sports reporter, member of the honor society and a top-rated ROTC cadet, and that he went on to win a Rhodes scholarship and went to Oxford University to study English literature. When he joined the army, he went through jump school, Ranger school and flight school and was then assigned to Germany as a helicopter pilot. Although he volunteered for Viet Nam duty, he was assigned to teach English literature at the United States Military Academy at West Point. At the age of twenty-nine, he gave it all up and went to Nashville to become a songwriter.

Yes, he can be persistent, that man of yours. You can learn a lot about life by just watching him operate. He has a deep wisdom that others eventually recognize. He is the point to which people gravitate to learn. They feel comfortable, taken care of, nurtured, in his presence. He is a teacher of teachers, training those who will go out into the world and train others. From deep within him surges a geyser of knowing, a fountain that rises to quench the thirst of others. He knows he must reach out to a wide audience, that his destiny lies beyond four walls. His sensitivity is so great that he can become trapped behind those walls that become a shell, shutting others out and himself in. At this point, he seems hard and uncaring but it is only a defense mechanism to protect his soft underbelly, like a crab with its shell and soft interior.

Your Twenty-Two Man is sensual. He may be very ticklish as well because his body antennae are so sensitive, aware and alert at all times for the slightest change in your moods. Don't let that sarcastic or disdainful look fool you. He loves to be loved, fondled. It alerts all the cells in his body. His central nervous system sends messages to his brain where signs flash off and on, red alert. That doesn't mean danger, unless you consider lying in the arms of a wonderfully passionate, handsome male who is aware of your every desire and ready to fulfill it, a dangerous condition!

When he finds his centering point, he is the perfect mate. He exudes strength, wisdom, ability and general confidence about who he is and what he's here to do. You give him a job to do and it will be done, well. He is dependable and enduring. But he's not just another man with a beautiful body and a pretty face. He is also contemplative, intuitive, creative, talented and understanding of you and your feelings. He cares about what you think and what you want from your relationship with him. When he's at his best, he is loving and adaptable to most situations, without giving up one iota of his personal independence and individuality, without jeopardizing his strong foundation and basic beliefs. His loyalty is enduring, like the bristle cone pine which was old when Methuselah was a baby. If you like quality in a product and value for your money, you're wise to invest in a relationship with a Twenty-Two Man.

The Twenty-Three Woman

Where does one begin to describe this bubbly, creative, delightfully social, energy-filled dream who dashes in and out of your life? She's hard to describe for many reasons, not the least of which is the fact that she's always riding on overdrive with the motion of a whirling dervish. If she seems blurry around the edges, it's not your eyesight. Anything that moves that quickly usually gives off such an illusory image, like a moving fan that appears to be a disc but, in reality, is three separate blades. But you'll never know what your Twenty-Three Woman is really comprised of because she doesn't have an off button. She whisked through the pre-natal assembly line so quickly that the angel on duty that night never even noticed. That's not to say she was born with a few missing parts although there may have been times in her life when a few exasperated heads shook that thought around for a few minutes. No, she's got it altogether. Probably, more together than most women you'll ever encounter.

There's no question about the fact that she's a quick thinker. She was ecstatic when the typewriter was patented in 1868, on the 23rd no less!, because now there's finally something that can attempt to keep up with her thought processes. Communication is the motivating force behind everything she does, and she is most adept at it. Whether she's reaching out to people, problems, or ideas, she is performing mental calisthenics that would make Nadia Comaneche look clumsy. She is a natural-born sleuth with a catlike curiosity. There isn't much that can stump her. She can put together a solid yellow banana puzzle in which the corners don't match or solve a Chinese puzzle in record time while more ordinary humans are left behind in a freezing frenzy with ragged cuticles and dark hollows under their glazed eyes. She has a remarkable insight and understanding, and a mind that can twist and turn through the darkest and most unsolvable labyrinths. She can connect intricately hidden or complex ideas with ease seldom seen. She can always think of a better way to do things, how to improve the conditions in her environment. If she decides to put this energy into her home, she'll run it like an Army sargeant with a smile. If she happens to work for you, she'll have your desk drawers organized like a honey comb with the rubber bands separated according to color and the paper clips according to size. She knows a hundred ways to increase the efficiency of the office, restaurant or shop, and if those in charge are wise, they'll listen to her. It would be impossible not to listen to her, she tends to be quite verbal.

Motion and time are points of interest to your Twenty-Three Woman. She likes speed in most areas of her life. However, she must be careful she doesn't sacrifice solid virtues and time-tested techniques for the promise of getting the job done more quickly. Faster is not necessarily better, and if she's more concerned with timing than quality, she will waste her energy and not perform at her best.

The one undeniable fact about your Twenty-Three Woman is that she is exciting. She lives life to the nth degree. She finds life an adventure, a safari into the jungles of emotion, accomplishment, entertainment and sociability. She loves freedom and the space in which to express herself. A dull, drab existence is impossible for her, as you have most likely found out by now, because, if there isn't any excitement, she will create it. The party will never be dull when she's around because she can always come up with an idea for some fun, such as rolling a hula hoop across the mayor's lawn at one in the morning. "Why not," she laughs gaily, "He's always talking in circles anyway."

Speaking of talking, there's one way you can get even with her. Confine her in a room with Jimmy Stewart for one hour and you'll return to find a stark raving lunatic on your hands. Her mind operates like a machine gun, and sometimes her stream of conversation keeps up with it, so when she's confronted with someone who trudges through the English language like a fly in molasses, she's literally beside herself with frustration. And you wouldn't want that. You can hardly handle one of her.

If she's one of the speedy talkers sometimes found in this group, you won't ever have to worry about telling the end of a story, or even finishing a sentence. You just start it and she'll take it from there because, somehow, she always knows exactly what you're going to say anyway. She steps in for one of two reasons, perhaps both. The first is that you're not telling your story fast enough. She can hardly wait to get to the punch line or the point of the telling. The second is that she knows she can tell it with more drama and humor than you ever could. Her mind moves so quickly that she wants it told so you can all move on to the next topic of conversation. Have you ever noticed the length of her attention span? She's like a Mercedes on the Autobahn. She speeds to her destination, absorbing and computing information so quickly that she makes the rest of us look as though we're standing still.

Your Twenty-Three Woman is a social person. She is popular, outgoing and fun to be with. She has a magnetic charm that draws people to her. Because she is so adaptable, she can fit in with almost any type of people and any situation. By nature, she is kind, sympathetic and sensitive to the feelings of others. She's a good diagnostician or psychiatrist because she has the uncanny ability of intuiting what's wrong in the body or the mind, in business, politics or any social setting. With a touch of the dramatic and a way with words, she effectively and eloquently communicates her findings.

The Twenty-Three, fiery, civil rights leader, Bernadette Devlin, who became one of the twelve Northern Ireland British Parliament members in April 1969 shortly before her twenty-second birthday, has been called the "Pasionaria of the Ulster civil rights movement," a "mini-skirted Fidel Castro," and a "Joan of Arc." She has laughingly said of herself, "I am no saint, and not even an interesting sinner."

23

On a scholarship to college, she changed her major to psychology during her second year. Subsequently, during her participation in a civil rights demonstration, a young man was seriously injured by a policeman while trying to protect her. She later recalled, "I was in such a state of anger that I just went back and poured forth at the students for two hours and I haven't stopped since."

Your Twenty-Three Woman cares, and she will be very vocal about her feelings. She may write them down as Devlin did in her book, *The Price of My Soul.* And your woman has a way of getting attention. It is practically impossible for her to go unnoticed. Sooner you could hide the sun behind a pebble on the beach than be able to eclipse her positive, creative, moving energy. She is a doer, no question about it. Because she is so talented, she has a vast array of areas in which to express herself—writing, acting, singing, lecturing, teaching, demonstrating—but always in a way that will make the multitudes sit up and listen. She has so much charisma that she becomes recognizable around the world—a Shirley Temple or Sarah Bernhardt.

Do not think that she doesn't have a care in the world, there is a part of her that is most reflective and aware. She has her moments when she'll stand back, look, feel, think, and generally wait until the situation is absorbed somewhere in her brain cells. This survival mechanism saves her from being totally impulsive and active, plunging into the surf without first testing the water with her big toe. She's nine-tenths plunger, granted, but her dependable instincts tell her when to toe-test. That's why she'll never be predictable. There are little clues, however, as when she takes off her socks at the opera theatre or rolls down her Hanes in a posh restaurant. She's not preparing to grind and bump, but rather to test the environment.

Your Twenty-Three Woman does have to watch out for the fun and games, however. She loves to go to a party and can go all night, driving a splashy BMW from one frolicking spot to another, her hair, long scarf and dress blowing in the night air. She's an extended metaphor, striving to experience everything at once, to describe many lives in one. The danger is the "playgirl" syndrome, where she becomes swept up in the need for continual excitement and motion for the sake of action and not accomplishment and fulfillment. She is in greater danger of wasting and scattering her energies than her Five sisters, the 5 and the 14.

Talk about emotional. This woman of yours runs the gamut of emotions more quickly than the Road Runner with the coyote in pursuit. Her emotions can range from almost inebriated enthusiasm to the black pits of hell and then back again in the time it takes you to say Tiddleywinks. You'll probably end up saying more than Tiddleywinks but only because she surprises you so. Unpredicted typhoons do elicit a few expletives. Expletives, bleeps and deletions follow in her wake like seagulls follow a trawler. She may be totally unaware of the activity she stirs up and the emotions she arouses, most of which is positive however. The responses come from being startled, not necessarily from negative reactions.

Good things come in small packages, and your whirlwind of energy was once a little girl. If you think she likes to have fun now you should interview her mother. She's the panting, exhausted woman over there on the stretcher. The one who is still trying to catch her breath after twenty years of living with your irascible Twenty-Three Woman. As a child, your woman wanted to do everything. To the surprise of many, she could. She didn't have to be coaxed to get up in front of relatives or the class to perform. In fact, if you didn't move quickly enough, you were likely to get trampled as she made a dash for her debut. When she was in front of nine hundred people to perform she was in her glory. The more quiet types would write the play or speech for someone else to read.

As a teenager, the music club, acting group or student council, and probably all three, were graced by her attendance. She was always the first one to volunteer before she even heard what the mission was. A constant diet of this behavior tended to temper her somewhat—not much, but a little. She's also the one who, on a dare, got up on a table in the school cafeteria and to the accompaniment of the squishes of peanut butter and jelly sandwiches and the slurps of Pepsis, sang the Star Spangled Banner, first and second stanzas.

Of course, that's all behind her now. She's grown up, right? She has her priorities today. Housecleaning may be on the bottom of that list but that's only because she has so much to do, things that are much more important and much more fun. Besides, she can get her housework done in about twenty-three minutes.

She can run any place better than any one. Just ask her. She'll toss a stimulating, captivating smile your way and agree most readily, and then march you off on your appointed task. She is efficient when she applies herself, and she can get more done in one day than most can in a week. You'd better recognize this fact because she does need recognition and positive feedback from you. She bathes in your approval and admiration which refreshes her for more action and excitement. She's not keen on routine, balking at a steady nine to five life style. What she really wants is to be her own boss, set her own hours and clean up the mess others have made of this beautiful world. In the meantime, she'll find time for you. Remember, she can do a lot of things at the same time. When you're the object of her sparkling eyes, you'll feel every cell in your body come to attention. She'll make you know what it's like to be alive. When she throws her arms about your neck and beams up into your happy face, you'll understand that, although everything can be improved, she's the next best thing to perfection. After all, no one's perfect. Except maybe...her.

The Twenty-Three Man

Now you see him, now you don't. Your Twenty-Three man is as quick, adaptable and elusive as quicksilver. His mercurial qualities are legendary. His sneakers are specially made to conceal the wings on his heels, and the rubber in his footgear grounds his tremendous electrical energy. You must have noticed it. The way your hair stands on end when he's nearby, and the way people automatically turn toward him when he enters a room, as if they expect something is about to happen—which it is of course. He doesn't just make things happen—he is a happening. Wherever he goes, his curious, magnetic energy creates excitement. People may not know why they feel suddenly energized and alert when he's around but, at some level, they are responding to his mind power, which whirls at incredible speeds.

At one level, many Twenty-Three Men are very social creatures. Your man may love the crowds, the parties, the stage and his central position there, entertaining the multitudes. He tends to be the focal point of any gathering because he is so witty and clever. His lightning-quick repartees astonish, captivate and mesmerize his friends and any available audiences. One part of him thoroughly

23

enjoys this exchange of energy because at heart he is a communicator and showman. He is the type to bound out of bed, that is, if he hasn't danced into the wee hours of the morning, which is very likely, and be up and out of the house before you can say Jack Sprint. There might be something going on out there that he wouldn't want to miss. He's not likely to miss anything anyway because his five senses are always on alert, picking up information with the keen sense of a campaign manager awaiting a blitz from the opposing candidate.

He is wired for sound. Whether he appears calm and controlled on the surface or fidgets like a released Jack-in-the-box, you can be sure that his nervous system is highly activated. He runs on his nerves, therefore he needs time by himself, away from the active, moving crowds with which he usually associates. This seeming dichotomy produces a Twenty-Three type that may be described as reclusive and quiet but you will inevitably find that they still need social contact in large doses. Even if they are loners, they could never become hermits because they need contact and feedback from others. On a regular basis, such as through their professions, they will mingle, socialize and generally express their keen and lively wit and engaging conversational abilities because that is what feeds their furnace. But your Twenty-Three Man must take periodic rests or he will burn himself out.

To understand all the facets and implications of this man is to try to solve Rubik's cube. He has so many twists and turns in his personality that capturing a view of one solid and unmoving side of him is a major accomplishment. Closer examination reveals, however, that his other sides are still not matched.

You'll retain a saner view on life if you just flow with him and enjoy the trip. To say that he'll make your life interesting is a study in understatement. You won't have a dull or restful moment. He has a curious way about him that seems to stir other people into motion. He's the yeast that's added to a recipe. Suddenly the dough is rising, expanding, and forces are set in motion. The most apt description of your Twenty-Three Man is he's a catalytic communicator. He gets things moving and changes the status quo, sometimes without being the least affected himself. He'll stand in the midst of the melee with an innocent look on his face, wondering why everyone is so excited, what caused all the commotion. There are times when he's not aware that he's the one who unraveled things, everything was running smoothly and quietly before he came upon the scene and now everyone's running around like kittens chasing their tails wondering why they're going round and round and not accomplishing anything. They're probably picking up his dizzy energy.

The Twenty-Three Man Johnny Carson has been called "the sharpest mind in America today." His "Tonight Show" has been dubbed "NBC's answer to foreplay." The "King of Late Night Television," the quick-witted Carson has won out over late night rivals such as Dick Cavett, Merv Griffin and Joey Bishop, and even topped the CBS Late Night Movie. He keeps up a frantic pace, chain smokes and is an exercise nut. Even though he is described off screen as quiet and reflective, his life style depicts a man who needs to throw off tremendous excess energy and one who thoroughly enjoys his professional role as entertainer.

Your Twenty-Three Man has a curious mind. Like Carson, who scans the *New York Times* and the *Los Angeles Times* each morning for monologue material, your man can scan wide ranges of information, absorb and digest it, then spew it out for popular consumption. He knows how to communicate the information once he has gathered it. Because he is interested in almost every phase of living, he is a veritable Ft. Knox of knowledge. This awareness, in conjunction with his ability to intuit information that is not readily available in the ordinary way, gives him uncanny diagnostic talents. He has a way of just "knowing" what's wrong in the physical, social or political body. Not only does he know, but he wants to tell everyone what he knows, and will eventually do so in a masterful manner.

His sexual magnetism is legendary. His ability to communicate spills over into every area of his expression. He is a warm, affectionate and demonstrative lover. You won't find the same old thing every night with this man. Nothing bores him more than routine, day or night. He is curious and likes to investigate the new and untried.

Some Twenty-Three Men may live the sexual facet of their personality vicariously, as did Alfred C. Kinsey, author of the best-selling book, *Sexual Behavior in the Human Male* (1948) which was roundly condemned from many pulpits, to be followed by the even more shocking, *Sexual Behavior and the Human Female* two years later. (Women weren't thought to have sexual thoughts or feelings in 1950.) Although Kinsey was "upright," "responsible" and serious, he didn't go out with a woman until he was twenty-seven and then married her, and conducted exhaustive studies on the gall wasp, an insect which reproduces without sexual encounter. His curiosity about relationships was very evident, as was his ability to relate that information to the public in a dramatic manner. He also gave lectures where his "wry sense of humor" came to the surface. When asked what he thought of a doctor who wrote that a man reached his sexual peak at forty-eight, Kinsey replied, "My opinion would be that the doctor was 48." Kinsey went on working eighteen hours a day despite criticism from the "moral" community.

Regardless of the restrictions others try to place upon him, your Twenty-Three Man must have his freedom, to do, think and express himself in his own inimitable way. He needs a big playground—perhaps the entire planet—in which to roam. That's not to say he is not loyal. He can be the most devoted mate in the world but he has to feel free, he has to know he has room to move within that relationship, that he isn't smothered or watched or followed every moment of his day. He doesn't like small spaces where he feels crowded.

For you to try to keep him from expressing his opinions would be like an ant trying to muzzle a great dane. Don't even try. This doesn't mean that he's always talking. Some Twenty-Three Men are surprisingly quiet—they find other ways to get their messages across—but when he does decide to speak, just move back and let it happen. Discretion is the better part of valor. Besides, there's nothing else you can do anyway. His inner motivation to communicate in some manner is so strong that it would be as useless to stem it as it would be to shovel you-know-what against the tide.

Because the Twenty-Three Man is so versatile and talented, you are apt to find him in almost any profession but his work will always be stamped with an agile versatility and a charming way of getting across to other people. What he has to be careful of is becoming temperamental and explosive, letting his emotions get the better of him. Sometimes he gets too many things going at the same time, neglecting to do any one of them well. This will increase his frustration, bringing on moodiness and unpredictability. But when these facets of his multi-dimensional personality are

23

under control, he is the most amazing of men, able to do just about anything and publicize his feats at the same time.

As a child, he was either physically or mentally performing calisthenics. Naturally, one is much easier to identify than the other. The first is the type who easily twists caps off child-proof bottles, who wants to know where babies come from and is the first youngster in the family to find daddy's "bunny" book.

In his teens, as did Alfred Kinsey, he may be one of the first eagle scouts in the country, writing papers such as "What Do Birds Do When It Rains?" Who else but a Twenty-Three Man would want to know what a cuckoo does in a downpour? Rest assured, he didn't enter adulthood until he found the answer to that fascinating question.

Your Twenty-Three Man may be the type who is extremely agile physically, as are dancer-actor Gene Kelly and Pele, the world's most celebrated athlete. The big problem with them seems to be shutting off the energy. At seventy years old, Gene Kelly says: "My only problem is in learning how to loaf. I'm a little better now but I still find it hard to relax for more than one day at time." Pele was so restless in the classroom that he finally left school at the end of the fourth grade. Both men made successes of themselves because they could think. Kelly devised a new form of dance from ballet, tap, modern dance and athletics that revolutionized the art of motion picture choreography, and Pele had the ability to plot elaborate offensive plays on the spur of the moment. Like them, your Twenty-Three Man is mentally quick, and often, just as quick on his feet. See how easily he tap danced into your heart.

In spite of the socially inclined aspects of this man, there is a deep, hidden side to him that is often mystifying to those who, at first meeting, find him so charming. He can be exceptionally protective about his private thoughts—those he wants you to know about you will know about—and his private life may be classified Top Secret, but because he can carry on a lengthy conversation, you feel as though you've known him all your life without really knowing anything at all. Though he often appears to act quickly, without much thought, he is more often reacting. His thought processes move so quickly that he can assess a situation with lightning speed, then counter with the missing elements. He is naturally intuitive and psychic but he may translate that as just being logical. He often wonders why everyone doesn't move and think at the same speed he does. If people or things move too slowly around him, he can become most impatient. Sitting around is not his idea of a fun thing to do, unless he's heavily into researching a pet idea or project, in which case he'll die with his boots on, covered with a thick layer of dust.

Your Twenty-Three Man has a magnetic force that pervades his environment, touching everyone and everything that comes in contact with him. Most people love him—a few may not—but one thing you can be sure of is that he won't go unnoticed. It's rather difficult to turn your back on the winged messenger of the gods. Mercury has a way of turning heads, piquing your curiosity, exciting your senses and raising your temperature. Your thermometer's rising steadily. It's that sensual glint in his playful eyes and the element of surprise and the unknown that lies in his waiting arms. You know you can't resist his charms. The lights are low, the music soft, he's coming toward you, your heart's thumping like a bongo drum. You can't imagine what delights lie in wait for you. He might even take off his sneakers.

The Twenty-Four Woman

That curvaceous female on the beach gingerly sticking her meticulously polished big toe into the ocean to test the temperature is your Twenty-Four Woman. She isn't about to dash higgledy-piggledy into the pounding surf to discover that the water's too cold and the waves are too overpowering. Such uncertainties disturb her. But once she's made a positive determination, she enters the ocean with full appreciation of the feel of the waves on her body, the taste of salt on her lips and the sensation of the sun on her skin. She will enjoy the experience to the fullest.

Basically, your Twenty-Four Woman takes life seriously. She feels responsibility toward any duties assigned to her. In community and civil work, she is the solid citizen, the cooperator and builder, the one who wants a strong foundation under her and just laws to govern those structures she builds and within which she lives. She has a cosmic egg mentality. She sees everything as her duty and everyone as her responsibility, and she hovers over both with the same devotion as a mother hen.

There's a big part of her that's a homebody. The natural nurturing instinct surges up in her every time a stray cat walks through her yard. The stray is probably well-tended and loved, but she'll whisk it into the house and give it a good meal just in case, then watch it prance, well-satisfied, down her driveway on its way to tell all its friends about the soft touch in the neighborhood.

Her house is already well-populated. She's the one who phones in everytime there's a call for help over the television. She now houses three adopted children, cares for four children overseas, fifteen dogs, six cats, a pet skunk and a baby tarantula, besides being a scout leader and a member of the PTA and the Save The Baby Seals Organization. She just got off the phone and now she's filling the bath tub. "But they have such beautiful, big eyes," she explains.

Your Twenty-Four Woman may also be a perfectionist and, with the household she's got, that could drive her to reading the telephone book for pleasure. The columns are so neat. You can tell if she has this exacting malady if, after you shower, she expects you to chin yourself on the shower rod and drip-dry. Spots on the newly scrubbed bathroom floor just won't do.

But she has such a pleasant way of saying things that you find it hard to resist her logic. Her sultry voice slips over you like a silk blouse over a powdered body. You can feel the lilting waves wash around you hypnotically. There's a poetry, an art, a captivating rhythm in her delivery that has you listening more to the melody than the meaning, which is usually fortunate because the meaning often escapes you. She may be musical, like the perfectionist Twenty-Four Woman, Barbara Streisand, whose million dollar vocal chords have captivated the world.

This woman of yours may be an antique "nut." She puts a high price on things made by hand, appreciating the feeling and love that goes into them. They also give her a sense of continuity with the past, a feeling of belonging and security. The sensual beauty of an exquisite antique really turns her on. Sometimes you wish she would get as excited over you as she does over nineteenth century Satsuma porcelain. You may not have that aged look but you do have good lines and you weren't made in Taiwan—were you? Anyway, you were made with love so that makes you quality.

24

Friends and family are especially important to your Twenty-Four Woman. She sees her life in terms of relationships and she needs constant feedback from others to ensure her identity and safety. Some Twenty-Four Women have highly developed egos and must be careful they don't become stubborn and argumentative, believing they have the correct solution to every problem that arises. Then their fine nurturing and caring qualities degenerate into fault-finding and worrying.

Your Twenty-Four Woman can be a very hard worker. She's willing to assume many obligations and carry them through, efficiently and well. She has strong organizational qualities so she can handle groups, whether they be family, friends or large corporations, with a firm, orderly but loving hand. Part of her success in this area is her power of observation through which she learns quickly. She can see the whole picture as well as the parts, and she knows how to bring it all into a harmonious balance. What she lacks, if anything, in any other area, she more than makes up for in perseverance. It was persistence that ensured the Twenty-Four Woman, Belva Ann Lockwood, her right to practice law before the United States Supreme Court, the first woman to do so.

As does Ms. Lockwood, your Twenty-Four Woman has pronounced social feelings and a desire to see justice done for all peoples. When those emotions are aroused and rise within her, she surges up like the Almighty Cosmic Mother whose relentless poundings cannot be denied any more than the shoreline denies the storm waves. She makes her point. When she moves in righteous anger, she is an impressive sight but don't be lulled into false security if she appears as calm as the most placid of waters on a sparkling sunny day in summer. The waves are still washing in, and little by little, she works her wonders.

Your Twenty-Four Woman has a personality that attracts others because she is basically a loving person. That loving nature emerges through her actions and envelopes all those who meet her in person and get to know her as a friend. Because she has such warm and earthy energy, she should go after her goals personally, meet people face to face rather than use the telephone, the mails or emissaries. Her personal charm and magnetic voice will win the day every time. When she reaches out to shake, women feel they have a friend and men wish to kiss her hand. Her touch conveys subtle messages of love, compassion and empathy.

When she was a little girl, she probably liked playing doctor, not only because of the nature of her strong desire but because she has an innate healing energy that needs to be expressed. A play first aid kit, complete with bandaids, red-colored water for iodine and candy pills, would have delighted her on any occasion. How she managed to get bandaids to stick to the angora cat was beyond everyone's understanding. And she had the only cat with a continuing case of what appeared to be the mange—all those bare spots. "Ouchless" bandaids hadn't been invented then.

Through her teen years, she may have been somewhat shy and retiring. If so, she was only biding her time, getting her bearings, feeling her way around life's corners, nooks and crannies. She may have allowed others to take advantage of her good nature so that she ended up with the dirty jobs, the ones that no one else wanted to do. But she is observant and soon learned that there are more ways than one to earn the respect and friendship of others. She discovered her diplomacy.

Now, as an adult, she uses her powers of persuasion and her charming manner of dealing with people to good and proper advantage. She will hold up her end of any arrangement, even if she finds the task distasteful, because she believes in the rules. This behavior may continue until she reaches a point where she feels she has been pushed too far, used too much, then she will make decisions to correct the problem and no amount of cajoling or threatening will change her mind. The Twenty-Four Woman and novelist, Edith Wharton, as a debutante in 1880 in New York society, moved "dutifully through the social rituals, (even though she) secretly hated it; or better, she saw through it." Her "subtle and ironic novels satirized the aristocratic New York society into which she was born—and from which she escaped." She was totally unprepared for the inadequate sexual relationship in her marriage, common for women in her time, and the dominant theme of her writing was the "entrapment of women—in an ill-chosen marriage or simply within the constraints of society." She produced book after book for an appreciative audience and the ensuing enormous sums allowed her to divorce her husband and live a "quietly luxurious existence."

Was it mentioned that your woman may have a taste for the finer things in life? She may have excellent taste in clothes and the jeweled accessories, or in decorating her home, the community or public buildings and offices. She feels the need to put her extreme artistic tendencies into some kind of form. Whether this expresses in creative productions of her own or collections of beautiful objects is hard to say but you will find out soon enough. Some people may be satisfied with a piece of the rock but when she starts investing in pieces of the Taj Mahal and having it shipped to her place, you'd better nip those tendencies in the bud.

Close loving and sexual relationships are important to your Twenty-Four Woman. She thoroughly enjoys the physical contact but she needs more than a body in her bed. She wants your love and tenderness and understanding. She needs a completely balanced partnership. This is the spiritual side of her, manifesting in her need to share all of herself with you. Her warm, sensual, physical contact with you, coupled with the sharing of her love and devotion, gives you the best of both worlds. She is ready to be your partner, on an equal sharing and loving basis, to go through life with you facing the good times and the bad. She is strong and enduring, not falling by the wayside the minute adversity strikes. Often, she will do more than her share but don't take advantage of her because then her justice issues rise up and you'll have more trouble than you can handle. And when the "weaker" sex gets riled up, at least in the animal kingdom, the males know enough to back off.

There is a very practical side to this woman, that's if and when her desire for luxuries isn't predominant in her life. But, even then, the practical, conservative woman will shine through. She will clip coupons and search the papers for sales. Her dollar bills have unsightly stretch marks because she values things of the earth—like money. She works hard for it and, as a rule, spends it with caution.

Your Twenty-Four Woman is not the type to get carried away by every new fad and idea that comes bopping down the pike. She wants time to absorb and process new approaches, time to carefully test the possible repercussions of any act. To her, rash means those little red bumps that break out on the body. And that's not a rash or fingernail polish on her big toe after all. It's the mercury in her thermometer for testing climatic conditions.

Tradition is as much a part of her as feathers are of a duck. And what's an eider without down. She will faithfully carry out the little rituals during holidays and in the running of her home and raising of her children that her mother and grandmother did. In a positive sense, the book *My Mother, My Self*, is more true of her than most women because she so identifies with her past and her roots. To continue these traditions bestows a sense of security in her life. It is a familiar, safe, loving and secure way to live. So, if every Thanksgiving you have to go on a Fox and Geese hunt, following a trail of newspaper strips through the woods to capture the "goose," or have to hang Christmas stockings on the mantle, not only the entire family but also, for the gerbil, parakeet and the pet tarantula, you'll understand why. Although you may have trouble helping Santa fill the arachnid's stocking. What do you give a tarantula who has everything? And knowing her, it will. Can you believe that at one time you had trouble shopping for your woman.

One thing you won't have any trouble with is the way she looks at you with those secret, intimate glances, when the room is full of people. You can feel each other's presence as a deep longing about to be filled. You move toward her, bend down and whisper, "What are you looking at?" She lifts her long lashes up toward you and says huskily, "You." Every circuit in your body is suddenly on alert. And if these people don't leave soon, you will teach her another meaning for the word rash.

The Twenty-Four Man

All the world loves a lover so no wonder your Twenty-Four Man is in such demand. He can pen a pretty poem, arousing your most libidinal instincts because there is a sensuality in his approach that is right in the bosom of Mother Earth. He feels his way through the words like an accomplished woodworker caresses the wood he will fashion into a thing of beauty. He has an on-going love affair with the things that belong to the earth, the things that fill his senses with wonder and awe at the symmetry and balance so obvious in the natural running of this beautiful green planet. Coupled with his poetic nature is a basic need for order.

He shares nature's need for an orderly system—it wouldn't do for spring to follow summer or the trees to bud in the fall—and your Twenty-Four Man wouldn't think of omitting a comma, semi-colon or the proper syntax. What would a passionate love poem be with itinerant plural possessives and dangling participles? He attacks such defacing oddities with the full vigor and energy he possesses, which is considerable.

The Twenty-Four Man, Robert Graves, author and poet, has established himself firmly in literary halls. Once dismissed as a "minor poet" because of his "adherence to traditional metrical form," he eventually became recognized as a master in his field. His poetry has been described as "hard-edged, vigorous, precise and clear in its diction, sensuous in its imagery and ironic in its wit." And when Graves says that "the main theme of poetry is properly the relations of man and woman rather than those of man and man," he is expressing the true Twenty-Four Man's outlook on life. The man-woman relationship theme in poetry is his perception of poetry's purpose because he sees life in those terms.

Firm foundations will always be obvious in your man's approach to this world. He explores the perimeters of his world with a cautious exactness so that he won't fall off the edge—just in case the International Flat Earth Research Society is right and the world really is flat. This is one of the reasons that the perimeters of home, family and relationships are so important to your man. They give him a sense of belonging, an identity that is reflected in the reactions of others to him. They are a quantity in his life he can see, feel and measure because they are there, around him, loving him. He responds to the security these facets of his existence lend him.

Even if he is charming and social, witty and clever, there is a part of him that often needs to close the door to the outside world. You will often find him walking through the woods or along the beach or the river when he is in this frame of mind. Getting in touch with nature soothes his high energy level. However, most of the time he needs people. He is the partner, the helper, the builder, the creator.

A number of factors join in your Twenty-Four Man to create an individual with an appreciation of art in some form. There is a sense of drama in him that comes out at the most unlikely moments. He has a talent for magnifying his emotions so the stage or music or writing is a fine outlet for him. He learns a great deal about human nature through his powers of observation and can often mimic others in comical ways. His warm, earthy personality and pleasant tone of voice and manner of speaking draw others to him. Once he is aware of these innate characteristics, he will be a success in whatever field he chooses and these qualities will shine through.

Health is an issue that can interest a Twenty-Four Man in some way. His hands are a special part of his anatomy. They can feel the vibrations of the things they touch and caress, they know an object or person better after they have touched it. For this reason, your Twenty-Four Man may have healing powers in his touch. A hand on the forehead of a sick child or friend may work wonders and transmit his tremendous healthy energy without him ever knowing it. His presence lends a stabilizing factor to the disrupted energies of the sick. For this reason, the field of medicine, especially chiropractic care, or the ministry may beckon him. At any rate, at some level he is interested in and aware of his state of health, and that his body is a precious resource, which he should value. Whether he cares for it or not, he is aware that he should.

Your Twenty-Four Man can be exceptionally effective in business as well. He is not afraid of work. It's no accident there are twenty-four hours in a day, and sometimes your man thinks he should be working through all of them. He does need to be busy, to channel his energies into an active life style because, if he doesn't, those energies will build up inside him and cause physical problems. He is a person who should never retire. If, for some reason, he isn't working, he can do an about face and become very lazy, lying around worrying about this, that and the other, until you're ready to truss him up and drop him in the Salvation Army box. So, encourage him in his work, help him find his true niche, because, once he does, he will share it with you.

He is very family oriented. His family, personal possessions and comforts can be of utmost importance in his life because he has a strong, loving nature. He will go to all lengths to protect you and his domain because his home is his castle. Even his trash is his until it lands in the town dump. Watch him react when a strange car stops in front of your house and a man steps out and starts examining the trash you put out that morning for collection. A furrow appears over his eyes, his head thrusts forward as he peers out the window.

"What's that guy doing, going through our trash?" he asks, accusingly.

"I don't know," you reply. "Maybe there's something there he can use."

"Yeah, but that's my trash," he retorts, still glaring intently at the stranger, as

24

if his stare would disassemble the unsuspecting man's atomic structure. "He's got no right pawing through my stuff." He's reaching for his coat now. He doesn't let go of things too easily.

Your Twenty-Four Man can be a wonderful promotor because he has a sense of what the public needs and likes, and how to present those products. His sense of theatrics may come out in the way he publicizes his business while he himself can play very low key. In one way or another, you will see his flair in handling people and making them like it. The mystery of him is that you don't know whether you're about to meet a quiet, sedate individual or a demented gypsy violinist. It may not be a question of either/or with him, but of when. Sometimes he'll be the first and at other times he's the second. You'll hold your breath more than once waiting to see which side will surface. If you embarrass easily, wear red when he's around. The contrast won't be so stark.

As a child, your Twenty-Four Man needed to belong, to feel a part of the family and its activities. Part of his security was being noticed so he would find ways to get attention. A little soft shoe, reciting poetry, maybe even helping with the housework—there's a part of him that's very orderly—and if that didn't work, he may have resorted to more dramatic means like painting murals on the walls. It wasn't until much later that his mother appreciated his artistic endeavors.

Through his teens, his need for camaraderie was stronger than ever. His warm, down-to-earth personality attracted all kinds of people. He may have begun then to realize that his talents lie in expressing his abilities in personal ways as did the Twenty-Four Man, Jim Henson, who, in high school, joined a puppet club. Henson's voice and his ability to communicate basic feelings and attitudes was his forte. Today, the majority of the more than five hundred Muppets of television and film fame "owe their voices to Henson." Everyone identifies with these lovable bits of cloth and ping-pong balls because of the loving care their creator has bestowed on them. Henson commented that owning the Muppets was like having an "international nursery school."

Your man has carried these same qualities with him into adulthood. It is the window through which he views his world. Therefore, he should instill these feelings in everything he does, including his work. If he runs his own business then he should follow his natural inclinations and treat his employees as one big family. They will respond to his caring nature and be loyal and persevering. His faith in the basic goodness of people will be well rewarded, and he can make a success of any business he goes into. Who would have thought the Muppets would gross $15 million annually? So, don't be alarmed if he decides to start a rent-a-jogger franchise or a National Ghost Adoption Agency. Besides, he can stand the jeers and taunts of less imaginative types. He is sensitive, yet he doesn't ruffle as easily as some.

There is very little that gets past his observation and instinctive awareness. He has a feel for things, situations and people, knowing just how to handle them to bring out the very best they have to offer. He stores the subtle nuances he observes in the people he meets so that, if he is of a mind to do so, he is the perfect mime. This quality in Jim Henson is what gives his Muppets their human personalities and appeal. Your Twenty-Four Man uses this stored data at a later date, when the need or occasion arises, even if he does so unconsciously. He is instinctively aware of how he should respond to each person. Whether he chooses to do so is another matter. Most of the time he does, because he basically likes peace and a comfortable life style and environment.

Your Twenty-Four Man knows that, as Bacon said, "Nature, to be commanded, must be obeyed." He has an innate respect for the rules that lend stability to the world he so loves and with which he identifies. When he lives with the rules, he no longer needs them because they become a natural part of his way of life.

When he lives up to the best within him, his principles are admirable and unshakable. He believes in truth, hard work and accomplishment. He values love, loyalty, family, friends and compassion. He is the one who listens to your problems with an understanding ear and can give wise counsel if needed because he truly understands your feelings. He has the added advantage of being practical enough to not offer you inappropriate platitudes when what you need is good solid advice. He is unafraid to stoop to wipe a small tear or bandage a tiny knee yet he is a pillar of strength, unbending in a battering storm. He will love you with a devotion and tenderness that brings tears to your eyes and a prayer of thanks to your lips. You know you must have done something special to warrant such a man. And if height were given out for merit, your Twenty-Four Man would be breathing a most rarified air. Speaking of breathing, notice how yours changes dramatically whenever he's around!

The Twenty-Five Woman

You knew from the beginning that your Twenty-Five Woman was different. Was it because she was sitting in a lotus position on the public transportation system uttering faint ommmms or was it merely your superior awareness that alerted you to the fact that here was someone you'd like to get to know better? You've never quite been able to figure out that first meeting just as you've never quite been able to figure out this woman you call love. There's no question "she is woman." You haven't seen that many lush rolling hills and dales since you were in Vermont. But you've since found out that this woman is a dangerous combination of beauty and brains. There should be a law forcing women like her to wear bright blue arm bands so they can be easily recognized before men are inexorably drawn into their subtle, magnetic aura. But it's too late now. You've made your bed so you must lie in it. The next question is: how are you going to deal with this gorgeous creature?

You could turn on the charm, maybe you'd fool her. But that won't work because she has an ability to see right through any false pretensions or tomfoolery. The normal tactics won't work with her. You see, she has more than five instincts and they're always working overtime. Her mind is as busy as a shopping mall the day before Christmas, but she's not the type to buy just anything. She's a very selective shopper. She knows what's quality and what isn't so a little wining and dining is fine but don't get too carried away with your technique because she knows exactly where you're coming from. The best thing you can do is try being you. She'd like that.

Your Twenty-Five Woman likes the message to be clear. Helen Reddy, born on the 25th, composed and sang the hit song, "I Am Woman," against the advice of her producer. Included on her first L.P., it was only mentioned by music reviewers of the feminine persuasion. But, in a month's time, it sold over a million copies, 80

25

percent to women. Ms. Reddy said that she had experienced a lot of life and one night realized that she couldn't have survived if she hadn't been strong so she wrote a song that "reflected the feminist consciousness." Her song spoke of her personal philosophy, strengths, and belief in herself. This woman of yours is no faded lily.

Her intuitive responses will leave you bubbling in your beer more than you care to admit. No one can be right that often. But then, you're trying to apply the law of averages, logic and statistics to her, and that's like applying Robert's Rules of Order to Michaelangelo's sculpting of *The Pieta*. One has little connection with the other. So, just relax and enjoy her. Don't try to figure out how she does it. As Napoleon said when questioned about his one-night vigil inside the Great Pyramid, "You wouldn't believe it anyway."

But talk to her. She wants to communicate, and she does it well. Be sure to focus on that word "communicate" because it means the information goes both ways. She isn't about to sit like a bump on a log and listen to you expounding about the superiority of the patriarchal world and its myriad accomplishments. Expect some feedback. As a matter of fact, expect a lot of feedback, like a copy of Webster's complete, unabridged, modern, up-dated dictionary making resounding contact with your pituitary (which is located right between your eyes). She can be most graphic when she puts her mind to it. And you'd better believe she has the mind to do it.

Every Twenty-Five Woman is a philosopher, overtly or not. She is in touch with mystical worlds that are hidden from many others. The unknown fascinates her. Helen Reddy studies philosophy and psychology, and curiously enough, her first hit song was "I Don't Know How To Love Him," Mary Magdalene's poignant love song from the rock musical *Jesus Christ Superstar*. The Twenty-Five Women, Ella Fitzgerald, Aretha Franklin and Anita Bryant have strong religious ties. Carly Simon and Sissy Spacek are into meditation and TM. It would be impossible to keep a Twenty-Five Woman away from investigating and discovering the hidden psyche, the inner self and the higher Self. It is a deep-seated compulsion with her. So, you'd better get used to her chanting mantras, droning ommmms, proclaiming the Word, and tramping over forbidden ground. She's a vagabond wonderer and wanderer, but not in an aimless and shifting pattern. She seeks knowledge, therefore her feet may tread strange and confusing paths, from your point of view, but she innately knows where she's going and her ultimate goal will prove the journey worthwhile.

Because of her journey there is a part of her that remains aloof. In the midst of the most charming conversation and social interplay, she remains an island, shimmering like an emerald in the heart of an expansive sea. The waves may lap at her gently, caressing her tenderly under the warmth of the sun, or toss and surge with frenetic motion, whipping into a frenzy on her shores. She will stand stolid, deep and enduring, knowing that outside forces can never disturb or alter the core that resides deep inside her being. It's a thing she knows but cannot explain. She just knows that she is woman.

By now you've found that out too. You've discovered that she can carry on animated conversation with the butcher, the baker, Dolly Parton or Golda Meir with equal ease and consumate skill. She is a highly intelligent woman, with a quick mind and penetrating insight. If you have a secret, forget it. Before you're seven sentences into the conversation, you'll find those guarded words slipping through your lips like a silk kerchief from a magician's sleeve. She has a way of subtly guiding you through troubled waters to the source of the problem and before you know it, it's out in the open where you can all examine it. One feels rather naked around her.

The Twenty-Five Woman, Barbara Walters, overcoming a slight speech impediment, has become one of the "most astute interviewers in TV history." She's conducted newsmaking interviews with every President since Lyndon Johnson as well as with world figures like Anwar Sadat, Henry Kissinger and Menachem Begin. Her quick wit caught TV talk show interviewer David Frost by surprise when she told him, before the cameras, that she succeeded in the difficult television business by "hard work, determination and sleeping with the producer." This woman can parry words with the best. So, in your woman you find a baffling mixture of curiosity and stimulating conversation combined with silence and aloofness.

When she slips out of her meditative frame of mind, she can be the life of the party. She injects zest, enthusiasm, fun and excitement into each moment as if it were her last and she is going to live every sweet beat of it. There's a cry of "wagons ho" resounding deep inside her so she creates a feeling of adventure in everything she does. Her enthusiasm and charm captivate you. Before you know it, you're perusing the ads in the Sunday paper for your own Conestoga. Any woman who can talk a man out of his four-wheel drive has something going for her.

She loves nature. Surprisingly enough, behind that glamour, charm and intellect, lies a very simple woman. She finds peace in the rustle of the leaves and bubble of a brook, solace in the incessant beating of the surf against granite cliffs and wonder at her own immortality in the pinpoints of light that glitter in the canopy of the midnight skies.

Your Twenty-Five Woman can extract nature's secrets like no other. Because she has pronounced intuitions and analytical ability, she is a natural detective, whether she is in the laboratory searching for the cure to rampant disease, teaching and stretching young minds in a classroom, attempting to bring reason and sanity to an unstable political world or guiding her children through this wonderful journey called life with their eyes wide open and aware. She recognizes the similarities in Mother Nature and human nature.

She can be very analytical. She thinks in ways that no one else does, following circuitous routes that would amaze a Minotaur. When, looking for a friend, you ask if Joe's around, she's apt to pause, gaze into space a moment, then reply thoughtfully, "No, actually, he's more complex than that. If I had to use shapes to describe him, I'd be more apt to call him a sphere with many facets." It may take you a moment or two to figure out what she's said, but you have to remember, she takes life seriously, thinks seriously, and puts deep meaning into the things you say.

If you think you're lost at times when she's around, watch her when she's involved with a book. Seventy-six trombones and a clarinet blaring full force seven feet behind her would not disturb her concentration. You've probably noticed this if you've ever tried to get her attention during these moments. She effectively builds an invisible, soundproof bubble around herself and floats off into the sacred pages of the book she has carefully selected. Like a computer, she'll store that information into neat little drawers for further reference.

Your Twenty-Five Woman must be aware that her analytical abilities can turn critical if she expects that same response to high ideals from others that she often sets for herself. She must learn not to be judgmental about the life-styles of others.

Sometimes she sets her principles so high that she finds it difficult to live up to them herself. She finds herself fluctuating between vowing to adhere to her standards with every ounce of her strength and giving them up entirely as impossible goals. Here, the Twenty-Five Woman becomes vacillating, erratic and brooding. This can degenerate into preaching morals but practicing a very different life-style herself, rather like a "Do as I say and not as I do" syndrome. However, her "doing" can be very private.

But most often your Twenty-Five Woman sets standards that she knows she can attain and she lives up to them gracefully and admirably, setting a fine example for others. This mind-set began early in her life when, as a child, she loved playing courtroom scenes. Wearing last Halloween's witches' robes, carrying a Bible under one arm, she would climb up on top of stacked wooden boxes and proceed to listen to the grievances of her neighborhood friends. After weighing and measuring the evidence, she would either sentence them to CC (clubhouse clean-up) or award them damages (so many black jelly beans—the black ones tasted best).

Teenage years saw her struggling more than most of her friends with what was "right" and "wrong." She didn't find it as easy to flaunt the rules or forget what she knew in her heart was right for her. Even if she were center stage, in the midst of the action, she suffered the torments of the damned when she failed to live up to the best within her.

Today, grown-up and in control of it all, she has evolved into a thoughtful, intelligent, witty and mystically magnetic woman. She can find total comprehension in philosophical and spiritual principles when her life seems to be falling apart. She has an inner strength that defies the ploys and seeming disparities in the outer, physical world. Her mental resiliency will continue to astound you as the years dance by. She will bring you a rare understanding of the meaning of life that will serve you well when you wander into a pot hole here and there, throwing your entire psyche out of alignment. With delicate mental fingers, she will move disjointed fragments into place, then massage your being into vibrant glowing health. She will give you a reason for being, a place in her life and in the universe. She is a banquet, a source of sustenance in a hungry world. Forget the two-dollar coupon at the pizza parlor and the free fries under the Golden Arches. From now on, you dine at the Ritz.

The Twenty-Five Man

You can tell a lot about your Twenty-Five Man by the two stone Sphinx that flank either side of his doorway. They would be rather forbidding if it weren't for the big red bows tied jauntily around their necks. Their silent, mysterious eyes omnisciently observe a harried, hurried, unknowing world. Their unmoving stone bodies seem untouched by the activity of life. Yet, the splash of red ribbon lets you know that they are not entirely immune from devilish impulses themselves, given the proper mood and circumstances. All of which is an accurate picture of your Twenty-Five Man.

There is a part of him that's aloof, removed, given to periods of quiet introspection. By understanding that these moments are essential to his health and well-being, you can avoid much misunderstanding. He is a thinker, a researcher, a detective whose curiosity impels him to seek the secrets of life. When he's in one of these moods, you'd be madder than a March hare to try to entice him into a party or conversation. There are other men whose tongues, like a hummingbird's wings, flap eighty times a second but your man is not about to flap unless he's got something important to say.

But let's correct one impression right now, lest you think you've got a living zombie on your hands. He can be a witty, charming and delightful conversationalist when he chooses to be so. His conversation is littered with glittering gems of information, polished to brilliance by his quick mind and made thoroughly captivating by his rare charm. He is a supersalesman, able to imbue his ideas with an excitement that washes over his listeners. Because his mind is his greatest resource, he is very rarely without an idea, a project or a goal which will be effectively communicated to the public.

The unusual combination of extrovert and introvert, fun-loving and serious, was evident in the Twenty-Five Man, Anwar Sadat. In *A Man With A Passion For Peace,* Henry Kissingeer, who knew him well, wrote: "Any simple assessment of Sadat is therefore likely to be mistaken. Dozens of visiting Americans were charmed by him. But he was also aloof and reflective and withdrawn. He could hold his own with small talk, but on deeper acquaintance it became clear that it bored him. He much preferred to spend his idle time in solitary reflections in his restless perigrinations around his beloved country." A *Time* article written after his assassination commented on his "uncanny discernment. He handled fourteen American Presidents with consummate psychological skill." This peasant's son was the "originally underestimated politician" who had the "wisdom and courage of the statesman and occasionally the insight of the prophet."

Whatever you do, don't underestimate your Twenty-Five Man. He tends to do that himself in the beginning and, because he projects that image of himself to others, people may overlook his great potential. But once he gets his sea legs under him, it's full sail ahead.

Very little remains hidden from your man. When he trains his fine mind, he can parry and thrust with the best of them because his penetrating insight reveals the hidden aspects of the most complicated problems. He observes life with an all-seeing eye, stores the information in his computer-like brain and is able to pull it out at any given time in the most disarming manner. He is a formidable opponent. But he knows where the real battle is fought and won. As Sadat said, in one of his favorite quotes, "In the end, the sword is always conquered by the mind."

The Twenty-Five Man has amazing intuition and should learn to follow his "hunches."

This man is also a wanderer, physically as well as intellectually. He must be careful that his purpose in life doesn't fluctuate like a double Libra trying to make a decision. This type moves through life with varying degrees of intensity, playing his destiny by ear. This is fine if it is what he consciously chooses but if he finds it discomforting, then he must learn to focus his attention. Besides, this approach is hard on the lobes.

Playing by ear can be beneficial, as it was for the Twenty-Five Man, Elton John (born Reginald Kenneth Dwight), who learned to do so on the piano at four years old. Before he started writing songs he wrote poetry, and although he can't play any instrument but the piano, he says that he can "hear melodies in my head when I write." He went on to say "My roots are listening to records. All the time, I live, eat, sleep, breathe music." He composes a song in an hour, an album in two days. He has been called a "musical computer" but a "creative one, turning his vast musical knowledge into works that are distinctively his."

Your man's roots may not be in records but they are in a mystical realm where unheard melodies play, unseen colors splash brilliantly across the mind and formless thoughts roam wide and free. He can create something out of nothing. Give him a blank piece of paper and he'll create a picture, a story or a song; hand him dry words on that paper and he'll bring to life the characters contained within as he speaks their lines; hand him a piece of wood and he'll carve a tree; or hand him a problem and he'll produce a pearl.

If he is good with his hands, he can fix anything. You won't need a plumber, electrician, carpenter, painter, paperer or gardener because he knows enough about all of them to start the job, and his intuition and natural technical know-how will carry him through to its completion. And he'll probably invent something along the way. Remember...you've got the only plumbing system that gurgles when the bathroom light is turned on. But, you've got plenty of hot water, nothing leaks, and it is a conversation piece...just like your Twenty-Five Man.

When he was a little boy, he invariably could be found wandering down to the fishing hole with a wooden pole over his shoulder, to spend quiet, contented, sunny hours, dangling his hook and probably his toes in the cool stream. Undisturbed, his mind wandered through the leaves overhead, the bubbles in the brook, and up into the cottony clouds in the sky. He thought and wondered and imagined.

He may have been extremely restless in high school, finding it difficult to settle down to studies unless he had exceptional teachers who could motivate him. He might have found more excitement in raising Cain, Abel and the police chief's dander than in dusty tomes. Guaranteed, he had more excuses than you could shake a stick at, and most of them were thoroughly convincing.

Today, as an adult, that adventurous streak is still in him, though it may be hidden by years of experience and his natural reticence to speak of the things that are meaningful to him. If, one day, on an impulse, he decides, as did Bilbo Baggins in *The Hobbitt,* to break all tradition and go on an adventure, you'll know from whence the impulse arose. You'd be smart to throw a few things in a big hankerchief, tie it to the end of a stick and follow him because, one thing you can be sure of, the journey won't be dull. Besides, he'll need you along. He doesn't always plan things too well before he makes decisions. He needs to think things over, weigh matters carefully before he goes adventuring. By now, of course, his years of experience may have taught him that. Maybe it's because he's had more than one travel-bureau computer suggest that he hitchhike. Luckily, the Twenty-Five Man, Admiral Richard Byrd, didn't take that advice. It would have been a rather damp trip to the Antarctic.

If his standards are too high in the beginning and he fails, he takes it personally and his own self-esteem suffers. He then begins to worry and grow moody. He must learn to be less critical of himself and others. Usually, he overcomes these moods because he does have a good philosophy and the ability to reason

25

intelligently. In fact, his intellect is quite superior when he chooses to train it. Therein lies the key word. Training. Once your man decides to focus his considerable strength and talents, to train his technical abilities and allow his instincts to have full rein, there is very little at which he cannot succeed. The only difficulty lies in choosing a path because so many will be open to him.

You can be a great asset in his life if you recognize his sensitivities. He really needs you. Even if he comes on like gangbusters, he lacks confidence. A partner who understands him and supports these emotional moments in his experience will be rewarded in so many ways. Helen of Troy may have had the face that launched a thousand ships but, if you stand beside your man, you'll have the sastisfaction of knowing that you launched a thousand ideas. And those are just a few off the surface. He'll continue to justify your belief in him and to surprise the world with his creative talents. He is a bottomless font.

It wouldn't be surprising to find him dipping into metaphysical and philosophical realms of thought and action. Like the Jesus Christ lizard that walks on water and the Oxford swift that remains in flight three years, your Twenty-Five Man has powers that would astound you if you only knew. They might surprise him too. He certainly has the ability to change the thought patterns of a generation and more. He recognizes the spiritual essence of the individual and, whatever he does in life, through the whisperings of his conscience, he is constantly reminded of that higher side of self.

The Twenty-Five Man, lecturer, poet and essayist, Ralph Waldo Emerson, was the leading exponent of Transcendentalism and developed his own personal version. While an ordained Unitarian minister, grief over the death of his first wife led him to question his beliefs and subsequently resign his ministry. He then began to develop his Transcendentalism, attempting to humanize science by explaining that "the whole of nature is a metaphor or image of the human mind." In 1835 he moved to Concord, Massachusetts and remarried. There his circle included Bronson Alcott, Margaret Fuller and Henry David Thoreau. For fifty years, this eminent group met regularly creating an atmosphere that dubbed Concord "the Athens of America." So, if your man begins wearing a short white toga, laced knee-high sandals and an olive branch perched rakishly on his brow, and starts preaching on "the divine sufficiency of the individual," you'll know where he's coming from. As long as the men in the short white jackets don't come for him. Customs do change.

He may agree with the Italian proverb that "Once the game is over, the king and the pawn go back into the same box," but he also knows that the human being is more than the body, more than the sum of its parts. His faith has more facets than the Star of India and the Hope Diamond combined. His friendship is a priceless gift because it will teach you the wonders of yourself, your rhythm, poetry and your absolute necessity in the cosmic plan.

He knows a lot more than he lets on. Why do you think those Sphinxes flank his doorway? How many people know their significance? Even if they did, chances are they wouldn't understand as he does. The Sphinx, a combination of a human, a lion, a bull and an eagle represents the four fixed laws of the universe: to do, to dare, to know and to be silent and are symbolized by Taurus, Leo, Scorpio and Aquarius. They are also the four symbols on a relief on Chartres Cathedral translated as Matthew, Mark, Luke and John. Yes, your Twenty-Five Man's roots run deep. He

25

knows he must abide by the laws. His conscience is a constant prick in his side, reminding him. He has more to gain and more to lose than most, but because he is aware, he'll be good, he'll follow the rules. . . .

What about those red bows tied round the silent necks of the stone creatures? He put them there himself because, in the final analysis, we always reveal our true selves. He is the mystic and philosopher, the poet and musician, the explorer, the moralist and the keeper of the keys of wisdom, but he's no prude. See that crooked smile. What do you suppose he's up to now.

The Twenty-Six Woman

Your Twenty-Six Woman is what you'd call physical. It's not just the deep, veiled eyes, the sensual lips or the body that calls like a warm featherbed after a cold day's work that caused that motion in the pit of your stomach when you first laid eyes on her. She glanced your way and an invisible hand flung a fistful of stars at your mind. With dawning delight, you realized a connection had been made that promised more than ordinary pleasure. You somehow knew that here was a woman who could consummate your most secret fantasies. Your instincts were right on target.

You were a few steps ahead of most men because your Twenty-Six Woman often presents a cool exterior that belies the sensitivity and compassion that lies beneath. She can appear an ice maiden, distant and unperturbed, as does Jaclyn Smith, whose beauty beckons yet forbids. But if you're a wilderness man, those shivering tingles racing up and down your spine are just a challenge. You know the floods that result when the spring thaw hits the frozen peaks, washing down over the earth, preparing it for the explosive burst of nature's birth. You're not about to let that controlled exterior fool you.

On the other hand, don't underestimate her strength. Whether her physical body is slight or sturdily built, she has a resiliency, a persistence, a determination that is the stuff of which the world is built. Creation may have taken place in seven days with a well-earned recess at the end but who do you think started building up this planet when the initial construction was completed. Her Twenty-Six adds up to an 8 and it was on the Eighth Day that the nails and hammers, the nuts and bolts, and the steel and cement took over. Even the atomic number of iron is 26. Her world is built upon an orderly system that has no room for leaning towers. She respects the strength and discipline that is the structure of society and the family. She knows that laws are the glue that holds all of life together.

She may pour her vast energies into her body as did Mildred "Babe" Didrikson who was chosen by an Associated Press Poll in 1950 as the outstanding woman athlete of the first half of the twentieth century. Ms. Didrikson excelled in the 80 meter hurdles, shotput, broad jump, javelin throw, basketball, baseball, billiards, swimming and diving. In 1932 she set two world records at the Olympics and went on to championship golf where she won every woman's title at least once. She married a wrestler.

You don't have to be a wrestler to keep up with your Twenty-Six Woman, although is could be helpful. She does know some pretty interesting holds. Your Twenty-Six Woman may not choose to put her time and effort into sports but she surely will put it into the physical world in some manner. Sexual contact is an important part of her life. She wants to explore and experience the limits in personal relationships. She's a person of emotional extremes, with a calm exterior that should never fool you.

Your Twenty-Six Woman's home forms an important part of her existence whether as the home of her childhood or the one she has created for herself as an adult. It's her fortress and she'll run it as a feudal baronness. She has a strong hand, an urge for power and control that can have family members meeting secretly in the dark of the night composing a modern *Magna Carta.* You'll have to remind her occasionally that serfdom went out with jousting and suits of armor. She tends to get carried away.

On the other hand, she is stubbornly loyal. She can rant and rave and roust her loved ones but let one foreign hand touch a lock of any family member, and the hordes of Genghis Khan will descend in all their bloodcurdling fury, decimating the countryside for miles around. That sweet, quiet woman, you're saying, shaking your head in disbelief. No way. Oh well. No one can say you weren't warned.

Your Twenty-Six Woman is fond of show. She likes to make some kind of impression before she leaves, a lasting impression that will sweep down through the centuries, or at least, a few generations. Domestic products would appeal to her business sense. She has the wherewithal to create an empire out of the most unlikely items. A needle and thread, scissors and a few yards of quilting and she's off and running. First, she'll give her hand-made items as gifts, then sell a few at the church fair. The stores downtown will want a few dozen and, quicker than the songs from *Saturday Night Fever* made number one in the Top Forty, she'll have you and the kids lined up doing piece work. When you show up at work with a few common pins stuck through your shirt front and your left hand hidden in your pants pocket because the thimble got stuck on your middle finger and you haven't been able, short of surgery, to remove it, you'll know it's time to cross the family line and hire outside help. God knows, she's making enough money now to do so.

The tenacity she shows in her work carries over to her home. She likes her roots. If she loves her home and feels good in it, trying to get her to move is like pulling teeth from the mouth of a recalcitrant woman wrestler. You wouldn't want to try. When she's house hunting, she'll know when she walks into a house if it's the right one for her. She has unconscious awareness of when she's "home." She feels those comfortable, secure stirrings right through the soles of her shoes, as if she were a wandering willow whose long thirsty roots have finally found nourishing soil and life-giving water. She'll probably plant a willow outside the house and in the winter, after cutting the twigs and removing the bark, dry them and weave the rods into baskets and wicker furniture and start another business.

If she has the mind to, she can turn any item to profit, including her creative talents, with which she is well endowed. The Twenty-Six singer, Olivia Newton-John, born in Australia, won a talent contest when she was fifteen. The prize was a free trip to England. "Despite her initial reluctance to pull up roots," once she arrived in England she decided to make it her home and embark on a musical career there. "In spite of the apathy of music critics, her albums carried the Midas touch," an apt description of a fully-operating Twenty-Six. Ms. Newton-John enjoys country music, gardening and animals, she once wanted to be a veterinarian. In the spring of

1978 she cancelled a very lucrative tour of Japan to protest the slaughter of dolphins by Japanese fishermen. Her feelings run deep.

26

Your Twenty-Six Woman identifies the feelings and vibrations contained in matter, form, objects. She soaks up the nurturing warmth of the soil, the accepting harmony and joy in animals and the feelings that go into the making of a piece of furniture or jewelry. In fact, she is a natural at psychometry, the ability to divine information about a person or object by touching or holding it, as Johnny Smith did, in *The Dead Zone* by Stephen King. That may be the motivation behind her need to own certain objects—she is picking up the particular vibrations of that object and finding it pleasing to her own psyche. Her feelings toward animals are based upon the same reactions. She learns about her own feelings through her senses, through touching objects and people and the earth.

As a child, she would have been a prize pupil in the Montessori Method of education, in which young children are encouraged to learn through their senses. It would have alleviated some of her frustrations from hearing her parents admonishing mantra, "Don't touch that, please leave that alone." How could she not touch when there were so many wonderful things around her about which to learn.

Her teen years saw her experimenting with the seeming disparity between the rigid structures she saw and with which she identified and the playful voices that whispered in her ear. Too often she was taught that experiences were for either saint or sinner, and that pleasure belonged to those in the latter category, a horrifying discovery because she is a sensual person.

As an adult, she has come to understand the spirituality in matter, the higher self uncovered in a physical relationship between two loving individuals. The Twenty-Six Woman, poet and best-selling author of the book, *Fear Of Flying*, Erica Jong, has been called the "bad girl of American letters or still worse, a pornographer." She is astonished because her novel is "all about unfulfillment but apparently we live in a society which is so absolutely crazed on the subject of sex that a book like mine can be regarded as sensational." Other Twenty-Six descriptions about her are that she is "a dreamy yet graphic, seriously playful, wanton, and earthy addition to the small stock of women poets who celebrate their sex," and that "inside her rigid frames of syntax, a playful metaphorical mind is at work, busy in plentiful inventions of little fables."

The Twenty-Six Woman has to be careful she doesn't get caught within the structures she builds. Brooding over a past that can't be or should have been changed is a waste of her fine talents and drive. Domineering others in a need to create strong perimeters of protection about herself can kill the true love and fulfillment that can be hers in an open and equal relationship.

Your Twenty-Six Woman was born with the spirit of cooperation. It shows in all that she does. When she has her strong will and emotional nature under control, she sees her world in terms of pairs or opposites, and she comprehends and is sensitive to the other people's ideas, feelings and position. If you feel you'd rather do something yourself, she'll adopt a laissez-faire attitude although it may be difficult. It is her nature to want to help solve problems, to roll up her sleeves and dig in, but she will respect your wishes. If you want someone to support you emotionally, to offer creative ideas and practical ways of utilizing them, to work beside you without complaint and with full faith that you will succeed, then you have chosen the right woman. Her good judgment and keen sense of balance, her awareness of the public pulse and her Midas touch will insure your success in the business world. Jaclyn Smith has "considerable talent as a money manager." One of her interests is finance. "She is a tax expert." Your Twenty-Six Woman is always testing her limits. She likes to see just how far she can go, as if an invisible but cautious hand were nudging her ahead, one step at a time. As each step is secured, she needs to take another, then another, until her accomplishments take on mythic proportions. She even surprises herself. Her progress can be so gradual that often, when she stops and turns around to see how far she's advanced, she's almost to the top of the mountain and she's not even puffing.

Experiences will come to her through her senses, her physical body, through relationships and the trials and successes of the material world. Money, sex and power are aspects of her life that take on meaningful proportions, aspects that can have rewarding and spiritually uplifting results in her evolutionary path. They are a part of her being so she needs to recognize their inherent virtue regardless of the misconceptions of a misguided world. When she learns to use her talents and her physicality to best advantage, she is in a position to give loving and enduring service to the world through the example of her life or as the result of her physical accomplishments.

At this moment there are only the two of you and whether she's laying aside her stock market reports or her needle and quilts, you know that your time has come. The love that she's not inclined to display toward you publicly wells up in her eyes. This intimate moment is meant only for you. She's not going to share it with anyone else. In the background, as the radio plays "Physical, let's get physical . . .," she looks at you and whispers, "Yes. Let's."

The Twenty-Six Man

It's no accident that the atomic number of iron is 26. That four-letter word just about sums up your Twenty-Six Man's attitude, principles, body strength and will power. He's a man of extremes, constantly testing himself in the physical world. He's in tune with his number which represents the ultimate extension of the physical. English has twenty-six letters, the extent to which we can express ourselves verbally or through the written word. When we speak of *the* marathon, we are talking of the most famous Boston Marathon, which is twenty-six miles, representing an extreme challenge to the physical body. Esoteric writers have called the twenty-six degree slope of the Hall of Truth in the Great Pyramid the symbol of evolutionary progress, or our fullest evolutionary expression. A deck of playing cards, which contain hidden numerical information, is comprised of twenty-six black cards and twenty-six red cards, representing the extremes (the yin and yang, the negative and positive) to which the human being is subjected and within which he or she must find a balance during the fifty-two weeks of every year. To top it all off, the number of the cube, which the ancients used to symbolize the body and the material world is a 26 (8 points, 6 planes and 12 lines). It is the stone which must be worked, shaped and perfected in the building of the temple (the human body). Even the earth has a

26

twenty-six mile buldge around its middle. So, you see, your Twenty-Six Man is planted in the land like a tree with roots digging deep into the rich soil for sustenance and security. He is intimately familiar with the earth in all its manifestations—money, power, sex, physical strength, security and comfort and he is also aware that he has the opportunity to use the Spirit that resides within these things to express his own talents as well as to benefit and aid humanity.

Wow! That's an armful, and so's your Twenty-Six Man. He has tremendous power and energy and it would take quite an individual to fill his shoes. He knows how to work and he can identify with those who struggle to maintain a foothold in life through the sweat of their brow. When he puts his mind and body full force behind a project, he draws success and money by the barrel-full because he has good common-sense and practical instincts. Besides, when he gets an idea in his handsome head, he's like a very large dog with a particularly meaty bone. No one would dare try to take it away from him. You'd have to be either crazy or invisible to try. He'll take an idea and pound and batter it until it has no choice but to go the way he wants it to. This is the iron number.

If you're getting the idea that he can be stubborn, that's your own interpretation. Let's just say that he doesn't give up easily. That's his advantage. When others are ready to throw in the towel, he's just getting warmed up. He enjoys exercising his biceps in more ways than one. He sees the world in terms of power and control and, since the 26-cube represents the body, much of that control needs to be exercised over his own body's needs and desires. His body can become a haven of peace and pride or a prison in which he is trapped by his own attitudes and beliefs.

The Twenty-Six Man, Johnny Cash, singer and composer of country music, sparked a revival in country-western music. As a child he was exposed to "songs of work and lament." Plagued by his use of drugs and alcohol, his popularity waned until the late 1960s when he was rediscovered by a more diverse audience. Aptly enough, his return was on the wings of his *Johnny Cash at Folsom Prison* album. His "powerfully simple songs of elemental experience" created a new and bigger audience. Johnny Cash knows the sorrows and joys of life because he's a Twenty-Six Man.

Your Twenty-Six Man has an aura of independence about him, as if he can handle anything thrown his way. Look at James Arness and John Wayne, both born on the 26th. In their roles as motion picture stars, both of these men presented a powerful image of tough, aggresive self-sufficiency. Your man may come across this way without even realizing it. And in public he may wish to portray that very image because innately he enjoys his influence. But, in private, he can be the most tender of lovers. He has a sensitivity to your emotions that can be absolutely spooky. He almost absorbs your feelings so that he becomes a mirror-image of your needs, fulfilling them with a tenderness too deep for words. And he does enjoy the physical, you lucky woman! The added bonus is that he's so good at it. Practice makes perfect, right?

Your Twenty-Six Man does have to learn to keep the lid on his emotions, otherwise they will bottle up inside him and blow in one fell swoop. He must learn to work with them because, more than most others, the negative emotions he keeps inside will eventually manifest through sickness or physical disabilities. His body reacts keenly to his mental attitudes and emotions. He should go on occasional one-to three-day liquid fasts to cleanse his body of clogged passageways where his emotional state has caused debris to lodge in an "I won't let go" attitude.

Letting go is one thing that your Twenty-Six Man finds hard to do. At the extreme end of this trait lies the danger of being overbearing and power-hungry, trying to possess everything and being unwilling to share anything. This person can get caught where he believes security lies, in a past of his own choosing, but the past holds only restriction and fear.

Your Twenty-Six Man has learned to handle his power in positive ways. He thoroughly enjoys the big deal of big business and Wall Street and the stock market, and even if his inclinations run along artistic lines, his practical good sense and Midas touch will ensure a commercial success. He is always testing limits. He wants to know just how far he can go, just how much he can influence the course of events. He has to know where the perimeters and boundaries are because they make him feel secure yet he doesn't want the boundaries to be too restrictive. He needs a lot of room in which to move and operate because he has a big job to do, one that will influence the multitudes.

The Twenty-Six Man, Robert Ripley, of *Ripley's Believe It Or Not*, also had a fascination with limits. Ripley's first "Believe It Or Not" cartoon appeared in the *New York Globe* in 1918. Aptly, it illustrated "seven athletic oddities." His cartoon expanded into a series of films, books and radio programs, and became syndicated in papers around the world as the public not only became fascinated with the oddities but with the extremes in this physical world.

He needs to watch his appetite, being so tuned in to physical delights. As mounds of potatoes dripping with butter and Italian pizzas leaning with layers of pepperoni and mushrooms pass through the portal between his nose and chin, he should remember his fasts and how he hates them. It could help curb those primitive little cells, the taste buds, that can take over his life. He could end up like the hummingbird who eats twice its weight each day and has to go into a torpor at night so it won't starve but, of course, the hummingbird doesn't have to worry about its girth. Being aware of this facet of himself, he may decide to play the opposite extreme, and be stern and extremely disciplined about his dietary habits. There is a happy medium that he should seek since balance is a necessary part of his outlook.

As a boy, he was either bent over a bug collection or out making physical contact with his beloved mother, Earth, probably rolling around in the mud, wearing his new sneakers and jeans. Heaven forbid if the kids thought he was wearing something new.

In his high school years, he was as fully involved as a twenty-six alarm fire, earning money, dating, going on camping trips, playing sports, identifying fully with the reality of his everyday life.

Today, he may be measuring the emotional reaction of this planet, as does Charles Richter, originator of the Richter magnitude scale that measures the intensity of earthquakes. When offered a job in the California Institute of Technology's Seismological Laboratory, Richter, with a Ph.D. in theoretical physics, quickly immersed himself in the studies of geology and geography. After amassing a mountain of data, he devised a scale for measuring the difference between large and small earthquakes. Richter's interest in physical extremes is obvious in his work as is his need for physical contact with the earth. As an elderly man, he still likes to camp out on the ground.

26

Your Twenty-Six Man finds that home and family are important support systems in his life. Behind every good man...right? Females, don't rise up in righteous anger. The same can be said of the Twenty-Six Woman—"Behind every good woman..."—because in the case of the Twenty-Six it happens to be very true. Your man requires the harmony of a loving relationship with the people he cares about in order to function well in the world. You form a link to family and family, for him, is his continuity with the past, its structure and security. He'll fight to deserve and protect your love. An early marriage can be beneficial for him because it helps stabilize his intense emotions and also draws upon his sense of responsibility and his work ethic.

What you've got here is a saint or a sinner and maybe a little of both. It's a relative judgment. But it can't be denied that your Twenty-Six Man has more facets than a Rubik Cube has possibilities and trying to color-coordinate them leaves weak women in pools of hysterical tears and strong women gritting their teeth. Once in a blue moon you'll twist just the right way and he'll suddenly appear before you in all his complex simplicity. In one dazzling moment you'll see his tenderness and strength, his vulnerability and practicality, his devotion to humanity and to himself, all as one viable, compatible package. He's really got it all, you'll whisper to yourself. Then the moment passes and, as human nature demands, he slips back into being more human. Your Twenty-Six Man can really get into being physical. That's his speciality.

The Twenty-Six actor, Leonard Nimoy, famous for his portrayal of Mr. Spock in the long running television series "Star Trek," has been called a very physical actor. Early in his career, after playing the part of a young disfigured boxer, he experienced the effects created by heavy foam-rubber makeup. Nemoy said that he began "to identify with the internal life of this face. I began to respond to my new appearance." Because he absorbs so much of the physical aspects of his role, to this day he is still caught up in the Vulcan speech patterns, social attitudes and patterns of logic and emotional suppression. Curiously enough, the character Mr. Spock is much like the Twenty-Six Man in the respect that he presents a stoic, efficient exterior while inside emotional battles are waged.

Your man's sensitivities often lead him to take on more than he should—no one would dare say could—handle. He sees social disparities as a personal responsibility, and will pour his considerable energy, endurance and dynamism into correcting these imbalances. Because his decision-making abilities are keen and because people look to him for leadership, he is in the position to make positive changes in society.

Your Twenty-Six Man has a love affair going with the world. He understands the drive of the senses to find fulfillment whether it be in the world of business, the arts or professions, or in the arms of the woman he loves. He will show you, in the tenderest moments, the meaning of unity. At the peak of your most intimate touching, you will joyfully discover what he has known all along, that the driving concentration for fulfillment is search for union with the Creator and the final letting go is the ecstasy of Oneness. He releases the Spirit in Matter and shows you the purest pleasure in a physical relationship. A word of warning. Don't tell anyone. You want this man all to yourself.

The Twenty-Seven Woman

You need to get one thing clear from the outset. Your Twenty-Seven Woman can do almost anything but she doesn't do windows. Not that she can't, it's just that her mind is attracted to less domestic tasks where Windex and crumpled newspaper play no role. Those are the key words—her mind. Now, put her on the other side of the Windex—say, promulgating the clean air act—or that crumpled newspaper—writing the editorials—and you may capture her spirit.

There's no doubt that she's captured your interest however. You don't usually pant when you're standing still. She is a magnetic woman, no doubt about that, but, initially, you were hesitant about those two tiny antennae that periodically rise out of her head like periscopes, sweep the area once or twice, then descend silently back amongst the waves of her lovely hair. She looked quite normal—above average but normal—so you decided to shrug off this tiny defect. And that's how it was when you first met.

You've subsequently discovered the purpose of her antennae. She's sharper than a card shark at a Wednesday Whist party. There isn't a hair on your head or a thought in it that she hasn't counted or accounted for. Did she ever tell you she ran a computer check on you before she accepted your invitation to dinner? Those deceptively simple questions she asked you when you first met were not designed to boost your male ego, even if you thought she was fascinated with your life's story. She knew you like a well-read, dog-eared book before you had gotten past puberty in your telling. Computer verification merely confirmed what she had already deduced.

It's obvious by now that your Twenty-Seven Woman has good taste. Look at the company she keeps. She's taken you to more museums, libraries, historical sites and theatres than you care to count. While most women are home observing the basrelief from piled-up fingerprints on the woodwork, she's admiring reliefs on Chartres Cathedral and examining eighteenth-century French rococo. She has an innate appreciation of beauty, art and symmetry because she senses the mystical messages hidden there, messages that move her spirit and touch her feelings.

Your Twenty-Seven Woman is a curious combination of feelings and intellect, rhyme and reason. She often feels like she's on a see-saw or in a tug-of-war between her instincts and her analytical mind. On one hand, her initial contact with a person or situation is responsive, reactive, instinctual and laid back. She gets all kinds of subliminal messages. Then, as if a bucket of ice water had just washed down over her, she holds out a mental hand and says to herself, "Hold on. Wait a minute now. I need to analyze this situation." So, out comes the microscope and the notebooks, and she's settled in for a long, cold night's patient observation. She tends to rely heavily upon her intellect as if she felt more safety resided within those perimeters. Heaven forbid she should allow strange feelings and intuitions to guide the responses of an inteligent woman like herself. After her initial regrouping, her sharp analytical mind begins to logically probe the dark corners of her feelings, a little at a time, just as far as and as long as she can neatly color-key the bits and pieces. Any similarity between her initial response and the end result is purely coincidental. The day that she finally admits to herself the validity of her instincts and the value of using them in conjunction with her intellect, she is on her way to performing miracles.

27

You'll soon discover that your Twenty-Seven Woman can talk on almost any subject when she's in the mood. Where some people can easily see both sides of a question, she navigates around six sides, then floats calmly in the center, recording and filing its cosmic import. As a result, you'd swear she has a photographic memory. Her vast storehouse of knowledge is enviable and a bit intimidating. You may not be used to a woman who has total recall and can remember every word you've spoken to her since you first met. You rather enjoy the phrases she plucks from history and literature to colorfully illustrate the moment but to be reminded in graphic detail of promises (catalogued as to time, place and circumstance) made in less than intellectual moments can be more than disconcerting. It might even make an honest man out of you, an aspect she would surely admire.

She has high ideals, a nobility of character and a deep integrity that permeates everything she does but she's not a namby-pamby sentimentalist who dissolves into a tearful flailing of the breast in times of stress. She's a quiet determined center of calm in the midst of turmoil and strife, confusion and bedlam, insanity and hopelessness. Her leadership is not the kind that forces itself down your throat as would an overzealous mother forcing a pill down the throat of a sick but recalcitrant child but rather a quietly determined authority that creeps up on you as Carl Sandburg's fog did, on little cat's paws. You find yourself turning to her more and more as time goes on and her advice proves wise and productive.

As people begin to recognize her inner power, she emerges a Cassandra, freed from the curse of not being believed. People go to her for help, drawing sustenance from her font of wisdom and practical application from her repository of fact. Because she is a thinker, and thinking requires time alone, solitude and reflection, a part of her remains aloof from the busy, hectic, scattered business of the everyday world. Therefore, she's drawn reluctantly into her role as counselor. It's not one she actively seeks but one into which she is ineluctably drawn.

Nature is an important segment of her world because there she finds the rest and peace that is so conducive to her metabolism. The Twenty-Seven Woman, Rachel Carson, writer, biologist and conservationist, said, "I can remember no time when I wasn't interested in the out of doors and the whole world of nature... I was a rather solitary child and spent a great deal of time in the woods and beside streams, learning the birds and insects and flowers." Her "prophetic and influential" book, *Silent Spring* (1962), created a world-wide awareness of pesticide pollution that set off a controversy that resulted in further research into the effects of pesticides and the birth of the modern environmental protection movement. She has been described as intellectually ambitious, quiet, self-contained, an earnest scholar. She abandoned an English career for biology only to realize her literary dreams in a series of books about the environment.

At home or on the job, your Twenty-Seven Woman needs space and privacy, a room aside to do her own thing. She should work alone or within a group where she has the option to operate on her own frequency without interference. She doesn't like to account to anyone for her actions which makes her a rather independent worker. Part of this phenomenon is that she wants to see a task through from beginning to end. Her clarity of thought and keenness of perception enable her to work out the best possible way of handling a job. To hand her project over to someone who could botch it goes against her grain. She is a bit of a perfectionist as well.

As a child, she was probably more serious than other children, taking life without the proverbial grain of salt. Reading, study and moments by herself when she could get in touch with the wonders of the new world around her awakened the deep wells of her curiosity.

She carried these qualities into her teens where her interests could have broadened into literary or artistic lines as well. Regardless of how immersed she was in a social life, she still maintained a controlled reserve, a place within herself that others knew was off limits.

Today, as an adult, some areas are still off limits and always will be but she has learned to temper her cloistered periods so that she doesn't become too introspective and self-concerned. She has strong moods during which her clever tongue can give you a painful case of whiplash. Her superb vocabulary contains words you've probably never heard so unless you're collecting for Webster, don't impinge upon her solitude. It is a necessary outlet for her intense energy.

She can talk a door off its hinges, opening up her world and the world of those she encounters. Tiny (five feet tall), slight Mother Teresa of Calcutta, is a bundle of energy who has dedicated her life to "the poorest of the poor," inspiring the world with her loving devotion to all God's children. Her leadership formed a community of twelve in 1950 that has mushroomed to over seven hundred sisters and one hundred brothers in houses around the world working with poor children and sick and dying adults. In the book, *Something Beautiful for God,* Malcolm Muggeridge says, "I never met anyone less sentimental, less scatty..." One reporter observed, "She looked tough and alert, no saintly madonna." Another said, she has a "calm, straightforward manner," and while she "can break easily into laughter...she can also be insistent, even salty in her low, soft voice if this will benefit the needy." She is "mesmerizing and charismatic," moving "like a still point in a whirlpool of poverty and misery."

Long range projects intrigue your Twenty-Seven Woman. She is not the least daunted by the length of time or size of a task. Distance, time and dimension fascinate her. The time element became obvious when she noticed the seven year pattern in her bouts with poison ivy. She has stock in Calomine lotion and can talk with great experience about the seven year itch. Certainly not all Twenty-Seven Women are susceptible to poison ivy but they are susceptible to the seven year itch. You can see why, in a world of instant oatmeal and plastic credit cards, she is considered an anomaly. She knows her work will have far-reaching and enduring repercussions. If a job's worth doing, it's worth doing right.

She is extremely observant even though she doesn't always appear so. Sometimes, in the midst of a charming, witty dialogue—yours—you find her staring blankly into space. It couldn't be the conversation, you reason, she must be malfunctioning. So you wave your hands frantically in front of her eyes, yell "Fire!" clash a pair of symbols, and don't earn one tiny flutter from her eyelash. You've sworn more than once that she was parked in the dead zone. But you can see her chest rhythmically rising and falling. So, muttering a few oaths, you continue your dialogue. It is interesting and it would be a shame to waste it. At least, you can hear it. The incident is long-forgotten when, next year at this time, she will curl your meticulously casual, blow-dried hair into tight little ringlets when she repeats, verbatim, your entire conversation. Entire. She can be dangerous.

Your Twenty-Seven Woman knows that her mind is her greatest resource, a moving creative force in this world of form. That's why she remains cool in the midst of crises. She is plugging into inner space where all answers are available and where cosmic reinforcement assures her that life is an ongoing reality before and after this "parenthesis in time" known as one human life span. She sees the universal life flow as surely as if it were in 3-D on wide screen. No wonder she spends so much time gazing into space.

But she's also affectionate, loving, sympathetic and totally captivating. She has been a mystical transfiguration in your life. Billions of suns, bound together by gravity, burn in her eyes. Her essence swirls about you like the "blue arms of spiral galaxies." She is a thought of the gods, formed of gossamer clouds. She will transport you to worlds never seen. If she has chosen you, you too have been touched by the gods. So, until the next black hole and the big bang come along, wouldn't it be absurd to ask her to do windows?

The Twenty-Seven Man

You're convinced you're the one who turned around first and noticed your Twenty-Seven Man. You had a warm feeling wash over you, you say, so you looked in his direction. Before you congratulate yourself on your ESP ability, as well as your good fortune, think back carefully. Remember how the little hairs on the back of your neck stood up and you had a tingly feeling around your shoulders? You stopped in the middle of a sentence as if a thought were trying to push its way into your mind. It was then you turned and saw him looking quietly at you from across the room. Even from your position, you could feel his subtle magnetism moving in slow waves over you, silently, powerfully. So perhaps your meeting was more ordained than you knew. You could ask him, although whether he'll tell you is another story. Sometimes he doesn't even kiss on the first date.

He's a man whose first contact is laid back. While other men come on like gang-busters, laughing, back-slapping, strutting like primo dons before admiring audiences, he remains cool, calm, unperturbed on the surface, observing their performances with his characteristic reserve. His air implies that whatever other people do or say is totally irrelevant to him. However, behind that far-away facade lies a sensitive, sometimes nervous, self-critical soul who is much more responsive to outside stimuli than you can imagine or he would care to admit. But, because he's a born philosopher believing in a live-and-let-live attitude toward life, he reasons that what others do is fine with him as long as they don't interfere with his life style. You see, your Twenty-Seven Man has a mind of his own and, as the little boy does with his shadow, he carries it with him wherever he goes, along with a collapsible spade.

Have you noticed that little black pointy thing hanging from his key chain? You've seen rabbit's feet, zodiacal emblems and gold initials adorning those keepers of keys, but a spade? Relax. He's not Digger O'Dell, the friendly undertaker from early radio days, he's just a digger. He's been at it since his little hands first clasped a sand shovel and by now, he's dug his way through mounds of gravel and bed rock. What he can't dig up and uncover, when he's a mind to, isn't worth knowing. If you have a suspense account—one of those accounts where the balance is always a mystery and the monthly statement arrives with maddening regularity to prove again that the butler didn't do it (you did)—don't try stuffing the evidence in the mattress or down the garbage disposal. He knows. He always knows.

Your Twenty-Seven Man knows a lot of things. He's an intellectual with a strong drive toward literary and artistic achievements that express his high ideals and moral code. He understands the essential worth of a human being regardless of his station in life and he has the ability to express in ways that will be heard by the masses. The Twenty-Seven Man, John Steinbeck, aroused wide-spread concern about the problems of migratory farm workers in his greatest novel, *The Grapes of Wrath*. Before he became a success, he worked as a laborer while writing. His firsthand "observations lent authenticity to the working men in his stories." His Nobel Prize citation praised his "social perception and realistic and imaginative writings."

Your Twenty-Seven Man also has a powerful imagination. Who else would stick their arm down the kitchen PIG looking for your checkbook? The point is he understands human nature all too well. He has a universal awareness of what makes people tick—he's checked out your clockworks too—so he is more tolerant, sympathetic and impersonally caring than most. As the Twenty-Seven Man, Louis Auchincloss, Wall Street lawyer and writer, once said, "If a human being is described completely, his class makes little difference. He becomes a human being on the printed page, and other humans, of whatever class, can recognize themselves in his portrait."

The world is like a mirror-image to your Twenty-Seven Man, a place where he sees reflections of himself in the lowest and the highest of individuals and their actions. It's as if he had a Third Eye, which probes into the soul of things, revealing the innermost meaning of its existence. He approaches his investigations like a laboratory scientist wearing a white jacket and holding a gleaming scalpel in his freshly washed hands. He's going to do things by the book to make sure the conditions are perfect because then, he reasons, the results will be accurate and provable. Somewhere along the line however, Heisenberg's Uncertainty Theory raises its little metaphysical head and your Twenty-Seven Man is left staring nakedly at his own mystical and esoteric leanings. As scientific and analytical as he tries to be, his own emotions and feelings lie in wait to emerge at the most inopportune moments, forcing him to believe in impossible things.

Inevitably, just as Alice said in *Through the Looking Glass*, your Twenty-Seven Man cries, "One can't believe impossible things." And just as inevitably, he will answer, as did the Red Queen, his own anima, the receptive, believing side of himself, "I daresay you haven't had much practice . . . When I was your age I always did it for half-an-hour a day. Why, sometimes I've believed as many as six impossible things before breakfast." He's had his six impossible things to believe by now so he's had to come to terms with the fact that he is an intellectual psychic.

The Twenty-Seven Man, Charles Lutwidge Dodgson, mathematician and author, is remembered by most of the world as Lewis Carroll. He wrote a number of mathematical treatises, including *Euclid and His Modern Rivals* (which we all remember) but he has continued to live in the minds and hearts of millions through his children's stories, *Alice In Wonderland* and *Through the Looking Glass*. It is said that the books' subsequent appeal to adults was based upon Carroll's "ingenious mixture of fantasy and reality, irony and absurdity." There are those today who

27

claim that Carroll included metaphysical messages in his whimsical characters and their adventures. He did manage, at any rate, to construct a beautiful window through which he could view the best of both worlds, symbolic of left and right brain functioning, reason and fantasy, a window which your man needs to consider if he doesn't want to go down the drain with your checkbook.

Your Twenty-Seven Man is particular. In some areas of his life, he's a perfectionist. At times he can be exasperatingly fussy as was Lewis Carroll who, when traveling, carried a trunk in which he wrapped each item in a separate piece of paper. Your man will tell you he's just thorough and careful. He wants things well researched so that he knows where he's going before he steps out, and he will step out. Travel and adventure appeal to him because they stimulate and contribute to his pursuit of wisdom. Even when he was little, he was ready to explore the wide world. He collected experiences and ideas the way the other kids collected baseball cards.

As a teenager, he was friendly but more serious than his peers. If he played sports, he would have had the game well thought out and his moves planned ahead so that he was eventually recognized as a thinking player.

Today, as a strategist, he's hard to checkmate. He can sense and react to an opponent's moves with lightning rapidity. The Twenty-Seven Man, Bruce Lee, considered the greatest martial artist in the world, knew what his opponent thought and, almost simultaneously, was able to react to that thought with exact precision. He was devoted to the perfecting of the technical particulars of his art as well as the philosophy. His book *The Tao of Jeet Kun Do,* combines his style and personal philosophy which, he warned, worked for him but not necessarily for the reader. Readers should only take what applied to them. He recognized the universality of the technique while maintaining his own individual application of it.

Your Twenty-Seven Man falls naturally into leadership roles because of his uniqueness. He doesn't hire trumpeteers or take out a full page ad in *Variety* to announce his capabilities, he just quietly goes about his business with a determination and vision that invariably leads him to the top. He likes to see a job through to the finish once he starts. While others are busy jostling each other on crowded, well-worn paths, struggling toward the summit, he has found a hidden trail and climbed the mountain with little apparent effort. He gets ahead in life faster than most because he learns so quickly. His perceptions are keen and accurate. He doesn't have to be told over and over because he gets it right the first time.

Since he has a keen intellect, he must be careful he doesn't use it to bluff his way through life. Loose lips sink ships, and he's got a fleet of ideas to be concerned about. It would be a shame if his ships never came in because he turned his extremely active mind to self-serving pursuits at the expense of others.

But your Twenty-Seven Man has feelings for others. He has a sensitivity to your moods that runs deep. Your love is important to him because he gives so much of himself to others through his work that he needs to be refilled, comforted and sustained by the knowledge of your love and companionship. No one can empty their well continually without having it run dry. He needs periodic respites during which his source can be rejuvenated. During these cycles, he may whisk you off to the mountains or the countryside without warning so you'd better carry a collapsible toothbrush in your pocketbook.

If he needs to get away by himself, don't feel hurt or abandoned. He has his solitary moments when he closes up tighter than a bar on Sunday morning. You won't be able to drag a word out of him anyway so back off gracefully and wait for him to break out of his catatonic condition and rejoin you in the world of the living. His regeneration will do wonders for your relationship.

One thing you have to realize is that you must share your Twenty-Seven Man, not with another woman, but with the world. If he lives up to the best within him, he has an important destiny to fulfill. His understanding and patience, strength of character and moral fiber, and deep compassion and wisdom will eventually lead him on paths that few have known and some fear because they require so much from the individual. He'll save his personal love for you but the universal love that mushrooms from the depths of his being must be released. His work, his life, his ideas and principles become a beacon in a fog-shrouded world.

Your Twenty-Seven Man collects ideas not as a collector who pins butterflies to a board to admire their dead beauty in the solitude of his room but as a lover of life who nets the butterfly for just a moment, becomes one with its delicate patterns of color and grace of movement, then releases it to travel its miles through the sunlight to bring awe to the mind of a child or, perhaps more precious, to the mind of an adult who has not lost the ability to wonder. The thoughts and experiences your man collects can change a life or many lives, can live through the ages on the printed page for generations to read long after he has gone. His life can make a difference.

And you make a difference to him. He has elegant tastes and he's scrutinized you as carefully as Vincent Price examines a masterpiece. You're his work of art, a complex combination of color, form and radiance, the epitomy of womanhood. He would choose no less. So, take his hand and journey with him through a world of wonder and achievement. Together you will explore the universe.

The Twenty-Eight Woman

It isn't that power, money and sex are the *only* things in your Twenty-Eight Woman's life, because they're not, but she *does* enjoy them. You may find that hard to believe because your woman may be very subtle, but don't let her fragile femininity fool you. She's about as harmless as a fox in an unattended chicken house. She has distinct ideas and a will that won't quit. It's useless to say no to her because, if she has made up her mind, you might as well tell cats not to have kittens or mothers not to care.

Your Twenty-Eight Woman has an air of vulnerability about her that brings out all your protective instincts. You tell yourself that she obviously needs your strong protection and will succumb to your irresistible advances. When it's a bit too late, when you're past the point of no return, you'll suddenly realize that, like a bug in a Venus Flytrap, you are the one who has succumbed to her magnetic charms and struggling is useless. There's no way out, even if you were looking for one, which you aren't. Who is crazy enough to give up a package like her?

Her personality can change in the most disarming ways. In 1962, at the 34th Academy Awards Presentations, the Twenty-Eight Woman Ann-Margret sang the

Oscar-nominated song, "Bachelor in Paradise." *Show Magazine*'s Rowland Barber later wrote, "What she appeared to be was a girl in her first formal...who set out for the Junior Prom...she wore a scared, sweet smile. Then she began to sing...and a transformation took place: from Little Miss Lollipop to Sexpot-Banshee. Her rendition...was definitive. She squeezed it out, ground it out, belted it out, wrung it out and flung it out... In the space of three minutes, Ann-Margret became the hottest name in town." The Twenty-Eight Woman Bridgette Bardot is no slouch in this area either.

28

The 28th does have sexual overtones. It was on this day in September of 1979 that Barbara Streisand "won her breasts back." A federal court ordered the publishers of *High Society Magazine* to remove Ms. Streisand's breasts from photographs taken on the set of *The Owl and the Pussycat.* A rather tiring task since wholesalers had to cut the "offending organs" from over two million copies with a pair of scissors. Sexual, your Twenty-Eight Woman is, but you're walking on your brains if you think that she is only a sex kitten. First of all, she is a hard worker. She'll even do windows if she has to. In fact, she rather enjoys a challenge. It brings out the tigress in her. She can work long, hard hours and still be going strong, well after others have tossed their panty hose on the floor and are sprawled on their beds, out like proverbial lights. But your woman's still burning the early morning oil because she has a purpose, a goal, that strange, catalytic vision that drives her onward and upward.

Second, she's a devoted, loving and sustaining mate. When you come home from the office exhausted because the computer broke down and you had to think all day, she'll be waiting for you, full of sympathy and understanding. As she listens to you babble incoherently because your brain's on overload, she'll know intuitively what happened and what you need. She'll find ways to make you feel good, to divert your attention, like a little bacchanalian feast with flowing wine and grapes a-dangling. She's very creative.

Your Twenty-Eight Woman is full of very different ideas. She is serious about those ideas because she wants to be recognized for her individuality so you'd better not laugh at them or put her down too often unless you want to make a habit of checking under your hood each morning before you start your car. She can be serious about her dislikes as well. Count the scars on her adversaries, and count your blessings at the same time. She doesn't notch her gun.

She is tenacious by nature because she wants to excel. There is a part of her that, in spite of her need to belong, to be a part of the group, must stand separate and apart, and all the jellybeans in the Oval Office aren't going to change that. She'll hang on long after you've cried "uncle" and you'll seldom hear her even whisper "aunt." When Ann-Margret took a twenty-two foot fall from a platform onto a stage while performing at The Sahara at Lake Tahoe, she almost died. But within three months, although she had sustained many serious injuries, she made a triumphant comeback in Las Vegas. So cancel your woman's big insurance policy. She isn't going to let go that easily.

If you think you've got a hit woman on your hands, look again. More likely she's a stunt woman. Despite her appearance, she has amazing physical strength and an agility that would embarrass an accomplished gazelle. When these two characteristics are combined with her drive and her natural instincts for reacting, her boundless energy and her daring, she's unbeatable.

Speaking of daring, she is. She seems to need to test her physical limits, to see how far she can go, how high she can climb, how much she can accomplish. She rather enjoys the unusual and will seek it out, as you have probably discovered by now.

She wasn't always this way. In fact, as a child she might have been quite timid and shy. She certainly would have needed the close companionship of family and friends for support. Relationships were very important to her, as they are today, even though they might have been hard for her to begin or maintain when she was very young.

She began to understand in her teens that by expressing her own unique talents she could captivate and entertain others. It was her method of drawing the companionship from them which she needed. Her self-awareness began to emerge in the midst of relating outside herself.

Today she is a leader of people, an executive of groups, the head of a clan. She seems to be the focal point around which myriad lives, interests and fortunes swirl. And the strange part of it all is that she does it so unabtrusively. She's the contented tigress, putting down one soft paw after another, moving cat-like through life without disturbing a leaf or branch, moving with the quiet grace and sleek beauty of the jungle cat, seemingly unaware of her surroundings or the power she carries so lithely in her body. But every other creature in the jungle is aware at some level that when she is angered or hungry, it's time to turn tail and make for them thar' high vines and far plains. She can teach you the true meaning of having a tigress by the tail.

Your Twenty-Eight Woman can be very playful however. There's a clown lurking behind those captivating, innocent, lost-looking eyes. No matter how sleek and sultry, or warm and round your Twenty-Eight Woman is, she seems to have the "muppet factor" that producer Lorne Michaels attached to Gilda Radner, born on the 28th. Radner soared to stardom with Chevy Chase on NBC's "Saturday Night Live" series. At ten she decided to be funny and was encouraged by her father. He took her to plays and shows every week and they were very close until he died when she was fourteen. She is said to have a "vulnerable child-like quality," "a thirty-three-year-old woman who appears to have a band-aid on her knee," "a compulsive toucher and hugger" who "exists largely on a diet of sugarless Bazooka bubblegum." Sally Struthers has this same "muppet factor," which calls upon every red-blooded male instinct to want to protect this vulnerable creature. Even Gilda Radner is described as being "fun to hug because she is so fragile and brittle at the same time."

The contrast between the soft vulnerable maiden and the ice maiden is confusing to most men. But the Twenty-Eight Woman, who appears aloof and untouchable, has built walls of protection around a very sensitive, soft interior. This woman can come across as so independent that others disregard her needs. They believe she can handle almost anything—which is very true—and that she doesn't need or want anyone, which is most untrue. Because this type of Twenty-Eight Woman sends out such messages, she can find herself in self-imposed isolation. She may then mentally build on the situation, magnifying the restraints in her life which, in turn, feeds her attitude and she's got a negative Catch 22 situation revolving around her. She finds herself starting many projects but finding it hard to finish any of them. She often throws her hands up and sits back, waiting for life to present something to her rather than going out after it.

28

But your Twenty-Eight Woman has a handle on things. She really is an executive by inclination and she is willing to work behind the scenes. Her motivating force is to be the best, to be distinctive and different, to stand out within the crowd, and she has the drive and the tenacity to get exactly what she wants out of life. A certain amount of publicity is acceptable along the way but she does enjoy her privacy. She can become as elusive as Jackie Onassis when that private space is invaded too often. She takes that space seriously. Ms. Onassis has taken a reporter to court several times for allegedly invading a thirty-foot distance imposed upon him by the courts in previous cases. She's no paper tigress.

Your woman has a bearing, a certain carriage, that permeates her environment like an expensive French perfume. It is subtle and sexy as well as regal and commanding. It invites yet holds at arm's length. You don't know whether to sweep her into your arms and cover her delectable body with kisses or fall at her feet and adore her from there. To first know her is to be drawn ineluctably by her magnetism and vulnerability. To know her better is to recognize her core of inner strength and spirituality, her sense of self and others, her individuality within her companionability.

She is a people person, there's no doubt about that. She needs you but you must learn to give her space. She wants you on equal terms, beside her. None of this female walking twenty-eight feet behind business. She may physically walk behind you or stay out of the limelight but she will always be your equal. If you don't know that by now then she will let you know in no uncertain terms. She not only speaks her mind when she feels she must, but she backs up words with action.

She does make your life exciting. She has drawn a huge square in her life—she loves large perimeters because they give her the sense of containment she needs as well as the freedom of space she requires—and placed all the things she needs and owns within that square—you, her money, possessions, property, passport and Visa card—and now she's happy and contented. She'll make your home a playground of sensual enchantment and intrigue, spiritual comfort and fulfillment. And to top it all off, you have visiting hours from 1:00 A.M. to midnight from Monday through Saturday, just as long as you remember, never on Sunday.

The Twenty-Eight Man

Are you really ready for a Twenty-Eight Man? You'd better work your way up to five miles a day and cold swims in the North Atlantic before you take on this James Bond in a business suit. He's strong, sometimes silent and very, very sexy. His odor eaters have more sex appeal than most Playgirl centerfolds. And if you feel yourself turning white-hot because of his radiations, join the multitudes. He has a wide audience of admirers.

He has a strong awareness of his physical body, just as you and every other woman does. How many men walk down the street followed by women with telescopic lenses? The Twenty-Eight film star, Dirk Borgarde, often, on public occasions, "had his flies sewn up to protect him from his more enthusiastic female fans." It's the subliminal messages your man sends out that draw women because, somehow, he doesn't feel complete by himself, he needs someone else to fill the voids in his life. Because he's so sensually tied to his body, his needs express in physical contact with the opposite sex. Aren't you glad! He finds satisfaction as well as wholeness and balance in your arms. He could never understand the Puritan ethic or denial of his sexuality in any way because, to him, sex is a very enjoyable part of life, a very important part.

The famous German poet, Goethe, born on the 28th, enjoyed his first literary success with his book, *The Sorrows of Young Werther*, which drove hundreds of young men to suicide in imitation of the book's hero who took his life over an unfulfilled love. Goethe's own life, however, was quite different. It is said that one of his trips to Italy prompted the comment that "he left no petticoat unturned." The Twenty-Eight Man, Ian Fleming, creator of super-sexy spy, James Bond, said he wrote for "warm-blooded heterosexuals in railway trains, aeroplanes and bed" and that his stories were "straight pillow fantasies of the kiss-kiss, bang-bang type." Fleming lived like his Bond hero until he reached his forties when he finally married. Not all Twenty-Eight Men are rakes, hopping from one bed to another, but they are strongly tied to their sexuality and find great joy and satisfaction there.

Your Twenty-Eight Man has strong ties to loved ones and family and, once committed, is the most loyal, devoted and satisfying mate you could ever imagine. It's no accident that chewing gum was patented on the 28th because, like Wrigley's, your man will stick to you like gum in a child's hair. When everything else seems to be falling apart at the seams, he'll be there, holding your life together with his sticktuitiveness, assurances and confidence. He knows he can do it because he's practically impossible to pry loose once he's assumed a stance. Did you ever try to get the gum out of a child's hair?

Discipline is a major influence in your man's life. He may use it as Bruce Jenner does to train his body in an athletic career. He has an amazing physical strength and he possesses a good sense of balance with an instinct for the right move at the right time. Behind it all, he wants to be the best at what he does and it's this drive that transforms him from a fine player to an outstanding athlete.

He can be a compulsive worker like the Twenty-Eight Man, Alan Alda, who says that "work is love." Your man knows that if he pours his considerable talents and strengths into a project or toward a goal, he will make it. Who is going to step in front of a single-minded steam roller? He doesn't view work as a distasteful task to be swallowed quickly and forgotten as was the sulpher and molasses of childhood days. Work is an ethic with him wherein he can express his creativity and become personally involved with his creations. Personal involvement is always important to him.

Alan Alda exemplifies the Twenty-Eight Man through his devotion to his wife and three daughters, his work and his interest in health (he once wanted to be a doctor). "Work is at the heart of health," Alda said. Your man instinctively recognizes this body-mind connection. He may often state, "Busy hands are happy hands," and "I'm too busy to be sick." His intense interest in life, work and health keep him healthy long after others are pushing up daisies. As he passes you for the eighth time on his jog around the one mile track, he'll grin like a Cheshire Cat. He's just got a runner's high. And all along you thought those people jouncing along the sides of the road with their baggy drawstring pants, T-shirts and sweatbands were just stoned.

He'll make you laugh. He can be very funny. Sometimes his humor has the

28

slow, smooth impact of a few Brandy Alexanders. Sometimes there's a delayed reaction and you find yourself chuckling at your friend's news that her pet canary got loose from its cage while her daughter was slipping a paper super-bird cape over its head and it finally checked out on the picture window. Not very funny news, granted, so you'll have a hard time explaining to your friend that you were thinking about something funny your Twenty-Eight Man said three nights ago at supper.

Some part of your Twenty-Eight Man recognizes the healing power of laughter. He may use humor to convey social messages that, in themselves, are serious. Alan Alda sees the humor in "M*A*S*H" as a way the actors and actresses have of "constantly fighting...the insanity of war as best they can." Soldiers have been known to laugh when their buddies were killed beside them in battle. Audiences at horror films laugh during frightening scenes. Laughter is the body's way of releasing tensions that cause physical problems.

But you'd better believe he has a serious side. Alda's not the "skirt-chasing surgeon" character he created and developed as "Hawkeye" on "MASH." He's an outspoken member of Men for ERA. The following statements show his awareness of the necessity for equality. "Everybody suffers when you squash one-half of the population." "How can you have a happy life with someone who is swatted down like a gnat? I think we need to come to a new awareness of each other."

Your Twenty-Eight Man's awareness started early. It's one thing to find a three-year-old gazing at his father's *Penthouse* magazine but it's quite another when he begins repeating the jokes and pinching the baby sitter. In some areas he was quite precocious.

He was always an affectionate type and through his teens, his circle of admirers grew by leaps and bounds. He loved being part of the group but he always stood out. His drive to be different and his capability of being so began to emerge. Besides, you had to laugh at him because he was either so funny you couldn't help it or so strong you didn't dare not to.

That's not to exclude the more serious, quiet Twenty-Eight Men. You'll find a sense of humor lurking beneath their quiet exteriors and a bit of deviltry as well. Regardless of how laid-back he can appear, there's still a little boy in him who wants recognition for personal achievements. So, go to the stationery store and buy a box of gold stars. Slip one to him once in a while and you'll have him eating out of your hands.

There is a bit of a contradiction in your Twenty-Eight Man. He wants his privacy and solitude but he also wants personal recognition for the uniqueness of his achievements. He has leadership qualities and enjoys power but wants to be free of the restrictions that fame necessarily imposes on the famous. He is alternately shy and bold, retiring and commanding, a collaborator and an independent, often managing to find himself between the devil and the deep blue sea when he tries to define his motives and his needs. On the one hand, if he attempts being too independent, assertive and ambitious, he courts the real danger of alienating his friends and loved ones who interpret his actions as exclusive of them. He appears too self-sufficient and self-absorbed. Conversely, if he becomes too passive, laid-back and dreamy, of which he is capable, he gets lazy and merely trifles with the unique gifts he possesses. He then builds sand castles in the wake of an onrushing tide.

Your Twenty-Eight Man must avoid starting projects and not finishing them or, as is more likely, seeing a project through to a successful conclusion then dropping it before his success stabilizes. Sometimes he loses interest the minute he succeeds and begins to look elsewhere for new fields to conquer because he craves a certain amount of newness, excitement and challenge.

You see, there's a conservative liberal peeking out from behind those startlingly brilliant eyes. You did notice that he set up his corporation as: The Twenty-Eight Man, Inc.—that's not black or India, but representative of the many men he carries inside him. He has a strange compulsion to be unconventional within the framework of conventionality. Another contradiction it would seem but nonetheless true. He really needs the safety of boundaries, perimeters and foundations in his life. Once within them, however, he may do the most unorthodox things. He's a libertine with a ball and chain clamped firmly around one unflexible ankle, moving stoically through the streets of life calling out, "Stop it, I love it." His "stop it" cries are to be interpreted as "I don't want all these burdens and responsibilities. I'm not an Atlas meant to suffer the weight of imponderable events," and the "I love it" finale means he wouldn't have it any other way. After all, where would we all be without Atlas? He is a rather necessary figure, separating the heavens from the earth as he does. If he weren't there, the sky would come crashing down with a sickening splat! and we'd all be in flatland. So, he's important and he's noticed. On occasion, your Twenty-Eight Man needs that kind of attention. So, humor him. Every eighth week, stand back on your heels, drop your lower jaw and stare disbelievingly at his latest accomplishment. It shouldn't be hard. He'll probably evoke that kind of response from you anyway.

Money's only important to him when he doesn't have it. Regardless of his protestations to the contrary, a high-paying job is a symbol of his self-esteem, a measurable quantity in direct proportion to his self-worth in this material world. This is true of most everyone but more so with your Twenty-Eight Man because the physical world and his place in it are key factors in his view of life. The life-style he adopts is no indication of this attitude. He may dress to the teeth or just to the waist—with him you never can predict—but the clothes don't prove the man, as he'll tell you, deeds do. And your Twenty-Eight Man dares to do them, as long as you're behind him, and his mother and father, and the kids, and the million and a half he has stashed up the chimney. And all along you thought the only reason he wouldn't let anyone use the fireplace was because he was nasty neat. Fooled again.

But you were no fool when you decided he was the man for you. He is the most loving, sensitive and affectionate of the One Family (1, 10 and 19). He loves to love you, making an art of it as he uses his creativity in the most personal and rewarding ways. Although you can't take that to the bank and deposit it, it's still worth all the ticker tape on Wall Street. He's given you the best of all worlds—physically, mentally, emotionally and spiritually. Is it any wonder you walk around with that foolish grin on your face, regardless of K.O.'d canaries? You're not sauced or souped up. You've just got a runner's high.

The Twenty-Nine Woman

Notice how your heart pounds like a war drum whenever your Twenty-Nine Woman is near. One thing's for sure, you know your blood's circulating. But there the certainty ends. When you're with your woman, there's nothing on God's little green planet that you can really be sure of except the law of physics which states that the only constant is change. Now, if you're a man who likes to come home at night to pipe, slippers and the *National Enquirer,* spaghetti on Wednesdays and beans on Saturdays, you might as well toss in the towel and hang up your gloves right now. Because she just isn't going to cut it. She could do it for a while, even a long while, if she wanted to—and therein lies the secret—but there will come a day when the natives will revolt and you'll have an insurrection on your well-manicured hands.

Ingrid Bergman, the Twenty-Nine Woman, was given one chance by the grandfather who raised her to attain the acting career of which she dreamed. She auditioned at the Royal Academy of Dramatic Arts. After everyone else had chosen Shakesperean roles, she selected the part of a girl who made her entrance on stage in one flying leap. She said later that she did this to get attention. She did, and the rest is history. Believe it—this woman of yours can be unpredictable.

If you like to plan what you do and do what you plan, and you are still attracted to this Twenty-Nine Woman, better make friends with a philanthropic psychiatrist who'll treat you for free because you're going to need all the help you can get. It's not that she means to drive you crazy, it's just that she does. If the sweat's beading on your lip and you're feeling a little nervous, it may be because you're getting an image of the beauty and the beast in this woman of yours. And guess what! You've got an extremely accurate imagination. But when you're in public, don't worry, she won't sprout facial hair and grow long in the tooth!

Understand, if the pressure's on, she's at her best, performing like a seasoned trooper. The more difficult the problem, the straighter she stands. When she starts wearing epaulettes to bed at night, expecting a salute from you instead of a kiss, you won't have to ask if something is bothering her. It'll be obvious. But you won't worry because she can handle it. What you won't like are the 2:00 A.M. drills on the back lawn. When she takes control, there's only one general, and she doesn't want to do it alone so guess who is elected?

She does need you, although you would never have suspected that when you first met her. She can come across as the most confident of women, self-contained, calm, serene and totally at peace with the world. You'd never believe the thoughts and urges that toil and bubble beneath that controlled exterior. She feels lost and alone by herself and, though she can live alone, she prefers companionship. It brings out the best in her, helping maintain her balance by presenting a mirror image of herself through her partner. We are attracted to our opposites.

Your Twenty-Nine Woman is something of a mystery and a contradiction. People instinctively like her, and she draws them in droves. However, though she has many acquaintances, she has few close friends. She can handle casual relationships because they don't demand too much from her but close personal relationships require care and effort, and there's a danger of getting too close and being hurt. She is very sensitive so she often draws the line at emotional intimacies because her emotions are too intense. She can become involved in friends' lives in ways that overwhelm her and the effort drains her energy. Arguments and differences can arise that disturb her need for quiet and peace. Sometimes she unconsciously sets up these conflicts to break a relationship that has become too intimate. It's like waving a red flag in front of a bull but her anger is a symbol that something vital in her is feeling vulnerable so rather than take a chance of being hurt, she closes the door.

Her life is a series of unexpected events as if the cosmic plan were to see just how quickly she can react and how adaptable she is. The unexpected can appear to be good or bad, the only certainty is that it is sudden. In some cases, the unexpected can take on extreme proportions, from vast public recognition and approval to notoriety and back again within a matter of years. Such was the case with Ingrid Bergman who, by 1950, had become a world symbol of virginal and saintly qualities through her roles in films like *Joan of Arc* and *The Bells of St. Mary's.* When she had an extramarital affair with film director Rossellini and bore him a child, the public reacted with a scorn and vengeance that seems incredible today. In 1950, Senator Edwin Johnson of Colorado delivered an extraordinary and passionate harangue from the Senate floor, not against political vice or foreign enemies but against a movie actress whom he labeled a "free-love cultist" and a "powerful influence for evil." Sermons tolled from pulpits and groups picketed theatres showing Ms. Berman's films. The public's idol had fallen with a resounding crash and they were angry and disillusioned. But eventually, the furor abated and today, Ms. Bergman is again a respected talent in her field.

You'll find that it's easy to set your Twenty-Nine Woman on a pedestal. She is warm, responsive, understanding and broad-minded. Behind her quiet, cooperative nature lies a strong sense of idealism which she can express very eloquently given the right circumstances. She's an extremely persuasive individual because her knowledge comes from a place of knowing, which transforms it into wisdom. Her persuasiveness can be subtle, on one hand, but that doesn't diminish her effectiveness one iota. When righteous indignation is kindled within her breast, the warrior steps forth in full armor, brandishing the two-edged sword of truth and justice. She is magnificently terrible. As long as she maintains her sense of perspective, she is an effective force but when her indignation becomes anger, she throws caution to the four winds and becomes erratic and destructive. She is a powerful woman, therefore when she's good, she's very, very good and when she's bad, she's very, very naughty: the beauty and the beast syndrome. Eat your carrots every day so that when you come to the breakfast table, your eyesight will be perfectly clear. If she appears her lovely, serene self, relax, drink your Postum and thank your lucky stars—astrological or otherwise. But if she looks rather shaggy and disheveled, beat a hasty retreat or you may be seeing stars. Under those conditions, it's not wise to antagonize her. A wise man rules his stars and discretions's the better part of valor, which simply means run! to the nearest exit. The blood you save may be your own.

If you've talked with people who knew her as a little girl, they'd say you had the wrong person. She was a shy, quiet child who certainly was not the devilish, wacky person you've been describing. Of course, she did receive undue attention as a first grader when she correctly spelled the longest word in the English dictionary, antidisestablishmentarianism, and was promptly whisked off to the capitol for the state spelling bee contest. She seems to know things that surprise people.

Because of this innate wisdom, as a teenager, she could have exhibited more forceful traits, like arguing and debating, more frequently. It would be hard to convince her of your point of view because, regardless of how pliable she seemed, when she walked away, you knew you hadn't made the slightest impression on her. She could be quite focused. But she still had her sense of humor. A teenager who

29

secretly ties the teacher's shoelaces together under the desk is not one's idea of a shy student.

Today, she may have worked on developing her nutty side. It certainly wouldn't need much help. One of Hollywood's "most talented and wackiest character actresses," the Twenty-Nine Woman, Madeline Kahn, knew she was good when she began singing opera at Hofstra University but she soon discovered "her undeniable ability to crack people up with her neurotic comedy routines." Probably best known for her roles in Mel Brook's *Blazing Saddles, Young Frankenstein* and *High Anxiety,* Ms. Kahn says, "I've played all the crazies. I could ride bareback down Broadway and nobody would recognize me."

That's debatable but there's the subtle element in your Twenty-Nine Woman, to be up front, making a difference, impressing people, leading them yet somehow, in some way, maintaining a sort of anonymity, a mysterious role, as if, no matter how conversational and social she is, you never really know her. Life just isn't all that simple with this woman of yours. Oh well, who wants simple?

Part of your Twenty-Nine Woman's complexity is the extreme fluctuation she experiences in her attitudes and outlooks. She can be totally concerned for other people, for their welfare and state of mind, and spend all her energies in the pursuit of that goal, then suddenly, without warning, get caught up in extreme ego identification and power struggles so that it's no longer the outcome of the situation that matters but the part she plays in the scenario. Here she gets caught in anger and force and unwise use of her influential authority. Her eloquence aids this position so she can convince herself as well as others as to the rationality of her actions. But your woman has learned to handle this part of herself. The resulting recognition, awards and perhaps notoriety that she ultimately receives because of her fine qualities is the outward manifestation of her effect upon the world. But beneath her accomplished exterior lies a forest primeval, "where the murmuring pines and the hemlocks, bearded with moss, stand like Druids of old." When the outside world has drawn too much, she needs to retreat to her forest, to go within and find that stream of consciousness that will refresh and revitalize her.

She can only keep her intense energies buried for so long. If they aren't examined in moments of meditation or communion with nature, and expressed in controlled and useful ways in the world, they will erupt like a super nova and you will be in for a severe case of sunburn.

Your Twenty-Nine Woman should rely upon her pronounced intuitions to tell her when it's time to pull in her bed, pick up her shell and scurry off to her soft, moss-covered forest where nature's melody will soothe her. Because she is an observant person, she sees the parts, envisions the whole and has the energy to put it all together. Like some cosmic puzzle addict, she's always doing it for other people so she might as well do it for herself as well. You have noticed her "intuition," haven't you? That's the only way most people can explain her thought processes. But you were smart enough to have recognized that right from the start. What else can you say? You're intelligent and you can hardly keep up with her so it wouldn't do to downplay her abilities.

You've made a unilateral assessment and decided that she is some woman. She may not follow all the rules all the time but that's what makes her so exciting.

She's a paradox of unpredictability. Your life together has been running beautifully, harmoniously and on an even-keel but you know better than to take that for an established pattern. Your motto ever since you've known her is anything that can happen, will! And it usually does!

The Twenty-Nine Man

Calm down. Don't get hysterical. It's not really as hopeless as you may think. There is one technique that can help you with your Twenty-Nine Man. We all learn through repetition, right? One times two is two, two times two is four, three times two is six, remember? Even though the only numbers that multiply to 29 are one and twenty-nine—not much repetition there—there may still be a way to get to him. Take the word "moderation" and embroider it on his Fruit-of-the-Loom, write it in shaving cream across his windshield each morning and finally, tatoo it on his inner eyelids because there are times when he needs this reminder in large doses. This is a man who does not like to sit still.

Basically, what you've got here is a first class nut. Oh, it's not all that obvious at first. If you observe him during his more staid and sedate cycles, which tend to be longer in duration than his cashew, almond and Brazil nut cycles, then you will wonder who in the world this character sketch is about. "Certainly not about my conservative, cooperative Twenty-Nine Man," you'll mutter, a bit protectively. "Nothing could be further from the truth." Don't think this is an attempt at character assassination. Give your relationship a little time before you make that judgment and above all, be prepared, expect the unexpected and carry a first aid kit with you at all times. The smelling salts are for you.

Let's say you're at a concert with your Twenty-Nine Man. He didn't really want to go but he went to please you. He's very considerate. You're in the plush lobby during intermission, drinking champagne, admiring the furs and elegant gowns some of the society women are wearing. This is a very dangerous moment because your Twenty-Nine Man is bored. Never let him get bored. He looks around uninterestedly, shifts from one foot to another, puts a finger inside his shirt collar and tugs on it as he stretches his neck like some great crane. You can see he longs to escape. A deep sigh, then an idea flashes in his head, an impish grin plays at the corners of his mouth. This is red alert. Suddenly he hunches over until his hands are sweeping the floor, then, dragging one leg behind him like a modern-day Quasimodo, he humps off through the startled and parting throngs screaming, "Sanctuary! Sanctuary!" Red-faced, you scurry after him explaining weakly, "He's auditioning for a part in *The Hunchback of Notre Dame.*" When you get outside, you're going to kill him.

But the fact of the matter is, when you get outside, he is leaping and gesturing wildly to passers-by with such fervor and realism that you burst into laughter. The contrast between the disdainful shock and disbelief inside the concert hall and the complacency with which the pedestrians on the street receive his performance is so extreme that you cannot help but see the comedy in it. City pedestrians are used to just about everything, just as you will have to be if you plan to spend time with this lovable, unpredictable creature born on the 29th. When he gets into these moods, you'll have to get him into blinders and a straight jacket and, in nose to nose contact, direct a good dose of hell fire and damnation at him just to get his attention. He can become fixated.

29

Generally however, when he is good, he is very, very good. He has a lot going for him because he is loving, sentimental and caring. He understands people instinctively so he makes a fine counselor, mediator and peacemaker. His perception is broad, all encompassing, like the Twenty-Nine Man, Dag Hammerskjold, Swedish statesman and second secretary general of the United Nations, who called himself "citizen of the universe." With "self-effacing restraint and great patience," he developed the Secretariat as "a stable, effective agency for peace" while serving as peacemaker "in many explosive political disputes, often on his own initiative." Keying into the need to contact the inner self, he established a meditation room at the U.N. When your man is operating on his highest frequency, he is capable of unifying major differences among peoples because he genuinely sees and recognizes the value in all sides and opinions, arriving at solutions that don't show favoritism but are made in the best interests of everyone concerned.

Your Twenty-Nine Man has the ability to attract crowds of people. In fact, he often draws so many that he can be spoiled by the attention that is paid to him. People often fawn over him, drawn by his charisma and personal power. He has strong leadership qualities and a double energy reserve that drives him to use his unique personality as an effective tool in achieving his goals. It is not his money or position, although he may have both, that draw the people and resources he needs, but rather the unique individuality of his person that captivates others. He is a most convincing man when he sets his sights on a goal.

Even when he is quiet, meditative and preoccupied with other things, his intense energy field is vibrating at such a high frequency that people cannot help but be aware of him. Tie his hands behind his back, tape his mouth and lock him in a dark, soundproofed closet in a back room of the house, and you'll have people banging on the closet door wanting to know what you've got in there.

Your Twenty-Nine Man is constantly tested. It's as if he sends a silent challenge out into the universe that places him in the position of arm-wrestling with the gods. He often wonders how he gets himself into such situations because he is not always consciously aware of his innate competitiveness. His test is to find the balance between the two worlds of which he is a part—the creative, sensitive, cooperative role and the assertive, individualistic, pioneering path. His life is a constant see-saw, up and down between these two positions. Occasionally an extreme action on his part knocks his partner off the other end of the see-saw whereupon he finds himself fanny-down with a thud on the other end, with the difficult task of defending that posture. He is quite competent to do so however, because of his expressive talents.

The Twenty-Nine Man, William Randolph Hearst, American publisher, "held views which were subject to remarkable alterations." His ideals and concern for others showed when, through his editorials, he fought for women's suffrage, anti-trust legislation and an eight-hour work day. Then he strongly opposed Roosevelt's New Deal Reform. Favoring the war with Spain in 1898, he vehemently opposed the United States' entry into World War I. In 1932, he was instrumental in capturing the presidential nomination for FDR but afterward he became his bitter opponent. His power was unmistakeable. He took his father's newspaper, the *Daily Examiner,* and made it the "most enterprising, brilliant and sensational newspaper San Francisco had ever seen."

Your Twenty-Nine Man can be moody and changeable, partly because he can see both sides so clearly and searching for a middle ground frustrates his need to get things done quickly. When this pressure builds up, the energy spurts out and he takes intense stands that he'll stick to until the cows come home and neither you nor anyone else will change his mind. Only he can, and often does very suddenly, finding himself just as securely cemented in the opposite stance. So the best thing to do is take a vacation until he sees the error of his ways.

Doesn't he sound like fun? He really is, you know, because most of the time he is very reasonable. It's just that he is such an adventurer, a pioneer, a seeker of new places and new experiences that his drive needs more than one outlet. He should never sit around doing nothing. You know what happens when he gets bored. Hobbies are really necessary to help him find that precarious balance he is always seeking. Such interests will serve to calm his nerves. It's better if his hobby is something entirely different from what he does every day. If he works with his logical mind on a daily basis, he needs to exercise his creative side. If creative work is his profession, he should systematically exercise his body and delve into practical accomplishments. Because he can be intense, it is essential that he maintain a balance, learn to function with both his right brain, the creative, receptive, imaginative side, and his left brain, the practical, logical, assertive side, because, to get stuck in one side at the expense of the other is to develop a lopsided view of life.

The Twenty-Nine Child often finds his life disrupted in some way through many residential moves, family separations or siblings that force him to learn to cooperate and understand on a broader scale.

As a teenager, again it's either learn to cooperate or rebel. Poet Rod Mckuen left home at eleven and Hearst was expelled from Harvard for "undue horseplay."

Your Twenty-Nine Man may have found the balance early but at least he's got it all together now. That explains why he won't leave home without it—his balancing beam. It's rather bulky and hard to explain but necessary unless you're into public scenes. But whatever incidents occur in his life, whether perpetrated by others or merely the result of his own energies boomeranging, his life is one of experience. He challenges the world because he needs a place to deposit his vitality in the search for the experiences life has to offer him. Without this broadening effect, he courts the very real danger of getting caught in his tremendously strong ego. When ego identification occurs, the power that he wields becomes a dangerous weapon rather than an instrument of peace.

Your Twenty-Nine Man has the potential of becoming an example for others. People look to him—how can they help it! He is a bit of a clown and if they don't notice him voluntarily, he'll find extraordinary ways of making sure they do—so, one way or another, he will be recognized. His power can be awesome, therefore, it's essential that he get both heads screwed on correctly—the right and the left. He can function out of both but the trick is to do it simultaneously.

Once he does, however, he is an extremely responsive, loving human being, as is Rod Mckuen, who at sixteen, after landing a job as a late night disc jockey on an Oakland radio station, lamented over the air about his romantic problems and was

29

promptly written to by troubled teenagers who recognized his genuine empathy and understanding. Mckuen ended up dispensing advice to the lovesick along with music. Your man has this quality of true understanding although he'll always be "irregular," different and a bit unpredictable. That's what makes him so exciting. Rod McKuen has been described as "irregular," and he says himself that he's never married because no woman could put up with his pace. In your man's calm, free-flowing moments, you can reflect on that side of him, wondering if it really exists, because he is so even-tempered and considerate of your needs most of the time. He is a font of deep emotions that even he is not aware of most of the time, although he needs to explore these hidden depths if he is to be introduced to the wonders of himself. You've had glimpses of that wonder, tastes of his greatness and wisdom, and you feel privileged to be in his company, to know that he chose you as his companion to walk—run, or perhaps dash, all depending on the circumstances—through life, and you couldn't be happier. He's no stick-in-the-mud. He'll try just about anything. You say you've got tickets to the opera for tonight? Well, make sure he doesn't get bored, and take another look at *The Phantom of the Opera.*

The Thirty Woman

How you ever got tangled up in her scarf you'll never know. To begin with, no one but a Thirty Woman would wear a scarf thirteen feet long. But there you were, shopping in a crowded department store, minding your own business, when suddenly a long, buttercup yellow woolen scarf came whipping around one side of your neck, disappearing around the other, and you found yourself struggling back to back with a stranger who began screaming "pervert!" In the midst of the jostling crowd and against the back of this anonymous, hysterically screaming woman, you almost panicked. Your hands flew to your neck to pull at the offending article. You were suddenly certain the government had sent a hit woman out to garrot you. You knew you should have claimed everything on your IRS return last year. Eventually however, you disengaged yourself with all the skill of a child disentangling himself from the ghastly embrace of a Halloween skeleton, and you whirled about angrily to confront this kook. There she was, your Thirty Woman, hair tousled about her lovely shoulders, eyes confused and upset, filling with sparkling tears, sporting a rather askew, long yellow scarf full of rips and rents. You took a deep breath, hesitated and then, within minutes, you were both laughing warmly, carrying on an animated conversation reserved for those who've known each other for eons. She apologized effusively, noting that she was in the habit of whipping her scarf rather dramatically about her neck. That was the beginning of your life.

    Whenever you think of her now, which is often—she's not a person you put out of your mind easily—you remember that first meeting because it seems to epitomize your Thirty Woman. She's so extraordinarily full of life, vitality and exuberance that it makes your heart ache with joy. Being near her is like lying on your back in the meadow on a warm summer's day with the sun pouring over your body; heat bugs, like air-raid sirens, whining their lazy songs, a velvety Monarch butterfly lighting on your wrist for a golden second, then lifting off like dandelion fluff on a wafting breeze. She brings a new awareness into your being, you see joy and beauty wherever you look, life bursting forth from the earth. Even your Thomases' taste better.

It's strange how she can transform the most ordinary event into a memorable experience. Like shopping in a department store. But there have been many more moments since then, perhaps not all as public but still quite theatrical and memorable nonetheless. What you are really experiencing is life through her eyes. She genuinely enjoys living, doing, being, loving and sharing, and her enthusiasm has rubbed off on you like the magical glow from a lightning bug. Now, by osmosis, you walk around all lit up.

By now, you've realized that she has a wonderful imagination. She has an imagination that far exceeds any other mortal and has no historic parallel. While you don't often draw your breath well, she draws pictures of universes and worlds of which you've never even dreamt. Her imaging can lead her onto many unusual pathways, some star-strewn, others deception-laden. Because she is basically optimistic and truthful, expecting the best from everyone she encounters, she must be aware that there are those who would deceive her. However, her trust and faith are usually rewarded. The law of physics and metaphysics—what you send out comes back to you—applies here as well. Your Thirty Woman feels justified in trusting others and believing the very best is about to happen.

Your Thirty Woman may love to talk. All Thirty Women are very expressive in some manner. The Thirty Woman, actress Jill Clayburgh, has been in therapy since she was nine years old. She's still talking about the emotional range of her expression. She said that, as a child, "I loved the fantasy of movies and the theatre... I used to perform every day at home." An early classmate said of her, "She was an elegant, tall little girl with a summer house in Greenwich, classes at Mr. Barclay's dancing school, and a big smile."

This effervescent woman of yours may not always seem totally all together. Like the clothing she leaves strewn about the house, she often leaves parts of herself scattered here, there and everywhere for others to enjoy. She may seem scatterbrained at times but that's only the result of the many facets of her talent seeking expression. You can catch her off guard, when her mind is wandering the cosmos and perusing the akashic records, and get the impression that she's flighty. Far from it. She has a serious side, an intelligent side that takes to philosophy, religion and literature like a hungry baby to a bottle. It feeds her soul. At those moments, she may seem blissed out but she's connected to a cosmic pool of information that nourishes her imagination.

No one had a more cosmic connection than the Thirty Woman, Helena Petrovna Blavatsky, a Russian-American theosophist, who co-founded the Theosophical Society in 1875 in order to "counter materialism and agnosticism and promote research on the secret laws of nature." Reports had it that supernormal phenomena happened in her presence, to which she attributed her understanding and "manipulation of superphysical forces." Her famous writing, *The Secret Doctrine,* is a mind-boggling account of the beginnings of creation and the laws of the universe. Jill Clayburgh is no slouch in this area either. Philosophy, religion and literature were subjects of special interest for her at Sarah Lawrence College.

30

No, there's nothing petty about your Thirty Woman. When she does things, she does them in a big way, with style and in a manner that's sure to draw the attention of every individual with at least three working faculties. She seems to have an idea for every party, a smile for every person, a word for every occasion. The cat's never had her tongue or even considered it as part of the menu. Any event, however minor, is a stage for her expression. When the cat's climbing the back door, jiggling the knob, yowling plaintively, she'll call out across the kitchen, "We gave at the office," then revel in the chuckles she has stirred. She's something of a showwoman. The Thirty singer, Linda Ronstadt, when recalling her early parochial school days, said, "The nuns hated me. They hated the way I talked about boys. I was too giggly, too loud, and wore too much makeup, and dressed too sexy." You notice how many "too's" Ms. Ronstadt used in her description. The Thirty Woman wants to experience all of life in one fell swoop, and more conservative types might consider that "too much." You can see what your woman could have been like as a teenager. Although there are quieter types, they are still bubbling over with the need to express the fullness they feel inside.

In her early childhood, the Thirty Woman was leading up to this state of being, perhaps experimenting with a babysitter tied to the kitchen ladderback, firewood piled at her feet, in the unwilling role of Joan of Arc under the Thirty Child's imaginative direction. But the night this Thirty Child considered setting a match to the firewood—for realism, you understand—was the last night her parents ever got a babysitter. Word spreads fast.

Today, she's set aside her childhood fantasies and replaced them with adult fantasies. Which is the more dangerous is hard to tell. Dangerous to whom is another aspect of this relationship you might want to test out. Through experimentation, you'll find out if you can pass her tests. Just keep one eye on her. Your Thirty Woman loves adventure—she is one—and the call of distant places, faces and paces. Association with foreign countries, peoples and ideas adds fuel to the fire that burns within her. She's not regional or narrow in any sense of the word. She's a citizen of the cosmos with the accompanying broad ideas and tolerances. With her family tree she has to be. Her mother was probably the original Auntie Mame.

A natural mate to her cosmopolitan approach to life is the innate need for freedom. She needs room with a capital "R" and 90 degrees worth of latitude in both directions so don't crimp her style unless you want to end up with a body like a wash board. Remember, she's emotional and can get carried away. What she does, she does in big ways. By giving her plenty of space in your relationship, you'll not only save yourself a messy body cast but you will develop and ensure a place for yourself in her larger-than-life heart.

She wants nothing more than to leave a lasting impression on you and everyone else she meets. That's one reason she feels she has to have the last word. Leaving a room full of people can be a traumatic experience fo: her. Leaving the room with just one person in it is harrowing enough. Jill Clayburgh, in therapy, is still trying. Watch her at a party. It's time to leave. She glides through the room toward the door, tossing off kisses and compliments like so much confetti, then stepping through the exit, she hears a parting phrase from a friend. She pops back in through the doorway like the Pillsbury doughboy for a final wave and goodbye, then back through the exit, only to hear another voice from the midst of the crowd and back in she pops. Heaven forbid she should leave a gesture unacknowledged. Someone might remember that person instead of her. Revolving doors were made for people like her. She hates good-byes. They are so tiring—literally. But her natural charm and genuine lovingness transform what might be considered egotistical in another into a delightful exchange of emotional feelings and good will.

You do have to watch your Thirty Woman because she's just liable to take your life savings and put it on Foxy Grapes to win in the third. "It's a sure thing," she exclaims as you plunge your head between your knee caps and beat the earth in overwhelming fear and frustration. Of course, Foxy Grapes wins by a whiff and pays ten-to-one. You're comatose by now but the thought of all that lovely money does wonders to revive your flagging physiology. But, you warn her, wagging a rather limp forefinger, "Don't you ever do that again."

"I told you it would be fine," she smiles at you. She may not tell you, however, about the times when Foxy Grapes staggered last across the finish line, like a wino on a three day binge. Sometimes she's strangely silent. But most of the time, she's right.

However, your Thirty Woman has an understanding, an insight into the natural laws behind the workings of the world. Because of this, she can rise above mundane problems to see the beauty in the cosmic creative plan. She'll make you see the advantages within the most desperate situation and she'll have a packet full of creative ideas that she'll willingly share to help you work out your dilemma. Her faith and laughter will embue you with new hope.

"Why worry about it," she'll exclaim, throwing her arms about your neck. "A hundred years from now it won't make any difference."

You know what, she's right. It probably won't make any difference next week. You find yourself laughing again with this amazing woman you so love. You look into those vibrantly alive eyes and that exuberantly hopeful face and your heart expands three sizes. She is so very theatrical, extravagantly emotional, incorrigibly adventurous, insanely free and open, zany, wild and wonderful. And that's during her more conservative moments. Imagine what's in store for you when she really lets her hair down.

The Thirty Man

There's something rather magnificent about your Thirty Man. Perhaps it's the way he gesticulates, pontificates or generally emulates—all verbs he is familiar with because they have a grand, regal sound, and he's nothing if he isn't grand and regal. Even if he doesn't know their meaning, he's apt to flourish them before bedazzled listeners because they have the flair that fits his image.

Your Thirty Man is something of an actor. He views life as a drama with him playing the lead role. He knows that he has a special destiny, ordained by the gods and in keeping with his vast reserves of talent. Zeus himself had a hand in his making and, if you don't believe him, check his birth certificate. It's bound to be marked with the royal seal. Your Thirty Man doesn't deal with underlings.

If you've fallen in love with this wonderful creature, you're in for a merry-go-round adventure, with mirthful music, flashing lights and gay crowds of people. He likes to socialize. Eat, drink and be merry is his motto as his waistline will attest if he doesn't exercise some discipline over his appetites. But contact with people and social issues are the real meat and drink of life for him because he needs an audience. He's got something to say and isn't the type to want to expend precious energy before an empty theatre or even one that's half-full. He really expects the place to be jam-packed full, standing room gone, hanging from the chandeliers room only. After all, he is the one who is performing. Who'd be foolish enough to miss such an opportunity to learn and grow, and be entertained at the same time?

There's no question about his entertaining you. He has an easy flow that captivates audiences. You feel as if you've always known him although you may have just met last night. Of course, he did keep you up all night talking about his adventures and misadventures so that by now, you even know what flavor toothpaste he sweeps across his ivories but he doesn't tell that to everyone so he must really like you. You inspired his confidence and you're a good listener. That's important with this man.

Your Thirty Man needs a mate who not only listens but appreciates him and his efforts, talents and accomplishments, which are too varied to try to list. He's like the Sun which has no choice but to shine indiscriminately on everyone and everything because it is its nature to give life, light and warmth. Even with no one around to enjoy these qualities, the sun still shines. One can't imagine not taking advantage of such a source of light, to bathe in its life-giving rays and feel warmed by its benevolent attention. We can understand why the ancients looked upon it as a symbol of deity and worshipped its life-giving light as one of creation's highest manifestations. Your Thirty Man has these same qualities. Notice how people are drawn to him, sit beside him and talk, or more often, listen. They feel warmed and comforted by his mere presence. Like the sun, he has a healing effect upon their bodies and souls. And all he wants in return is a little, simple genuflecting and prostrate worship.

The wide open spaces—physically and mentally—beckon to your Thirty Man. He has a broad philosophy, an all-encompassing view of life. When he's tuned in to his altruistic ideals, he gives generously of his time and resources to social groups and organizations, asking nothing in return but the joy of giving and the satisfaction of knowing he's helped someone. Strangely enough, this may be a part of his life he doesn't talk about, as if sensing that idle chatter or boasting would somehow diminish his giving.

He also needs room in his life-style to express the many facets of his being. He's not what you'd call a focused individual. In fact, he has to be careful of just the opposite point of departure—the scattering of his energies and talents. He can do many things, wear many hats and wear them with style. Flamboyant is his middle name, and the devil-may-care attitude he seems to possess often fools people into overlooking his more serious side. Trying to suppress the exuberance that wells up inside him, however, is like trying to cap a gushing oil well with a hair net. It's an exercise in futility.

Remember the first time you met—before the all-night conversation? You can hardly forget it. He entered the room—he doesn't just walk in, he makes entrances—immediately capturing almost everyone's attention. That small knot of people in the far corner heatedly discussing some political issue were soon diverted from their conversation by a joke your man began telling about Vincent Van Gogh.

You must understand, your Thirty Man doesn't just tell a story, he acts it out with larger-than-life realism. He is an inveterate and absorbing story teller but it wasn't just his tale that caught the corner people's attention. It was your Thirty Man's theatrical climax as he swept a jack knife from his pocket, snapped it open and began brandishing it wildly about his head, realistically threatening to emulate the great painter and slice off his ear. You guessed it—Van Gogh was a Thirty Man too. These men do get carried away. He laughed later at your suggestion that he might have done it but you never know what he might do to get attention. Ah well. . .it's all academic now. . .that is, until the next time.

The only time he sulks is if he's not noticed. His feelings get hurt when his efforts at entertaining or socializing fall on fallow ground. It seems his ego is fed by the attention others pay him. This is a constant need in his life. He finds being alone an empty and hollow experience. He's certainly not the type to be snowed in a closed hotel in the mountains for the winter, taking care of the boiler room by himself. He'd go bonkers and begin typing page after page of such old truths as "All work and no play makes Jack a dull boy." And your Thirty Man is not dull.

His eyelids can be drooping over his cheekbones but when the evening repast is put away, he's up and out, seeking excitement and camaraderie somewhere out there in the night. He's not just going to one place for the evening either. He'll hit three or four places before he's through his nightly meanderings, not necessarily to drink but to socialize, to be with people because he basically likes people and needs to be with them.

And he'll attract them as well. There can be thirty guys in the same room but, unless they're Thirty Men, they stand little chance of drawing the glances, smiles and friendly back claps that this man of yours will. He'll also draw all the women in the room. Although he's fundamentally a loyal type, he is inclined to be flirtatious and fun-loving, happy and exuberant, all of which can be misconstrued by the opposite sex. You might want to shave his head and paint "taken" over his bald pate in bright scarlet letters. It could deter the less persistent female types but it certainly won't diminish the Cheshire Cat grin or the captivating sparkle of his ivories across the crowded room any more than midnight can blanket a brilliantly flashing neon sign on a country road. He's the one people will notice. In all truth, there are times when he'll shake his head and wonder why he attracts so many women. It isn't always fun. His wardrobe costs are astronomical—torn shirts and all.

Age has nothing to do with his appeal. He can be young, slender and ordinary-looking or older, heavier and dashingly handsome, he still exudes a special charisma and a youthfulness that is obvious either in his appearance or thoughts, mannerisms and expressions. The Thirty Man, "American Bandstand's" Dick Clark, at age fifty-two, is "seemingly ageless and mercurial." He has overseen two generations of "rock'n'rollers" and is still going strong. He looks young, thinks young and communicates as well with the youth of today as he did thirty years ago. The Thirty Man, Mark Twain (Samuel Clemens) also maintained his youthful good humor and deep appraisal of the ageless truths of childhood through his immortal *Tom Sawyer* and *Huckleberry Finn*. Twain's social commentaries were often hidden beneath a delightful wit and a pleasing yarn so that the public took their medicine eagerly and with a chuckle. A spoonful of sugar does wonders.

Your Thirty Man can get caught up in his story-telling, enlarging his own exploits to the point of surpassing both Agent 007 and Superman in order to draw attention to himself through dreams of things yet to be. And when he's in this frame of mind, he can also magnify the little negative things in his life beyond proportion. But because he's innately a happy type, he seldom gets sick. He merely ends up dawdling on petty things that can make him extremely nervous and prone to fritter away his valuable talents in shooting the breeze. This is when his attention-getting antics are at their worst because it is pure ego need on his part, unmindful of others.

But when he's truly functioning at peak efficiency, he's not just another pretty face. He is unmatched in the annals of history. He has a vision and the talents to express it. Van Gogh has been called the "archetype of Expressionism, the idea of emotional spontaneity in painting." His strokes were bold and sweeping, brilliant and daring, just as your Thirty Man is when he attains a comfortable position in life and has the freedom, time and room to move and express himself. When this happens, if it hasn't already, you will see a visible change come over him. His genuine altruism emerges along with a deep sense of peace, contentment and pure enjoyment of life. He dares mighty things, knowing he will succeed and his knowing makes it so.

As a child, he probably drove his parents up one wall, across the ceiling and down the other wall, either in pursuit of him or escape from him. It's always hard to tell.

By his teens, if his parents weren't committed, it's probably because he had left home for broader horizons. Of course, you can't take that literally. He could have just left mentally, exploring worlds others knew little of and believed in even less. But that never stopped him. He isn't one you can convince easily, especially if your ideas are the least bit confining. You might as well erase "you can't do that" from your memory bank because it will only serve to intrigue him as to why and prod him to prove you're quite incorrect, not because of any pioneering instincts but out of pride and belief in his own greatness.

But now he's grown up—you think. Yes, he is. Look at the size of his feet. They are bigger than his baby shoes which are now bronzed and standing like the royal guard, flanking the entrance to his home, offering a silent challenge to all passers-by to try and fill them, which he knows is quite impossible. But they are rather cute. See how the shoelaces fall jauntily over the red-carpeted steps. Oops! Is one untied? You stop to examine and the next thing you know, the Thirty Man is out on the steps, sitting next to you, and you're telling him all about the sewer back-up in your apartment, your married boss who has been trying to compromise you, the five stitches that were taken in your head last week when your new car was just about demolished at an intersection and the denial of funds on your Mastercard, two weeks before Christmas. And you know what, you'll be laughing about it, genuinely seeing the humor in the whole human drama of getting so caught up in the material side of your existence. This wonderful man of yours has the ability to lift you out of the mire and mess of everyday complications and, with his panoramic view of life, change the doldrums into the social event of the year. He sees the dawn in the midst of darkness, maintains an abiding, comforting faith when all else fails and has total confidence in the goodness of each event that fate sees fit to toss your way. For your Thirty Man, anything is cause for a party. He's going to make you smile, no matter what. Look! There's a smile tugging at the corner of your mouth. It's coming, coming...there it is. Thank goodness. Now he doesn't have to cut off his ear to get your attention.

30

The Thirty-One Woman

How many women do you know who got a cruise control in their Christmas stocking? Santa knows what good little Thirty-One Girls need. And she is good, most of the time, obeying the rules, staying within the perimeters of social acceptance. But she has a strange physical imbalance. Her right foot weighs considerably more than her left. It's called a lead foot, and she knows how to put the pedal to the metal. Check her speeding tickets. Placed end to end, they would make an impressive belt stretching the girth from New York City to the Golden Gate Bridge, if you included all the ones she should have received along with the ones she did receive. But you see, she has another unusual physical piece of equipment—a golden tongue. Oh, it may not look like spun gold but it can spin quite a tale when it's called upon. Ask any thirty-one police officers along that paper belt.

You may find your Thirty-One Woman confusing at first—how can anyone stay within the rules yet break them—and when you begin to describe her to your envious male friends, the adjectives you use seem to contradict each other. But that's the fun and mystery of her. It's like buying a grab bag each morning when you first arise, one that will set the tone for the day. You never know what you're going to get or what's going to happen. It's not that she's unpredictable, she's just changeable, and she isn't always going to perform the way you expect, although she is dependable. There, you see how confusing and contradictory she seems. A little explanation is in order here.

First, she is a creature of habit. She enjoys routine and schedules because they lend a sense of security to her existence, a key word for your Thirty-One Woman. Much of what she does is toward this end. Because breaking a schedule offends her innate sense of order, she may find herself speeding toward an appointment so she won't be late or racing along the highway because she has allocated a specific amount of time to get X number of things accomplished, and neither heaven nor high water will deter her from her appointed rounds. You see, she is dependable.

Second, she is also quite thorough and precise. Her cupboards will be stocked with everything from alphabet soup to Brazil nuts. She'll have it all inventoried and stocked in an easy-to-find manner. Even the letters in the soup will be in alphabetical order. Then, she'll hire the Palace Guard to watch her larder. She knows how to cover all contingencies.

She is so efficient that wherever she finds herself she fast becomes the one to whom people look for direction. You'd have to be blind in one eye and failing in the other not to recognize her sterling leadership potential. She's the type who glides into an office practically unnoticed—only because she can be so quiet about herself—then takes over the entire operation before anyone knows her last name. She wouldn't tell them anyway but now they know it because it's written in gold letters on a frosty pane across her office door. Her potential is quickly recognized so promotions are a natural. In the rare cases where her abilities go unnoticed for too long, she has effective remedies. Thirty-one strong men with a battering ram pounding on your frosty-paned office door will gain her a quick and well-advertised entry. By the way, her middle name is perseverance.

The Thirty-One Woman, Jane Pauley, co-anchor woman on NBC's early

31

morning "Today Show," climbed from the job of unknown cub reporter at WISH-TV in her hometown, Indianapolis, to the prestigious and long-running, early morning national news program "Today" in four short years. Audiences responded positively to Miss Pauley's "Proctor and Gamble good looks, authoritative delivery, relaxed manner and honest Midwestern image." Her second week on the job helped the "Today" program to grab its highest audience in six months, even though it was competing with ABC's new entry, "Good Morning America." Miss Pauley is also very thorough; she "assiduously researches each of her assignments."

Yes, your woman has that honest, clean and golden-tongued delivery that captivates. She knows how to talk with people, to mingle and put others at ease. She wants to make a good impression because acceptance is important to her, as well as recognition for her individual achievements and contributions to her world.

Your Thirty-One Woman cannot help but stand out in a crowd. She's most expressive, talented and creative, and her drive to achieve, to be the best at what she does, energizes her potential into a moving, vibrating force that is hard to stop. She rolls inexorably forward, like the wheel of life, rhythmically, steadily, surely. Hard work is a welcome outlet for her intense energy, it's a place she can pour her ideas, talent and determination. Once she starts rolling, you'd sooner stop to discuss the merits of falling with an onrushing avalanche than try to convince her that what she's doing needs more thought and consideration. She's already examined every crevice of argument so what you're trying to say, tactfully, is that you disagree with her conclusions. And that will make about as much impression as a whistle in a wind storm.

She wasn't always so certain, however. As a little girl, she was probably quite shy, self-contained, unwilling to reach out to strangers for fear of upsetting the status quo, which is familiar, therefore safe. She may have had a protective, nurturing home—many Thirty-One's do—but she was still cautious, feeling her way into the future.

By her teens, her expressive individuality drew such warm responses from people that her confidence began to build. She may also have forced herself to overcome any self-doubts through sheer will power. At any rate, she noticed that people were starting to take note of her in favorable ways.

Today, she is noticeably different but in comforting, pleasing and self-confident ways that others do not take offense at because they sense her truly deep caring nature. She respects life and energetically pursues it, but always with a respect for its rules. The Thirty-One singer, Donna Summer, said, "I don't drink, snort cocaine, take Quaaludes, or sleep around town... My whole life is work and it's always been work. Even when I'm home relaxing, I'm playing the piano or singing. I've got to be doing something recreative or constructive."

Your Thirty-One Woman believes in the work ethic, pouring much of her energy into her profession inside or outside the home. She's the type who can handle both with considerable ease. Because she follows the rules, sees the results of logical, well-planned efforts, she succeeds. She never doubted she would and neither did anyone who watched her along the way.

Of course, sometimes you may lose track of her. She'll disappear for hours or days at a time, or maybe she'll just barracade herself in the house, nailing up the doors and windows and cement-screwing heavy chicken wire over the chimney. She doesn't want you playing Santa Claus and surprising her. Solitude is a necessary part of her existence. She needs to be alone to recharge her batteries, so if you have a date and arrive to find large keep out signs stuck all over the lawn and one on each doorway, don't take it personally, even if one does read, "This means you," with a large pointing finger poking directly at your heart. Occasional retreats do her a world of good, and you too. Just think how glad you'll be to see her when she finally emerges.

She is a very private lady. She's not going to tell you anything about herself unless she's good and ready. This characteristic often seems contradictory but, as you know, she does contradict herself, she contains multitudes. She is personable, charming and can be a flowing conversationalist as long as sacred areas are not approached without invitation. Step too far and your life's not worth a plugged nickel. Or an unplugged one for that matter. It's best to wait for an invitation.

You see, getting too close too quickly upsets her balance. She has to know where she stands, exactly, marked out in chalk on the floor like directions in a school play. It's her security and order syndrome. If she understands what's happening, she can handle anything but she doesn't like surprises. She needs time to adjust her body, mind and routine to new circumstances. When affairs go awry, her body can react in negative ways because she is innately tuned to the concept that the mind rules the body. If she's consciously aware of this truth, then she will make a supreme effort to practice positive thinking. Donna Summer is a firm believer in faith healing, in which the mind heals the body.

A negative Thirty-One Woman tends to shut herself off from the joy that can be hers in the mainstream of life. Anti-social and reclusive, she can alienate friends and family by holding on to ideas and beliefs long after they have outlived their usefulness and even to the point where they become destructive. She becomes suspicious of other's motives and selfishly protective of her possessions like the dog in Gibran's *The Prophet*, burying bones in the shifting desert sands for a future security which the desert quickly erases.

But your Thirty-One Woman has learned to develop her inborn faith and optimism, to trust the present, the future, and the goodness and bounty of life. She can give freely because she knows life will provide for her. If it doesn't, she'll march on out there and find what she needs through hard work. She's certainly not afraid to roll up her sleeves. In fact, she rather welcomes the challenge. It builds spiritual muscles.

Health becomes an important issue in your woman's life, not necessarily because she is unhealthy but more because she has an interest in a properly-functioning body. She has a mission to accomplish that requires a healthy physical body. It is said that a busy person hasn't time to be sick. She understands this concept and works toward keeping her body fit so she can continue toward her goals with every physical advantage. That's why you'll find your Thirty-One Woman involved in exercise—Ms. Summer dances, Ms. Pauley jogs—or in health foods, performer Carol Channing carries her own into restaurants. Ms. Channing also has the reserve characteristic of this number. Although it seems incredible from her interviews, she has said, "I am terribly shy but, of course, no one believes me."

She's a person worth having on your side because she is resourceful, loving, dependable and she never forgets a kindness. You know that generous contribution

31

she made to the Oakwood Nursing Home. The old man who fixed her bicycle chain when she was ten years old is in there now. He was crotchety and never spoke much to anyone but he helped her once and she remembers. You do want to watch out for her memory, however. It's a two-edged sword which she wields with deadly certainty. But she'll remember the nice things you've done as well. Although she isn't always openly demonstrative about her feelings, you know they're there, hidden beneath the many wonderful layers that are her.

Her moods can change as often as New England weather—which can experience a temperature differential of forty degrees in twenty-four hours—and with considerable force; but then, you're a hearty breed, enjoying changes in the weather. Sunny, calm conditions, day after day, cross the border into the land of monotony as far as you're concerned. Monotony, however, is a state of affairs you'll have little danger of encountering as you journey this lifetime with your Thirty-One Woman. But you're not afraid of what the future will hold. Your Thirty-One Woman invites your trust. She knows things about your family that you don't even know, not because she pried or asked but because they confided in her. You didn't know that, did you. Well, don't bother asking her about it. The lasting torments of hell could not drag one single word from her silent lips. There's no sense in getting upset. After all, this is one of the qualities you most admire in her. It also reassures you that your deepest secrets are safe with her. And that is one big relief. What if people knew about...never mind. She is special. You smile broadly. You are a lucky man.

The Thirty-One Man

You met your Thirty-One Man in the drugstore. You were bent over a shelf, investigating the virtues of a straight-handled as compared to an elbow-handled toothbrush when you heard a resonant voice say to the clerk behind the counter, "I'd like some bag-balm please."

Bag-balm? you thought. What in the world is bag-balm? You straightened up, stood on your toes and peered over the dental floss display and there he was, your Thirty-One Man, paying for a brightly decorated can containing this unknown substance. You were immediately interested. In him and the bag-balm. Always quick to react, you immediately moved to the counter, smiled at the salesgirl and said, "I'd like a can of bag-balm please."

In the midst of turning away, he stopped and glanced your way. Bag-balm enthusiasts are a rare species. "Wonderful stuff," you added, as the clerk reached for a can. In the back of your mind you were praying he would respond and, at the same time, you were wondering how you could fudge your way through the conversation if he did. You thought about dropping the can with the hope it would open, so you could get some idea of what the stuff looked like. Therein might lie a clue to its use.

He smiled at you. A thousand pins pricked at your heart. "So, you use bag-balm too. Not many people even know what it is."

"Oh, really," you returned, taking your package from the clerk. "I thought everybody knew about it. Such good stuff too." Oh God! you thought. Now what?

"It sure is," he continued, reminiscing now. "My grandmother used it all the time on the cow's udders whenever they got sore or infected. She had a big farm and swore by the stuff. I wouldn't be without it." He shifted his weight to one foot, obviously interested in anyone with such a vast repetoire of knowledge.

"I wouldn't be without it either," you assured him, wondering what it was you wouldn't be without. In your best Sherlockian manner, you rummaged through your mind and finally realized it had to be some kind of a preparation that cleaned up infections.

You did discover that he's into old-fashioned remedies, treatments that have been tested by time and proven effective. He has an innate understanding of natural healing processes so his interest in health foods, exercise and mental disciplines, one or all of them, are a natural offshoot of this awareness. In fact, he may have a creative approach to combining herbs or drugs in alchemical or chemical ways, originating a whole new concept in healing. But if he starts drinking foaming cocktails out of laboratory crucibles, you may have to put your foot down. A little originality can go a long way.

He does have this thing about his body. In some way, he makes the connection between what he believes and how his body reacts. It's as if they were one, and what one does, the other follows naturally. The Thirty-One Man, Michael Landon, actor, writer and director, as a young man, had developed a Samson-like belief in the "mystical, strength-giving powers of his thick, long hair." Though he was small, he earned national recognition in javelin hurling by breaking a national school record, and went on to the University of Southern California on an athletic scholarship. Soon after his arrival on campus, he was cornered by a few disgruntled jocks who gave him a crew cut. The next day, Landon's throws were consistently fifty feet short of his average. Persisting, he finally tore the ligaments in his arm and his javelin career was over. What his mind believed, his body believed as well.

The power of positive thinking is a necessary part of your Thirty-One Man's life because he so strongly identifies with his belief that it becomes a sacred commandment, not to be tampered with, unless you're prepared to counter the forces of nature and a deep, disembodied voice. He is a focused individual, rather disinclined to alter his opinions, once they are formed, or his ways, once they are chosen.

Your Thirty-One Man is also quite persistent. He doesn't give up easily. He may go down occasionally but he never goes out so don't turn away on the count of ten because he doesn't know when to quit. When he believes in himself, he can move heaven and earth, overcome the devil and the deep blue sea with an ease and grace that belies the effort behind the act. People seldom know the strength, agony and just plain hard work the Thirty-One Man invests in his life because he makes it look as easy as falling off a log.

He may appear social, gracious and charming, or at the very least, he sends out an alluring charisma that promises fun and flirtation. And he can be all these things. But the truth of the matter is, he is somewhat of a loner. He needs consistent and regular periods of retreat and solitude to bring his body and mind back into harmony. During these retreats he may find himself drawn to mind-body disciplines like Transcendental Meditation, Est, Meditation and aikido. Surely a copy of the Thirty-One Man, Norman Vincent Peale's, *The Power of Positive Thinking,* graces his night table in that little house on the prairie.

31

Your Thirty-One Man also needs these periods of respite because he tends to over-work, to put too much of himself into everything he does. You want a blanket chest for Christmas? He isn't just going to go to the lumber yard and buy the wood. Oh no! He'll plan a trip to the Canadian wilderness where you and he will tromp for weeks through miles of towering fir until you find just the right pine. He's so thorough and exacting that he wears himself out, not to mention you and the boots you both wore on your wilderness trip. Think what might happen if you asked him to add a room on to the house. On second thought, maybe you should have it done when he's off on one of his retreats. He wants control of every project from beginning to end. Michael Landon is pictured on the cover of the January 9–15, 1982, issue of *TV Guide* with a subtitle under his name reading "The Star Who Must Have Control."

There is a pool of creative ideas sloshing around inside your Thirty-One Man. His imagination should be channeled into constructive pursuits so that this talent isn't frittered away. He has a lot of energy to put behind his ideas and, being a tireless worker when he applies himself, he can accomplish what others would call miracles. But he does need to latch on to a positive belief in himself. The Thirty-One Man is in danger of becoming so routed in routine and set ideas that he allows opportunity to pass him by. His persistence can become bull-headed stubbornness with no rhyme or reason behind it. This attitude can narrow down his mental scope and his circle of friends.

But your Thirty-One Man has dealt with that side of himself. He's had to work at getting out of himself and breaking the molds which hold him. There is a basic part of him that is very structured and rule-oriented, and this structure can be inhibiting, can close him in. Even the cool, macho film hero, Clint Eastwood, remarked, "I like to play the line and not wander too far to either side." The Thirty-One Man, Gabe Kaplan, said, "I'm inhibited and shy," and Richard Chamberlain, born on the thirty-first, told reporters, "Getting out of my shell was my biggest problem."

Rules and boundaries are a necessary and good ingredient in your Thirty-One Man's lifestyle. When they are used properly, they guide his creative drive and talent into useful and worthwhile pursuits. Staying within the perimeters set up for himself is necessary, but your man still needs to find ways to vent his powerful drive so this energy may go into his work, physical exercise or leisure activities. He may love to drive fast, like Chamberlain, Eastwood and James Coburn, to vent his internal combustion. Or he may become a workaholic like Gabe Kaplan or a fitness fiend like James Coburn, but you'll find his intensity focused in some area of his life.

As a little boy, he was driven. He could have been the skinny little kid who had to fight his way through grade school with an inferiority complex, as did Norman Vincent Peale. At any rate, his body and his pride went hand in hand.

In his teens, he may have begun to become aware of his ability to converse with people to ease any relationship conflicts. He does have a way with words even though, today, he realizes he doesn't need many to get his point across. James Coburn is still best know for the "mean-faced cowhand who ordered Schlitz Light on television, getting the most money for the fewest lines in the history of the medium." So whether your man's a motor mouth, which is unlikely, a well-balanced charming conversationalist or a man of few words, which is more likely, you can bet your grandmother's jewels, he'll be heard. It's all in the delivery, and he knows how to deliver. Besides, there may be money in it.

Yes, your man may aim to please but his purpose is profit. Money means security, and security fits in nicely with his divine sense of order and rules. He has good business acumen, a sense of the practical and useful, and he likes to build. He enjoys planting the seed, nourishing it, watching it grow and finally, producing the finished product. He's there from start to finish because it's his baby, he's put his energy and faith into it, it represents a part of him, so it's got to be good. The money he makes is a reflection of his self-worth. If he makes a boodle, he feels worthy. He has to be careful, however, that he doesn't judge himself by his wallet.

Your Thirty-One Man enjoys comfort. He doesn't necessarily need to be rolling in greenbacks or even wading through them as long as he has enough set aside to feel secure and supply the necessities, plus a few luxuries. Of course, what makes one man feel content may not be nearly sufficient for the next. If this need gets away from him and begins to run rampant, he may start pinching pennies, nipping nickels and denting dimes. If he's had as many marriages and children as the Thirty-One Man, Norman Mailer, he'll have to squeeze a lot more than loose change just to keep up with family payments. Journalist and novelist Mailer admits that his alimony and child support payments total $150,000 a year.

A home and supportive family are very important for your Thirty-One Man. Because he is not always demonstrative, tossing off compliments, pats on the back and dazzling smiles, he is often misunderstood by the people he loves. His quietness, silent moments and periods of retreat can be misconstrued as a lack of interest in others. But you know he cares, that he's loving, loyal and genuinely in need of your love and understanding. Beneath that stoic exterior, he is sensitive and finely strung, like a priceless Stradivarius that needs a gentle touch to release the heavenly melody waiting in its quivering strings. His emotions often lie too deep for tears so he rarely shows his feelings. Not every woman has the wisdom and insight to look beneath this placid exterior. He knows his feelings are strong, real and meaningful so he is honestly confused when others don't respond to him the way he feels he responds to them. Once he learns to open up, to keep trying no matter how often he seems to be rebuffed, he will eventually emerge like the brilliant sun after days of gloomy weather.

You respond to him with every fiber of your being. He makes you feel good. In fact, you warmed up to him the very first time you saw him. Who else do you know who uses bag-balm?

Acknowledgments

Our grateful thanks to Bill Teschek, a 28, our local librarian, who we found slumped over his desk every time we approached him (we think it was because of us); Judy Dubois, a 7, for her keen discernment and generous help; and Alta Dubois, a 27, for her humorous observations. Our thanks to Budd Perry of Memories Studio for a fine photograph. Just what we'd expect from a 2.

Barbara Aultz
Jo Ann Aultz
Debbie Bacon
Douglas Baird
Karen Baird
Richard Berard
Dr. Robert Berube
Michelle Blanchard
Tom Boyd
Matthew Bunker
Reid Bunker, Sr.
Sarah Bunker
Virginia Bunker
Brenda Byrne
Robert Campbell
Ann Marie Cardarelli
John J. Cardarelli
Mary Cardarelli
Michael Cardarelli
Robert Castle
Louis Catinchie
Doris "Mimi" Colby
Glenroy Colby
Stephen Dadabo
Laura Decato
David Deshon
Michael Dickens
Raileen Dickens
Richard Dickens
Richard Dickens, Jr.
Todd Dickens
Paul Dougherty
Angelia Drake
Gayle Dyment
Nancy Edwards
Holly Enright
Angelo Faro

Claudia Faye
Bonnie Finnagan
Ronald J. First
Georgia Fitzpatrick
John Fitzpatrick
Adam Freeman
James Freeman
Mark Freeman
Matthew Freeman
Patricia Freeman
Robert Gillespie
Steven Gray
David Haddad
Beatrice M. Harmon
David Hartness
Brenda Hayes
Francine Hayes
Leslie Hoziel
Mathus Hoziel
Priscilla M. Hussey
Steven Iannalfo
Meredith Jordan
Joan Kahl
Phil Kane
Jay King
Allan Knowles
Allan Knowles, Jr.
April Knowles
Bonni Knowles
Bruce Knowles
Charles Knowles
Christopher Knowles
Elisebeth Knowles
Lucy Knowles
Venus Knowles
Eben Lambert
Kim Larkin

Tom Larsen
Shaun Levesque
Kris Limont
Dorothy Limont
Mark Limont
Stacy Limont
Bruce MacIntyre
Mary McGill
Melanie McIlveen
Richard McIlveen
April Merriam
Barbara J. Michel
Jay Millard
Joan Mukuska
Elizabeth Munson
Jack Murphy
Terrance Murphy
Lillian Murray
Fred and Marilyn
 Muscara
Charles Newbold
Lena Newbold
Kathy Nudd
Debra O'Leary
Gloria Oldfield
Heidi Ouellette
Jane Persh
Jonathan Persh
Faith Peterkin
Don Picard
Martha Porier
Sean Powers
Robert Preston, Jr.
Shirley A. Rider
 and the Chief
Helen Robinson
Jeannette Sawyer

John Shay
Elizabeth Spence
Medra Tilton
Maureen Vaughn
Noris Viviers
Shawn Viviers
Allan Wanderlich
LuAnne Wanderlich

Ronald Wanderlich
Susan Wanderlich
Dianne Wardle
Galen Williams
Kevin Willie
James Willwerth
Trisha Willwerth
April Worley

Dixon Worley
John Wyman
Julie Wyman
Grace Zibell
Hugh Zibell
Hugh Zibell, Jr.
Sally Zibell

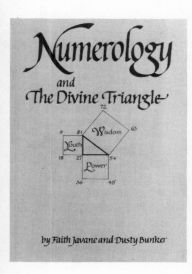

NUMEROLOGY & THE DIVINE TRIANGLE

Faith Javane & Dusty Bunker

Now in its fifth printing, this major work embodies the life's work of Faith Javane, one of America's most respected numerologists, and her student and co-author Dusty Bunker, a teacher and columnist on metaphysical topics.

Part I introduces esoteric numerology. Topics include: the digits 1 through 9; how to derive your personal numbers from your name and date of birth; how to chart your life path; the symbolism of each letter in the alphabet; the life of Edgar Cayce, and more.

Part II delineates the numbers 1 through 78 and, illustrated with the Rider-Waite Tarot deck, synthesizes numerology, astrology and the Tarot. *Numerology & The Divine Triangle* is number one in its field.

ISBN 0-914918-10-9
280 pages, 6½" x 9¼", paper $14.95

NUMEROLOGY AND YOUR FUTURE

Dusty Bunker

In her second book, Dusty Bunker stresses the predictive side of numerology. Personal cycles, including yearly, monthly and even daily numbers are explored as the author presents new techniques for revealing future developments. Knowledge of these cycles will help you make decisions and take actions in your life.

In addition to the extended discussion of personal cycles, the numerological significance of decades is analyzed with emphasis on the particular importance of the 1980s. Looking toward the future, the author presents a series of examples from the past, particularly the historical order of American presidents in relation to keys from the Tarot, to illustrate the power of numbers. Special attention is paid to the twenty-year death cycle of the presidents, as well as several predictions for the presidential elections.

ISBN 0-914918-18-4
235 pages, 6½" x 9¼", paper $12.95

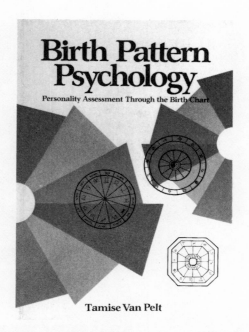

Tamise Van Pelt

BIRTH PATTERN PSYCHOLOGY
Personality Assessment Through the Birth Chart

Tamise Van Pelt

Birth Pattern Psychology presents a holistic method for looking at the birth chart that combines some of the basic tenets of astrological measurement with the type of personality research basic to psychology. The book takes the reader through a step-by-step method for understanding the effect of birth on the developed personality.

The basis of Tamise Van Pelt's application of astrological principles to personality assessment is the division of the twelve astrological houses into four major triangles. When a planet appears in one of the houses that makes up one of these trines, it influences one of the four basic psychological needs: Growth, Security, Stimulus and Love.

Van Pelt postulates that a preponderance of planets in a specific "Need Triplicity" will cause the search to fulfill that need to be a primary motivating factor in the person's life. Lack of planets in any of the triplicities does not indicate a lack of desire in that specific area; it merely means the need will not be stressed in the individual's personality or actions.

In researching *Birth Pattern Psychology*, Van Pelt analyzed hundreds of charts to formulate and test her theory. Numerous charts of noted people are included in the book to help the reader understand the traits and needs the author discusses.

ISBN 0-914918-33-8
256 pages, paper

$14.95

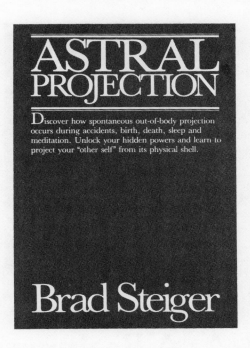

ASTRAL PROJECTION

Brad Steiger

Parapsychological researchers have established that one of every one hundred persons has experienced out-of-body projection (OBE). These experiences are not limited to any single type of person, but rather they cross all typical boundaries.

In *Astral Projection*, Brad Steiger investigates the phenomenon of OBE and correlates those events into broad categories for analysis and explanation. In his clear and non-sensational style, Steiger relates how these spontaneous experiences occur and when they are likely to re-occur. In addition to the standard and well-documented categories of spontaneous astral projection at times of stress, sleep, death and near-death, Steiger devotes considerable time to the growing evidence for conscious out-of-body experiences, where the subject deliberately seeks to cast his or her spirit out of the physical shell.

Along with his study of astral projection, Steiger sets guidelines for astral travellers, tells them the dangers they may face and how this type of psychic experience might be used for medical diagnosis, therapy and self-knowledge.

Author Brad Steiger is your guide to controlling astral projection and using it for your own benefit.

ISBN 0-914918-36-2
234 pages, 6½" x 9¼", paper $12.95

HUNA: A Beginner's Guide

Enid Hoffman

As author Enid Hoffman recalls, "I began to feel with rising excitement that I was on to something very valuable and real. I learned that this concept was at the bottom of all the practices of the Kahuna. Their miracles and magic were the result of their profound knowledge of energies and substances, visible and invisible. This knowledge enabled them to control their life experiences instead of having events control them, and made it possible for them to assist others to do so. I became aware that they were expert psychologists with a thorough understanding of human nature. Their understanding of interpersonal relationships and relationships between the selves and the physical world gave them incredible power.

"For me, these were very exciting realizations, holding the potential for everyone to grow in knowledge and power. My enthusiasm grew because I knew that if the Kahuna had done it, we could do it by studying the Huna concept, practicing their techniques until we were as skilled as they. Then we would be able to produce miracles, too."

Centuries ago, the Kahuna, the ancient Hawaiian miracle workers, discovered the fundamental pattern of energy-flow in the universe. Their secrets of psychic and intrapsychic communication, refined and enriched by modern scientific research, are now revealed in this practical, readable book. Learn to talk directly to your own unconscious selves and others. It could change your life.

ISBN 0-914918-03-6
220 pages, 6½" x 9¼", paper

$12.95

DEVELOP YOUR PSYCHIC SKILLS

Enid Hoffman

Psychic skills are as natural to human beings as walking and talking and are much more easily learned. Here are the simple directions *and* the inside secrets from noted teacher and author Enid Hoffman.

Develop Your Psychic Skills gives you a broad overview of the whole field of psychic experiences. The exercises and practices given in this book are enjoyable and easy to do. Use them to strengthen and focus your own natural abilities and turn them into precise, coordinated skills. You'll be amazed at the changes that begin to happen in your life as you activate the right hemisphere of your brain, the intuitive, creative, psychic half, which has been ignored for so long.

This book shows you how your natural psychic powers can transform your life when you awaken the other half of your brain. It teaches you techniques for knowing what others are doing, feeling and thinking. You can see what the future holds and explore past lives. You can learn to locate lost objects and people. You can become a psychic healer. It is all open to you.

Develop occasional hunches into definite foreknowledge. Sharpen wandering fantasies and daydreams into clear and accurate pictures of events in other times and places. Choose what you want to do with your life by developing your psychic skills. When you finish this book you'll realize, as thousands of others have using Enid Hoffman's techniques, that the day you began to develop your psychic skills was the day you began to become fully conscious, fully creative and fully alive.

ISBN: 0-914918-29-X
192 pages, 6½" X 9¼", paper $9.95

COMPLETE
MEDITATION
Steve Kravette

Complete Meditation presents a broad range of metaphysical concepts and meditation techniques in the same direct, easy-to-assimilate style of the author's best-selling *Complete Relaxation*. Personal experience is the teacher and this unique book is your guide. The free, poetic format leads you through a series of exercises that build on each other, starting with breathing patterns, visualization exercises and a growing confidence that meditation is easy and pleasurable. Graceful illustrations flow along with the text.

    Complete Meditation is for readers at all levels of experience. It makes advanced metaphysics and esoteric practices accessible without years of study of the literature, attachment to gurus or initiation into secret societies. Everyone can meditate, everyone is psychic, and with only a little attention everyone can bring oneself and one's circumstances into harmony.

    Experienced meditators will appreciate the more advanced techniques, including more sophisticated breathing patterns, astral travel, past-life regression, and much more. All readers will appreciate being shown how ordinarily "boring" experiences are really illuminating gateways into the complete meditation experience. Whether you do all the exercises or not, just reading this book is a pleasure.

    Complete meditation can happen anywhere, any time, in thousands of different ways. A candle flame, a daydream, music, sex, a glint of light on your ring. In virtually any circumstances. *Complete Meditation* shows you how.

ISBN 0-914918-28-1
309 pages, 6½" x 9¼", paper, $12.95

COMPLETE
RELAXATION

Steve Kravette

Complete Relaxation is unique in its field because, unlike most relaxation books, it takes a completely relaxed approach to its subject. You will find a series of poetic explorations interspersed with text and beautifully drawn illustrations designed to put you in closer touch with yourself and the people around you. *Complete Relaxation* is written for all of you: your body, your mind, your emotions, your spirituality, your sexuality—the whole person you are and are meant to be.

As you read this book, you will begin to feel yourself entering a way of life more completely relaxed than you ever thought possible. Reviewer Ben Reuven stated in the *Los Angeles Times*, "*Complete Relaxation* came along at just the right time—I read it, tried it; it works."

Some of the many areas that the author touches upon are: becoming aware, instant relaxation, stretching, hatha yoga, Arica, bioenergetics, Tai chi, dancing, and the Relaxation Reflex.

Mantras, meditating, emotional relaxation, holding back and letting go, learning to accept yourself, business relaxation, driving relaxation.

Family relaxation, nutritional relaxation, spiritual relaxation, sensual relaxation, massage and sexual relaxation. *Complete Relaxation* is a book the world has been tensely, nervously, anxiously waiting for. Here it is. Read it and relax.

ISBN 0-914918-14-1
310 pages, 6½" x 9¼", paper

$10.95

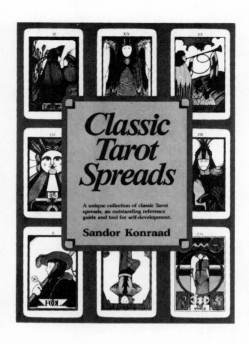

CLASSIC
TAROT SPREADS
by Sandor Konraad

Classic Tarot Spreads presents one of the most comprehensive collections of card spreads available in one book. It includes 22 classic spreads that provide a key to the history, mythology and metaphysical meanings of the cards.

The book not only covers the practice and ritual of card reading, it treats the Tarot deck as a magical tool and counseling medium that can be used to resolve basic life issues. Sandor Konraad includes spreads for opening a reading—answering questions about health, love, marriage and money—as well as spreads for ending a reading.

Illustrated with the beautiful Oswald Wirth deck, *Classic Tarot Spreads* provides clear and essential meanings for all 78 cards of the Major and Minor Arcana. Also included are seven esoteric spreads rarely found in print.

A 30-day program uses repetition and slow, methodical addition of each new card to provide an easy method for learning the entire deck. And the author has included sections that introduce beginning students to the basic concepts, and sections with spreads designed to challenge the technique of Tarot experts.

ISBN 0-914918-64-8
160 pages, 6½″ × 9¼″, paper

$12.95

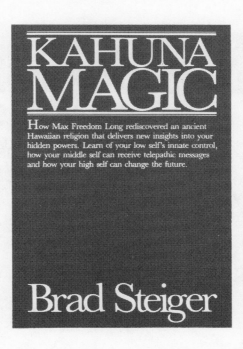

KAHUNA MAGIC

Brad Steiger

Based on the life work of Max Freedom Long, *Kahuna Magic* lays open the secrets of the Kahuna, the ancient Hawaiian priests. Long used the secrets of the Hawaiian language to unlock the secrets of this powerful and mystical discipline.

Long was a much-respected psychic researcher. His student Brad Steiger chronicles Long's adventures on the way to understanding the magic of the Kahuna. By following Long's trek, the reader will learn how the Kahunas used their magic for both the benefit of their friends and the destruction of their enemies.

Central to the Huna beliefs was the thesis that each person has three selves. The Low Self is the emotive spirit, dealing in basic wants and needs. The Middle Self is the self operating at the everyday level. The High Self is the spiritual being that is in contact with every other High Self.

The subject matter of *Kahuna Magic* is contemporary and compelling. The book incorporates many of the concepts and concerns of the modern Western psychological tradition of Jung and Freud while bringing in subjects as diverse as Eastern philosophies and yoga in a manner that will help the readers understand themselves and those around them.

ISBN 0-914918-34-6
127 pages, 6½" × 9¼", paper

$10.95

HOROSCOPE SYMBOLS

Robert Hand

Horoscope Symbols, Para Research's latest book by leading astrologer Robert Hand, explores astrological symbolism. Hand, with twenty years experience in the field, analyzes traditional meanings, considers alternatives and uses his own experience to develop and clarify these symbols. He thoroughly explains astrological symbolism—its history as well as its application for modern astrologers. In this new work, Robert Hand continues to build his reputation as the major new voice in humanistic astrology.

The author covers such basics as signs, planets, houses and aspects, illuminating their core meanings. In addition, Hand discusses midpoints, harmonics, the effect of retrograde planets and other often confusing areas for the astrologer.

Previously announced as *Planets in Synthesis*, *Horoscope Symbols* is the culmination of four years work. If you are new to astrology, this is the book to grow with. If you have already studied the basics, Robert Hand's approach will give you new perspective, insight and wisdom.

To quote the noted astrologer Alan Oken reviewing Robert Hand's *Horoscope Symbols*: "As usual, his writing is very clear, . . . what is most noteworthy is his ability to synthesize his comprehensive understanding of astrology from his basic scientific viewpoint . . . in humanistic prose.

ISBN 0-914918-16-8
400 pages, paper, 6½" x 9¼"

$19.95

NUMEROLOGY KEY TO THE TAROT

by Sandor Konraad

In *Numerology: Key to the Tarot,* Sandor Konraad investigates the cosmic connection between the art of reading the Tarot and the hidden meaning behind numbers. He reveals the secret of that relationship in a way that will appeal to beginning students as well as experienced numerologists and tarot readers.

Using the card readings and numerological analysis for Sherlock Holmes, the author presents both these arts in a lively, informative and instructive manner. By teaching the tarot spreads and numerological interpretations for a familiar character, Konraad shows you how to use the same techniques to deal with money, career, creative endeavors—most matters of life.

Through the connection between Tarot and Numerology, you'll discover why Holmes was given to drug abuse and why Holmes' brother had even greater powers of deductive reasoning. From the analysis of Holmes, you'll learn to construct an astro-numeric chart based on the numeric vibration affecting your life.

This book provides numerological guidance for anyone thinking about changing his or her name. Konraad discusses numerological identity and examines what might have happened if Sir Arthur Conan Doyle had used the name he originally intended for Sherlock Holmes.

Numerology: Key to the Tarot offers an eclectic approach to these two popular disciplines and makes learning the Tarot much less formidable than other books. Sandor Konraad calls the Tarot the great "unbound bible" of Numerology and his book will help you use both disciplines.

ISBN 0-914918-45-1

234 pages, 6½″ × 9¼″, paper,

$13.95